Juan Luis Vives: Politics, Rhetoric, and Emotions

By looking at rhetoric and politics, this book offers a novel account of Juan Luis Vives' intellectual *oeuvre*. It argues that Vives adjusted rhetorical theory to a monarchical context in which direct speech was not a possibility, demonstrated how Erasmian languages of ethical self-government and political peace were actualised rhetorically and critically in a princely environment, and finally, rethought the cognitive and emotional foundations of humanist rhetoric in his late and famous *De anima et vita* (1538). Ultimately, towards the end of his life, Vives epitomised a distinctively cognitive view of politics; he maintained that political concord was not a direct outcome of institutional or legal reform or of the spiritual transformation of the Christian world (an optimistic Erasmian interpretation) but that concord could only be upheld once the dynamics of emotions that motivated political action were understood and controlled through responsible rhetoric that respected *decorum* and civility.

Kaarlo Havu works as a postdoctoral researcher at the University of Helsinki, Finland. He specialises in early modern intellectual history and has published on Renaissance humanism, political thought, and the history of rhetoric.

Routledge Studies in Renaissance and Early Modern Worlds of Knowledge

Series Editors:
Harald E. Braun (University of Liverpool, UK) and Emily Michelson (University of St Andrews, UK)

SRS Board Members:
Erik DeBom (KU Leuven, Belgium), Mordechai Feingold (California Institute of Technology, USA), Andrew Hadfield (Sussex), Peter Mack (University of Warwick, UK), Jennifer Richards (University of Newcastle, UK), Stefania Tutino (UCLA, USA), Richard Wistreich (Royal College of Music, UK)

This series explores Renaissance and Early Modern Worlds of Knowledge (c.1400–c.1700) in Europe, the Americas, Asia and Africa. The volumes published in this series study the individuals, communities and networks involved in making and communicating knowledge during the first age of globalization. Authors investigate the perceptions, practices and modes of behaviour which shaped Renaissance and Early Modern intellectual endeavour and examine the ways in which they reverberated in the political, cultural, social and economic sphere.

The series is interdisciplinary, comparative and global in its outlook. We welcome submissions from new as well as existing fields of Renaissance Studies, including the history of literature (including neo-Latin, European and non-European languages), science and medicine, religion, architecture, environmental and economic history, the history of the book, art history, intellectual history and the history of music. We are particularly interested in proposals that straddle disciplines and are innovative in terms of approach and methodology.

The series includes monographs, shorter works and edited collections of essays. The Society for Renaissance Studies (http://www.rensoc.org.uk) provides an expert editorial board, mentoring, extensive editing and support for contributors to the series, ensuring high standards of peer-reviewed scholarship. We welcome proposals from early career researchers as well as more established colleagues.

For more information about this series, please visit: https://www.routledge.com/Routledge-Studies-in-Renaissance-and-Early-Modern-Worlds-of-Knowledge/book-series/ASHSER4043

Juan Luis Vives: Politics, Rhetoric, and Emotions

Kaarlo Havu

LONDON AND NEW YORK

First published 2022
by Routledge
4 Park Square, Milton Park, Abingdon, Oxon OX14 4RN

and by Routledge
605 Third Avenue, New York, NY 10158

Routledge is an imprint of the Taylor & Francis Group, an informa business

© 2022 Kaarlo Havu

The right of Kaarlo Havu to be identified as author of this work has been asserted in accordance with sections 77 and 78 of the Copyright, Designs and Patents Act 1988.

All rights reserved. No part of this book may be reprinted or reproduced or utilised in any form or by any electronic, mechanical, or other means, now known or hereafter invented, including photocopying and recording, or in any information storage or retrieval system, without permission in writing from the publishers.

Trademark notice: Product or corporate names may be trademarks or registered trademarks, and are used only for identification and explanation without intent to infringe.

British Library Cataloguing-in-Publication Data
A catalogue record for this book is available from the British Library

Library of Congress Cataloging-in-Publication Data
A catalog record has been requested for this book

ISBN: 978-1-032-14669-0 (hbk)
ISBN: 978-1-032-14671-3 (pbk)
ISBN: 978-1-003-24045-7 (ebk)

DOI: 10.4324/9781003240457

Typeset in Times New Roman
by KnowledgeWorks Global Ltd.

Contents

Acknowledgements   vi

Introduction   1

1 Becoming a Humanist: From Paris to Louvain (1514–1520)   19

2 Conversation and the Rhetoric of Counsel (Around 1520)   59

3 Managing Discord: Vives on Politics (1523–1529)   97

4 Redefining Rhetoric in *De disciplinis* (1530–1531)   137

5 Rhetorical *Decorum* and the Functioning of the Soul (1532–1540)   174

Conclusion   212

Bibliography   222
Index   249

Acknowledgements

There are several people and institutions I wish to thank for their support without which finishing this book would have been impossible. The European University Institute, the University of Helsinki, and the University of York have provided a stimulating atmosphere for the development of my thought. The Academy of Finland, the Alfred Kordelin Foundation, and the Niilo Helander Foundation have all believed in my work.

There are also a number of colleagues who I want to thank for their intellectual and emotional encouragement throughout the project. At the EUI, Martin van Gelderen and Antonella Romano, both in their own ways, helped me to broaden my understanding of early modern intellectual culture. At the University of Helsinki, I am particularly grateful to Markku Peltonen and Kari Saastamoinen for their comments and healthy criticism. I have also greatly appreciated the intellectual and moral support of Jonas Gerlings, Matti Lamela, Brian Olesen, Alan Granadino González, Tupu Ylä-Anttila, and all those who attended the intellectual history working group seminar at the EUI and the seminar of history at the University of Helsinki.

I owe a particular debt of gratitude to my lovely parents Eva and Jukka, to my sister Laura and her family, and to all my other relatives. Last but certainly not least, Eeva, Tuomas, and Mikael have offered me love and support throughout the project.

Introduction

In 1538, towards the end of his life, Juan Luis Vives (1492/3–1540) wrote in his preface to *De anima et vita* (hereafter *De anima*) that knowledge of emotions was 'the foundation of all moral philosophy, whether private, or public'.[1] The explicit link indicated between the understanding of emotions, ethics (private moral philosophy), and politics (public moral philosophy) in this well-known passage has often been praised as one of the many signs of the modernity of Vives's psychology.[2] In many of these accounts, *De anima* has been seen as the moment of the emergence of an anti-metaphysical and ethically orientated interpretation of the operation of the soul, which anticipated a distinctively modern and experimental attitude to psychology. With a focus on *De anima* as a moment of striking originality that hints at things to come, these readings have primarily been future orientated, and, consequently, less interested in the historical (conceptual, political, cultural) framework within which questions of the soul arose.[3] Because of this, they have largely ignored the extent to which late medieval philosophy had inspected the operation of mental faculties in a metaphysical vacuum, and they have rarely elucidated the complexity of the moral and political questions that *De anima* was seeking to answer.[4]

The purpose of this book is to offer a historical account of Vives's political and ethical thought by placing it in the context of his views on rhetoric. The study sustains that rhetoric, with its powers to shape and direct the mind, provides a link between humanist practices of ethical self-cultivation, civic participation, political concord, and Vives's theory of emotions as it was outlined in *De anima*. It suggests that Vives, who never developed a systematic political or ethical philosophy, engaged deeply with the cognitive and emotional basis of ethics and politics in his encounter with rhetoric. This, I believe, is more than of anecdotal interest and has broader significance for our understanding of humanist political thought, which, as James Hankins has recently argued, has often been brushed aside as 'mere rhetoric'.[5] Through Vives, I aim to show that much of his work was intended as a reflective take on the most pressing political and religious issues of the time.

My main argument is that Vives, in a particularly tumultuous moment in European religious and political history, gradually developed a view of

DOI: 10.4324/9781003240457-1

rhetoric that came to underscore the pivotal significance of what in classical rhetorical theory was referred to as *decorum* (appropriateness, propriety).[6] As I will show, Vives's interpretation of *decorum* linked the standard modern meaning (propriety of conduct and speech) with a promise that only through *decorum* persuasive speech was possible. This *decorum* was more than a rhetorical principle; it served as a nexus between his theory of ethical self-government, political concord, and rhetorical practice.

In scholarship on Vives, it has been common to emphasise that ethical self-control and virtue resulted from the control of harmful passions, and that political concord followed from the virtuous behaviour of those in power. As I aim to show, these issues were intrinsically linked with rhetoric since language played a pivotal role in the construction of emotional dispositions and in the activation of specific emotions. In stressing the suitability of one's speech to socially accepted rules and the avoidance of open verbal confrontation, Vives wanted to secure that strong and harmful passions were suppressed, which contributed to the ethical self-government of the speaker and his/her audience and, consequently, to political and religious concord. Yet this rhetoric of *decorum* simultaneously implied that, when one combined knowledge of socially accepted rules with a meticulous understanding of the emotional dispositions of one's audience, one could speak convincingly, realise the humanist ideal of an active life in the service of the community, and enhance political concord. Lastly, I argue that this interpretation of the *ars rhetorica*, formulated most clearly in the 1530s, must be seen as a solution to the political and religious discord of the time which, for Vives, was partly due to the potential of adversarial rhetoric to divide humans and destabilise concord. These concerns, I suggest, provide a significant context to much of what is stated in *De anima* about the connection between knowledge of the soul and moral philosophy.

Vives and Northern Humanism

One of the underlying hypotheses of the study is that rhetoric offers an interdisciplinary perspective on Vives, which enables us to go beyond internal histories of political thought, the mind, or the emotions, whether contextual or *longue durée*. The book does not, however, merely reconstruct a systematic or thematic account of Vives's theory of rhetoric and politics. It rather aims to show that Vives's attempts to delineate a rhetoric of *decorum* and to connect rhetorical and moral philosophy with knowledge of emotions can be seen as a historically specific reflection of the educational, rhetorical, ethical, and political projects of a generation of Northern humanists. Reading Vives in the context of Northern humanism illuminates what he was doing in his rhetorical works and in *De anima*, but it also allows us to better grasp a particularly interesting take on the rhetorical and emotional presuppositions of the broader Northern humanist reform movement. As Margo Todd has argued, this reform movement, epitomised by Erasmus's work, aimed at 'the moral reconstruction of the social order' both in spiritual and earthly matters.[7] I, therefore, trace Vives's attitude towards ethics, politics, and rhetoric in a close connection with the faith of Northern humanism from its early optimism of the 1510s about the malleability and perfectibility of humankind to the gloomier late 1530s. I contend that Vives's work brings to light a largely unknown strain of Northern humanist thought that, in the 1530s, outlined a distinct approach to rhetoric as an art of *decorum* and grounded this interpretation of the *ars rhetorica* in a theory of the soul.

To read Vives in the context of Northern humanism, while not a highly controversial move, is not without its problems. In the first place, Vives is undeniably a peculiar figure in the historiography of Northern humanism. It is often pointed out that he was considered a member of the leading triumvirate of transalpine humanism alongside Desiderius Erasmus (1466–1536) and Guillaume Budé (1467–1540), and many of his works, especially *De disciplinis* (1531) and *De anima*, have been praised for their scope, quality, and pivotal importance for humanist culture.[8] Still, while his stature as a humanist is recognised, he has been omitted even from companions to Renaissance humanism. Indeed, in comparison to Erasmus, Thomas More (1478–1535), or even Guillaume Budé, he remains a largely unknown thinker in the Anglophone world despite being the second most frequently printed Catholic humanist in the sixteenth century after Erasmus.[9]

Perhaps the primary reason for this neglect is that in the aftermath of the formation of national traditions of historiography, there has been some confusion as to the intellectual context in which Vives should be placed. Whereas a strong Belgian tradition, originating in the work of Henry De Vocht, has considered Vives a Northern humanist, many Anglophone scholars have willingly adopted him into the circles of Tudor reformers, and, more importantly, Spanish scholarship has often sought a place for Vives within a distinctively national narrative.[10] This was particularly important for a well-established nineteenth- and twentieth-century Spanish conservative tradition – epitomised by Marcelino Menéndez Pelayo and Adolfo Bonilla y San Martín – which saw Vives both as an orthodox Catholic thinker and as a strikingly original Spanish philosopher who anticipated some of the major developments of later European philosophy (Baconian empiricism, Cartesian method, Scottish philosophy). When the conservative paradigm was challenged in the 1960s due to new findings that proved the *converso* background of Vives's family, Spanish history did not lose its centrality.[11] In the most influential work on Vives in the twentieth century, Carlos Noreña's *Juan Luis Vives* (1970), the Iberian element was not forgotten, although it was given a distinct reading within the Jewish strand of Spanish history. Noreña, who was acutely aware of Vives's European dimension and focused extensively on his Central European connections, still placed his basic mentality inside the Spanish *converso*-tradition.[12] In a similar spirit, and despite the rapid opening of Spanish academia to international currents in the post-Franco era, it has been quite common to acknowledge Vives's prominent

4 *Introduction*

place in Erasmian circles, yet to discuss the wider significance of his work within a national story of intellectual evolution.[13]

One of the underlying convictions of this book is that there are compelling biographical and intellectual grounds to discuss the evolution and significance of Vives's thought primarily in the Northern humanist context. He was the son of a *converso* family in Valencia who left his hometown to study at the University of Paris in 1509. In the academic environment of Paris, he became acquainted with new currents of humanism and, after moving to the Low Countries in 1514, he was adopted into the humanist circles of Louvain University, Bruges (he married into a local family), the court, and to the printing activities of the Republic of Letters around Erasmus. Indeed, Vives became a major humanist with the help of Erasmus, Guillaume Budé, and Thomas More, and he frequently associated his work with these figures, especially early in his career when his personal relationship with all three was friendly. In the late 1510s and 1520s, he worked for a dynastic peace close to seats of power in the Habsburg and Tudor courts. In around 1528, following his failure to make an impact on the divorce negotiations of Henry VIII (1491–1547) and Catherine of Aragon (1485–1536), he became increasingly detached from everyday politics and dedicated his later years mostly to the completion of larger treatises on politics (*De concordia et discordia in humano genere*, 1529, hereafter *De concordia*), education (*De disciplinis*), rhetoric (*De ratione dicendi*, 1533; *De conscribendis epistolis*, 1534), and the soul (*De anima*).

If Vives's biography intersected with major Erasmian moments – the enthusiasm of the 1510s, the disillusionment with dynastic warfare and religious discord in the 1520s, and the gradual loss of momentum and influence in the 1530s – his intellectual trajectory also engaged with typical Northern humanist themes. He wrote extensively on the need for reform in the Church; he was fierce in his criticism of scholasticism and in his call for a renewal in all arts and disciplines; and his moral and political writings discussed at length the utter futility of warfare, the fruits of peace, the importance of ethical self-government, and the significance of a virtuous life for the performance of political and ecclesiastical *officia*. Yet, in one crucial aspect he was different from Erasmus and many of his followers. While he was profoundly influenced by Erasmus's philosophy of Christ and deeply concerned by the religious antagonism of the time, he decided not to focus on theology (or Biblical scholarship) partly because he considered it a dangerous discipline due to the increasingly conflictual atmosphere of the 1520s and, more importantly, due to the problems his *converso* family was having with the Spanish Inquisition in the Iberian Peninsula. After decades of persecution, his father was trialled in Valencia (1522) and burnt at the stake in 1524 and his mother's ashes (she had died in 1508) were exhumed and suffered the same faith in 1530.[14] Because of all this, he mainly moved in academic and courtly environments and wrote extensively on ethical and political philosophy and their links to education, rhetoric (he, together with

Erasmus, was arguably the most important Northern humanist writer on rhetorical theory), and theory of the soul. All this makes him a particularly interesting case to study the political dimension of Northern humanism.

The second problem with the placement of Vives in a Northern humanist milieu is perhaps even greater since it does not concern Vives but the very meaning of Northern humanism and its close neighbouring concepts (e.g. Erasmian and Christian humanism). These terms were traditionally associated with relatively stable intellectual positions, such as inner spirituality, reforming zeal, evangelism, conciliarism, or the study of Biblical languages. In the past decades, a much more complex interpretation of their meaning has emerged due in part to theoretical developments that have problematised the employment of general categories – both those used by contemporaries and those elaborated by historiographical traditions – as ready-made contexts that explain specific intellectual trajectories. Accordingly, concepts such as Northern humanism are now used not as fixed entities but as places that allow a complex set of meanings, receptions, and appropriations.[15]

Taking its cue from this criticism, the book uses Northern, Erasmian, and Christian humanism only in a loose sense that leaves room for different appropriations of similar themes. If employed in this spirit, they continue to be useful in offering a context in which Vives's thought was formed, developed, and read by contemporaries. For Vives, to be a follower of Erasmus was an identity (he described himself as a follower), but also a cultural and social position that enabled him to develop his work and to make it public in print. Furthermore, some very general ideas, both thematically (reform of the Catholic Church, inner spirituality, criticism of warfare) and conceptually (evangelism, critique of merely legal interpretations of politics, interest in ethical self-government, concern with education), despite divergent opinions of their exact content, were largely shared by a generation of humanists. Consequently, Vives's work is seen here as an appropriation and continuation of Northern humanist, especially Erasmian, concerns with rhetoric and political philosophy.

Humanism, Rhetoric, and Politics

The emphasis put on rhetoric throughout the book draws on a widespread scholarly interest in Renaissance *ars rhetorica*. In the past few decades, the idea that humanists were first and foremost rhetoricians has been heartily endorsed and its implications for religion, politics, subjectivity, self-representation, literature, art, and several other fields have been extensively explored. With respect to early modern political thought, the growing interest in language and rhetoric has prompted some ground-breaking research, which has gone far beyond Paul Oskar Kristeller's powerful description of humanist rhetorical concerns as primarily professional and literary in nature.[16] This scholarship has linked rhetoric with politics in a myriad of ways. One strand, originating in Quentin Skinner's and John Pocock's work, has analysed the reception of Ciceronian rhetoric as an essential element of early modern civic culture. Rhetoric, with its ability to come up with arguments on both sides (*in utramque partem*) of any question debated, implies difference of opinion which, for its part, implies politics.[17] Others, such as Wayne A. Rebhorn, have emphasised the commanding dimension of early modern rhetoric as brute verbal power through which the minds of the audience could be reached and ultimately dominated.[18] Yet another strand, evident in Marc Fumaroli, has read the appropriation of classical rhetoric to diverse political environments (e.g. republics, courts) as a political project in itself since it reveals a great deal about the ways in which the power of rhetoric could be realised in different institutional and cultural settings.[19] Despite their at times significant differences, all have underlined that rhetoric lies at the centre of the political self-interpretation of the early modern period as a dialogical practice of politics, as a theory of argumentation, or as a persuasive power that dominated the emotions of the audience.[20]

There is no doubt that the current enthusiasm for rhetoric has shaped our present understanding of Northern humanism. Often with a specific focus on Erasmus or Thomas More, it has inspired innovative work on humanist philology and literature.[21] It has also made us much more sensitive to the rhetorical canons through which Northern humanists both interpreted their own actions and communicated themselves to others.[22] Yet it is undeniable that the reassessment has most forcefully concerned religious thought and theology, as witnessed by the ever-growing scholarship on the most famous Northern humanist, Erasmus. Ever since Jacques Chomarat's monumental *Grammaire et rhétorique chez Érasme* (1981), it has become common to argue that the interpretive key to Erasmus's thought lay in his interest in classical grammar and rhetoric rather than in any specific theological position. For Chomarat, Erasmus was a pious orator who tried to replace the abstract, ahistorical formalities of scholastic philosophy with a living *logos*, a rhetorical, decorous truth that was embedded in a historical language, that respected individual differences, and that accommodated itself to different situations in the spirit of tolerance.[23] In Chomarat's footsteps, several studies have underscored Erasmus's interest in classical rhetoric as decisive for his views on theology (Manfred Hoffmann) and religious toleration (Gary Remer and Marjorie O'Rourke Boyle).[24]

When we turn our attention to Northern humanist political thought, it is evident that nothing close to this has taken place. Unlike theology, politics was, of course, never a dominant theme in studies on Northern or Erasmian humanism. Following Marcel Bataillon's highly influential *Érasme et l'Espagne* (1937), most historians have portrayed Erasmianism and Northern humanism as a spiritual movement that, through Biblical scholarship, channelled a great yearning for ecclesiastical reform within the Catholic world.[25] Within this paradigm, politics has undoubtedly been present, but mainly as a secondary field the dynamics of which mirror the more important developments in theology and religious thought. As the argument goes, the Erasmian call for spiritual or ethical self-transformation could be turned into a demand to put one's virtue into the service of others in a range of duties, both scholarly (reform of texts, philology, writing of treatises), and activist (counsellor, educator).[26]

Admittedly, there are studies that shed light on the critical potential of Erasmus's work in religious and civic issues. Reception studies have shown that many of Erasmus's readers took up the potentially radical implications of his work in order to articulate socially, politically, and religiously subversive ideas.[27] Erasmus's political treatises have occasionally been interpreted as rhetorical interventions that defended the Dutch political system of consensus between the princes and towns against the monarchic aspirations of the Habsburgs.[28] It has also been highlighted that Erasmus's *Adages* (1500) were political and religiously subversive essays; that the aspiration of *Institutio principis Christiani* (*On the Education of a Christian Prince*, 1516) was to direct the rulers to virtue through epideictic rhetoric; and that normative ideals could serve as a rhetorical model to criticise those in power.[29] Still, while it is becoming obvious that Erasmus and other Northern humanists employed the discourses of ethical and spiritual self-control to comment on the political concerns of their time, this element remains understudied and poorly understood.

One consequence of disregarding the interconnections between rhetoric and politics is that it becomes difficult to appreciate the rhetorical framework within which humanists themselves interpreted their texts.[30] The omission of rhetoric and the reading of Northern humanist texts through the prism of systematic political theory has, more often than not, resulted in a distorted picture of the scope and nature of their political views. It has been common to describe Northern humanists, in a dismissive tone, as exponents of a distinctively ethical interpretation of politics according to which virtuous disposition is everything, whereas systematic investigation into legal, institutional, and constitutional matters amounts to very little. Indeed, the undeniable ethical flavour of their political thought, often embedded in rhetorical interventions, has meant that they are largely absent from the broader history of political thought. Since it is debatable whether they produced a coherent or original theory of, say, sovereignty, law, justice, institutions, constitutions, rights, obedience, resistance, political freedom, or citizenship, Northern humanism, apart from More's *Utopia*, has been largely neglected even in general presentations of Renaissance/early modern political thought.[31]

The prevalent interpretation of Vives fits the picture very well. In classic studies of Vives's political views, ranging from Bonilla y San Martín and Noreña to José A. Fernández-Santamaría's, Francisco Calero's, and Philip Dust's more recent work, three typically Northern humanist themes have been repeatedly underscored. The first of these is that Vives, fully in line with an ethical account of politics, thought that political problems and discord could be traced back to a lack of individual virtue, especially of those

8 *Introduction*

in powerful positions. As Noreña put it, 'all social evils, especially poverty and war, are passional disorders of individual citizens which have burst forth into the social dimension'.[32] In this narrative, there was a direct route from the violation of Christian or Stoic ethics (subscribed to by Vives according to Noreña) to political discord. The second point is that all political and other institutions (family, religious organisations) appear as redeeming devices that primarily enable the moral perfection of humans through laws and education. Thus, unlike in neo-Augustinian traditions in which politics was conceived above all as a remedy against sin, in Vives, institutions are both a sign of the social and benevolent nature of human beings and a natural context for the further cultivation of that nature. The third aspect is more historically specific and points to immediate political goals which, in Vives's case, were peace among Christian states, the restoration of the unity of the Church through a council, and the reform of manners across the spectrum of social associations (Church, state, family). These were the external signs of inner virtue.[33]

Rhetoric and Politics in Vives

As I suggest, this picture can be modified if we consider rhetoric. In order to clarify the relationship between rhetoric and political thought, I will engage with three themes which, as I seek to illustrate, are closely interlinked. First, I approach Vives's political texts as rhetorical acts. Second, I examine Vives's reception of rhetorical theory and his stress on rhetorical *decorum* as a continuation of his political concerns. Third, I aim to show that Vives's theory of the soul and emotions in *De anima* can be seen as an extension of his rhetorical and political work. In other words, I examine both how rhetoric functions in politics and how reflections on politics, in turn, motivate further reflection on rhetorical theory and theories of the soul. Since I do not approach his views on politics and rhetoric as a theoretical system but as the outcome of separate interventions in diverse discussions, I have adopted a chronological approach where specific themes are emphasised in different chapters. This allows us to see the interconnections between separate problems within different genres of writing (rhetorical handbooks, treatises on the soul, education, and politics), but without harmonising them into a systematic theory. In this way, Vives's *oeuvre* appears both as a situated answer to specific questions and as an attempt to connect replies to these questions to a larger interpretive framework.[34]

The first theme – the reading of political texts as rhetorical acts – is dependent on showing that Vives himself conceived of rhetoric as a political practice. Here I partly build on earlier research on Vives's rhetorical views. This scholarship has shown Vives's pragmatic approach to rhetorical theory and analysed the ways in which specific literary compositions drew on rhetorical precepts.[35] It has also been stressed, in a slightly different key, that Vives's theory of monarchy presupposed wise counsel, liberty of speech, and the active participation of humanists in the courtly environment.[36] Despite its merits, this literature has only sporadically linked rhetoric to contemporary political discourses or to the deeper socio-political concerns of the time. Consequently, while the study takes its cue from existing research on Vives's rhetoric, it goes beyond it in arguing that he conceptualises rhetoric as a form of active participation. This has some implications for our view of Vives and Northern humanism more generally. It shows how the abstract political discourse of ethical self-government is performed in critical endeavours with specific goals, which challenges a classic view that portrays Vives and other humanists as backward-looking naïve moralists, alien to practical issues, and mostly irrelevant to early sixteenth-century concerns.[37]

This rhetorical element of Vives's political texts is prominently present in Chapters 1 and 3. Chapter 3 discusses Vives's understanding of rhetoric in his early encounter with humanism. I situate Vives in the emerging humanist academic milieu of Paris and Louvain in the 1510s and aim to show that Vives's polemical writings on the arts of the *trivium* (grammar, rhetoric, dialectic) make more sense when we see that he thought of language, especially rhetoric, as a medium through which an active life in the service of the community (*negotium* in classical thought) should be realised.[38] I show that the lack of practical utility is Vives's central criticism against the scholastic curriculum, and that some of his educational materials – most importantly *Declamationes Syllanae* (1520) – teach about the possibilities of rhetoric in politics. In Chapter 3, I analyse Vives's numerous political texts of the 1520s as critical interventions against the ambition and power for domination of the secular rulers of the time, most importantly Charles V and Henry VIII. These works certainly stemmed from a humanist and Christian philosophy that emphasised the ethical self-government of those in power as the key to political concord. Yet, when they are analysed as rhetorical interventions, they appear as much more critical in their assessment of those in power than what has been usually thought. We are also able to connect Vives's criticism to the aspirations of Dutch provinces to control the warfare of Habsburg princes by referring to the duties and virtues of rulers, a point that has thus far been largely ignored.

Now, to argue that politics is conceptualised rhetorically requires some clarification because of the potentially radical nature of the claim. I do not contend that Vives thought of politics in a Roman sense as an autonomous field of civic action in which differences of opinion were mediated rhetorically among citizens who mutually recognised each other's right to participate in a debate.[39] The civic dimension of rhetoric was quite systematically merged with a moralising worldview, in which rhetoric enabled, in the hands of a self-transformed Christian humanist, the enhancement of virtue and reform in politics, religion, academic disciplines, and education. Because of this, politics was not merely an autonomous field of civic action but comprised some preconceived notions about the very nature of politics (e.g. the ethical nature of politics, God's providential plan for humankind). Still, as I aim to show, political texts can go to considerable lengths in rhetorically and critically accommodating these ideas to different questions and audiences since eloquence was supposed to enable civic action in practices of political counsel in rigidly hierarchical regimes.

The second theme of the book – the reception of rhetorical theory – does not engage with politics through rhetoric but with rhetorical theory through politics. In other words, rhetorical views and theory are considered as a reflection on political concerns. While Vives's rhetorical works are admittedly not merely political since they engage with a wide range of issues (e.g. correctness of language), much of their content becomes more intelligible in the context of political thought and practice. Here I partly draw on the work of Edward George and Peter Mack, who have shown that Vives's originality within the rhetorical theory is visible in his focus on contextual appropriateness (*decorum*), but, unlike them, I argue that this move can be interpreted in the context of politics.[40]

I will engage with rhetorical theory in Chapters 2, 4, and 5. In Chapter 2, I explore the discursive culture of Northern humanism on two levels. First, I outline the significance of friendly, symmetrical conversation (*sermo*) for the definition of the reciprocal relations between Erasmian humanists. Second, I describe how Erasmian humanists conceived of their relations with those outside learned circles through more vertical, asymmetrical rhetoric between the wise and the ignorant and, through a close analysis of Vives's *De consultatione*, examine how the tradition of deliberative rhetoric, republican in its origins, was appropriated into a princely context. Chapter 4 focuses on Vives's treatise on education, *De disciplinis*. I claim that *De disciplinis* can be seen both as a critique of an overly optimistic understanding of rhetoric in the aftermath of the traumatic 1520s and as an attempt to delineate a new role for rhetoric as a responsible practice. In *De disciplinis*, Vives ultimately criticised all forms of open confrontation because they evoked strong destructive passions but incorporated a predominantly civic curriculum into a new kind of rhetorical culture that mediated difference of opinion without making discord conspicuous. Chapter 5 examines Vives's rhetorical works in the context of Erasmian rhetoric and claims that they exemplify what he was calling for in his *De disciplinis*. More specifically, I maintain that the emphasis put on *decorum* in *De ratione dicendi* is an ingenious answer to the problem of rhetoric since it simultaneously suppresses open confrontation and proposes that it is only when openly adversarial rhetoric is avoided that rhetoric can be truly persuasive. In this way, it provides a solution to some of the problems with the divisiveness of speech and the possibilities of persuasion that had been central in rhetorical performance in the 1510s and 1520s, in critical reflections on the history and nature of the *ars rhetorica* in *De disciplinis*, in instructions on political counsel (*De consultatione*, printed in 1533), and in letter writing (*De conscribendis epistolis*, 1534).

The stress put on the civic and practical dimension of rhetoric sets the study apart from some of the most influential interpretations of Erasmian rhetoric, which, often with a focus on Erasmus, have largely emphasised the spiritual dimension of eloquence. This approach is epitomised by Chomarat's depiction of Erasmus's transformative *sermo* that imitated the healing word of Christ, although Chomarat was by no means unaware of the political dimension of some of Erasmus's work.[41] Unlike Erasmus, who composed an influential treatise on homiletics (*Ecclesiastes*, 1535), Vives wrote his rhetorical works for educational, practical, and civic contexts. In his reflections on language (e.g. *De concordia*), Vives could admittedly discuss speech and rhetoric in the context of God's providential plan for humankind, but his practical advice reveals a remarkably subtle adaptation of classical rhetoric into an early sixteenth-century context. This appropriation could certainly underscore the importance of transforming the audience or recipient spiritually or morally through religious speech or what is traditionally called epideictic rhetoric centred on praising and blaming the moral qualities of a given person or action. The kind of speech that aspires to character formation will be referred to as transformative rhetoric throughout the study. Yet not all rhetoric was concerned with the moral and spiritual guidance of one's audience; as classical rhetoricians well knew ever since Aristotle, deliberative (political) and judicial rhetoric aimed at immediate persuasive effect not by changing the dispositions of one's audience but by using them as starting points in an argument.

As I will argue, this idea was not lost on Vives. While he, like many humanists, stressed character formation through education and responsible rhetoric, his actual advice on rhetorical practice discussed extensively how to produce more immediate effects in one's audience in works such as *De consultatione*. Indeed, some of the ethical dispositions that were presented in dubious light in Vives's moral philosophy, such as ambition, were treated as starting points for persuasion in his rhetorical works. This implied that those in power did not always have to be good in order to do good. This emphasis on the practicality of the a*rs rhetorica* is no minor claim since Vives was arguably the second most influential Northern humanist writer on rhetoric after Erasmus, and especially because of his *De conscribendis epistolis*, one of the most studied authors on the art of eloquence in the sixteenth century. Interestingly, Erasmus's and Vives's rhetorical works could be incorporated flexibly into different contexts that did not subscribe to Erasmian views on Christian reform in any direct way. Both the emerging civic culture of Tudor England and the Jesuit curriculum understood their civic possibilities but discussed them within radically different worldviews.[42]

The third theme that links Vives' rhetorical *oeuvre* with politics concerns the connection between the art of eloquence and the theory of emotions. To my knowledge, Nancy Struever's work is the only attempt to link Vives's interests in rhetoric and the soul, but she has not focused on the historical and contextual dimension of this link.[43] Since Vives's rhetorical works are, in place of ready-made precepts, marked by an interest in *decorum* and in the details of a specific situation (speaker, theme, audience, context), a closer examination of the emotional dispositions of the speaker and the audience appears as a major issue. As I will argue in Chapter 5, Vives's late *De anima*, while participating in many discussions on the soul, can be seen as a reflection on and culmination of his ethical, political, and rhetorical concerns. On the one hand, it develops his views on moral philosophy by offering a particularly psychological account of ethical politics dependent on the control of harmful passions. In other words, *De anima* shows that virtuous action can be enhanced if we comprehend the natural limits to the possibilities of self-control.[44] On the other hand, the treatise was viewed by Vives as the foundation of rhetoric since it offered an account of those emotions and passions that a speaker had to understand as a precondition for persuasive speech. Furthermore, it also provided an explanation as to why a speech that hid open confrontation in the spirit of *decorum* was, in most cases, the best way to convince, especially when writing to those dominated by pride.

All these ideas – that Vives's political interventions are mediated through rhetoric, that rhetorical theory is appropriated to princely environments, and that interest in rhetorical persuasion was linked to an interest in cognition and emotions – reveal, I believe, a distinctively emotional and rhetorical attitude towards politics and, consequently, should be studied together. Indeed, when these themes are included in the same study, we get a much clearer picture of how and why Vives develops his understanding of rhetoric but also of how the rhetoric of *decorum* mediates rhetorical practice in political interventions (theme 1), conditions the accommodation of rhetorical theory and education (theme 2), motivates knowledge of emotions (theme 3), and, in the end, provides an antidote to the political and ecclesiastical discord of the time. It brings forth a civic and classical perception of rhetoric that is driven by political concerns and that motivates research in other disciplines.

In underscoring the emotional and cognitive dimension of politics, I engage with broader debates on the role of emotions in early modern political thought.[45] Some of the scholarship on early modern emotions, which has challenged a more restrictive focus on institutional and normative questions in the history of political thought, has delineated a metanarrative in which the period appears as nothing short of decisive in the redefinition of the place of emotions in political life. According to the most famous of these interpretations, those emotional impulses that were traditionally associated with vice were increasingly seen as natural and positive incentives to action and reflection, and they were said to play a crucial part in the formation of commercial society or the rise of a new political theory based on self-preservation.[46]

This book does not argue that Vives anticipates these developments by adopting a merely descriptive view of emotions that could be exploited for the interest of the state or commerce. Rather, his understanding of emotions is supposed to function within a largely moral outlook on politics that stressed an already classical connection between ethical self-government and politics, a connection that James Hankins, in accordance with a substantial scholarship on humanism, has recently described as 'virtue politics'.[47] Yet Vives's rhetorical works clearly problematise this philosophy and explore its limits. It is obvious that in his rhetorical works, he often takes as the starting point the less-than-perfect nature of the audience/recipient. If this rhetoric was to enhance political concord – and surely that was what it was supposed to do – then concord was not a transparent outcome of the virtue of the audience but rather the result of the management of the emotional dispositions of the audience on the part of the orator. This shows that Vives, in actual rhetorical practice, was inclined to play with the problematic emotional dispositions of those in power in order to enhance concord. In other words, it shows a tension between rhetorical practice and the philosophy of ethical self-government and self-transformation so central to Erasmian humanists.

Yet the flexibility of rhetoric should not be overemphasised since the aim to enhance religious and political concord clearly set limits to rhetorical performance. In other words, the flexibility of rhetoric could only be justified as a temporary concession to the realities of a life of *negotium*. It had to enhance political and religious harmony, but it could not be employed to defend the more immediate interests of the princes of the time. This view remains sceptical and critical of passional impulses such as ambition and merely tries to harness them to rhetorical performance in what is a markedly critical discourse of the interest of the state (or the dynasty in power). In retrospect, it is perhaps possible to sustain that in the attempt to use harmful passions as motives to compete for virtuous, ethical glory rather than actual political power, Vives and others failed to account for those emotions and passions that really motivated the powerful of the time and largely neglected the growing logic of the reason of state. Despite this failure, Vives's view of the role of emotions in decorous rhetoric was clearly developed as an extension of a distinct, rhetorical approach to politics that this book seeks to uncover.

Theoretically, the book participates in a tradition of contextual intellectual history originating in Quentin Skinner's methodology that tries to reconstruct authorial intentions by situating them in historically specific linguistic circumstances. In the past few decades, there has been a lot of theoretical discussion on the theoretical underpinnings and relevance of intentional history. It has been pointed out that the kind of intentions we recover are potentially manifold and analytically tied together with the reconstruction of an adequate context, which, for its part, cannot be separated from the kind of questions we are interested in. But when the close relationship of authorial intentions to our research questions is acknowledged, they continue, I believe, to serve as a fruitful analytical framework for thinking about the meaning of texts for their writers in a specific historical setting.[48] Consequently, I intend to analyse Vives's position on rhetoric as answers to historically situated questions that must be reconstructed.

In most cases, I have used modern editions of Vives's works whenever available. In addition to Brill's Series of Vives's (mostly early) writings, I have employed Tristan Vigliano's edition of the first two parts of Vives's *De disciplinis* (2013), José Manuel Rodríguez Peregrina's edition of *De ratione dicendi* (2000), Charles Fantazzi's edition of *In pseudodialecticos* (1979), and Mario Sancipriano's reprint of the first edition of *De anima et vita* (1959). When there is no reliable modern edition, I have used sixteenth-century editions that are available in a digitalised form and can be accessed, for instance, through the database entitled Universal Short Title Catalogue (USTC). I have employed Gregorio Mayans y Siscar's eighteenth-century *Opera omnia* (1782–1790) only when I have not found a reliable or readily accessible modern or sixteenth-century edition of a specific work, as in the case of the 1529 political compendium built around *De concordia*.

Notes

1. Vives, 1959, *praefatio*, last page: 'quod est de Affectibus speculatio, quae tertio libro continetur, fundamentum uniuersae moralis disciplinae, siue priuatae, siue publicae'. I have generally used the translations offered by bilingual editions (such as the Loeb editions of classical literature) and other reliable translations, which are indicated in parenthesis in the notes, but some translations are also mine. Regarding Vives's works, I have used the translations of Brill's critical editions whenever possible. With *De ratione dicendi*, I have mostly used my own translations, since I did not have access to David Walker's edition of the treatise until recently. With *In pseudodialecticos*, I have mostly used Fantazzi's translations but some translations are also mine (this is indicated in the note). Translations from Vives's other works are mine. 'Emotion' will be employed as a general concept for all affections throughout the work, and 'passion' is used when reference is made to intense and destructive affections that were negatively valued. Vives's main term for all emotions is *affectio*, but throughout *De anima*, Vives employs various terms for emotions such as *passio*, *perturbatio*, or *motus animi*. Some of these, mainly *passio* and *perturbatio*, have negative connotations and are reserved for disturbing, often strong passions.
2. Following Aristotle, moral philosophy comprised ethics, politics, and economics for most humanists. To these Vives, in *De disciplinis*, added the study of those duties (*officia*) that were related to the customs of specific regions, Vives, 2013, 452.
3. Bonilla y San Martín, 1929, 2:246–7; Noreña, 1970, 254–5; Sancipriano, 1958, 3–7; Sancipriano, 1959, v–vii, Watson, 1913, xciv–xcv, xcix, cxix–cxii; Watson, 1915; Abellán, 1986, 114–20. In Noreña's more detailed *Juan Luis Vives and the Emotions* (1989), *De anima* is read both in the *longue durée* tradition of the soul stretching from Antiquity to Descartes and Spinoza, and as a result of his own psychological experience; see Noreña, 1989, xvi, 219–27. For a criticism of the tendency to focus on *De anima* as a moment of anticipation; see Del Nero, 2008b, 279–80.
4. The first point is emphasised by Casini; Casini, 2006a, 21–3.

5. Hankins, 2019, xi–xii.
6. The Latin noun *decorum* will be spelled in Italics in order to distinguish it from the English word. It is a derivative of *decor* (comeliness) and the adjective *decorus, a, um* (graceful, becoming), and it was frequently used in the ethical, poetic, and rhetorical discourse of the time to refer to the propriety of one's speech and/or actions. While some expressions in rhetorical theory were close (such as *apte dicere*, to speak appropriately), *decorum* was the most often used term.
7. Todd, 1987, 22.
8. For the triumvirate of Northern humanism, see González González, 2007, 9–10. Regarding *De disciplinis*, Kristeller has argued that 'Vives made the attempt to replace the scholastic tradition in all fields of learning with ancient and humanist scholarship, and this attempt had considerable influence on later educational theory and practice'. Kristeller, 1990, 133. The importance of the work as an overall assessment of Western culture is often repeated. See Noreña, 1970, 116–7; González González, 2007, 57; Roest, 2003, 143; Guy, 1972, 151; Vigliano, 2013, xi.
9. He is not mentioned in 1996 *The Cambridge companion to Renaissance humanism* (ed. Kraye). For the number of printed editions; see Universal Short Title Catalogue (https://www.ustc.ac.uk/).
10. IJsewijn, 1988, 160, 170–80; Adams, 1962.
11. González González, 2007, 320–41; Menéndez Pelayo, 1953–1954, 34–5, 116, 119. Menéndez Pelayo considered Erasmus an insignificant figure in the history of philosophy in comparison with Vives; Menéndez Pelayo, 1948, 43. Bonilla's assessment of Vives is much more nuanced and he deliberately rejects the idea of a Vivesian school of thought (*vivismo*). However, he is keen to demonstrate Vives's significance for wider currents of European thought and for the critical spirit of the Renaissance; see Bonilla y San Martín, 1929, 2:246–7, 339–50. The Jewish background of Vives's family was proven by Miguel de la Pinta y Llorente and José M. de Palacio. In de la Pinta y Llorente – de Palacio y de Palacio the link to Castro's work is made on the very first page in the so-called 'nota importante'; see De la Pinta y Llorente – de Palacio y de Palacio, 1964, 9. Before this, the famous historian Américo Castro had already hinted at Vives's Jewish background; see Castro, 1984, 646–8. See also González González, 1998.
12. Although Vives appears as a thinker permeated by a certain Spanish *converso* spirit in Noreña's classic study, the significance of his thought is still measured by comparing him to some of the authentic heavyweights of later European thought, such as Montaigne, Kant, Bacon, Descartes, and Locke (yet without some of the glaring exaggerations of a segment of early twentieth-century scholars); Noreña, 1970, 19–22, 76–104, 122–47, 176, 228, 275–99.
13. In his monumental *Historia crítica del pensamiento español*, José Luis Abellán argued that Vives belonged to a Spanish tradition by claiming, among other things, that the emigration of thinking is an integral part of Spanish history. Abellán is aware of Vives's connections with Central European humanists, yet situates him within a Spanish current of Erasmianism interpreted in the spirit of Marcel Bataillon; see Abellán, 1986, 108–9. See also Abellán, 2005, 12. Bataillon himself was much more ambivalent about Vives's place in the Spanish Erasmian tradition. He described Vives as a disciple of Erasmus and treated him extensively in his *Érasme et l'Espagne* but was well aware that Vives's proper context was not Spain; see Bataillon, 1991a, vi, 674–5. See also Hidalgo-Serna, 2002, xiv–xv.
14. González González, 2008, 25–7.

16 *Introduction*

15. Seidel Menchi, 1987, 16–7; Rummel, 2001, 57–64. For a discussion on Erasmianism, see Koryl, 2013, 43–50; Mout, 1997.
16. Kristeller emphasised the continuity from medieval *ars dictaminis* and *ars arengandi* to Renaissance letter-writing and oratory. Kristeller was, of course, knowledgeable on a range of manifestations of Renaissance rhetoric across the spectrum of cultural life; see Kristeller, 1979, 23–5, 112–6. For the development of Kristeller's thesis, see Monfasani, 2000. For eloquence as a stylistic ideal linked to social, political, and economic greatness, see Baker, 2015, 4–5, 27, 29–30, 174–5, 234–6. For humanist Latin as a form of social distinction, see Waquet, 1998, 246–72. Early modern political texts are now often read through the metalanguage of rhetorical theory, see Skinner, 1996; Peltonen, 2012. For the clarification of the linguistic circumstances within which early modern writers operated in their engagement with texts, see Blair, 2010; Moss, 1996; Moss, 2003; Cummings, 2007; Mack, 2002, 2–3.
17. See especially Skinner, 1996, 15–6; Pocock, 1975, 58–60.
18. Rebhorn, 1995, 15.
19. Fumaroli, 1980, see esp. 17–34; Fumaroli, 1983, 253–4.
20. Many of the leading works on the history of rhetoric explicitly make a plea for the revival of rhetoric as a contemporary practice. See, for example, Fumaroli, 1999; Skinner, 1996, 15–6; Vickers, 1988, vii–xi.
21. Their ability to engage with the rhetorical canons or culture within which they were formed is ultimately what makes them works that can be placed in the broader context of literature; see Kahn, 1985, 89–114, 183–4; McCutcheon, 2011, 52–7; Kinney, 2009, 115–8. It has also been argued that the focus on grammar and rhetoric has prevented us from understanding the literary side of Erasmus's texts as literature in which our humanity is revealed; see Cummings, 2013, 29.
22. Erasmus's self-presentation portrayed by Jardine emphasises it as a deliberately constructed self-image; see Jardine, 1993. Others have analysed processes of self-interpretation and public presentation as being much more closely intertwined; see Scott, 2009; Greenblatt, 1980, 1–9. The post-modern question of how to read through the different layers of humanist rhetoric has been raised by James D. Tracy; see Tracy, 1995. This self-presentation can also be collective. Indeed, in Hanan Yoran's *Between Utopia and Dystopia: Erasmus, Thomas More, and the Humanist Republic of Letters*, the very creation of a Republic of Letters around Erasmus has been seen as a source of authority and a claim to intellectual autonomy. Yoran does not describe this as a straightforward process but as a project that is ridden with internal tensions between the humanist yearning for intellectual freedom from patronage and their epistemological and ethical presuppositions that denied the very possibility of a transcendental and rational sphere as distinct from social reality; see Yoran, 2010. Some of this literature has portrayed them as much less tolerant than Chomarat; see Baumann, 2015, 98–9; Laureys – Simons – Becker, 2013.
23. Chomarat, 1981, 1:13–25, 2:1159–73. For the significance of Chomarat; see Mansfield, 2003, 151–73.
24. Remer, 1996, 41; Chomarat, 1981, 2:1162–4; O'Rourke Boyle, 1983. In contrast to Chomarat's aversion to theological systems, Manfred Hoffmann has stressed that rhetorical language in Erasmus mediated and revealed an underlying ontological or theological design; Hoffmann, 1994, 6.
25. Bataillon, 1991a, v–vi, 845–9. The idea of a spiritual Catholic reform spearheaded by Lefèvre and Erasmus was already central to Augustin Renaudet's famous *Préréforme et humanisme à Paris pendant les premières guerres d'Italie*

(1494–1517), Renaudet, 1916. See also Mansfield, 2003, 43–52; IJsewijn, 1975, 223; Ijsewijn, 1988, 2:164–5, 169–70; Rabil Jr., 1988a, 216, 257; Nauert, 2006, 155, 158–67.

26. Tracy, 1996, 87–90, 94–100, 104–26; Léon Halkin describes Erasmus's thought as a *mélange* of critical Christianity (*christianisme critique*) and the *philosophia Christi*. While his idea of criticism is more attuned to ecclesiastical matters, it comprises other aspects of life as well; see Halkin, 1987, 425–35. For the connection between inner spirituality and a life of *negotium* in Erasmianism, see Todd, 1987, 22–43; Adams, 1962; McConica, 1965.
27. Seidel Menchi, 1987, 11–24. Bietenholz's *Encounters with a Radical Erasmus* presents the reception of some political views, namely Erasmus's pacifism, Bietenholz, 2009, 3–10. See also Gilly, 2005.
28. Tracy, 1978, 6–7, 51–66.
29. Mann Phillips, 1964, 37–8, 101–5; Stacey, 2007, 23–72, 196–204; Pollnitz, 2015, 82–7, 106–12; Bradshaw, 1991, 122–31.
30. Some have deliberately tried to set aside the rhetorical element. Erika Rummel, for instance, has attempted to separate Erasmus's political thought from mere rhetoric by grounding it in his more systematic and less eloquent theological works; see Rummel, 2014. In her article, rhetoric has almost completely lost its political dimension; it is portrayed as a virtuoso expression of platitudes.
31. In Skinner, the focus is mostly on More's *Utopia*, although his famous *Foundations of Modern Political Thought* dedicates a large section to the political thought of Northern humanism; Skinner, 1978, vol. 1, 193–263; Skinner, 1990, 442–52. In *Renaissance Humanism* (ed. Rabil), there is no separate section on the political thought of Northern humanism; see Rabil, 1988b. In *Republicanism, a Shared European Heritage* (ed. Van Gelderen and Skinner), Vives is not mentioned, and Erasmus figures mainly in Tilmans' article, 'The Burgundian-Habsburg Netherlands (1477–1566)', Tilmans writes that Erasmus 'called upon a Ciceronian language' in his *Institutio*, but her focus is not on Erasmus; see Tilmans, 2002, 107–8. In Hankins's 'Humanism and the Origins of Modern Political Thought' More's *Utopia* figures, but Erasmus is mentioned only once; Hankins, 1996, 137–40. In Janet Coleman's *A History of Political Thought. From the Middle Ages to the Renaissance* (Blackwell, 2000), Northern humanism is completely absent. In Haddock's *A History of Political Thought*, the chapters dedicated to the sixteenth and seventeenth centuries move from Machiavelli to Bodin, Filmer, Hobbes, Grotius, Pufendorf, Althusius, and Locke, Haddock, 2008, 70–113. A notable exception is Pierre Mesnard's *L'essor de la philosophie politique au XVIe siècle* where Erasmus's integral humanism and union of classical knowledge with Christianity is not only presented but also very positively assessed; see Mesnard, 1936, 86–140. Vives, however, plays no role in Mesnard.
32. Noreña, 1970, 212. See also Strosezki, 2014, 534; Kohut, 2014, 563.
33. See Bonilla y San Martín, 1929, 2:291–304; Noreña, 1970, 212–27; Fernández-Santamaría, 1998, viii, 6; Calero, 1999, 12, 44–53. In Philip Dust's *Three Renaissance Pacifists*, Vives is described as the most philosophically minded pacifist critique of dynastic warfare; see Dust, 1987, 7–11. See also Curtis, 2011. A further dimension of the tendency to interpret institutions as possibilities for enhancing good is said to be his call for a civic welfare system formulated in *De subventione pauperum*; see, for instance, Abellán, 1986, 123–5.
34. This sets the study apart from a prevalent trend in the histories of rhetoric, the mind, and political thought to focus on one theme or concept. For the history of rhetoric, see Mack, 2011. In the history of politics, we have histories of

freedom, constitutionalism, virtues, casuistry, and a range of other topics; see Jonsen – Toulmin, 1988; Skinner – Van Gelderen, 2013; Van Gelderen – Skinner, 2013. For philosophy of mind, see for instance Knuuttila – Sihvola, 2013; Kaukua – Ekenberg, 2016.
35. See Rodríguez Peregrina, 1995; Rodríguez Peregrina, 1996; Rodríguez Peregrina, 2000; George, 1989b; George, 1992; George, 1997; George, 2000; George, 2008; Mack, 2005; Mack, 2008; Abbott, 1983; Abbott, 1986. For Vives's flexible approach to rhetorical theory, see George, 1992, 114.
36. Curtis, 2008, 114, 132–3; Curtis, 2011.
37. Mansfield, 2003, 34–9; Kisch, 1960; Monzón i Arazo, 1992, 315–6; Noreña, 1970, 213.
38. In classical thought, *negotium* referred to the active life of a citizen and it was contrasted to a solitary life of contemplation (*otium*). Vives's conception of active life did not concern the duties of a citizen to a specific polity but emphasised work for the common good of humanity in different spheres of life. See pp. 43–4.
39. Skinner, 2002, 3:69–70.
40. George, 1992, 114; Mack, 2008, 238, 275.
41. Chomarat, 1981, 2:796, 1083, 1119–20.
42. Peltonen, 2012, 1–9, 42–7; Skinner, 1996, 19–40; O'Malley, 1993, 253–64; Moreno Gallego, 2006, 571–7.
43. Struever, 2009, 244–7.
44. The idea that the understanding of emotions provides the basis for education and self-cultivation is made in Curtis, 2011, 33–4.
45. This literature is growing fast. For the early modern period; see James, 1997; Kahn – Saccamano – Coli, 2006; Sharpe, 2011.
46. A famous account of how passions were harnessed to the interest of the state either by turning vices into interests or by playing some vices (or passions) against others is portrayed in Albert Hirschman's classic *The Passions and the Interests*. These developments largely take place in the seventeenth and eighteenth centuries; see Hirschman, 1977, 9–31. See also Kahn – Saccamano, 2006, 2–6.
47. Hankins, 2019, 36–45. In Italian scholarship on humanism, the connection between virtue and politics has been made for decades; see Cappelli, 2017, 83–5. For Machiavelli's relation to virtue politics, see Fubini, 2009, 273–83.
48. For the intentionalist position, see Skinner, 2002, 1:57–102; Bevir, 1999, 27, 31–77. For recent discussions, see Hyrkkänen, 2009; Butler, 2012, 164; O'Neill, 2012; Martinich, 2012; Miglietti, 2014.

1 Becoming a Humanist

From Paris to Louvain (1514–1520)

Vives's Quest for Wisdom

In 1514, a young Spaniard named Juan Luis Vives entered the European literary scene by publishing his first writings, some of which were gathered in a larger volume entitled simply *Opera*.[1] The central text that offered an interpretative framework for the eight pieces of *Opera* was a playful dialogue, *Sapiens*, the short preface of which (*In suum sapientem praelectio*) served as an introduction to the whole *Opera* as well as to the dialogue itself.[2] In the preface, Vives contrasts the current ignorant state of learning to the wisdom of the ancients and early Christianity that had produced large numbers of wise men. He writes that 'formerly the tongue of philosophers was free' and that in the free cities of Athens and Rome as well as in early Christianity, it was allowed to speak against deformation and vice while also professing particular admiration for satire capable of truthful speech.[3] The dialogue proper was in fact a satire, which was performed by Nicolás Bérault (c.1470–c.1545), Gaspar Lax (1487–1560), and Vives himself, who offer the reader a fictional tour around the halls and corridors of the colleges of the University of Paris in a quest for true wisdom.

The quest is, however, full of deceptions. One after another, the masters of different disciplines fail to produce a satisfactory answer irrespective of whether they come from a humanist or scholastic background. While the dialectician, the philosopher, the physician, and the mathematician are criticised for their technical, scholastic language, the exponents of the linguistic arts are hardly portrayed in a more satisfactory light. The grammarian interrogates the three main interlocutors on scattered biographical and orthographical details in a confused manner which leads Lax to exclaim to Vives that he should 'not expect wisdom' from this dull man of letters.[4] The poet, for his part, mumbles a confusing sequence of poetical sentences, where, to use the words of Lax, 'the profane, the humane and the divine are entangled', which counts as true mockery of the 'sacred theology' the poet had claimed to possess.[5] The rhetorician is not much better. Vives's call for a Ciceronian or Quintilian orator embellished with wisdom and capable of moving all emotions is not responded by a rhetorician hopelessly unable to move even the emotions of his students.[6] The search for a wise man versed in the 'circle of disciplines' is finally fulfilled by a theologian who pronounces that 'true wisdom is the Son of God', which is contrasted with temporal and bodily goods.[7] This true wisdom would provide one with a tranquil soul free of harmful passions. The path propagated by the theologian highlights the contemplative – even monastic – dimension of wisdom as an exercise in inner spirituality.

Despite its ambiguities, the contents of the dialogue and its attitude towards learning as a quest for wisdom that would manifest itself across all disciplines resonated well in the academic *ambiance* of Paris of the time, as this chapter will reveal. By expounding on the academic milieus of Paris and, later, Louvain, the aim is to show what was at stake, both conceptually and in practice, in the nascent rivalry between the scholastic and humanist strands of learning. These have traditionally been seen as two competing educational paradigms with scholasticism emphasising dialectic and focusing on formal questions of reasoning and humanism paying more attention to grammar, rhetoric, and the historical dimension of semantics. The reconstruction of the academic debates on education and developments in the *trivium* will enable us to understand better what Vives himself thought he was doing not only in the introductory dialogue to his *Opera* but also his other 1510s texts centred on language teaching. This also puts us in a better position to comprehend how Vives came to think that a reformed *trivium* could serve as a basis for an active life in the service of the community and how that connection was thought to function. The link between the renewal of language teaching and active life was occasionally made in his 1514 Parisian writings, but, as we will see, it was much more fully expressed in his 1519 *oeuvre* (printed in Louvain) and in his 1520 *Declamationes Syllanae*, which offered a more comprehensive account of the significance of humanist studies for a life of *negotium*.

Grammar Teaching and Poetry at the University of Paris

Vives had moved from Valencia to Paris most likely in 1509, and the printing of his 1514 *oeuvre* represented the culmination of his Parisian experience.[8] For a long time, it was believed that he stayed in Paris for three years, until 1512, studying at the conservative and scholastic minded Collège de Montaigu. This interpretation was challenged by Enrique González González who, in his *Joan Lluís Vives: De la Escolástica al Humanismo* (1987), convincingly demonstrated that Vives's activities in Paris continued until 1514 and were most likely not solely focused on the Collège de Montaigu.[9] As González González has shown, in Paris Vives attended courses at different colleges, collaborated with printers, gave courses on classical and humanist materials, published inaugural lections to his courses (*praefatio*), and cultivated friendships with the humanist circles of the French capital centred on Nicolas Bérault.[10] Vives's enthusiasm for some of the currents of humanist learning and his experimentations with different literary styles have effectively opened up the intellectual context within which he can be placed.

The widening of Vives's intellectual milieu in Paris does not, of course, mean that his writings can be understood by employing a conventional notion of humanism. The significance of humanism as a historiographical category has, as is well known, been hotly debated in scholarship and the very existence of a deep gulf between humanist and scholastic cultures has become increasingly problematic.[11] More importantly, the meaning of humanism or humanist education was very much a question for contemporaries themselves. Although the discourse of the time frequently invoked a dichotomy between *bonae litterae* and scholastic barbarism, by 1514 there was no open confrontation between two clearly defined forms of knowledge in Paris. In fact, prior to the emergence of the famous Reuchlin case, which dealt with the application of Jewish studies and humanist philology to scriptural exegesis, the disputes between scholastics and humanists were not very heated in the French capital.[12]

The relatively peaceful coexistence was facilitated by the fact that humanism developed at certain colleges within the propaedeutic Faculty of Arts, whereas the higher faculties, especially the theological faculty, continued to work in a scholastic fashion. Indeed, individual scholars such as Josse Clichtove (1472–1543), a doctor in theology and an associate of Jacques Lefèvre d'Étaples (1450–1536), could draw on both traditions.[13] Vives's 1514 works were also rather ambivalent in their portrayal of the scholasticism – humanism debate. Although his *Sapiens* is often read as a humanist critique of scholasticism, a sort of an early version of his polemical and more famous *In pseudodialecticos* (1519), the text did not amplify on the differing academic backgrounds of its protagonists Gaspar Lax and Nicolas Bérault. The prominent French humanist Bérault seemed to be in total agreement with Lax on the deficiencies of Parisian academic life. Lax was a scholastic specialist in dialectic and a relatively well-known student of the most famous member of the theological faculty, the dialectician John Mair (1467–1550). As a matter of fact, in his 1514 *Life of Jan Dullaert* (*Vita Ioannis Dullardi*), dedicated to one of his own scholastic-minded teachers who had studied under Mair, Vives wrote, in a tone that was by no means critical, that Mair had been 'certainly the best philosopher of his time'.[14]

The absence of an open confrontation did not mean, however, that the Parisian academic community was unaware of the popularity of new humanist materials and how these could imply change for the teaching of the *trivium* (grammar, rhetoric, dialectic) at the Faculty of Arts.[15] Since the Faculty of Arts was heavily based on the linguistic arts of the *trivium* and since it served as a propaedeutic faculty that prepared students for the higher faculties, the way in which reading, speaking, and arguing was taught was considered relevant to the whole circle of arts and disciplines. Already in 1509, the theologian John Mair was irritated by some of the developments of humanism that were potentially threatening to the scholastic process of clarifying truth through its dialectical methods. By referring to a famous epistolary dispute between Pico della Mirandola (1463–1494) and Ermolao Barbaro (1454–1493), he reminded his readers that even Pico had defended the technical language of scholastics as the appropriate tool for this task. In 1516, Mair was more worried about recent developments and implied that the Faculty of Arts was not preparing students for the study of theology in a suitable manner. He affirmed the necessity of other arts for theology yet complained that 'although such things are treated in certain faculties, perhaps, however, they are not treated sufficiently'.[16]

Mair was right that some of the strongholds of nominalist scholasticism were affected by new materials. In 1516, François du Bois (c.1483–1536), a teacher at the Collège de Montaigu, published his *Progymnasmatum*, a contribution to the humanist trend of looking for an abundant, eloquent, and versatile style. The influence of humanist handbooks on grammar teaching is further confirmed by the curricula of the Collège de Montaigu. As Noël Beda's (c.1470–1537) statutes for the Collège from 1509 show, traditional scholastic works such as Alexandre de Villedieu's (c.1170–c.1240) *Doctrinale* (c.1209) or Donatus's *Ars minor* and *Ars maior* were coupled with humanist authors on grammar such as Niccolò Perotti (1430–1480), Agostino Dati (1420–1478), and Guy de Jouenneaux (d. 1507), who had composed an increasingly popular version of Lorenzo Valla's (1407–1457) *Elegantiae linguae latinae* (1444).[17] Moreover, the extracurricular courses offered by independent teachers such as Bérault or Vives revealed a strong presence of humanist texts in the classroom.[18] The change in grammar teaching was noticed by printers who were making humanist materials available at a swift pace. Josse Bade (1461/1462–1535), who contributed greatly to the propagation of humanist works in the French capital, hinted in his introduction to Iohannes Balbi's (d. c.1298) *Catholicon* (1286) of 1506 – the scholastic grammar *par excellence* – that it was old-fashioned and becoming outdated.[19]

As John Mair's comments about the propaedeutic function of the Faculty of Arts indicated, the changes taking place in grammar teaching had philosophical, semantic, practical, and cultural implications for the whole spectrum of knowledge. Indeed, grammar teaching had been intrinsically tied to a whole culture of approaching language and argumentation. In the late Middle Ages, the purpose of grammar had not been limited to the teaching of linguistic skills for the use of language, but it had predominantly evolved into an investigation into the meaning of words linked closely to a highly developed tradition of formal semantics and dialectical reasoning. While Alexandre de Villedieu's *Doctrinale* had provided a pedagogical grammar in verse for students, other treatises such as Balbi's *Catholicon*, Donatus's *Ars Grammatica* or Priscian's grammatical works accentuated the study of language as deep semantic analysis.[20] The *raison d'être* of what was in its thirteenth-century heyday called speculative grammar was often stated in the introductions to and commentaries on treatises and referred to the Aristotelian idea of unveiling the semantic relations of a mental language.[21]

In this way, some aspects of medieval grammar could be understood as propaedeutic elements leading to formal and terminist dialectic (logic), and many semantic problems expounded in terminist logic were born out of grammatical commentaries.[22]

The pedagogical tools of *quaestio* (question) and *disputatio* (disputation) equally fostered a practice of reading that was connected to the formal aspirations of grammar teaching. The *quaestio*, or set of *quaestiones*, enabled one to amplify and contextualise problems arising from a text through a dialectical treatment. It also provided a method of presenting separate questions for a disputation and a model for exercising argumentative and analytical capacities.[23] The *disputatio* was the active treatment of a *quaestio* through arguments for and against, followed by a refutation and a final solution to the problem posed. Like the *quaestio*, the *disputatio* could serve as an active oral exercise or as a way of exploring a problem arising from a commentary on a text. In its different forms, it was primarily an exercise in formal reasoning and semantic precision that accentuated the importance of the formal validity of arguments according to the semantic and propositional rules of dialectic. Despite their highly formal nature, both exercises also had a practical task: they showed how problems arising from authorities and other texts could systematically be clarified and bound together with the unity of other knowledge through a dialectical treatment of questions.[24] The connection between dialectic and grammar meant that the grammar course had to prepare students for formal reasoning, which explains Mair's anxiety at the introduction of humanist materials. As another theologian, Josse Clichtove, claimed, grammar was the 'nurse of other arts'.[25]

New humanist materials not only replaced scholastic ones but also redirected the focus of language teaching from formal semantics to a semantics of use (*usus*) and literary abundance (*copia*). Although scholastic and humanist works could coexist in curricula and in accounts of grammar as in Josse Bade's *Introductio in grammaticen* (1510), there was a marked shift in emphasis for humanist textbooks overwhelmingly discussed the semantics of words as a web of relations of meaning within authoritative classical and Christian literature.[26] In Niccolò Perotti's *Cornucopiae* (printed in 1489), a humanist dictionary based on an *enarratio* of Martial's poetry, every definition of a word brought to the fore other possible uses of the term as it was applied by a number of classical *auctores*, enabling verbal abundance and rhetorical invention. The semantics of *Cornucopiae* and other works on grammar were intrinsically linked to what is usually known as the *enarratio*, a formally loose practice of reading and commenting on texts that, rather than explaining abstract semantical relations, made them understandable in the context of other knowledge a student might have possessed about the *auctores*. Its implication was that words could only be properly understood when their uses in authoritative texts were discovered.

There can be little doubt that Vives was aware of these discussions around grammar. In 1514, he edited Battista Guarino's (1435–1503) *De ordine docendi ac studendi* (1459), one of the central treatises of humanist pedagogy, and was genuinely enthusiastic about it.[27] In a humanist vain, Guarino distinguished between the 'methodical' part of grammar which dealt with the 'paradigms' of different parts of speech and the historical dimension of grammar which focused on 'historical knowledge and 'past achievements'.[28] While Guarino offered prescriptive rules for grammar teaching, the more advanced part was dedicated to historical grammar. Here grammar teaching not only taught about language use but simultaneously introduced one to materials from which one could 'excerpt the customs, manners, and laws of various peoples, the various fortunes that befell individuals of genius and their vices and virtues'.[29]

Guarino's words implied that grammar teaching was not just an exercise in the reading and learning of classical Latin and individual words, but also that knowledge of words was a gateway to the wisdom of the *auctores*. This idea was widely shared in humanist circles. Naturally, the stress put on the context-bound meaning of words and syntactical rules in the texts of poets, historians, and other authors made it necessary to have a close familiarity with these authors since meaning could only be interpreted contextually.[30] The humanist *enarratio* also connected the familiarity with authors to the acquisition of wisdom. This wisdom did not primarily refer to ambitious argumentative schemes or to the elucidation of problems through the method of question and disputation, but to sentences, maxims, proverbs, and other short pieces of writing in which, through a certain sanctification of or reverence for the authority of the tradition, glimpses of truth were captured. Vives clearly believed that grammar was not just a question of words but also of wisdom. His printed introductory lecture on Francesco Filelfo's (1398–1481) *Convivia Mediolaniensia* engaged in a polemic with a possibly fictional scholastic-minded friend who claimed that the lecture was not about 'natural philosophy or astrology' but merely about grammar.[31] Vives, bitterly hurt, replied that what he was teaching could be useful not only for natural philosophy and astrology – subjects that had been treated with great eloquence in classical antiquity – but also to all other philosophy, whether civil or religious. Vives quotes a well-known metaphor, found in Seneca, Macrobius, and St Basil, about a bee that gathered nectar from different flowers and turned it into honey. Similarly, 'those scholars who know many disciplines and have tasted many flowers of various trees do indeed fly through many gardens' and, because of the spiritual nature of their products, 'their works' are 'sweeter than the honey of bees'.[32] Vives thus not only placed Filelfo's *Convivia* in the encyclopaedic tradition of Macrobius and Aulus Gellius, which emphasised eclecticism in collecting quotations, but also portrayed it as a path to wisdom.[33]

The idea that grammar was an exercise in wisdom somehow presupposed the ultimate harmony and concord of all knowledge and arts. The harmony of knowledge was encapsulated by the concept of a circle of disciplines, which underscored that all disciplines, rather than threatening one another, supported each other. As seen, the protagonists of Vives's *Sapiens* yearned precisely for a wise man versed in the circle of disciplines. The unity of all disciplines was made popular by the most famous French humanist, Guillaume Budé, who, in his *Annotationes in Pandectarum libros* (1508), claimed, drawing on Quintilian and Vitruvius, that all disciplines were intrinsically tied together.[34] The encyclopaedic ideal had practical implications for humanist educational materials. Since the *enarratio* wove single texts into the totality of knowledge, encyclopaedic works – such as Gellius's *Attic Nights* (*Noctes Atticae*), Macrobius's *Saturnalia*, or Filelfo's *Convivia* – were gaining in popularity because they provided a hands-on way to divulge the wisdom of tradition in a simple and condensed manner.

The unity of all arts was equally the presupposition of numerous attempts to put the humanist *enarratio* and other grammatical tools into play in philology. Jacques Lefèvre's work was perhaps the most famous example of this since it aspired to bridge all potential fractions between classical and Christian knowledge. He was one of the leading figures of Parisian intellectual life, and in a contemporary account of eminent men of letters, he was described as the French Cicero who had saved philosophy from barbarism, restored liberal arts to their former splendour, and joined unpolished philosophy with eloquence.[35] Between 1492 and 1506, Lefèvre had focused on shedding new light on Aristotle's work with humanist commentaries. Rather than merely purifying Aristotle from the interpretations of the scholastic commentary tradition through a neutral philological reading, he strove to harmonise Aristotle with a Christian worldview, referring to the Stagirite as *primus theologus*.[36] Lefèvre's work drew its inspiration not only from mystical philosophy but also from Neo-Platonism which had conceptually contributed to the sanctification of the philosophical tradition by portraying much of it as ancient theology (*prisca theologia*).[37] In the spiritualised excavation of truth, the wisdom of the ancients, if understood correctly and in a Christian spirit, could serve as an initial step on a path to true, mystical wisdom (*sapientia*).[38] The ideal of bringing classical wisdom into a Christian framework was linked to a widely held idea of education as a realisation of man's true human nature, a claim that was based on the integral union of *litterae* and *mores*.

Still, the incorporation of humanist and classical materials and methods into a Christian context was not without its problems because within specific disciplines the fractures were quite apparent. Since the late fifteenth century, many of the questions surrounding the moral nature of classical and humanist learning had been hotly debated with a specific focus on the ethical implications of classical poetry central for the linguistic training (grammar and rhetoric) of the Faculty of Arts. Already in a late fifteenth-century Parisian debate between two Italians, Fausto Andrelini (1462–1519) accused Girolamo Balbi (1460–1535) of an uncritical focus on classical eloquence and poetry and of indifference towards religious matters.[39] Robert Gaguin (1433–1501), the leading figure of French humanism in the 1490s, had likewise serious reservations concerning the moral nature of the philosophy of classical antiquity.[40] In his Parisian days in the 1490s, Erasmus was also irritated that many tried to imitate classical instead of Christian poets, and yearned for a poetry that would combine 'distinguished learning and an exceptionally high moral tone'.[41] This moral and spiritual interpretation of poetry is clearly the context for Vives's call for 'the sacred theology' of poets in *Sapiens*.[42]

As Erasmus's comments about imitation revealed, the threatening nature of poetry referred not only to its capacity to inculcate dubious moral wisdom into the mind of the student but also to its possible influence on the imitation of immoral verses. This was in line with many humanist curricula and works on grammar that claimed that the knowledge of words was ultimately directed towards one's own writing and speaking. Grammar teaching itself included written composition, and some of the pedagogical tools, such as commonplace books, already associated the reading and extracting of commonplaces with the possibilities of writing.[43] As Bade pointed out in his *Introductio in Grammaticen*, grammar was an art that taught one to speak and write correctly.[44] Indeed, the often-voiced humanist ideal of combining wisdom (*sapientia*) and eloquence (*eloquentia*) did not refer merely to rhetoric or oratory but to all writing, including poetry, a view that was reinforced by handbooks on the *ars poetica*, which, from the Middle Ages to more recent works such as Robert Gaguin's *Ars versificatoria* (1473) or Johannes Despauterius's (c.1460–1520) *Ars versificatoria* (1511), drew on rhetorical theory. Perhaps more importantly, the very duties of poetry were frequently described in terms similar to the genre of epideictic rhetoric that was centred on the praise and blame of a given subject or person. In this way, poetry was given a distinctively moral outlook that accentuated its capacities to laud virtue and condemn vice.[45]

For many, the ideal of moral poetry was incarnated in Battista Spagnoli (the Mantuan, 1448–1516), one of the most frequently printed contemporary writers of the first 15 years of the sixteenth century, who was quite systematically described as the Christian Vergil (Vergil was also from Mantua).[46] In a letter to Spagnoli printed by Bade, Giovanni Pico della Mirandola claimed that in Spagnoli's 'most saintly poems' the 'majesty of things' and 'splendour of eloquence' was such that they could be seen to demand the palm for their 'words and sentences'.[47] Josse Bade himself contributed to the fame of Spagnoli in Paris when he turned the Mantuan into a leading figure of a poetic tradition that, through its persuasive and emotional qualities, disseminated moral instruction.[48] Bade also propagated the image of a poet-theologian, epitomised by Spagnoli, in whose poetry one could see glimpses of divine wisdom and *prisca theologia*.[49] In a further evocation of the commonplace of the theology of the poets, Nicolas Bérault claimed in his commentaries on Angelo Poliziano's (1454–1494) *Sylva* (1480s) that poets were 'full of God, inspired by a celestial power, and moved by God's will'.[50] In this intellectual climate, Vives's quest for spiritual poetry in *Sapiens*, or his somewhat clumsy attempt to adapt classical rhetoric to the praise of Christ in a short 1514 text entitled *Veritas fucata* resonated very well indeed. The moral understanding of language use was equally perceivable in other genres; Vives's description of the capacities of satire to reveal the truth in his introduction to *Sapiens* also reflected a Christianised reading of classical genres within which ancient orators could rub shoulders with Christian writers in a mutual fight against vice. In fact, the link between satire and Christian truth had been made by Bade in his *Praenotamenta*, where he had likened classical satirists to the preachers of the Church.[51]

A Christian Interpretation of Classical Rhetoric

Although poetry was frequently discussed in the framework of eloquence, the primary art that taught students to put their knowledge of words into writing was rhetoric, the second art of the *trivium*. As we will see, despite an apparent tension between a Christian understanding of rhetoric as a transformative practice and a classical interpretation of eloquence as civic power, Parisian writers, in line with the general trend outlined above, strove primarily to harmonise different interpretations of rhetoric with one another. Consequently, it is not surprising that Vives, in these years, adopted a broad understanding of rhetoric as an expression of wisdom in all possible disciplines. This was to have a lasting impact on Vives. While his actual advice on rhetoric and emotions in his later treatises revealed an understanding of the differences between the transformative and civic dimensions of rhetoric, the ultimate compatibility of the classical and Christian traditions was throughout his intellectual trajectory taken for granted in his reflections on the art of eloquence.

Rhetoric was generally conceived of as a continuation of grammar. As Guarino's *De ordine docendi ac studendi* claimed, 'anyone trained in the aforesaid studies [grammar] is ready to pass on to the discipline of rhetoric'.[52] Just as in other disciplines, a union of Christian and classical eloquence was frequently called for within the art of rhetoric. Revealingly, Bade's *Inquiry* (*Disquisito Ascensiana*) described Cicero's diction as divine.[53] Thoroughly in this spirit, Vives's own introductory lecture to the fourth book of the Pseudo-Ciceronian *Ad Herennium* incorporated the Hebrew books of Isaiah into a classical corpus of eloquence.[54] But unlike in poetry, where Spagnoli could compete with classical authors, the primacy of classical orators was never really in doubt in rhetoric. Thus, in spite of mentioning Isaiah in the context of classical eloquence, Vives's lecture to the *Ad Herennium* clearly portrayed classical orators, most importantly Cicero, as the best examples of rhetorical skills.

The choice not only concerned the authoritative status of certain classical names but also affected Vives's portrayal of the nature of rhetoric. In the printed lecture on the part of *Ad Herennium* dedicated to figures and tropes, he did not describe rhetoric chiefly as a question of style and beauty, as a practice of teaching wisdom, or as a philological method of reading, but instead as dominion and power over the emotions and passions of the audience. Furthermore, he did not primarily emphasise the transformative capacities of rhetoric to bring about moral, Christian virtue but rather the ability to rule supreme in civic deliberations by the manipulation of the existing emotional dispositions of the audience. Vives explained that he tried to form an orator who could 'induce them [the audience] into any mood; he will have command of anybody's soul and will, and make them obey his words and speech without any resistance'.[55] The selection of exempla of good orators hailed Cicero as a king who was able to turn the collective mind of the Senate to whatever he wanted, and 'the choice of war and peace between the Athenians and Philip was in the power of Demosthenes thanks to his eloquence'.[56] Vives further instructed the reader that 'many if not all scholars of our time who want to be considered orators affect embellishments of style and the ring of fine speech-making', whereas a true orator selected his style according to the case at hand and mastered the emotions of his audience. He knew 'what words and technique he must use to rouse one's mind to hope, cast it down through fear or stir up wrath or envy, and other things of that nature'.[57]

The prominence given to Roman orators in Vives's introductory lecture was not exceptional since the corpus of authoritative texts on the use of words was largely inherited from antiquity. Ever since Guillaume Fichet's (1433–c.1480) *Rhetorica* (1471), the first printed French handbook on eloquence, the Parisian academic tradition had portrayed Cicero and Quintilian as the foremost *auctores* of oratory.[58] Their pre-eminence in the *ars rhetorica* was confirmed by their popularity in grammar and elementary schools and in the propaedeutic Faculties of Arts. As is well known, the Ciceronian corpus and Quintilian's *Institutio oratoria* were the most frequently printed rhetorical materials, outnumbering everything the Renaissance had produced, with several editions of Cicero's rhetorical works printed in Paris.[59]

It is hardly an exaggeration to claim that every early sixteenth-century student of classical rhetoric at the elementary level would have been acquainted with Cicero's *De inventione* and the pseudo-Ciceronian *Ad Herennium* – the book Vives was lecturing on in Paris. Both handbooks were schematic accounts of the basic content of rhetorical theory and served as standard introductions to the art of eloquence.[60] These works were complemented by Cicero's other introductory manuals, such as *Partitiones Oratoriae* (*A Dialogue Concerning Oratorical Partitions*), *Topica* (*Topics of Argumentation*), *Brutus*, and *Orator*, all of which were printed together with the *Ad Herennium* and *De inventione* in Josse Bade's 1511 Parisian edition of Cicero's rhetorical *oeuvre*.[61] Besides the pedagogic corpus, there were more sophisticated, complex, and philosophically challenging treatments of rhetoric that discussed its political role and its relationship to other disciplines. While it is unlikely that Vives possessed more than superficial knowledge of their content at this stage of his life, they became increasingly important for his reflections on the art of eloquence in his later work. Cicero's most complete work on rhetoric, *De oratore*, not only presented rhetorical theory as a schematic system but simultaneously reflected in a dialogue format on different aspects of oratory and its relation to other arts. Quintilian's *Institutio oratoria* wove rhetoric together with a comprehensive programme of oratorical education, discussing its relation to all aspects of public life. Aristotle's *The Art of Rhetoric* – the first systematic treatment of rhetorical theory – offered the reader the most complete treatment of emotions, while Tacitus's *Dialogus de oratoribus* (*Dialogue on the Orators*) provided insight into rhetoric's relationship to political developments and constitutions. Ultimately, the more advanced literature associated rhetorical theory with broader discussions on ethical, cognitive, social, and political issues.[62]

Despite the often-substantial differences between separate treatises, pupils across Europe would have received a largely similar overall picture of the basic structure of rhetorical theory. In these schoolbooks, students would learn that the duties (*officia*) of an orator were to teach (*docere*), to delight (*delectare*) and to move (*movere*) the audience. Moreover, they would have discovered that the three genres of rhetoric were judicial, deliberative (political), and epideictic, of which the first dealt with the normative judgment of past actions, the second attended to future-oriented decision making, and the third related to the moral assessment of persons or actions through the rhetoric of praise and blame. They would also have been told that the traditional skills of a successful orator were the invention of arguments (*inventio*) through topics (*loci*) and commonplaces (*loci communes*); disposition, or arrangement of arguments (*dispositio*) according to the six parts of an oration; style (*elocutio*) that referred both to the tripartite division of style into grand, middle, and low, as well as to the generation of ornaments through figures and tropes. Finally, they would have been informed that the two further skills of spoken oratory were memory (*memoria*) and delivery (*pronuntiatio*). This theoretical structure was not a clear-cut scheme of separate issues: the interrelations of different aspects of the theory were highlighted so that the invention of arguments (*inventio*) in the *Ad Herennium*, for instance, went hand in hand with the demands of disposition (*dispositio*) since different parts of orations aspired to specific goals.[63] What is more, rhetorical theory reminded students that the choice of specific rhetorical devices was always subject to the ultimate goal of oratory that could be defined as outright persuasion or, more reservedly, as speaking well on any matter proposed.[64]

Although there were some original Renaissance introductory works to the art of eloquence, such as George of Trebizond's (1395–1486) *Rhetoricorum libri V* (1433/1434), which in addition to Roman sources drew also heavily on Hermogenes, most Renaissance treatises served rather as complementary texts to a distinctively classical corpus.[65] Erasmus was a great example of this. His most famous rhetorical works – most notably a treatment of abundant style, *De copia* (*Foundations of the Abundant Style*, 1512); a letter-writing manual, *De conscribendis epistolis* (*On the Writing of Letters*, 1522); a set of proverbs, *Adagia* (originally printed in 1530); and his collection of exemplary dialogues, *Colloquia* (*Colloquies*, first edition in 1518) – all introduced stylistic, dispositional, and generic flexibility to a classical corpus. Within the genres of applied rhetoric, letter writing held a special place as witnessed by several popular handbooks produced by Erasmus, Despauterius, and many others. While letter writing as an art had long medieval roots in the *ars dictaminis*, the numerous Renaissance manuals drew abundantly from classical rhetoric, often incorporating the precepts of demonstrative, judicial, and epideictic rhetoric into their subject matter. For instance, Sulpitius Verulanus's (c.1470–1490) *De epistolarum compositione opusculum*, printed in Bade's *Epistolarum compositionem compendium isagogicum* (1501), offered considerable information about the stylistic, dispositional, and generic precepts of classical rhetoric.[66]

It should be remembered that rhetoric was not merely a technical art that provided advice for the generation of arguments and style but that it was always linked to a specific role eloquence was supposed to play in human life. There were various interpretations of its larger significance. In the classical tradition, as exemplified by *De inventione* and *Ad Herennium*, rhetoric was quite systematically linked to civic life. Not only was the focus on civic genres (judicial and deliberative rhetoric), but in *De inventione* Cicero classified 'oratorical ability as a part of political science (*scientia civilis*)' and offered a famous and often-quoted account of a first orator who 'assembled and gathered' men who 'were scattered in the fields' transforming them 'from wild savages into a kind and gentle folk'.[67] In this initial part of *De inventione*, a moral union of wisdom and eloquence demanded by different writers was achieved and given a distinctively social touch by insisting on its civilising element. Vives himself referred to the union of reason and words in his introductory lecture to the *Ad Herennium* when he asserted that what truly distinguished human beings from beasts was not that they conceived of rational ideas in their mind, but that they were able to communicate them to others through signs.[68]

Moreover, Cicero, in his other works, and most notably in *De officiis*, linked the imperative of the union of reason (*ratio*) and eloquence with the importance of active and prudential life. In *De officiis*, the most widely read book on moral philosophy in Europe already in the Middle Ages, Cicero reaffirmed that the natural bonds of society were reason and speech, 'which by the processes of teaching and learning, of communicating, discussing, and reasoning associate men together and unite them in a sort of natural fraternity'.[69] Furthermore, this rhetorical activity was united with the virtues of an active life for the common good (equated in Cicero with the good of the state), which was contrasted with a philosophical life that strove for the contemplation of eternal truths in relative isolation.[70]

Renaissance works that circulated in Paris frequently took up the idea that rhetoric was a part of a distinct civil science and affirmed the civic dimension of rhetoric. As one could read in the first lines of George of Trebizond's fifteenth-century *Rhetoric*, printed in France for the first time in 1512, rhetoric was 'the civil science by which we speak in civil questions with the assent, as much as possible, of the listeners'.[71] Josse Bade, following Cicero, similarly informed the reader that rhetoric dealt with forensic and civic matters.[72] Filippo Beroaldo's (1453–1505) often-printed playful *Declamatio Philosophi, Medici, & Oratoris* (1497) made a case for the supremacy of oratory over philosophy, arguing, in the spirit of Cicero's *De inventione*, for the pivotal importance of rhetoric for the 'founders of cities'.[73]

Yet there is another tradition, implicit in some classical and Christian materials, according to which rhetoric, rather than merely treating civic issues, taught about morals and spirituality, holding some transformative potential over its audience. In its different forms, this interpretation could place classical and other forms of rhetoric within the epideictic ideal according to which eloquence mediated virtue in a world of vice, which, as we have seen, was precisely the way in which poetry and satire were understood. Indeed, medieval writers, spearheaded by Giles of Rome (c.1243–1316), had already been conscious of an Aristotelian notion that did not ascribe to rhetoric its own subject matter (civic issues) but instead described it as a counterpart of dialectic that communicated persuasively about moral affairs.[74] In the Parisian context, the virtue that rhetoric was thought to transmit could be imbued with a Christian spirit. This was not altogether surprising since humanist commentaries on the most widely disseminated texts of political and ethical philosophy hardly ever accentuated the autonomy of these subjects. In his edition of Aristotle's *Nicomachean Ethics*, Lefèvre, for instance, wrote that the arts of moral philosophy and prudence were subject to divine *sapientia* and *bonitas*.[75] In contrast to Lefèvre, a scholastic tradition running from Jean Gerson (1363–1429) to John Mair affirmed much more clearly the autonomy of moral philosophical problems and developed responses to contemporary ethical and political questions.[76]

There were some conceptual discrepancies between the civic rhetoric of the ancients that often aimed at an instantaneous effect within the confines of a particular question and the Christianised eloquence of poets and pious authors that strove to inculcate virtue and bring about transformation in the souls of the listeners. As Vives's lecture to the *Ad Herennium* demonstrated, classical materials could foster a somewhat instrumental view of rhetoric as cognitive power. What was worse, they could also depict political and ethical vocabularies as suspiciously flexible. The very presupposition of classical rhetoric was that it was always possible to come up with arguments for both sides, *in utramque partem*, and in Cicero and Quintilian, we can find successful orators being praised for this ability.[77] For instance, within deliberative rhetoric, political issues were described as questions of honesty (*honestas*) and expediency (*utilitas*), but these terms served as general topics or headings under which every successful argumentation of one's case had to be placed. This was achieved by using the flexibility of key concepts to cater for a range of possibly opposite actions in an inventive way. In fact, the flexible capacity of rhetoric to provide believable arguments for every case was precisely the dimension for which it had traditionally been criticised. Echoing Plato's attack on rhetoric in *Gorgias*, the potentially deceiving nature of rhetoric, capable of masking and hiding truth, was sometimes voiced in Paris. The dedication letter to the 1512 Paris edition of Domenico Nani Mirabelli's *Polyanthea* (1503), a successful florilegia or reference work printed by Josse Bade, contained a highly ambivalent description of eloquence as an art capable of the best and the worst.[78]

Despite these Platonic concerns, most literature assessed rhetoric positively and saw no unbridgeable gap between classical rhetoric and Christian eloquence. Vives's writings echoed this view. Despite his description of rhetoric as a form of cognitive and political power in his introductory lecture to the fourth book of *Ad Herennium*, Vives himself was perfectly capable of equating the classical rhetoric of citizens with the Christian eloquence of virtue. In his introduction to *Sapiens*, Vives likened the orators of Athens and Rome to Christian speakers as preachers of virtue since all used their freedom of speech 'as it were to mutilate and tear deformities apart'.[79] Further reflecting this attitude, Vives reminded the reader in his introductory lecture to *Ad Herennium* that his work as a teacher of eloquence would be perfected by 'the Perfector of every good undertaking (God)'. He continued by hoping that the eloquence taught by him would not 'be turned to any person's ruin', and that it would make 'truth more beautiful, to propagate good and discourage evil'.[80] Equally as importantly, his introductory lecture to Filelfo's *Convivia* called for the union of eloquence and wisdom in all possible arts, ranging from moral philosophy to natural philosophy with no specific focus on the three traditional rhetorical genres. Vives not only praised Cicero but claimed that Plato 'wrote his philosophical works with supreme eloquence', that Aristotle 'composed all his works in a golden flow of speech', and went on to count Xenophon and Theophrastus among the eloquent.[81]

By 1514, Vives had associated humanist grammar teaching with rhetorical production. He had likewise witnessed considerable interest in the cognitive and emotional possibilities of rhetoric and professed great admiration for the powers of classical oratory epitomised by Cicero. Yet, in a reading that aspired to harmony, all possible fractures between civic and Christian rhetoric disappeared. His Parisian writings called for the union of *eloquentia* and *sapientia* through the range of disciplines in a universal fight against vice in all spheres of life.

Louvain, Erasmus, and Dialectic

While Vives encountered humanist currents in Paris, it was his familiarity with the humanist tradition of the Low Countries, and especially its most famous member Erasmus, that was to mark his understanding of language, the *trivium*, and the possibilities of humanist studies. In 1519, after years of relative silence, a work entitled simply *Opuscula* appeared from the Louvain printing house of Thierry Martens (1446/1447–1534), Erasmus's preferred printer in the Low Countries. The compendium of 15 texts, 5 of which were edited reprints of the 1514 works, displayed an awareness of typically Erasmian themes across the spectrum of intellectual preoccupations ranging from a fierce critique of the barbarism of scholasticism to the claim that true nobility stemmed from the excellence of character and virtue, not from one's ancestors.[82] Although the 1519 *Opuscula* exhibited intellectual and stylistic developments in various fields, in what follows, I want to foreground two issues that were significant for Vives's views on the links between humanism and a life of *negotium* and that both, I would argue, were connected to the civic dimension of his thought. The first one concerns the predominantly non-theological interpretation of dialectic in his satirical *In pseudodialecticos*, the most important text included in the 1519 compendium. While much of the debates on language teaching at the University of Louvain were centred on the relationship between Erasmus's humanism and biblical studies, *In pseudodialecticos* largely omitted theological exegesis and was rather structured as a plea for a humanist dialectic that could serve as the foundation of a humanist *trivium*. Secondly, I aim to show that this interpretation of dialectic was explicitly connected with the possibilities of a life of *negotium* not only in *In pseudodialecticos* but also in Vives's other writings of the time. I contend that his experimentations with the genre of declamation in *Declamationes Syllanae* can best be seen as an exercise in a distinctively political realisation of a life at the service of the community.

Vives's familiarity with Erasmian themes in *Opuscula* was not a coincidence since he was well acquainted with the Dutch humanist at this point of his life, and it has been rightly argued that around 1520, his career experienced a definite upswing.[83] He had probably had some connections to the Low Countries at least since 1512, and he might have been aware of some of Erasmus's work at the time.[84] What is certain, nevertheless, is that by late 1514 Vives had moved permanently to the Low Countries, and by 1516 he was already well connected both to the humanist circles of the Burgundian Netherlands and to the royal court in Brussels.[85] By the late 1510s, he was recognised as a humanist of great promise not only in the Netherlands but also by some of the leading European humanists such as Guillaume Budé. It is very likely that it was the support of Erasmus that had at least partly guaranteed Vives a favourable position at court, as well as academic visibility in Louvain and the services of the respected printer Thierry Martens.

Vives's incorporation into Dutch humanism occurred exactly at the moment in which Erasmus had just embarked on the most prolific phase of the development of his philosophy of Christ (*philosophia Christi*) in its various forms. *Philosophia Christi*, which united moral philosophy and theology, sought to cultivate a spiritual religion that would not only speak to the intellect through philosophical propositions but that could also transform, mould, and reconstitute one's spirit and way of living to the standards set by Christ himself in the totality of his life (*veritas vitae*). However, as Erasmus pointed out, this philosophy did not deal only with Church reform or the purification of sacred texts; in its perfect form, it would permeate all human activities, moving from theology to the moral, legal, political, and educational realms. In his *Paraclesis*, one of the fundamental texts uniting humanist scholarship to biblical studies and the introduction to his 1516 edition of *Novum Instrumentum*, he argued that if this philosophy reigned in princes, preachers, and schoolmasters, then the Christian republic would be free from discord on all levels of human intercourse.[86] Indeed, Erasmus pursued literary activities in the spirit of *philosophia Christi* on a variety of fronts, ranging from educational materials to political texts (*Institutio principis Christiani*).

The Erasmian worldview underlined learned piety (*docta pietas*) and further reinforced the union of humanist developments in the teaching of *trivium* and the incorporation of classical thought within a philosophy of Christ. The Erasmian syllabus, as it was outlined in *De ratione studii* (*On the Right Method of Study*, 1512), offered a decidedly classical curriculum for educational contexts. Erasmus's *Enchiridion militis Christiani* (*Handbook of a Christian Knight*, 1503), a presentation of a way of life and learning for any Christian, put forth a full-fledged humanist programme that not only provided the student with a necessary literary introduction to the secrets of allegorical, and ultimately true, levels of the Scriptures, but also served as a morally edifying educational pattern in itself. Although *Enchiridion* expressed some reservations with regard to poetry in a Parisian vein, the Erasmian programme was remarkably permissive as to the pagan tradition since it could adopt almost everything, provided that it was understood and interpreted in the right Christian spirit.[87] As has been seen, several of his works made a far-reaching attempt to incorporate classical genres and rhetorical precepts into the production of language. What is more, Erasmus described the importance of classical genres in a language not so different from that of the Parisian humanists. In the famous *Encomium Moriae* (*Praise of Folly*, 1511), he defended his liberty of speech and use of satire by claiming that he was offering advice and censuring vice without mentioning individual names; and in a letter to Martinus Dorp (1485–1525), he further endorsed his *Moria* by elaborating on how he aspired to bring forth moral improvement through amusement. He wrote that his 'purpose was guidance and not satire; to help, not to hurt; to show men how to become better and not to stand in their way'.[88] Ultimately, Erasmus put forward a conceptual framework within which a permissive attitude to humanist literary studies could be united with a theological and ethical programme.

Despite its Christian component, much of Erasmus's programme was outrightly polemical, and the years between 1514 and 1519 had witnessed a growing antagonism in the relationship between humanists and scholastics. The main reason for this was that Erasmus had followed the path set by

Lorenzo Valla and Jacques Lefèvre d'Étaples and turned humanist grammatical and philological tools to the use of biblical hermeneutics.[89] This approach to theology not only put into jeopardy the prestige of Europe's foremost theologians and theological departments, but it also questioned a whole tradition of discussing theological matters and problems arising from the interpretation of the Scripture through scholastic dialectical methods. The debate had an institutional setting in Louvain. While certain colleges at the Faculty of Arts in Louvain had a tradition of humanist teaching in grammar and rhetoric much like in Paris, the foundation of an autonomous institution, *Collegium Trilingue*, in 1517 led to serious tensions within the academic community of Louvain. The *Collegium* was a realisation of an older dream of providing students with the knowledge of all biblical languages, and its connection to Erasmus's own project of biblical studies was quite explicit.[90] Thus, in 1519, when Vives published his *Opuscula varia* in Louvain, he was in the centre of a polemic in which the dichotomy between scholasticism and humanism was transformed into a highly significant question of theology and, ultimately, of the limits and possibilities of humanist learning vis-à-vis the art that clarified truth: dialectic. Consequently, it is not a surprise that the central piece of the 1519–1520 *oeuvre*, *In pseudodialecticos*, deliberately engaged in a polemical debate with the dialectical method, the jewel in the crown of the scholastic *trivium*.

In *In pseudodialecticos*, Vives drew on the topics of the scholastic – humanism debate, a genre with an already long history in fifteenth-century Italy.[91] Some of the controversies, such as the famous epistolary exchange between Giovanni Pico della Mirandola and Ermolao Barbaro, were most likely known to Vives, but he was also aware of more current disputes in which Erasmus, supported by Thomas More, took on Louvain theologians. The first of these was Erasmus's exchange of letters with Martinus Dorp, a theologian not altogether unfavourable to humanities and the humanist circles.[92]

In a letter written in September 1514, Dorp denounced Erasmus's intention of applying humanist literary tools to the reading of the New Testament – a project that would lead to his *Novum Instrumentum* in 1516 – by insisting that 'truth and integrity' were 'qualities of the Vulgate edition'.[93] A philological reading based on Greek manuscripts would not only fail to fix the original version of the Vulgate but would also put its authority and the tradition of interpretation built on it into severe danger. As Dorp argued, Erasmus's project would be extremely harmful since a 'great many people will discuss the integrity of the Scriptures, and many will have doubts about it, if the presence of the least scrap of falsehood in them becomes known'.[94] After Erasmus's long response to Dorp, in which he affirmed the utility of humanist learning for the study of Scriptures, Dorp took the question to a more theoretical level that openly touched upon the relationship between humanist *trivium* and scholastic dialectic. He evoked the standard distinction of humanist studies as dealing with the elegance of the words while traditional theology

36   *Becoming a humanist*

was based on the science of things (*rerum scientia*) provided by dialectic.[95] Deliberately attacking the humanist union of eloquence and wisdom, Dorp argued that linguistic barbarism and wisdom were, in reality, compatible by posing the rhetorical question: 'But who except a perfect fool would not rather be wise even if he were to be a shining example of barbarism, than write beautifully without wisdom?'[96] Furthermore, he insisted that no philological reading could ever clarify all problems arising from the Scriptures (e.g. the correct administration of the sacraments) unless one employed dialectical methods.[97]

Erasmus provided a staunch reply to Dorp's first letter, underlining the uselessness of scholastic dialectic. His criticism was, however, largely based on the repetition of humanist commonplaces and it omitted methodological questions, which was hardly surprising given his strong distaste for dialectic.[98] The Erasmian union between literary studies, biblical languages, and theology became somewhat of a commonplace in humanist texts printed in Louvain, such as Petrus Mosellanus's (1493–1524) *Oratio de variarum linguarum cognitione* (1518), but like Erasmus, these works seldom took on scholasticism over the role of dialectic.[99] It was mostly in Thomas More's response to the second letter from Dorp to Erasmus that the debate was taken to the controversial question of the dialectical method. Against Dorp's accusations that Erasmus did not really understand dialectic, More claimed that Erasmus was actually superior to most dialecticians in the art of disputing. In More's redefinition of dialectic, several things converged. First, he argued that dialectic should be based on an analysis of the rules of propositions and argumentation as they happened in common language, challenging the very notion of a formal language central to the scholastic tradition.[100] Second, this reassessment was linked to a philological reading of Aristotle, the foremost authority on dialectic, who had been unaware of much of scholastic logic such as the highly developed formal semantics epitomised by the theory of supposition. In this spirit, More argued that dialectic should be a 'tool to the other branches of learning' rather than an end in itself.[101] Third, More, just like Erasmus, argued that traditional scholastic dialectic employed in theology was utterly incapable of enhancing concord since it could not transform its audience, and, what was perhaps even worse, because it provided heretics with material to 'strike back' by deploying the 'very problems with which they are assaulted'.[102]

Vives's *In pseudodialecticos* was heavily indebted to More's letter to Dorp, as More himself well knew.[103] Although Vives, like most humanists, agreed that dialectic was an art that dealt with truth, he presented a distinctively humanist philosophy of language focused on historical semantics to the detriment of formal ones. Like More, Vives emphasised that dialectic was effectively an analysis of semantic, argumentative, and propositional patterns of used language, and much of the argument was dedicated to the development of the different ramifications of this theme. As Vives claimed, 'the logician does not create new rules or expound the true essence of language, but rather teaches rules that have been observed in inveterate and familiar usage'.[104] Just as in a broad tradition of humanist interpretation epitomised by Lorenzo Valla, the standard of usage was not associated with spoken language but with the work of classical *auctores* and most importantly Cicero. Vives lamented that those who searched for linguistic rigor, 'that true and direct meaning of Latin sentences', did not look for it 'from Cicero, nor Quintilian' but 'from Peter of Spain or whoever preceded him'.[105]

Like More, Vives pointed out that a philological understanding of Aristotle, which More had connected to Lefèvre's project, would reveal a different philosopher altogether.[106] Vives asked sarcastically, 'is anyone of the opinion that Aristotle fitted his logic to a language which he had invented for himself, instead of to the current form of Greek which everyone spoke?'[107] Aristotle regarded 'senseless suppositions, extensions, restrictions and other petty terms' as 'extrinsic to the art of logic in that they contradicted man's common sense and habits of speech'.[108] Vives claimed that the *Organon*, a set of six books that contained all of Aristotelian logic and constituted the basis for the medieval commentary tradition, consisted entirely 'of a few brief precepts'.[109] According to him, the *Organon* should be taken literally as an instrument or tool with which 'the young boy proceeds to the other arts and sciences, since disciplines that are learned for the sake of other disciplines [...] should not occupy his studies for too long a time'.[110] Focusing solely on its perfection would be as stupid as if a shoemaker were to dedicate all his/her time to improving his/her tools.[111]

The dialectic of scholastics did not play its role as a tool. It failed to serve pedagogical purposes since it did not sharpen the mind and, more importantly, it severely detracted from the potential of language to carry out its social and communicative function. In a satirical critique of the conceptualist position, Vives instructed the reader that if words were to mean what each individual considered them to mean, 'no one will understand anyone else, since everyone will be using words in his own way rather than in the commonly accepted way'.[112] Whereas all other arts had a practical or contemplative end, dialectic could not claim either. The only people one could speak to using dialectical language would be ones' own disciples, and Vives brushed aside the argument that dialectic could produce certain knowledge (*scientia*).[113] The clarity and simplicity of Vives's own language were contrasted to scholastic dialectic, which aspired to a cunning victory in a debate, rather than to truth.[114] Like in More, this underlined that dialectic, rather than producing concord, unity of opinion, and truth, led to endless debates and division, violating the communicative duties of speech. Finally, knowledge of dialectic could not be put to use by other disciplines as it failed to perform its supportive functions for other domains of intellectual life.

These domains doubtless included theology. According to Vives, there were some theologians who thought that there could be 'no exactitude of speech' which was not 'adorned with horrid and rank barbarity, and stuffed with the vain devices of sophistry'. They were surprised to find out that in

Augustine there was nothing 'resembling the teaching of their logic textbooks'.[115] Still, it is extremely significant that, unlike More's letter to Dorp, the critique of dialectic found in *In pseudodialecticos* never brought theology into its main argumentative thread. Vives, for instance, omitted completely some of the most widely debated theological issues such as the study of biblical languages or the transformative philosophy of Christ so central to the Erasmian project in the late 1510s. Instead, *In pseudodialecticos* asserted that a technical restructuring of dialectic could serve as a new basis for all arts functioning in all domains of life. Within this wide-ranging critique, Vives linked dialectic to those humanist arts that he considered useful in an active life in the service of the community, a point strengthened by the selection of Cicero and Quintilian, to the detriment of Christian authors, as the foremost models of language usage throughout *In pseudodialecticos*.

Vives went to considerable lengths in his account of how professional dialecticians were completely ignorant of all practical matters related to a life of *negotium*. This criticism did not, perhaps, quite do justice to contemporary scholasticism, since it omitted the casuistic method that was employed for the resolution of current problems by many scholastics (e.g. John Mair). Yet, it accentuates the extent to which Vives connected a technical question of semantics to its relevance for active life. When confronted with social matters, 'you would think that they have been transferred to a new world, it is to that extent that they are ignorant about life and common sense'.[116] He claimed that, despite their external appearance, there was little humanity in these dialecticians[117] and went on to argue that 'they are most inept for undertaking negotiations, for taking part in embassies, for the administration of affairs, be they public or private, and for the handling of people's souls'.[118] The reason for this was their lack of knowledge on *studia humanitatis*:

> They do not cultivate the kind of arts that teach all these things, and that form the soul and human life: for example, moral philosophy, which adorns customs and minds; history, the mother of knowledge, and experience of things, namely prudence. Oratory, that teaches and governs life and opinion, and politics and economics on which the guiding of familial and city affairs is based.[119]

Although *In pseudodialecticos* mostly focused on criticism rather than on the presentation of a constructive alternative, Vives gave some hints as to what a reconfigured dialectic would look like. His main point was that dialectic should be an integral part of a humanist *trivium*, based on a descriptive rather than prescriptive analysis of language usage (*sermo*) in classical authors. Whereas rhetoric discovered 'ornament, brilliance, or gracefulness of expression', dialectic 'finds out truth, falsehood, or probability' in common speech.[120] Despite their separate tasks in the process of reading and writing, Vives repeatedly underscored the fundamental union of the *artes sermocinales* by criticising scholastic language for its rhetorical frigidity and Peter of Spain[121] for not knowing 'more about the force of individual [Latin] words than the Scythian, whom I just mentioned, would know about the essence of the Spanish language, which he had never seen written or heard spoken by anyone'.[122] This critique produced an extremely close union between dialectic and the rhetorical force of language, which had been dealt with as separate issues by scholastic writers, as exemplified by Dorp's claim about the compatibility of wisdom and linguistic barbarism.

The Evolution of Humanist Dialectic

Despite its polemical and critical tone, *In pseudodialecticos* was not just a vague call for a new dialectic but echoed larger developments in the field. Indeed, the critical dimension of *In pseudodialecticos* must be viewed in the context for a shared humanist quest for a renewed dialectic that would offer practical support for rhetorical composition.

Although Erasmus's 1512 *De ratione studii* did not mention any humanist treatises on dialectic, recommending solely Aristotle as a good introduction to the discipline,[123] and although the most prolific phase in the production of humanist dialectical manuals took place from the 1520s onwards, some works had developed a distinctively non-scholastic dialectic more suitable for humanist literary tasks. Valla's *Dialectice* (*Repastinatio dialecticae et philosophiae*), printed in 1509 by Bade in Paris, was outrightly polemical against the existing tradition, calling for a dialectic based on common language and subjected to rhetoric, the most noble art of the *trivium*.[124] Trebizond's *Dialectica* (*Isagoge dialectica*), printed in 1508 in Paris, offered a brief explanation of Aristotle's dialectic leaving aside much of the scholastic additions, at times underlining the usefulness of dialectic to oratory.[125] It was, however, Rudolph Agricola's (1443?–1485) *De inventione dialectica* (printed for the first time in 1515) that must have been Vives's main constructive reference point at the time. Vives did not mention Agricola in *In pseudodialecticos*, but he appears as the main authority in dialectic in Vives's (1522) commentaries on Augustine's *De civitate Dei* (*The City of God*) and in his later works. In the commentaries, he maintained that he had earlier written a short poem (*distichon*) in which he had praised Agricola's *De inventione dialectica* as the best extant Latin work on the subject.[126] This was not surprising. Agricola was perhaps the most famous Dutch humanist of the fifteenth century who, with extensive knowledge of Italian humanism, had played a crucial role in the development of humanism in the North and was greatly admired by the Erasmian circles.[127] In the 1510s and 1520s, many humanists in Erasmian circles promoted *De inventione dialectica* as an authoritative text on dialectic, and some – such as the jurist Claudius Cantiuncula (c.1496–1560) – even structured their works on the basis of Agricola's topical dialectic.[128] When it was printed for the first time in 1515 by Thierry Martens, it was prepared by a group of humanists from the Louvain circle, most notably Alardus

Amstelredamus (1491–1544), and officially supported by a theologian of the stature of Martinus Dorp, who, despite his disagreements with Erasmus, was favourable to many aspects of the Erasmian programme.[129]

New dialectical materials were eagerly praised for their contributions to other humanist linguistic arts. Josse Bade's short introduction to Valla's *Repastinatio* claimed that it could be of profit for both dialectic and rhetorical disputations.[130] Beatus Rhenanus's (1485–1547) prefatory letter to a Strasbourg edition of Trebizond's *Dialectica* (1509) also linked the reformation of dialectic to a broader narrative of the expulsion of barbarism from Germany and the rebirth of the liberal arts.[131] In another prefatory letter to Trebizond's treatise, Jacques Lefèvre described a meeting in Rome with two eloquent young men who, to his surprise, were not only educated in the *ars humanitatis* but also in philosophy and dialectic.[132] The union of dialectical learning and eloquence was also apparent in Guillaume Budé's *Annotationes*, in which his praise of dialectic (*laus dialecticae*) in the context of civil law (*ius civile*) was taken verbatim from Cicero's *Brutus*. This dialectic was extremely practical since it functioned in close connection with the rhetorical handling of particular questions. In the *Brutus*, Servius Sulpicius epitomised this dialectic, 'which teaches the analysis of a whole into its component parts, sets forth and defines the latent and implicit, interprets and makes clear the obscure; which first recognizes the ambiguous and then distinguishes; which applies in short a rule or measure for adjudging truth and falsehood, for determining what conclusions follow from what premises', and to all this Servius Sulpicius added 'a knowledge of letters and a finished style of speaking'.[133] Interestingly, Vives, in his *Praelectio in Leges Ciceronis*, quoted the exact same passage from Cicero, thus framing what was to be expected from useful dialectical learning.[134]

There were both practical and conceptual reasons for the propagation of a humanist dialectic. If one wanted to argue against scholastic dialecticians for the unbreakable union of wisdom and eloquence in all disciplines, then the central art of the curriculum that dealt with truth could hardly be passed over in silence. When humanism emerged as an overarching alternative to scholasticism across the spectrum of disciplines, it was no longer possible to let fundamental questions of method go untouched. But humanist dialectic was not just a necessary reaction against scholasticism; it provided a very hands-on method for textual analysis and the production of arguments that enabled a structured handling of argumentative topics (*loci*). Agricola's work exemplified this approach and showed how *loci* could be used in virtually all linguistic production.

Agricola's *De inventione dialectica* was not merely a technical treatment of argument but a work that taught the reader possible ways of reading, taking notes, and talking and writing in a convincing manner.[135] In all this, it was supposed to fulfil the rhetorical task of teaching (*docere*). As its name implied, it focused almost exclusively on one of the two tasks of dialectic: the invention of arguments (*inventio*), mostly disregarding the part that dealt with the judgment of the formal aspects of terms, propositions, and arguments (*iudicium*). Its system of topics offered headings for investigating terms in any question proposed, thus pointing towards all possible connections between the terms that could be used in the construction of propositions and arguments. It could be employed in the investigation of both general questions where no contextual elements were present (traditionally part of dialectic) and of particular questions where contextual elements were introduced (what a specific person should do/should we go to a war at this moment), and it underscored the interconnections between both types of questions since particular questions always imply general issues. For instance, 'should Cato marry?' is conceptually dependent on the more generally problem of whether a Stoic philosopher should marry, something that a successful orator should understand. As an example of a general question, Agricola analysed 'whether a philosopher should take a wife' by running through all possible topics from definitions to a range of other relations that could potentially offer information about philosophers and wives. This method provided a topical description of a given term (here philosopher and wife), and the aim was to find a middle term that linked or separated philosopher and wife and built a connection or a disconnection between the two terms depending on the formulated question and argumentative task at hand. In the case of philosophers and wives, the definition of philosopher described him as a 'follower of virtue', whereas the definition of a wife included the task of bringing up children. Since upbringing converged with care for virtue, one could, for instance, argue that the procreation of children was part of the duties of virtue (*officium*), which implied that a philosopher could take a wife.[136]

Agricola's system for analysing terms did not connect terms to any fixed set of categories but rather provided a flexible tool for the creation and refutation of arguments on any question proposed. The questions analysed were not stable, but they could instead be described as constructions of the orator and writer that referred to those points he/she had to make to produce convincing arguments for his/her case. The investigation of questions was connected to rhetorical viewpoints in several ways. The credibility of argumentation in a given question was related to the estimation the orator or writer made of his/her audience and of the opposition he/she would face, since it was only in relation to their beliefs and attitudes that the issues calling for argumentation or explanation could be determined in the first place.[137] Furthermore, Book Three of *De inventione dialectica* showed how dialectical topics could be put to use in the arousal of emotions, which had traditionally been part of the subject matter of classical rhetoric and especially of Aristotle's work.[138] Throughout the treatise, Agricola discussed dialectical invention and the treatment of questions as part of the duties (*officia*) and persuasive aspirations of classical rhetoric.

Agricola's insistence that all questions – both general and particular – could be analysed through dialectical topics both introduced dialectic into rhetoric and rhetorised dialectic. Rhetorical handbooks had traditionally been structured around task-bound tools and commonplaces that were classified according to the specific issues (questions, parts of speech) within the three genera of classical rhetoric. In *Ad Herennium*, for instance, deliberative questions have their specific topics catalogued under the honourable (*honestum*) and the expedient (*utilitas*), and very specific strategies for argumentation were offered. If one wanted to argue that considerations of safety (a heading under expediency) are more important than virtues and honour, one could state that 'no one can make use of his virtues if he has not based his plans upon safety' or that 'nothing ought to be deemed honourable which does not produce safety'.[139] Analogously, different genres of oratory possessed their own places for invention. In contrast, Agricola proposed that all questions could be analysed through a limited system of dialectical topics through which one could capture all the information provided by rhetorical handbooks if the case so demanded. The creative potential of these topics owed much to the fact that they provided a general index, an intertextual tool through which everything learned in grammar and rhetoric could be organised to produce speech and writing.

Agricola himself underlined that the topics were a continuum of all humanist literary endeavours. He not only emphasised the separate contributions of the arts of *trivium* to the same task – the successful production of speech and writing – but he also repeatedly linked his presentation of topics to an analysis of rhetorical pieces such as Cicero's speeches.[140] Moreover, Agricola was always unequivocal that topics could be of help in turning the authoritative statements extracted from valued texts and classified under topics into material for one's own writing and speaking. His highly popular *De formando studio*, printed by Thierry Martens in 1511, argued that one of the main goals of collecting and arranging topics and commonplaces was that it allowed the student to treat any theme in a personal and inventive way. Agricola claimed that if one did all this merely for the sake of acquiring information, we would be like books ourselves and that it was in one's own writing and speaking where 'seems to lie the main fruit of the long effort and care that we put into studying'.[141] In this process, dialectic could and should be the best organisational tool for the generation of writing and arguments.

The *Trivium* and a Life of *Negotium*

While humanist dialectical works offered painstakingly technical discussions and practical tools for argumentation in specialised treatises, these developments should also be seen in the context of the broader discourse on language. As we have seen, Vives mocked scholastic dialectic for the impracticality of its views on language for communication, and he strongly underlined the importance of an active life in the service of the community (*negotium*), largely dependent on the use of speech, in several texts from the same period. This offers another angle to the idea, already evident *In pseudodialecticos*, that dialectic should primarily be a tool that provided argumentative support for language use in practical situations. We can see this in Vives's assessment of the contributions of different disciplines, in the heroes he promotes (mostly Cicero and Socrates), and in his own interpretation of the meaning of his *Declamationes Syllanae*.

His short sketch of the history of philosophy, *De initiis, sectis et laudibus philosophiae* (1519), while underlining the ultimate unity of all philosophy as participation in truth and as a path to the 'immortal Prince of the Universe' (*mundi Princeps immortalis*), emphasised the usefulness of ethical philosophy for its ability to enhance virtue.[142] Following Cicero, Vives granted the palm for the invention of moral philosophy to Socrates, who was 'the first to take philosophy [...] and apply it to daily life and customs both of states and of individuals', and who promoted the idea that 'people should turn themselves wholeheartedly to the adjustment of their lives'. For this reason, he was considered the wisest man in Greece.[143] After lavishly praising the utility of natural sciences for social living, he came back to moral philosophy: 'the study of how each person is to order his life, of governing both public and private matters' that enabled our life to be 'restored to its humanity'.[144] Vives also strongly underscored the role of political philosophy, lawgivers, and rulers in the development of the medicine of the soul (*medicina animorum*) that could cure vice and lead to virtue.[145]

In addition to the figure of Socrates, to whom Erasmus referred as St Socrates in his *Convivium religiosum* (*The Godly feast*, 1522), Cicero often appeared as a hero who put his intellectual and literary competence at the service of the community.[146] Vives had already lectured on Cicero's *De legibus* and *De officiis* at Paris and professed admiration for Cicero's eloquence in his printed lecture on *Ad Herennium*. In 1519, Vives added an eloquent biography and appreciation of Cicero to a new edition of his *Praelectio in Leges Ciceronis*, originally printed in 1514.[147] He opened the description with a lengthy appraisal of Cicero's natural capacities for all the liberal arts and praised his adherence to and talent for 'poetry, philosophy, and oratory, which at the time in Rome was highly esteemed and considered', and underlined that Cicero put all his knowledge at the service of the Republic.[148] Vives defended Cicero's accommodation of his message to contextual requirements: he reminded those who accuse him of *leggerezza* (*levitas*) of 'the wisdom and cautiousness with which he acted in the *forum*, and his flexibility to adapt to circumstances'.[149] Ultimately, Cicero, with his eloquence and wisdom, was a fierce defender of the liberty of the Republic.[150] Thus, whereas Socrates epitomised the skills of a moral teacher and a physician of the soul, Cicero embodied the qualities of a prudent man who had to operate in the world of politics where contextual sensitivity was needed.

The life of *negotium* that one finds in Vives was in some crucial ways different from a classical interpretation of a civic life in the service of the community. In Cicero's *De officiis*, it was stated that 'the whole glory of virtue is in activity' and this idea was quite explicitly connected with the activity of a citizen.[151] Vives, on the other hand, clearly thought of civic life merely as one possibility to put one's knowledge at the service of the community. In the much later *De disciplinis*, in giving his fullest account of the life of an erudite, Vives certainly stressed the importance of serving others, claiming that the ultimate goal of studies is that we 'employ them for the public good'.[152] Unlike in Cicero, the public good was not, however, the good of a single political community but of the world: 'a wise man should think of the whole world as if it was a city whose citizen he himself is'.[153] He had made the same point already in his 1519 *Praefatio in Leges Ciceronis* and it referred to the Stoic-Christian idea of the world as a community of reason or spirituality in which a life of active participation, as depicted in *De disciplinis*, included different possibilities ranging from a political life as a counsellor to the teaching of the people.[154] But while a political life of *negotium* was just one realisation of one's service to others, several issues indicate that Vives saw it as quite a significant one. The stress put on *studia humantitatis* in *In pseudodialecticos*, the importance of Cicero as a model of a citizen, and, as we will see, the description of the contexts in which language should be used all imply that a political life was an important way to realise one's duties towards others.

Active life in its different forms was dependent on language. For those who wanted to put their linguistic competence to use in ethical philosophy as moral educators or transformative healers (like Socrates) or as citizens (like Cicero), humanist dialectical and rhetorical manuals offered organisational tools, but they had to be complemented with materials at which the topics used in *inventio* were meant to point. Since topics always referred to authoritative statements, they gathered texts and sentences confirmed by the tradition and divulged in the classroom. Consequently, an important way of introducing humanist commonplaces and wisdom into the educational context was through textbooks. Erasmus was perhaps the humanist who most clearly understood the value of schoolbooks. Much of his theological, ethical, and political precepts were included in educational materials the topics organised, which meant that they could be called on in the production of writing. Erasmus's *Adagia* and *Colloquia* were good examples of this. These works did not offer deep insights into the organisational principles of rhetoric or dialectic but provided ample content and examples for rhetorical production in the form of proverbs (*Adagia*) – that were sometimes amplified into proper essays – and exemplary dialogues (*Colloquia*).

In Erasmus's *Adagia* and *Colloquia*, a reader would find the basic message of Erasmian theological, moral, and political philosophy in a simple, compact, and easy to memorise form. *Adagia* was one of Erasmus's most popular works, an anthology where proverbs appeared as headings followed by an explanation or commentary on its meaning, origins, and possible uses.[155] Some of the main Erasmian ideas such as his philosophy of Christ, his Christian pacifism, and his ideas of Christian rule and rulers could be found in a range of adages such as *Dulce bellum inexpertis* (*War is treat to those who have not tried it*), *Sileni Alcibiadis* (*Alcibiades' Silenus*), *Aut regem aut fatuum nasci oportere* (*One ought to be born a king or a fool*), *Scarabeus aquilam quaerit* (*A dung-beetle hunting an eagle*), as well as in his most famous dialogue of the *Colloquia, Convivium religiosum*. *Dulce bellum inexpertis*, for instance, presented a condemnation of warfare in an approachable form to students. For anyone writing about war and searching for arguments for or against *bellum*, it would offer Erasmian commonplaces in abundance for the construction of one's own argument. Similarly, in *Scarabeus aquilam quaerit*, one found what was arguably Erasmus's most forceful denunciation of tyranny. The overtly critical political and social elements of the texts did not go unnoticed by Erasmus's contemporaries.[156]

The material extracted from texts and organised under topics could be reassembled into writing in various kinds of school exercises ranging from poetry to letter writing. In this way, Agricola's dialectical topics or the more rhetorical precepts on verbal and argumentative abundance (Erasmus's *De copia*) could be exercised in practice.[157] The pinnacle of oratorical training was the declamation, an exercise in argumentation for advanced students on a fictional judicial (*controversia*) or political (*suasoria*) case, the classical examples of which included Seneca the Elder's *Declamations* and pseudo-Quintilian's Minor and Major *Declamations*. Underlining the centrality of declamations, Quintilian, one of the foremost authorities on rhetorical and literary training, had claimed that declamation was the most refined rhetorical exercise which included all other exercises described in his *Institutio oratoria* and which, despite its fictional character, should 'provide the closest image of reality'.[158] In agreement with the declamatory exercise, Erasmus's *De copia* had described at length how one could come up with propositions and arguments in deliberative speeches (*suasoria*). *De copia* discussed the treatment of political themes in the context of current issues by showing, for instance, how one could persuade a king not to start a war with the king of France and how to persuade the pope not to make war on Venice.[159] This offered explicit advice on how to turn critical commonplaces on warfare into a speech.

By considering a range of contextual phenomena such as the relationship between the speaker and the audience or the relevant emotional dispositions of one's listeners, Vives's *Declamationes Syllanae* likewise showed how one could put everything learned in grammar, rhetoric, and dialectic courses into practice. The supposed political nature of the *Declamationes* has aroused some curiosity in modern scholarship.[160] It has been pointed out that there was a potential conflict in Vives's stated reasons for writing the work since, on the one hand, he stressed the fictional side of declamations and put great emphasis on the adaptation of arguments to characters and historically specific questions. On the other hand, he stated that one could draw political lessons from the *Declamationes*.[161] Considering Vives's own interpretation of his *Declamationes*, it is hard to see them merely as a fictional reconstruction of the classical past without any contemporary relevance.[162] This relevance could, in the traditional spirit of declamations, comprise a generic and a substantial dimension. The work can therefore be seen as an exercise in rhetorical politics: it taught political maxims, but it simultaneously showed how they should be moulded to specific situations in accordance with a contextual analysis.

Vives strongly underlined the political significance of the *Declamationes* in a dedication letter to the Emperor's brother Prince Ferdinand (1503–1564). The *Declamationes*, explained Vives, showed that a stable rule could only be based on 'the good will of one's subordinates' since in a regime grounded on fear even the slight possibility of free speech would make 'unfeigned opinions break out into the open'. The *Declamationes* would remind Ferdinand that 'the prince should do nothing which does not put the public interest above his personal welfare'.[163] A call for political rule based on virtue and love according to the common good was, of course, firmly in line with existing political literature and endlessly repeated in Erasmus's *Institutio principis Christiani*, a treatise that Vives mentioned in his letter to Ferdinand.[164]

Even more importantly, Vives highlighted the political possibilities of the *Declamationes* as a civic genre in his *Praefatio*. In keeping with the corpus of Vives's writings around 1520, all this was woven together with a critique of scholasticism and a call for a political life exemplified by Cicero. The scholastics to whom the philosophical and oratorical works of Pliny, Seneca, and Cicero were mere grammar 'are too narrow and low to embrace the admirable counsels, the lofty and wide-ranging prudence which one finds in Cicero's orations'.[165] Cicero's orations, Vives claimed, 'have disclosed and made visible the power of his talents and his advice, his experience in affairs and in governing the state', suggesting that perhaps scholastics wanted to leave to grammarians the task of developing 'the arguments and strategies for handling public affairs'.[166] Part of this was knowledge on how to 'gather what you have developed into an order whereby the parts of it will not get in each other's way, and everything you use will do more for your case in the location you assign than it would anywhere else'.[167] Whereas earlier Roman philosophers 'could have spent their days [...] in the magnificence of public life', and possessed 'knowledge of times past (*praeteritorum temporum cognitio*), a grasp of the principles of speaking (*praecepta dicendi*), and the celebrated art of living with their fellow citizens (*ars civilis*)', modern philosophers 'break down most pathetically' when 'they condescend to politics, or the study of the soul and human behavior, or home and family life'.[168] Declamations could be of help for Roman philosophers in their career; in the government of public affairs, Seneca 'occupied himself with others' declamations and drew ideas from them'.[169] Furthermore, Vives pointed out that in declamatory exercises, one did not necessarily speak one's mind but 'what is likely to persuade' since this was 'the ground-rule of declamation'.[170] Ultimately, as Edward George has argued, the *Declamationes* could be read as the dynamic and more eloquent counterpart of Erasmus's *Institutio*, composed very much as a collection of commonplaces, a point Vives made in his dedicatory epistle to the 1538 edition of the declamations when he argued that 'what is communicated in other works by precepts is tendered here by examples'.[171]

The focus on what could persuade trained one to use material drawn from topics according to all possible contextual phenomena, a point emphasised by both the rhetorical tradition and the dialectical work of Agricola. The *Declamationes* fulfilled this promise. Situated in the time of Sulla's tyrannical dictatorship (81–79 BC), the orations referred to historical circumstances but, despite some classical reference points, were fictional in nature.[172] One finds in *Declamationes* five different speeches, the first (Quintus Fundanus) and second (Marcus Fonteius) of which argued for the abdication of Sulla on both sides of the matter. The third was Sulla's own resignation speech, and the fourth and the fifth orations flowed from the mouth of Marcus Aemilius Lepidus and dealt with Sulla's condemnation and his possible public funerals respectively. The corpus of five speeches offered deliberations about future actions, assessments of the lawfulness of past actions, and moral evaluations of characters incorporating elements flexibly from different genres of classical rhetoric.

One can think of the second speech delivered by Marcus Fonteius as exhibiting the virtues of *decorum* demanded of a deliberative question debated under a tyrant. Fonteius built his case in order to dismantle the arguments made by Quintus Fundanus against the abdication of Sulla. Through a treatment of a sequence of questions formulated on the basis of Fundanus's claims, Fonteius argued that to abdicate was the right course of action because it was the honest and expedient thing to do for the Republic and clearly in line with Sulla's personal interest as well. Sulla should abdicate because his work to cure the maladies of the Republic was completed, and his adherence to dictatorship would constitute a fundamental threat to Roman political culture. If one was afraid of a civil war, one should not stick with dictatorship but abdicate since a defiance of Republican customs would lead to a boiling up of hatred that would burst into a civil war after Sulla's death. Moreover, instead of considering dictatorship as an anticipatory remedy for all possible threats, it was necessary to trust the mechanisms of the Republic, one of which was a temporally limited dictatorship, to solve its problems.[173]

In arguing for the case from Sulla's private point of view, Fonteius exemplified an argumentation that tried to consider Sulla's possible emotional dispositions by presenting his solution as the only path to a fulfilling life and immortal glory. Against Fundanus's argument that power was the supreme, godly good, Fonteius claimed that in a perfect, uncorrupted natural state this could indeed be the case since it would mean a happy life under the guidance of the best and the most prudent, but that in the current state of affairs leadership was a burden.[174] Since everyone strove for tranquillity and peace, a private life of *otium* was the only possibility because in a public life one was always burdened by the duties of the office and the fear of

48 *Becoming a humanist*

the people's anger.[175] Abdication would not only serve the interest of the Republic and the private interest of Sulla's family, protecting it from the hatred of the people, but it would also be a source of true glory in accordance with the Roman tradition. Although Sulla's actions as a dictator had been successful in the realisation of his ends – such as peace or the reestablishment and dignity of the Roman Republic – true glory did not stem from the possession of offices but from being commonly regarded as worthy of office, something only achievable through abdication.[176] In short, Fundanus played on Sulla's fears and thirst for glory by arguing that while he had so far acted correctly, a denial of abdicating would be interpreted as the action of a tyrant. A positive assessment of Sulla's deeds contrasted with Lepidus's post-abdication speeches where Sulla's actions during his dictatorship were described systematically as tyrannical at a time when the fear caused by his judgment had ceased to play any role and, consequently, Lepidus was able to speak more freely. In devising the speeches and the tone under Sulla, Vives could have drawn from Quintilian, the foremost authority on declamations, who, in *Institutio oratoria*, described situations where it was 'unsafe to speak openly'. These included school exercises where we were addressing an abdicating tyrant, in which cases we should employ the figure of emphasis to hide our meaning.[177] All this illustrates the extent to which the selection of arguments and the way they were presented was determined by contextual factors throughout *Declamationes*.

In some sense, technical issues related to grammar and dialectic, reverence to Cicero and Socrates, and Vives's own rhetorical compositions in *Declamationes* were, of course, separate discussions, and it would perhaps be too much to argue that the *Declamationes* have a direct textual relationship to Vives's understanding of dialectic. Still, as Vives himself pointed out in the introduction to the work, *Declamationes* revealed a participatory ideal that could not be realised through scholastic education and that was enabled by humanist methods. In *Declamationes*, the debates on the nature of language and meaning with the scholastics, humanist argumentative methods for producing text, and the stress put on the use of language in a life of *negotium* came together nicely. It displayed a rhetoric that employed dialectical topics (the general outline of arguments) and rhetorical accommodation in order to employ the persuasive possibilities of language flexibly in the treatment of concrete, politically loaded questions.

In the Erasmian discourse of the time, the declamatory exercise was not necessarily associated with passionate civic oratory in the mould of Vives's *Declamationes*. Indeed, already in classical thought, it had a philosophical interpretation as an investigation of general, philosophical questions.[178] Erasmus himself had introduced short political declamations (*suasoria*) into the classroom in *De copia*, but he had equally expanded on the declamatory exercise in his defence of the union of humanist studies and theology in his apology against Jacobus Latomus (1475–1544, *Apologia Latomi*, 1519). In the apology, Erasmus discussed the significance of rhetorical declamations in the context of the propagation of a cautious religious dialogue on non-essentials of faith as the right way to decide religious disputes. In this view, any discussion on a theme from two points of view (*in utramque partem*) could be portrayed as a form of declamation and could be contrasted with the dialectical methods of the scholastics.[179] But other than the acceptance of a multiplicity of viewpoints, Erasmus's ideal of dispassionate conversation on religious issues had little to do with the passionate and rhetorical nature of classical declamations.

Despite this, the political nature of Vives's *Declamationes* and his interest in rhetoric in place of theology was by no means a rebellion against the religious goals of the Erasmian movement. Rather, it was in line with the Erasmian ideal of applying the reforming project of humanist studies to all spheres of life and across the range of arts. In this spirit, Cicero and Quintilian could easily rub shoulders with Christian writers, and civic and religious issues could both be described as instances of speaking truth in Erasmian circles. In fact, in Vives's rewritten version of *Veritas fucata* from 1523, civic philosophers were incorporated into the troops of truth in a universal fight against error and vice.[180]

Ultimately, by 1520, Vives had acquired a more acute understanding of the political importance of the *trivium*, recognising that, rather than clarifying doubtful questions in a systematic way, it could communicate messages efficiently in different contexts through knowledge of man's cognitive possibilities. Simultaneously, Vives, who had professed admiration for a monastic ideal in some of his works from 1514, had clearly adopted the Erasmian conviction that one's inner transformation in Christ should be turned into an active life in the service of the community. The discussions on rhetorical *decorum* and politics would frame his own 1520s career and later reflections on politics.

Notes

1. The compilation is known through a possible reprint in Lyon. In addition to the dialogue *Sapiens*, the opuscula included three short pieces that had been printed earlier (*Christi Iesu Triumphus, Virginis Dei parentis ovatio, Christi Clypei descriptio*) and five introductory lectures to courses: *In leges Ciceronis, In conuiuia Philelphi, In quartum rhetoricorum ad Herenium, Veritas fucata*, and an introduction to *Sapiens*. For an in-depth description of the works, see González González, 1987, 165–7, 193.
2. The preface thus appeared twice in the work; see González González, 1987, 166. As a preface to the whole work, it was called *praefatio*, as a preface to *Sapiens*, it was entitled *prelectio*; see González González, 1987, 193. For the textual history of *Sapiens*, see González González, 2015.
3. Vives, 1555, 296: 'lingua philosophis olim libera'.
4. Vives, 1555, 298: 'hinc, Vives, sapientiam ne expecta …'.
5. Vives, 1555, 298: '… omnia prophana, humana divinis conmixta'; 'Haec est Poetarum sacra theologia …'.
6. Vives, 1555, 299: 'Non est qualem Cicero & Quintilianus oratorem uolunt, qui si esset, mirabili quadam ornaretur sapientia …'.

50 Becoming a humanist

7. Vives, 1555,, 297: '... Vives desideret sapientem, quem se habiturum arbitratur, si uir extet qui disciplinarum circulum quam optime calleat ...'; Vives, 1555,, 300: 'Nonne recte ego uos dixi in nomine Domini congregatos? qui sapientiam, id est, Dei filium quaeritis ...'. See also Vives, 1987, 32–4. For Budé's description of Erasmus as a man of encyclopaedic knowledge, see Erasmus. *Opus epistolarum Des. Erasmi Roterodami: denuo recognitum et auctum*, 12 vols., eds. Allen, Percy Stafford – Helen Mary Allen – Heathcote William Garrod (Oxford: Clarendon, 1906–1958. Hereafter Allen), 2:566 (Ep. 583, Budé to Tunstall).
8. In Valencia, he certainly came in touch with some currents of humanist learning before leaving for Paris in 1509. His youth in Valencia has not been included in the present study since no literary texts by Vives exist prior to 1514. For a reconstruction of the Valencian context, see Gómez-Hortigüela, 1998, chapters 1 and 2.
9. Noreña, 1970, 29–48; Mayans y Siscar, 1782–1790, 1:28; Bonilla y San Martín, 1929, 1:40–71. Jozef IJsewijn had already noted that Vives's printing activities in Paris had been broader than what had been previously thought, IJsewijn, 1977.
10. González González, 1987, 132–65; González González, 2015; Galand, 2015.
11. One strand of scholarship, epitomised by Eugenio Garin, has portrayed humanism as a philosophy that shifted the focus from abstract metaphysics and formal reasoning to a historicised understanding of man as a temporally situated being; Garin, 1965. Another tradition, dating back to Hans Baron's *The Crisis of the Early Italian Renaissance: Civic Humanism and Republican Liberty in an Age of Classicism and Tyranny*, has emphasised the civic side of humanism; Baron, 1955; Pocock, 1975. Finally, a strand looking for the minimal definition of humanism represented by Paul Oskar Kristeller has portrayed humanism primarily as a literary movement lacking in philosophical or political coherence and depth; Kristeller, 1979, 22. For recent discussions, see Baker, 2015, 3–15; Mazzocco, 2006. Recently, several studies have stressed the continuities between these two traditions; see Kraye – Stone, 1999.
12. Farge, 1985, 117–8. For a more thorough treatment, see Farge, 1992. The letter exchange between Giovanni Pico della Mirandola and Ermolao Barbaro was based on the implications of this dichotomy; see Pico della Mirandola, 1509. Pico's letter to Barbaro was printed frequently as part of a collection of letters entitled *Auree epistole*. In Paris, there are at least three editions of the work prior to 1514; see Universal Short Title Catalogue (https://www.ustc.ac.uk/). For the dichotomy between scholasticism and *bonae litterae*, see Rummel, 1995.
13. For Clichtove, see Bietenholtz, 1985–1987, 1:317–20.
14. Vives, 1991c, 14–5: 'Usus est praeceptore Ioanne Maiore, philosophorum sui temporis facile principe ...'.
15. Parisian humanism and especially the history of the Faculty of Arts has been a somewhat neglected object of study, but, for more information, see Renaudet, 1916, 90–159; Sebastiani, 2010; Nauert, 1998, 429.
16. Mair, 1509; Mair, 1516, fol. I[r]: 'Et quamquam tanguntur talia in caeteris facultatibus: non tamen fortassis sufficienter'. For the context of these quotes and the evolution of Mair's thinking on humanism, see Moss, 2003, 76–86. For a good account of Pico's argument, see Kraye, 2008.
17. Montaigu statutes of 1509, reproduced in Bakker, 2007, 91: 'Et sic in scholis suis se habebunt regentes in grammatica quod, cum inchoant in festo Remigii lectiones suas, primus regens in grammatica incipit de Alexandro in *Pandere*; capiet oratorem unum cum poeta de non prohibitis (quia tales prohiberi

debent: Terentius, Martialis, Iuvenalis, Naso in epistolis et similes); et insistet diligenter fundamentis in Donato, Alexandro, Peroto, Augustino et Guidone'. Already in the early sixteenth century, an MA from the Paris University was the most prestigious qualification for a master in humanist colleges in France. This would indicate an increasing presence of humanist learning in the university halls of the capital. See Huppert, 1984, 47–74.
18. González González, 1987, 132–42, 163–4. Vives lectured on the *Convivium* of Francisco Filelfo, on Cicero's *De legibus* and *De officiis*. and the pseudo-Ciceronian *Ad Herennium*. In 1513–1515, Bérault's lectures centred on Quintilian's *Institutio oratoria*, Cicero's *De legibus*, Angelo Poliziano's *Silvae* (a poetical introduction to the Georgics of Vergil and the Poet Hesiod), on Roman Law, astronomy, Cicero's *Phillipicae* (*Philippics*) and finally in 1516, on Suetonius's *De vitae Caesaris*. Extracurricular courses were common in Paris. Following the practice of Italian humanists, those who gave courses outside the usual college curriculum chose single authors or texts, often preparing an edition of the text in question; Fantazzi, 2006, 247.
19. Bade, 1506.
20. Unlike Donatus, Priscian's works were rarely used in elementary education in the Faculties of Arts due to the highly technical nature of their contents.
21. Aristotle, 1938, 115–7 (16a); Copeland – Sluiter, 2009, 14–28; Moss, 2003, 7. The significance of the change in teaching materials is discussed from a philosophical perspective already by Eugenio Garin; see Garin, 1968, 19–42. For a primarily negative assessment of humanist grammar, see Padley, 1976, 5–57.
22. Cummings, 2007, 115–8.
23. Weijers, 1995, 38–40.
24. Murphy has also underlined that the *disputatio* had a substantial, not just formal, role to play, and, consequently, it could be a way of treating themes of social and intellectual utility. Murphy, 2005, I, 12. More generally on *disputatio*; see Murphy, 2005, IV, 2–6.
25. Clichtove, 1501, ai: '... nutrix ceterarum disciplinarum'.
26. Bade mentions the heroes of scholastic grammar such as Priscian and Donatus together with humanist writers such as Lorenzo Valla; Bade, 1510a, the dedicatory entitled 'Iodocus Badius Ascensius Tossano Musceto Canonico insulano'.
27. De Schepper, 2000, 200.
28. Guarino, 1514, V[v]: 'Grammaticae autem duae partes sunt, quarum alteram Methodicen, quae breues omnium orationis partium formulas, id est methodus declarat, alteram Hisoricen, quae historias & res gestas pertractat, appellant' (Translation from Guarino, 2002, 268–9). Interestingly, Beatus Rhenanus's dedication letter placed Guarino's work in the context of Erasmus's programme; Rhenanus, 1514: 'Scribit de praeceptoris officio, & discendi ratione, quam rem ad Guil. Thaleium Erasmus, Rhodolphus ad Barbirianum, vterque doctissime explicarunt'.
29. Guarino, 1514, IX[v]: 'hinc varias hominum fortunas, ingeniorum & vitia, & virtutes excerpent ...'. (translation from Guarino, 2002, 286–7).
30. That grammar courses consisted essentially of the reading and understanding of authors was often pointed out; Bade, 1510a, Aaiii[v]: 'Tota grammatica consistit praecipue in intellectu poetarum, scriptorum & historiarum prompta expositione; et recte loquendi scribendique ratione'.
31. Vives, 1991a, 148–9: 'Ii omnes, inquit, qui has legunt cedulas, arbitrabuntur te aliquid vel in philosophia naturali vel in astrologia profiteri, cum solam grammaticam in eo libro interpreteris'; Seneca, 1920, 276–85 (ep. 84); Macrobius, 2011, 4 (1.3–5); Basil, 1902, 105 (IV).

52 Becoming a humanist

32. Vives, 1991a, 148–9: 'Volant, nec dubium, per plurimos hortos, qui plurimis ornati scientiis multos variarum arborum flores degustarunt; unde quae faciunt opera tanto sunt apum melle dulciora, quanto spiritalis dulcedo corporae praestat'.
33. Vives, 1991a, 144–8.
34. Quintilian, 2001, 1:212–3 (1.10.1); Vitruvius, 1931–1934, 1:16–7 (1.1.12); Budé, 1508, fol. IV^v: 'Cum autem animadverterint omnes disciplinas inter se coniunctionem rerum & communionem habere'. See also Bérauld, 2015, 32.
35. Trithemius, 1512, fol. CCXVI^v: 'Primus enim apud Gallos (vt Cicero apud Romanos) philosophiam rudem adhuc et impolitam cum eloquentia iunxit'. For the fame of Lefèvre, see Bedouelle, 1976, 47–8.
36. De Gandillac, 1973, 156; Bedouelle, 1976, 32–6.
37. The Neo-Platonic tradition of Marsilio Ficino and Giovanni Pico della Mirandola was well known in Paris; see Renaudet, 1916, 90–159; De la Garanderie, 1995, 118–21. For Lefèvre and reading as an ethical and transformational practice, see Rice, 1972, xvii–xxii; Bianchi, 2013, 140–3; D'Amico, 1988, 28–30. The idea that reading could itself be a moral act was shared by many; for Bade, see White, 2013, 240.
38. This happened preferably in monastic isolation. See, for instance, Josse Clichtove's *De laude monasticae religionis opusculum* (1513).
39. Renaudet, 1916, 124.
40. Gaguin himself had been in Italy and knew Giovanni Pico della Mirandola and Marsilio Ficino personally. Pico had also visited Paris in the 1480s.
41. Allen 1:163 (Ep. 49, Erasmus to Hendrik van Bergen. Translation from CWE 1:103). All translations from Erasmus's works are from *Collected Works of Erasmus*, 72 vols. (Toronto: University of Toronto Press, 1974–, hereafter CWE).
42. See note 5 (refers to the note 5 of Chapter 1).
43. For the history of commonplace books in the Renaissance, see Moss, 1996.
44. Bade, 1510a, Aaiii^v: 'Pomponius autem Laetus sic Grammatice est recte scribendi: recte loquendi: recteque poetarum cum emendata lectione interpretandi ars atque scientia'. Bade refers here to Pomponio Leto (1428–1498), who was one of the most famous members of Roman humanist circles in the 15th century.
45. White, 2013, 257.
46. In northern Europe, praise of the Mantuan was a commonplace between 1490 and 1510; for Erasmus's praise, see Allen 1:164 (Ep. 49, Erasmus to Hendrik van Berghen). For an overview of the treatment, see Severi, 2010.
47. Pico, 1507: 'sanctissima illa tua poemata: in quibus ea rerum maiestas/is splendor est eloquentiae/vt certatim in illis palmam sibi vendicare verba atque sententiae videantur'.
48. See White, 2013, 235–42.
49. White, 2013, 268–9.
50. Béraud, 2015, 72: 'Poetae deo pleni caelestique afflati numine, ac diuino spiritu perciti …'.
51. For Bade and satire, see White, 2013, 242–53. For satire in the 16th century, see Levi, CWE 27:xii–xiii.
52. Guarino, 1514, X^r: 'Perspicuum iam nimirum esse arbitror eum qui in praedictarum rerum studiis eruditus fuerit, ad Rhetoricen disciplinam posse transcendere, ex qua cum discendi artem fuerit assecutus, non modo Ciceronis orationes intelliget, verum etiam ex superiorum rerum varietate, & copiosam, & ornatam cum arte coniunctam habebit eloquentiam'.
53. Bade's *Disquisitio Ascensiana* in a 1508 edition of *Ad Herennium* refers at least twice to 'divina phrasis Ciceronis'; See Bade, 1508a. The adjective *ascensiana* refers to Bade's birthplace (Asse in Brabant).

54. Vives, 1991b, 132–3.
55. Vives, 1991b, 130–3: 'Vir tamen hic noster [...] tanquam in hortos per manus ducens hominum mentes in omnes affectus inducet, animorum quorumlibet ac voluntatum imperium habebit et sine repugnantia quaquam verbis illius ac orationi parentes'.
56. Vives, 1991b, 132–3: 'Penes Demosthenem ob eloquentiam Atheniensium ac Philippi saepius bellum atque pax fuit'.
57. Vives, 1991b, 132–5: 'Complures, immo fere omnes nostrae tempestatis litteratores, qui volunt oratores videri, verborum flosculos et tintinnum orationis dumtaxat affectant'; 'quibus etiam verbis et qua ratione animus erit in spem excitandus, deiiciendus ob terrorem, ad iram vel invidiam concitandus et id genus cetera'.
58. The status of Cicero as the prince of eloquence is often affirmed; see, for instance, Bade, 1508b.
59. For the popularity of these works, see Green – Murphy, 2006, 107–38, 351–60; Mack, 2011, 13–32.
60. They were often printed together. If one of them was printed on its own, it was usually the *Ad Herennium*: Mack, 2011, 14; Ward, 1983, 145–6.
61. Cicero, *Opera rhetorica, oratoria et forensia, premisso indice et Ad Caium Herennium rhetoricorum libri IIII. De inventione que et vetus rhetorica libri II. Topicorum ad Brutum* (Paris: Bade, 1511). There are six editions of these works in Paris from the 1510s, 1520s, and 1530s; see Green – Murphy, 2006, 110.
62. The reintegration of classical rhetoric in the Renaissance has been debated. For Brian Vickers, the Renaissance reintegrated classical theory after the fragmentation of the rhetorical culture in the medieval context. This view has been countered by scholars such as John O. Ward, who have emphasised the practical nature of medieval rhetoric. Vickers, 1988, 254–93; Cox – Ward, 2006, xv–xvi. See also Murphy, 1974, 361.
63. *Ad Herennium*, 8–10 (1.3.4–5).
64. *Ad Herennium* describes the duty of an orator to discuss civic and legal issues and 'to secure as far as possible the agreement of his hearers', *Ad Herennium*, 4–5 (1.2.2). Quintilian famously criticised the rhetorical tradition for defining its duty through mere persuasion, proposing a less ethically dubious definition as the art of speaking well; Quintilian, 2001, 1:350–69 (2.15).
65. For George of Trebizond, see Monfasani, 1976.
66. The work presented the six-part division, three genera of orations, and rhetorical stylistic precepts together with the Ciceronian three-part classification of letters into informative, familiar, and serious: Verulanus, 1501.
67. Cicero, 1960a, 4–7 (1.2.2), 12–5 (1.5.6).
68. Vives, 1991b, 130: 'Beluas, quas philosophi vocarunt irrationabiles, concipere mente pleraque ut homines nemo umquam sani sensus dubitavit. Ea vero aliis nota facere, nullis verbis queunt; significare nonnullis signis in quibusdam iisque perpaucis, difficulter quidem, satis videmus'.
69. Cicero, 1913, 52–5 (1.16.50): 'Eius autem vinculum est ratio et oratio, quae docendo, discendo, communicando, disceptando, iudicando conciliat inter se homines coniungitque naturali quadam societate ...'.
70. Cicero, 1913, 94 (1.26.92).
71. Trebizond, 1522, 2[r] (Translation from Monfasani, 1976, 267): 'Rhetorica est ciuilis scientia, qua cum assensione auditorum quo ad eius fieri potest, in ciuilibus quaestionibus dicimus'. The link between rhetoric and civic issues could also be found in some of the school materials that were becoming popular in Paris; see, for instance, Vergerio, 2002, 50.
72. Bade, 1510b, Aii[r]: '... in causis forensibus atque communibus ...'.

73. Beroaldo, 1514, next to last page: 'Equidem conditores vrbium/non tam philosophica doctrina: quam elegantia oratoria & illicio facundiae pellexerunt dispalatos homines ad ciuilitatem politicamque viuendi rationem'.
74. Copeland – Sluiter, 2009, 793–4.
75. Lefèvre d'Étaples, 1504: '... ut disciplinas emitterent/que vitam nostram cum privatam tum publicam divinorum conformi quadam bonitate formarent quam morales appellant'.
76. Bianchi, 2013, 143. The theological faculty had often functioned as a consultant body of Christendom in matters of doctrine and morals; see Farge, 1985, 115.
77. Carneades is the classic example of an orator speaking on both sides of an issue; Quintilian, 2001, 5:214–5 (12.1.35); Cicero, 1942, 2:64–5 (3.21.80); Skinner, 1996, 97–9.
78. Nani Mirabelli, 1512, AAii[r]: '... Vnde non immerito quidam gladio eloquentiam aequipararunt: quo & ad oppugnandum: & ad propugnandum tam male: quam bene vti possumus'. For *Polyanthea*, see Blair, 2010, 125–6.
79. Vives, 1555, 296: '... liberas [...] linguas, quae praua quasi discerperent ac dilaniarent'.
80. Vives, 1991b, 134–5: 'Perficiet inventum nostrum optimi cuiuscumque incepti Perfector'; '... in cuiusque hominis perniciem ...'; '... ad exornandam veritatem, ad persuadenda bona, dissuadenda scelesta ...'.
81. Vives, 1991a, 150–1: 'Quis enim Platonem summa eloquentia suam scripsisse philosophiam nescit [...] Quis [...] Aristotelem [...] ignorat aureoque orationis flumine [...] omnia opera composuisse'? The idea about Aristotle's golden flow of speech was a humanist commonplace that was first formulated in Cicero's *Academica*, see Cicero, 1933, 620–1 (2.38.119).
82. On nobility stemming from character, see how Vives describes Cicero's rise to consulship; Vives, 1984a, 12–3.
83. González González, 2008, 39–46, 53–4.
84. The exact chronology of Vives's movements between 1512 and 1517 has been a subject of some debate. For a good discussion of the evidence, see González González, 2003.
85. Vives, 1978, 110–1 (Ep. 3. Vives to Barlandus), 116–8 (Ep. 6, The town magistrates of Valencia to Vives).
86. Tracy, 1996, 110; Erasmus, LB V:141B-C (*Paraclesis*). This is reiterated in many of his works at the time; see, for instance, Erasmus, ASD IV/2, 80–2 (*Querela pacis*). *Novum instrumentum* was the first edition of Erasmus's New Testament. It comprised a Greek edition of the text, Erasmus's Latin translation, and declaratory annotations.
87. Erasmus, LB V:7E-9D (*Enchiridion*).
88. Erasmus, ASD IV/3 (*Moriae encomium*), 68 'Praeterea qui nullum hominum genus praetermittit, is nulli homini, vitiis omnibus iratus videtur'.; Allen 2:93 (Ep. 337, Erasmus to Dorp. CWE 3:115).
89. Rummel, 2008, 1–2.
90. For the renewal of grammar teaching in the Burgundian Netherlands, see IJsewijn, 1988, 168–71. On the foundation of the Collegium Trilingue; see De Vocht, 1951; Papy, 2018.
91. For the history of the debate in the Renaissance, see Rummel, 1995, 1–18. For Vives's *In pseudodialecticos*, see Périgot, 2005, 250–9.
92. On Dorp and humanism; see CWE 3:17–8; Bietenholz, 1985–7, 1:398–404; Jardine, 1993, 111–22. On the dispute; see Rummel, 1989 1:3–13.
93. Allen 2:14 (Ep. 304, Dorp to Erasmus. CWE 3:21).
94. Allen 2:15 (Ep. 304, Dorp to Erasmus. CWE 3:22).

95. Allen 2:133 (Ep. 347, Dorp to Erasmus).
96. Allen 2:128 (Ep. 347, Dorp to Erasmus. CWE 3:157).
97. Allen 2:135 (Ep. 347, Dorp to Erasmus).
98. Allen 2:98–100 (Ep. 337, Erasmus to Dorp).
99. Mosellanus, 1519, 5–6; Sowards in CWE 71, xxix.
100. More, 1986, 34–5.
101. More, 1986, 24–5.
102. More, 1986, 70–1.
103. Allen 4:268 (Ep. 1106, More to Erasmus).
104. Vives, 1979, 68–9: 'Neque enim dialecticus nouam facit traditque uim linguae, sed ex uetere & usitatissima regulas obseruatas docet ...'
105. Vives, 1979, 56–7: '... ipse rectus uerusque sensus orationum latinarum. At hunc ans quibus auctoribus petunt homines ignari? Non a Cicerone, non a Quintiliano [...] sed a Petro Hispano, seu si quis fuit alius ante ipsum'.
106. More, 1986, 22–3. In defending one's cause, it was common to appeal to the authority of a writer one's opponent would recognise. Using a similar strategy, Dorp argued that Erasmus's views on dialectic were against Erasmus's own heroes, St Augustine and St Jerome; Allen 2:133 (Ep. 347, Dorp to Erasmus).
107. Vives, 1979, 36–7: 'An putat quispiam Aristotelem suam dialecticam ad sermonem, quem ipse sibi confinxerat, & non potius ad uulgarem illum Graecum, quem totus populus loquebatur, accommodasse?'
108. Vives, 1979, 68–9: 'Neque intricat & detinet Aristoteles suum discipulum frigidissimis & stultissimis suppositionibus, ampliationibus, restrictionibus, litterulis [...] Verum ipse non censuit illa tradenda praeter omnem rationem artis dialecticae, utpote quibus communis hominum & sensus, & sermo non modo non utatur, sed etiam refragetur'.
109. Vives, 1979, 68–9: 'Cuius porro philosophi logica breuibus praeceptis tota constat?'
110. Vives, 1979, 68–9: 'Quo instrumento adiutum mox ad reliquas artes scientiasque transmittit. Nam ea quae aliarum rerum gratia discuntur, de quorum numero est dialectica, non diu occupare studia debent ...'.
111. Vives, 1979, 81: 'Quis ferat pictorem in componendo penicillo, in terendis coloribus, sutorem in acubus, in subulis, smiliis, ceterisque cultris acuendis, in torquendo incerandoque filo, in setis illi addendis, totam aetatem consumere?'
112. Vives, 1979, 50–1: 'Quod si legem unusquisque de uerbis feret, ut apud se significant, quid attinet, non dico latinam linguam, sed ne ullam prorsus addiscere, quum illud facilius sit uerba id demum significare, quod unicuilibet uisum fuerit, & quot erunt mente concipientes, tam varios habebunt significatus. Ita tandem, ut nemo alterum intelligat, quum unusquisque uerbis suo more utatur, non communi'.
113. Vives, 1979, 83.
114. Vives, 1979, 41, 85–7: 'Ita turbato eo, quicum certant, mira & insinuata uocabulorum forma atque ratione, miris suppositionibus ...'; '... quam etiam causam fore suspicor, cur hanc meam epistolam, tamquam rem nimis sacram atque reconditam non multi ex ipsis attingent, cum tamen nihil a me clarius, nihil apertius scribi latine potuerit'. See also the part on Augustine, Vives, 1979, 71–7.
115. Vives, 1979, 70–3: 'Quin & sunt nonnulli ex istis atque ex eorum numero qui theologi nominantur, qui nihil putant acute posse dici, nisi sit hoc amarissimo condimento conditum, horrida atque inculta barbarie concinnatum, istis sophismatum ineptissimis differtum tricis'; 'Miratum ferunt ipsum in homine tam logico, ne uerbum quidem esse de asinis [...] nec de aliqua ex iis rebus, quae traduntur in parum seu paruis logicalibus'.

56 *Becoming a humanist*

116. Vives, 1979, 5: 'In alium quendam orbem perductos eos esse credas, ita usum uitae & communem sensum ignorant'. The translation is mine.
117. In *De inventione,* Cicero highlights that man's ability to speak is what ultimately makes him superior to beasts; Cicero, 1960a, 12–3 (1.4.5).
118. Vives, 1979, 5: '… ut negotiis gerendis, legationibus obeundis, administrandis rebus aut publicis aut priuatis, tractandis populorum animis ineptissimi sint …'. The translation is mine.
119. Vives, 1979, 5: 'Neque enim iis sese artibus tradunt, quibus haec omnia percipiuntur, quaeque & animum & uitam humanam instituunt, cuiusmodi est Philosophia moralis, quae mores mentemque ornat; Historia, quae mater est rerum cognitionis & usus, id est prudentiae; Oratoria, quae vitam sensumque comunem & docet & moderatur; Politica facultas, & Oeconomica, quibus ciuitatum rerumque familiarium status & regimen constat'. The translation is mine.
120. Vives, 1979, 36–7: 'Dialectica itaque in hoc uulgari, & qui est omnium in ore sermo, uerum, falsum, probabilitatem inuenit, rhetorice uero ornatum, splendorem, gratiam'.
121. Peter of Spain was the author of the *Summulae logicales*, the most popular textbook of logic in the Middle Ages.
122. Vives, 1979, 66–7: '… uim tamen cuiusquam uerbi non magis sciuit, quam ille de quo modo loquebar Scytha uim sermonis Hispani, cuius nec uerbum uel scriptum legit, uel prolatum a quoquam audiuit'. The force of words was often linked to their rhetorical capacities, and Vives discusses this issue in his rhetorical works; see, for instance, Vives, 2000, 10.
123. Erasmus, ASD I/2 (*De ratione studii*), 118.
124. Valla, 1982, 175–7.
125. Mack, 2011, 46; Vasoli, 1968, 81–99. Monfasani has emphasised that it was not meant to be a polemical interpretation of dialectic but a short introduction to the art. It was, however, incorporated in the humanist tradition; Monfasani, 1976, 300–3, 328–37.
126. Vives, 1522, 60 (ii.xxi): 'Haec sunt Agricolae Phrysii dialectica docti / Quis non crediderim meliora extare Latina'.
127. Mack, 1993, 117–20.
128. Allen 2:90 (Ep. 336, Fisher to Erasmus); Cantiuncula, 1520, the part entitled *De origine locorum deque ipsorum utilitate, ex Rodolpho Agricola*, between the dedicatory epistle and the work.
129. For more, see Jardine, 1993, 83–98.
130. Bade, 1509: 'Prasertim cum multa insint & argute dicta & quae: si recipiantur: non parum ad Dialectices compendium faciant: neque pauciora quae ad rhetoricam disputationem conducant'.
131. Rhenanus, 1509, Aii[v].
132. Lefèvre d'Étaples, 1509, Aii[r].
133. Budé, 1508, fol. XXXVI[r]; Cicero, 1939a, 132–3 (41.152–3): '… artem quae doceret rem universam tribuere in partis, latentem explicare definiendo, obscuram explanare interpretando, ambigua primum videre, deinde distinguere, postremo habere regulam qua vera et falsa iudicarentur et quae quibus propositis essent quaquae non essent consequentia […] adiunxit etiam et litterarum scientiam et loquendi elegantiam …'.
134. Vives, 1984a, 6–7.
135. For an in-depth analysis of Agricola's *De inventione*, see Peter Mack, 1993, 117–302.
136. Agricola, 1992, 418–20 (2.XXIX): 'Definitio uxoris non multum dabit, nisi ea parte, qua ponitur in definitione philosophi cura virtutis, et in definitione uxoris causa liberorum quarendorum'; Mack, 1993, 183–4.

137. Agricola, 1992, 244–96 (2.VIII–XIV); Mack, 1993, 181–9.
138. Agricola, 1992, 216–24, 434–54 (2.IV, 3.I–III); Mack, 1993, 203–11.
139. *Ad Herennium*, 170–1 (3.5.8–9).
140. Agricola, 1992, 208–10 (1.II).
141. Agricola, 1532, 17: 'quando hic praecipuus esse videtur longi laboris, sollicitudinisque in studia collatae, fructus. Quid si nihil ipsi ad posteros mandare poterimus, nihil extra ea, quae didicimus, ad praesentes proferre, quid tandem inter librum, & nos intererit'. (Translation from Agricola, 2002, 213). See also Cave, 1979, 27.
142. Vives, 1987, 54–5.
143. Vives, 1987, 36–9: 'Socrates primum philosophiam […] ad civitatum atque hominum singulorum usus vitamque devocavit …'; '… ad morum compositionem […] totos sese converterent'.; Cicero, 1960c, 434–5 (5.4.10–1).
144. Vives, 1987, 54–5: '… cuiusmodi sunt de moribus uniuscuisque componendis, de gubernandis rebus et publicis et privatis […] Per haec enim vita nostra humanitati suae reddita est …'.
145. Vives, 1987, 30–1. Politics as medicine of the mind is a prominent idea in Greek thought; Aristotle, 1934, 61–3 (1102a). See also Fernández-Santamaría interpretation of Vives's *Fabula de homine* (1518) from the same time. For Fernández-Santamaría, *Fabula* sets the stage for man's journey from his post-lapsarian state to his true, God-like nature with the help of others, see Fernández-Santamaría, 1998, 1–8.
146. Erasmus, ASD I/3 (*Colloquia*), 254.
147. Vives, 1984a, 10: 'Iam vero illam partem video meae praefationi veterum interpretum instituto deesse, qua de auctore ipso nonnulla dicuntur; quam addam equidem ex more magis quam necessitate'. Vives was probably more familiar with Cicero than any other classical writer in his youth; Matheeussen, 1998, 107.
148. Vives, 1984a, 11: 'nactusque ingenium tale quale Plato fingit, liberalium omnium artium capacissimum, ad nullum litterarum genus ineptum, poesi, philosophiae dicendique arti (qui erat tunc in urbe ad summos honores gradus) totum sese tradidit'.
149. Vives, 1984a, 13: '… Ciceronis prudentiam scientiamque utendi foro et sese tempori accommodandi levitatem vocant …'.
150. At the time, one of the only Dutch texts praising a Ciceronian understanding of the active life was Jacobus Canter's late fifteenth-century *Dialogus de Solitudine*; Tilmans, 2002, 112.
151. Cicero, 1913, 20 (1.6.19), 80–3 (1.23.79–81), 94 (1.26.92) 'Virtutis enim laus omnis in actione consistit'.
152. Vives, 2013, 474: 'Hic est ergo studium ominum fructus […] ut […] eas in bonum publicum exerceamus'.
153. Vives, 2013, 478: 'Cogitabit uir sapiens mundum hunc esse uelut ciuitatem quandam, cuius ipse sit ciuis'.
154. Vives, 2013, 466–90; Vives, 1984a, 6: '… optimus civis huius universae civitatis, quae totum genus humanum capit …'.
155. Grant in CWE 30:1–83.
156. Allen 2:123 (Ep. 344, Zasius to Erasmus). For a political reading of the *Adages*; Mann Phillips, 1964, 36–8, 96–121.
157. For a comparison between Erasmus's *De copia* and Agricola's *De inventione*, see Cave, 1979, 3–34.
158. Quintilian, 2001, 1:324–5 (2.10.2): '… veritati proximam imaginem reddit …'. See also Quintilian, 1:310–5; 1:324–31, 2:140–9 (2.6, 2.10, 3.8.51–70).
159. Erasmus, ASD I/6 (*De copia*), 224–6.

58 *Becoming a humanist*

160. Some scholars have seen them as literary rather than political exercises. Lorenzo Riber, in his Spanish translation of the *Opera Omnia*, situates the *Declamationes* and the whole *Somnium* compendium in a section entitled *Obras filológicas* (philological works), emphasising their literary character. Vives, 1947–1948.
161. George, 1989a, 2–3; George, 1989b, 147–8.
162. As George has noted, Vives mentions three reasons for writing the *Declamationes*: 1. Against the inarticulate flatterers (scholastics), 2. An example of the art of declamation, not merely *Progymnasmata* linking grammar and rhetoric 3. Specific political lessons for Ferdinand. George, 1989a, 2–3.
163. Vives, 1989b, 96–7: '... bona subditorum gratia ...'; '... erumpere liberas voces et iudicia non simulata'; '... nihil debere principem agere quod non publica potius commoda quam sua privata respiciat ...'.
164. Vives, 1989b, 94–5.
165. Vives, 1989b, 102–3: 'Quod neminem mirari oportere arbitror, quoniam eorum angustissimi et humillimi animi admirabilia illa Ciceronis consilia, excelsam et late patentem prudentiam, quae orationibus continetur, non capiunt'.
166. The second quotation is presented in the form of a question, Vives, 1989b, 102–3: 'in orationibus vero vim ingenii et consilii, usum rerum regendaeque rei publicae [...] explicuisse atque ostendisse'; 'An censent grammaticorum esse [...] invenire argumenta illa et rationes, quibus res civiles tractes ...'.
167. This quotation is presented in the form of a question, Vives, 1989b, 102–3: 'Tum inventa eo collocare ordine, quo sibimet ipsa non officiant, nullumque sit quod non plus eo quo dictum est loco causae prosit quam alio translatum?'
168. Vives, 1989b, 104–5: 'Sed eos constat [...] magna cum laude potuisse in civitatibus et oculis hominum illoque publico vitae splendore versari ...'; 'Cum vero ad rem publicam, ad tractandos hominum animos moresque, cum ad rem domesticam et familiarem descendunt, ibi misere animis concidunt ...'.
169. Vives, 1989b, 106–7: '... in alienis quoque declamationibus versabatur deque eis sententiam ferebat ...'.
170. Vives, 1989b, 110–1: 'serviendum enim nobis est causae et non quid sentias, sed quid ad persuadendum faciat dicendum. Haec est declamandi lex'.
171. Edward George has studied the work in depth. He concludes that Vives's historical dramatisation, closely connected to the precepts of Quintilian and examples of Sallust, portrays a different and a more dramatised way of presenting Erasmian ideas compared to the Dutch master; George, 1989b, 144, 146–7. Vives, 1989b, 16–9: '... et quae alibi praeceptis traduntur, hic exemplis'.
172. Lepidus's speeches, for instance, refer loosely to fragments of Sallust's *Histories*, see George, 1989a, 5–6.
173. Vives, 1989b, 62–7, 90–1.
174. Vives, 1989b, 70–3.
175. Vives, 1989b, 76–9.
176. Vives, 1989b, 66–9, 72–3.
177. Quintilian, 2001, 4:72–4 (9.2.64–7): '... si dicere palam parum tutum est ...'.
178. Waith, 1988, 23–4.
179. Erasmus, LB IX:100C-F (*Apologia Latomi*); Erasmus, ASD I/6, 223–9 (*De copia*).
180. E.g. Demosthenes and Cicero; see Vives, Juan Luis. *Opera omnia*, 8 vols., ed. Gregorio Mayans y Siscar (Valencia, 1782–1790, hereafter Mayans), 2:520 (*Veritas fucata*).

2 Conversation and the Rhetoric of Counsel (Around 1520)

Erasmus and the Republic of Letters

In around 1520, Vives's place among the leading transalpine humanists was ensured. His prominent position within the Erasmian movement had far-reaching implications for the conceptual, social, and practical evolution of his works and career: it influenced the commonplaces and themes he drew on, accounted for his social status as a member of the Erasmian circle of friends, made him a man of *auctoritas* who could pursue a life of *negotium*, and integrated him into a reformative project that aspired to address different audiences. Finally, it offered him conceptual tools to understand how to speak and write within the humanist circles and when addressing those outside its boundaries.

In this chapter, I move from academic debates to discuss how discursive practices were supposed to work in real life. I will concentrate on two issues of this prolific phase in Vives's career. First, I situate Vives within the Erasmian circles, the famous early sixteenth-century Republic of Letters, by looking at the mechanisms with which it functioned and the civic dimension of its self-interpretation. Second, I connect this political element of the Republic to the ways in which the figure of the prince was conceptualised. Here I have a specific aim which is to shift, through a close analysis of Vives's *De consultatione* (printed in 1533) on political counsel, the perspective from the idealised view of an ethically self-governed Erasmian prince to a more practical view of the ruler as an object of persuasion in actual political matters. As I demonstrate, there is evidence that Vives, and some other humanists, had quite a practical view of the limitations of the rulers of his time, which not only played a fundamental role in *De consultatione*, but greatly influenced Vives's political inventions and reflections on rhetoric throughout the 1520s and 1530s. His position in the Republic of Letters and his views on princely counsel are undoubtedly two separate issues. Yet they shed light on each other not only because the construction of the Republic of Letters and princely counsel reflect two distinct interpretations of rhetoric – one emphasising symmetrical discussion and the other asymmetrical rhetoric – but also because it is precisely the presupposition of a humanist circle

DOI: 10.4324/9781003240457-3

of friends serving as counsellors that is the context for Vives's ideas on how rhetoric functions in princely regimes.

The collective aspect of Erasmian humanism is central for any attempt to interpret Vives's publications of the time. Indeed, works such as *Opuscula varia* (especially *In pseudodialecticos*) and *Declamationes Syllanae* not only established a conceptual connection between Vives's writings and the broader humanist programme around Erasmus, but they also revealed a social and cultural link to the discursive practices of the Erasmian Republic of Letters on various levels. One crucial issue here was the incorporation of new audiences into the literary debates of the time. *In pseudodialecticos*, in particular, mirrored a broader Erasmian attempt to address non-academic audiences in matters that were traditionally discussed only among the wise. Erasmus's scholastic adversaries were quick to point this out; they not only complained about the theological and philological points Erasmus put forward but also about the persuasive modality of his writing destined for non-specialists. In his first letter to Erasmus, Dorp recounted how the satirical *Encomium Moriae* had enraged many people and especially theologians who wanted to 'retain the respect of common folk'.[1] In his second letter to Erasmus, Dorp claimed that Erasmus should stick to the facts instead of using 'eloquent means of persuasion, by which I know you can make one believe anything'.[2] He also wondered, sarcastically, if Erasmus was 'short of subjects on which you could have won even greater reputation from the applause of the whole world'.[3] It was not just the scholastics who reproached Erasmus for his efforts to address larger audiences. Budé criticised him for writing trivialities when he should focus on distinguishing himself 'among special and exalted themes'.[4] Erasmus naturally recognised the popular element of his work but described it as part of his duty to serve as the supreme teacher of Christian humanism for a large lay audience. In his reply to Budé, Erasmus fiercely defended the usefulness of his popular works such as *De copia* since he was writing about liberal studies and other issues for 'children and dullards' and not for an educated readership.[5]

Although both Budé and the scholastics were critical of Erasmus's desire to reach a wider audience, the complaints were of different sorts. Whereas Budé disparaged Erasmus's choice of writing popular works instead of scholarly treatises, the scholastics bemoaned his habit of turning his readers and supporters into judges in scholarly discussions. Erasmus's scholastic critics, most notably the theologians Jacobus Latomus and Edward Lee (1482–1544), were keen to make the point that Erasmus altered the dynamics of discussion by turning attention from the issue under debate to questions of personal authority and *ethos*.[6] In a letter written in February 1520, Edward Lee, an English theologian with whom Erasmus engaged in a dispute on his New Testament at the turn of the 1520s, complained at length about his transformation of their dispute into an attack that blackened Lee's reputation, and made him 'unpopular with all learned men'.[7] Erasmus himself stated openly in his apology against Latomus, who was critical of his biblical hermeneutics, that sometimes 'falsely inflated reputations' needed to be punctured for 'the general advancement of scholarship'.[8]

Erasmus was not the only one who could turn scholarly discussions into attacks on the individual and collective *ethos* of scholastics using techniques of ridicule and satire that appealed to his audience. The commonplaces employed in Italian humanism to scorn scholastics had been widely taken up in transalpine humanism in the fifteenth century and were frequently employed by Northern humanists to portray scholastic learning as irrelevant sophistry devoid of intellectual authority.[9] In the context of the so-called Reuchlin (Johannes Reuchlin, 1455–1522) affair, which was central to Northern, especially German humanism in the 1510s, a debate on the heretical nature of Jewish literature was portrayed, in works such as *Clarorum virorum epistolae* (1514, a more extensive version including letters from Erasmus printed in 1519 under the title *Illustrium virorum epistolae*), as a debate between two academic cultures, to both of which a set of arguments, practices, and followers were attributed.[10] Much of the discussion during the Reuchlin affair did not aim to bridge the gap between scholastic and humanist cultures but rather, through heated attacks, turned the authority of the opposing faction into an object of ridicule.

In a similar fashion, in *In pseudodialecticos* Vives did not primarily open a dialogue with his opponents but picked up elements that made scholastic learning look ridiculous in the eyes of an audience that would often already have been favourable to the humanist position.[11] *In pseudodialecticos* was a rhetorical piece that, despite the force of some of its arguments, would not necessarily have been compelling on the internal impossibilities and contradictions of the dialectical system to a Louvain or Paris theologian. It was rather framed as an eloquent social critique that belonged to the satirical tradition of More and Erasmus in its portrayal of the outcomes of scholastic dialectic as an educational and epistemological paradigm. Revealingly, Vives presented the work as advice to a friend on the merits of scholastic and humanistic dialectic respectively, stating, 'if I have any good effect on you, I can also hope to exercise an influence on a great number of the young men who are your disciples'.[12] Furthermore, the structure of the work, based on a dichotomy of obscure scholasticism and humanism, accentuated the importance of *In pseudodialecticos* in a broader narrative about the rebirth of humanist studies and culture. Vives's personal story, which stressed the scholastic background of his own studies at Paris, gave a highly personal touch to the account. As he wrote, his conversion from the 'Cimmerian darkness' of scholasticism 'into the light' allowed him to 'see the true disciplines that are worthy of man' and which were called humanities.[13]

Both the collective ridicule of the scholastic tradition and Erasmus's (and other humanists') attempts to make some scholarly discussions public were decisively facilitated by the authority and reputation that Erasmus held as the supreme humanist of the time. Because of this, individual polemics against scholasticism did not take place in isolation but could presuppose a shared humanist authority that partly emanated from the popularity that the figure of Erasmus gave to liberal studies. The aspiration to address and educate wide strata of Christian people surely secured Erasmus's many easily approachable works visibility in Latin grammar schools, faculties of arts, and among a somewhat broader reading public across Central and Northern Europe. The printing of his work revealed a marked increase in his popularity somewhere around 1515 (less than 100 editions in 1505–1514, close to 1000 editions in 1515–1524)[14], and by 1520 he had become an authority whose value as a unique brand in Catholic Europe was well understood by printers such as Froben in Basel and Martens in the Low Countries.[15]

Erasmus's fame and reputation were not, however, merely the result of the selection of themes and the spontaneous popularity of his works; he himself participated in the crafting of his own reputation and authority. He recognised the importance of academic qualifications as a source of authority, and he even acquired a doctorate in theology at the University of Turin and explained in his correspondence that he did this largely to gain authority.[16] Still, by far the greatest source of Erasmus's authority as the prince of the humanist movement was the public praise of other humanists that was conveyed to a relatively large readership through the printing press. As Lisa Jardine showed in her *Erasmus, Man of Letters: The Construction of Charisma in Print* (1993), this humanist culture of reciprocal praise, drawing on classic humanist genres of encomia (e.g. demonstrative rhetoric, the depiction of one's life), was developed in introductions, prefaces, dedication letters, and commentaries that wove different humanists and their contributions together with a shared humanist programme. Erasmus's printed letters, which began to appear in 1515 (the first collection that comprised only letters was printed in 1516), were perhaps the clearest manifestation of the culture of mutual praise.[17] They invited readers to participate in the intimate friendship of humanist circles and to witness the construction of a European-wide community of scholars or, in other words, the Republic of Letters.[18]

It is perhaps no minor detail that Erasmus and the scholarly circles around him were the first intellectual movement that frequently employed the concept of the Republic of Letters as a form of self-interpretation. The term referred to a community of scholars who cultivated friendship, culture, and spirituality collectively and, consequently, it gave an idealised touch to the collective practices of the humanist circles around Erasmus.[19] The Republic was not, indeed, merely a creation of managerial reason meant to serve practical ends; its self-image always drew on classical ideas that stressed the equation between one's worth and public recognition. The self-interpretation of the Republic was essentially defined by two concepts: friendship (the Republic of Letters was interpreted as a consortium of friends) and conversation (*sermo*). Although one finds in Erasmus and Vives the ideal of a friendship among all Christians, which could serve as the basis for political and religious community, the friendship among the learned drew instead on a Christianised version of a classical and more exclusive discourse on friendship, the most widely read expositions of which were book VIII of Aristotle's *Nicomachean Ethics* and Cicero's *De amicitia*.[20] This discourse portrayed perfect friendship as an exclusive bond among the virtuous that made possible the cultivation of one's intellectual and ethical qualities in friendly conversation (*sermo*). *Sermo*, extensively described theoretically and in practice in Cicero's works, referred to a friendly conversation between equal friends in which the technical rules of rhetoric destined for the multitude did not apply.[21] The humanist love of *sermo* became often visible in Vives's correspondence. In discussing the life of an erudite man in *De disciplinis*, Vives described the spiritual friendship between the learned and differentiated between 'friendly conversation' (*amica sermocinatio*) suitable for the learned and 'hostile battles' (*pugna inimica*) associated with scholastic disputations.[22] Guillaume Budé, in a 1521 letter to Vives in which his relationship with Erasmus and the general obligations of friendship were discussed, declared that it was 'fair to love a man endowed with natural disposition, doctrine, refinement, and agreeable and pleasant use of conversation'.[23] Ultimately, friendship and *sermo* were closely interrelated since their respective definitions implied each other: *sermo* referred to a conversation between friends and friendship was inconceivable without conversation.[24]

Naturally, there were instances of friendship that did not live up to the lofty standards of virtuous friendship – Erasmus's and Budé's relationship was not very close and often descended into petty feuds – but that were still considered to be relevant to the public presentation of the Republic of Letters.[25] Erasmus's opponents understood that the Erasmian circle functioned as a collective space for reputation and authority. Edward Lee, for instance, claimed that the easiest way to glory would have been to associate with Erasmus, whom he described as a dispenser of immortality.[26] But despite the partly utilitarian connection between public friendship and reputation, the idealised model always emphasised that the reputation of the individual members of the Republic of Letters could be seen as a social recognition of true virtue and intellectual qualities.

Vives, the Erasmian Republic of Letters, and Political Life

It was precisely this Erasmian Republic of Letters, led by Erasmus, Thomas More, and Guillaume Budé, that took Vives, active in the humanist academic circles at Louvain, under its protection at around 1520. Although Vives had undoubtedly gained some reputation before, as witnessed by the letter from the town magistrates of Valencia in 1517, where he was described as someone capable of speaking at court for a matter concerning the Valencian *Studium generale*, it was especially in 1519–1520 that Vives's stature in the humanist movement was established in print.[27] The way in which he was welcomed into the Erasmian Republic took several forms, but a special place can be attributed to the praise (*laudatio*) given to Vives in the printed letters of the most prominent humanists of the time. It is highly probable that much of this praise was essentially written to be published in the first place. In February 1519, in a letter written to the physician of Prince Ferdinand, Juan de la Parra (d. 1521), Erasmus recommended Vives as a potential tutor for the Prince, who was Charles V's (1500–1558) brother. In the letter, which was printed for the first time in Erasmus's *Opus epistolarum* (1529), he claimed that Vives possessed 'more than common learning in every branch of philosophy' and that he was able to imitate the Ancients in such a way that one could mistakenly assume that his writings were from 'those fertile periods of Cicero and Seneca'.[28] In a letter to Budé (17 February 1520), published in *Epistolae ad diversos* (1521), Erasmus stated that Vives was successfully engaged in rhetoric, which seemed to be from another time and era. He furthermore indicated that when Vives took on a rhetorical case, 'it is not imaginary or academic, but true and serious'.[29]

It was hardly a coincidence that much of the praise centred on Vives's rhetorical and dialectical skills since it coincided with the publication of his two main works of the period: *Declamationes Syllanae* and *In pseudodialecticos*. Both Thomas More and Erasmus lauded *Declamationes Syllanae*, highlighting certain specific themes. They claimed that in the *Declamationes* an ancient ideal of the union of wisdom and eloquence had been achieved. In an introductory letter published with *Declamationes*, Erasmus wrote that he saw 'no one in whom you might find so much eloquence combined with such great knowledge of philosophy', and claimed that Vives had revived an ancient genre.[30] Although both Erasmus and More praised Vives's encyclopaedic knowledge of the different arts, they especially underscored his rhetorical capacities such as his ability to argue for both sides of the matter (*in utramque partem*). More also placed special emphasis on Vives's ability to create a tangible and visible presence. In an *encomium* of the work printed in the 1520 *Epistolae aliquot selectae ex Erasmicis*. More declared that Vives invested 'the stories [...] with such lively feeling' that he seemed to have 'seen it and felt it and been engaged in events as they happened for better or worse'.[31] Referring to *In pseudodialecticos*, Erasmus's introductory letter to the *Declamationes* instructed the reader that when Vives was engaged in 'those subtle but inarticulate subjects which are now so popular, no man showed more acumen in disputation or proved himself a better sophist'.[32] More too pointed out that he took a 'special kind of pleasure in his [Vives's] *In pseudodialecticos*' not only because it proved the absurdities of logic but because it also reminded him strongly of his own letter to Dorp.[33] Consequently, in the public praise of the time, Vives appeared as a supremely gifted orator well versed in philosophy and dialectic.

In a demonstration of the reciprocal nature of the culture of encomia, Vives himself returned the praise lavished on him by the older generation of the Republic of Letters. In 1519, he took the role of a public arbitrator in the epistolary disagreements between Erasmus and Budé. This was welcomed and promoted by Budé, who in June 1519 wrote to Erasmus that Vives was 'a keen supporter both of your reputation and of mine' and that he could 'prove a most effective link for the future, to support our friendship and hold it together' if any disagreements were to arise.[34] Although Erasmus was not overly enthusiastic about Vives's role and considered it somewhat unnecessary, in June 1520 Vives composed a long letter intended for Erasmus which was meant to bridge the gap between him and Budé.[35] Vives recounted the experience of a journey to Paris and depicted the success of the Erasmian theological programme there. Although he maintained that Erasmus did not want to be praised in a letter that was addressed to himself, Vives still could not help lauding his New Testament 'which has done more for Christian piety than a thousand years of declamation in the lecture-room'.[36] He also included an encomium of Erasmus's old friend Budé, whose intellectual work could rival that of the ancients, whose *De asse* (1514) had 'put to shame [...] the whole of Italy', and in whose character 'everything provokes admiration and respect'.[37] Moreover, he believed that their disagreements did not put into jeopardy their friendship and hoped that Erasmus and Budé had 'laid the foundations of your [Erasmus and Budé's] friendship so well and truly that it will stand forever in its own strength'.[38] This letter first appeared in print in Erasmus's 1521 *Epistolae ad diversos*.

Vives's praise of the most prominent names of Northern humanism also occurred in his scholarly writings. In his commentaries on Augustine's *De civitate Dei* (1522), a project commissioned by Erasmus, Vives lauded Erasmus, Budé, and Thomas More among many others. In the preface to the work, Vives connected his commentaries to Erasmus's attempts to purify St Jerome and Cyprian, aligning himself thus with Erasmian philological theology.[39] He further included in the commentaries a laudation of Thomas More and a long encomium of Budé (*Gulielmi Budei laus*), describing him not only as the leading jurist of the time but also as a man of universal knowledge and talent. As he wrote, 'France has never produced a man of sharper *ingenium*, acute judgment, precise carefulness, greater erudition. In these times, not even Italy'.[40] Vives himself was equally clear that the help of the humanist circles had decisively contributed to his own reputation and fame. In 1522, he, writing to Franciscus Cranevelt (1485–1564), one of his closest friends, maintained that his fame owed much to the support of Cranevelt, Erasmus, Budé, and More whom he called his 'recommenders' (*commendatores*).[41] In this circle of friends, he defined his rapport with the older generation simultaneously through bonds of friendship and through the more vertical relations between a master and a disciple. The position of friend-disciple that Vives adopted or sought to adopt with Erasmus was by no means exceptional since most of Erasmus's friends acknowledged both his special intellectual gifts and his authority as the prince of the Republic of Letters.[42]

While the framing of Vives as a skilled orator versed in all disciplines enabled many career alternatives, his preferred choice at the turn of the 1520s was to serve as a tutor or a counsellor to the powerful. Indeed, although

Vives enjoyed the favour of Europe's most prominent humanist theologian, Erasmus, and its leading legal scholar, Guillaume Budé, he did not immerse himself in these disciplines. Understandably, as a *converso* whose family had had problems with the Inquisition, he wanted to avoid theology. In his letters to Cranevelt in 1520, Vives expressed his opinion on the current state of theology in a very direct manner stating that for a free mind it was a dangerous path. In another letter, Vives declared that questions related to the burning of Jewish books – a direct reference to the Reuchlin affair – and to Martin Luther (1483–1546) 'do not concern me'.[43] It was mainly in his introduction to the commented edition of Augustine's *De civitate Dei* that Vives publicly united himself with Erasmus's theological programme of polishing the founts of Christianity.[44] Moreover, despite having a number of lawyer friends such as Budé, Nicolas Bérault, Cranevelt, and Thomas More, and despite showing interest in jurisprudence and composing some short pieces on law, Vives never studied the subject in depth.[45]

Although Vives was actively seeking disciplines and areas in which to demonstrate his intellectual qualities and even consulted Budé on the matter, he continuously manifested his desire to operate in a courtly environment rather than in the academic circles of Louvain.[46] Indeed, the authority of Vives as an orator well versed in philosophy not only enabled the use of *ethos* in scholarly debates (*In pseudodialecticos*), but it also provided him credibility in his interaction with the seats of civic and ecclesiastical power. Despite his scholarly pursuits at Louvain, Vives had gained some visibility at the court, served as the tutor of Guillaume de Croy (1497–1521), archbishop of Toledo and the nephew of the even more famous Guillaume de Croy (1458–1521, Lord of Chièvres), and he had even been presented as a suitable tutor for Prince Ferdinand who was destined for a political career. After Croy's unfortunate death in 1521, Vives, who was increasingly dissatisfied with teaching at Louvain, was eager to pursue activities close to actual seats of power.[47] When he was energetically looking for career prospects in the aftermath of Croy's death, he eventually chose to go to England in 1523 despite an offer from the University of Alcalá to be the successor of the famous Spanish humanist Antonio de Nebrija (1444–1522).[48] His English sojourn did have an academic dimension since he taught at Corpus Christi College in Oxford, but right from the start, Vives actively sought a place at court and frequently reported on his relationship with the royal family in his letters.[49] As a demonstration of his willingness to be considered a potential counsellor, in December 1523 Vives dedicated two translations of Isocrates's speeches on the respective merits of monarchy and republic to Cardinal Wolsey (1473–1530), the most powerful man at court.[50]

Problems with Erasmus and Concerns with Publicity in the 1520s

While it was partly with the help of the public support of humanist circles that Vives, short of any academic degrees, could emerge as a man of authority, it is worth noting that the praise given to him by other humanists was mostly concentrated in the years around 1520.[51] Although Vives continued to be connected to humanist circles at the French, English, and Habsburg courts throughout the 1520s and 1530s, his presentation as the rising star of the Republic of Letters declined around 1522. This was partly because of the general weakening of the Republic led by Erasmus, Budé, and More in the Europe of the 1520s, pestered by growing religious strife and war among European super-powers, but also partly because of the perceivable cooling down of the affinity between Erasmus and Vives following Erasmus's discontent with Vives's commentaries on Augustine.[52] Vives did continue to defend the Erasmian cause throughout the 1520s, for instance, during the debate over Erasmus and Erasmianism in Spain in 1527, and he never ceased to describe himself as a follower of Erasmus, whom he called his 'teacher' (*praeceptor*). Yet he was no longer printed by Erasmus's favourite Basel printers before Erasmus's death in 1536 and his works appeared without prefaces, dedication letters, or other paratext from members of the Republic of Letters.[53] Erasmus's reluctance to support Vives was glaringly exposed in the first edition of his *Ciceronianus* (1528), in which he critically assessed all major contemporary humanists yet left Vives unmentioned.[54]

As Vives's relationship with Erasmus cooled down and as the significance of the Republic of Letters diminished more generally, Vives never tried to turn himself into a public figure of Erasmus's mould and dimensions. Apart from a few notable letters destined for the most powerful men of Europe on selected civic and ecclesiastical issues, most of his letters were not written to be published and Vives never edited a collection of his correspondence for the purpose of printing. Furthermore, he never engaged in any aggressive promotion of his literary production through laudatory introductory letters from other humanists and he did not write such letters himself to others.[55] From what is known, his relations with the printing world were less intense than those of Erasmus, and he spent considerably less time in the actual production of books with printers than the Dutch humanist.[56]

There are many possible reasons why Vives did not try to become a new Erasmus in the 1520s. Personality traits might have played a part, and the tendency to think of Erasmus's position within humanism as nothing short of exceptional certainly accounted for the fact that no one within Catholic humanist circles came even close to his reputation. Still, Vives's handling of his own image was also conditioned by a deliberate decision to avoid overtly polemical topics and the publicity that came with it. Already in 1520, when Vives had consulted Budé about which field of study he should focus on, Budé, in his reply, stressed that the selection of expedient theological and philosophical themes would doubtless generate a critical reaction from the envious, referring to the example of Erasmus.[57] Vives's Jewish background and the problems his *converso* family was facing in Valencia did not encourage an open positioning in the religious debates of the time that were dominating the book market. More importantly, the Erasmian attempt to control public discussion through literary means, which often drew on Lucianic satire and ridicule addressed to a broader readership, was questioned when the popular and subversive tendencies of humanism were increasingly coupled with the Reformation.[58] Erasmus's engagement in bitter printed disputes with Lee, Latomus, Parisian theologians, and eventually Luther (with Luther, Erasmus's tone was markedly less aggressive) certainly did not appeal to Vives.

It is plausible to think that for Vives, Erasmus's inability to avoid public debates and attacks was connected to his prominent standing as the most famous representative of humanist studies and theological philology. Erasmus himself was increasingly aware of these problems and frequently engaged in self-censorship in the polemical 1520s and 1530s, when the use of satire à la *Moria* was becoming dangerous, but he never abandoned the genre and its ambiguous playfulness completely.[59] The failure of humanist attempts to control the discursive space through satire was more pronounced in Vives's choices. After 1519 and *In pseudodialecticos*, he seldom wrote in a satirical vein, moulding himself rather into an educated sage whose claim to authority was based on gravity and severity.[60] In the 1520s, Vives adopted *sine querela* (without complaint) as his motto, which emphasised the importance of self-restraint in the face of quarrels.[61] When Erasmus frequently complained about the misinterpretations his opponents made of his texts, Vives suggested that he should publish an edition of all his works in which he could make 'clear your definitive judgment on each point, so that we can be sure of the position you have taken', which would prevent confusion and disarray.[62] The supposed need for this was the textual divergences between different editions, but Vives's comments were undoubtedly also motivated by the debates Erasmus took, or was forced to take, part in. During the discussions, many of Erasmus's opponents pointed out his wavering on the burning issues that were being debated. They also bemoaned his propensity to avoid clear-cut statements and claimed that his persuasive style of writing allowed him to refrain from unambiguous pronouncements. Luther called him an eel that only Christ could grasp, and Ulrich von Hutten (1488–1523), whose friendship with Erasmus turned into a public feud in the early 1520s, complained about his habit to avoid positioning himself unequivocally in any of the significant questions of the time.[63]

Vives went even further in portraying the dynamics of debate among the learned as a form of discord, a criticism taken to its extreme in his 1529 *De concordia*. In *De concordia*, Vives described a battle between factions of learned men in which the people (*plebs*) served as judges, and which was fought with all the resources of the *ars oratoria* such as 'invectives, accusations, recriminations, epigrams, apologies, counter-apologies, epistles, dialogues'.[64] In a similar fashion, his reflections on the life of the truly erudite man in his 1531 *De disciplinis*, although drawing on a traditional discourse of an idealised Republic of Letters, clashed with Erasmus's choices on a number of things related to publicity. Vives still depicted the learned man very much as a member of the Republic who discussed his projects with others to get their opinions. But in doing this, he should avoid all disputes in his focus on truth, publishing little, and only after consulting friends in order to avoid overt attacks. He should also be careful not to re-edit his work too often because it obscured the intention of the writer. All this was important since the ultimate goal of the erudite man was to associate cordially and humanely with other scholars, and to guarantee that his life and manners, both individually and collectively, would testify to his self-government, innocence, and true authority.[65] The traditional depiction of the community of the learned as a model of concord that had ceased to perform its true function mirrored closely the development of printed debates and the rise of the pamphlet culture in the 1510s and especially the 1520s. Simultaneously, it also reflected what had happened to the great Dutch humanist during his public feuds, a fact that would not have gone unnoticed by the reader. By the late 1520s and early 1530s, Vives, the writer of the satirical *In pseudodialecticos*, who in his Parisian years had praised the ethical possibilities of satire, emphasised the threat posed by ridicule and all forms of open confrontation to concord.

Truth, Rhetoric, and Dissimulation

Vives's description of the culture of discord within learned circles in *De concordia* was naturally in stark contrast to the promise of harmony and friendship that framed the self-interpretation of the Erasmian Republic of Letters at the turn of the 1520s. As we have seen, this harmony was ideally nurtured by a non-confrontational conversation where others were accepted as equal partners in a dialogue according to the rules of *sermo*. Nonetheless, *sermo* was not restricted to the maintenance of the reciprocal relations of the circle of friends around Erasmus, but it increasingly emerged as a solution to some of the pressing problems of the time. Most importantly, in the religious debates of the 1520s, the ideal of conversation was proposed by Erasmus as a relatively tolerant model for discussing non-essentials of faith (*adiaphora*; this ideal was exhibited already in his *Convivium religiosum*), and he famously tried to frame his discussion on free will with Luther as a conversation or *diatribe*[66] between friends.[67] Vives too acknowledged the possibilities of *sermo* to mediate differences of opinion. In his 1522 letter to Pope Adrian of Utrecht (1459–1523), Vives had aligned himself with the Erasmian idea of defining a few essentials of faith through a Church Council and leaving non-essential issues open to debate. As he wrote, 'only those things should be examined and determined that concern the essentials of piety and moral behaviour' whereas debate should be allowed on other issues in which arguments existed on both sides (*in utramque partem*).[68]

Civilised conversation between friends did not, however, cater for all situations in which speech was needed; it was clear that in engaging with the world outside learned circles, one needed different kinds of discursive genres, many of which drew on oratory or incorporated oratorical elements into them. Since Jacques Chomarat's work, much light has been shed on the non-dogmatic, rhetorical nature of Erasmus's theology.[69] In studies that draw on Chomarat, it has been demonstrated that in Erasmus theological discourse took the form of a rhetorical language the transformative effects of which were supposed to resuscitate the spirit of Christ and transform Christianity on all levels of human intercourse.[70] It was in this spirit that Erasmus in his *Paraclesis* claimed that he yearned for an eloquence less ornate yet more powerful than Cicero's that, rather than inciting action, produced a spiritual transformation in the audience.[71] Furthermore, in equating Quintilian's definition of the orator as a good man skilled in speaking to a definition of theology as 'piety linked to skill in speaking of the divine' in his *Apologia contra Latomi dialogum*, Erasmus maintained that true rhetoric, based on the transformation of the speaker, could serve as the basis for a theology of piety.[72] In an extreme exposition of rhetorical theology, he claimed that the understanding and communicating of the message of the Scriptures were not two separate tasks but part of the very same mental process, an issue that Latomus failed to capture. Consequently, transformative rhetoric was ultimately inseparable from the transformation of the speaker.[73]

Yet the stress put on transformative rhetoric did not mean that that rhetoric should be transparent in any simple sense. As Peter Bietenholz has shown, Erasmus's ideas on the ways in which truth should be communicated in language were complex and he greatly stressed its accommodation to the particularities of a given situation.[74] This was in line with the classical rhetorical principle of *decorum* according to which one's sayings had to be adapted to the relationship and nature of the persons involved, the time and place of communication, and other contextual factors. While *decorum* as such was not a central concept in Erasmus's early manuals on rhetoric, such as *De copia* and *De conscribendis epistolis*, its main idea – the contextual accommodation of one's message – was quite important.[75] But perhaps more significantly, Erasmus stressed the contextual accommodation of truth in all his broader reflections on language, ranging from Biblical exegesis to his private letters. He thought that this is the way the New Testament, the Christ, and St. Paul had spoken and should be interpreted, and it is in this tradition that he clearly understood his own writings.[76]

Yet, as Bietenholz has argued, Erasmus's general emphasis on the contextual aspect of speech was intertwined with a more particular stress on what might be called ethical dissimulation. More precisely, out of respect for civility, one should often hide one's true opinions and show respect to the possibly erroneous opinions of the audience. St Paul epitomised this approach. In the classic debate on a passage in Galatians (2:11–4), in which Paul had rebuked Peter in public for following Mosaic dietary laws in order to please Christian Jews, Erasmus aligned himself with the interpretative tradition of Jerome and Origen who had seen the passage as an example of dissimulation. Unlike Augustine, according to whom both Paul and Peter had acted sincerely, Jerome had emphasised not only that Peter simulated the observance of Jewish diet for Christian Jews, but that Paul's critique was essentially a way to assure gentile Christians that they did not need to follow the Mosaic law in order to be saved. Indeed, Jerome had gone so far as to call the incident a feigned quarrel in which Peter and Paul had both dissimulated to their respective audiences.[77]

The idea of ethical dissimulation is fundamental to Erasmus's ideas of religious rhetoric and visible in his fierce and often-repeated criticism of Luther's lack of *decorum* and civility.[78] In a well-known letter to Justus Jonas (1493–1555) in May 1521, he bemoaned at length Luther's aggressive style and claimed that 'truth of itself has a bitter taste for most people', so that 'it would have been wiser to soften a naturally painful subject by the courtesy of one's handling'.[79] He maintained that 'the Spirit of Christ in the Gospels has a wisdom of its own', and, drawing on the rhetorical dichotomy between audiences composed of the wise and those made up by the people, he wrote that Christ himself said 'one thing to the multitudes, who are somewhat thick-witted, and another to his disciples'.[80] In a similar fashion, Erasmus elaborated extensively on the *decorum* of Peter and Paul, reminding the reader that the latter became 'all things to all men, that he may gain them all for Christ'.[81] While this rhetoric often concerned religious discourse, it was systematically extended to all rhetoric including speech destined to secular rulers. As he put it in a letter to cardinal Lorenzo Campeggi in December 1520, 'princes one should handle gently, for their majesty, if provoked too often, brings great disasters upon mortal men'.[82] Similar issues were applicable to satire. In his adage *Sileni Alcibiadis,* he described the Greek statuettes, Sileni, that, despite their comic exterior, held a hidden deity inside. The Sileni were explicitly likened to Socrates and Christ, but they clearly implied a form of self-interpretation, since the Lucianic or Socratic jester which Erasmus decided to play in works such as *Encomium Moriae* drew on the union of internal spirituality and a comic appearance.[83]

All this implied that truthful and ethical speech could draw on rhetorical accommodation and even dissimulation if it was necessary for persuasion.[84] There was, of course, a tension between truth and ethics, on the one hand, and dissimulation that could resemble flattery and deceit, on the other. Perhaps the central strategy to explain this was a recourse to one's conscience and intentions as an interpretive key to what was explicitly stated. Erasmus, for instance, maintained that, should the wise of his time and posteriority decipher his message in the spirit of *decorum*, the purity of his intentions and conscience would shine through.[85] In other words, while there might be some dissimulation and insincerity in the words used, the educated elite and future generations would understand that they stemmed from pure ethical dispositions and aim at enhancing the good. This reference to one's own conscience and intentions was not without its problems. It was often mocked by his adversaries ever since the time of his 1510s debate with Dorp, and Erasmus, although never abandoning his polemical way of writing completely, became increasingly aware of the impossibilities of controlling the interpretation of one's own meaning.[86]

Vives had certainly been thinking about the relationship between truth and words ever since his Parisian years. His 1519 edition of the *Clipei Christi descriptio*, originally published in 1514, included a reference to Paul's 'gentle yet effective' rhetoric which was contrasted with Peter's louder and more ardent speech.[87] However, unlike Erasmus, Vives did not expand greatly on the dissimulative tendencies of the New Testament but rather participated in older academic debates on the relationship between poetry, humanist learning, and truth. In 1514, he had framed his *Veritas fucata* as an attempt to enhance Christian virtue through humanist poetry. In a 1519 dedication letter to a new edition of *Veritas fucata* and the *Praelectio ad Catonem maiorem Ciceronis quae dicitur Anima senis* to Juan de Crommas, Vives explained that *Veritas fucata*, written in Paris, had essentially been an attempt to draw certain young people from 'vain and dirty poetry' to 'more saintly muses', and to 'more substantial disciplines'. He continued by explaining that he was a supporter of the muses yet opposed to 'empty words'.[88] Vives was also certain that the exposition of revealed truth could take different forms and was thus both rhetorical and interpretative. In a defence of his own meditations on the *Meditationes in septem Psalmos penitentiae* (1517–1518), he wrote in the dedication letter to the work (to Guillaume de Croy) that 'the words of the Holy Spirit are not tied to one sense', and that the Bible contained 'multiple and admirable senses' which were all correct because of the Spirit that had produced them.[89]

Still, Vives's greatest contribution to the dilemma of the union of words (*verba*) and things (*res*) was undoubtedly his 1523 *Veritas fucata*, which set out to delineate the conditions within which poetry and truth could coexist fruitfully. From the very start of the text, laid out as a dialogue between Vives and a well-known Spanish humanist Juan de Vergara (1492–1557), the difference from the 1514 treatment was clear.[90] Early on, the discussion was taken down from the initial heights of *philosophia Christi* by Vergara, who wished to talk to Vives 'in a simple manner and starting from the common use of words', moving on to a presentation of an allegorical story built around two camps, those of Truth, and those of Error.[91] In the story, the naked simplicity of Truth was juxtaposed to the extravagant, made-up, and twisted nature of Error, accompanied by many vices and a not insignificant number of people, all of whom decorated themselves with wrong names, 'denying proper ones', putting on a show of an ultimately flawed rhetorical redescription. Thus, among other lies, 'falsehood was called negligence, perjury the statement of truth, guile prudence'.[92] In striking opposition to this, in the followers of Truth no rupture occurred between the real nature of things and the names with which they were evoked. Here everything was 'naked, open, simple, certain, solid [...] truthful'.[93]

Unlike in the 1514 *Veritas fucata*, where the structure was static, here some notable developments took place and they were largely centred on negotiations between the troops of Truth and the soldiers of Error (*falsiani*). Whereas the spokesperson of Truth, Plato, failed to convince the party of Error, the delegation of Error led by Homer was more successful. Quite amazingly, Homer, in the negotiations, convinced Truth of the necessity of concealing its naked beauty, the unveiling of which, according to one of Homer's many arguments, would cause humans some additional satisfaction because of the effort put into it.[94] When Truth expressed its will to 'show itself naked', arguing that if it was perceived directly by humans it would excite love in everyone, Homer did not deny this. However, he argued that he 'knows the habits and character of his people', implying the necessity of concealment on these grounds.[95]

Truth accepted Homer's offer, albeit with ten different stipulations that were spelled out. The rules made perfectly clear that poetry was not interpreted as a narrowly defined metrical art but rather referred to a broader range of humanistic literary studies. Not only did the selection of authors such as Apuleius, whose satirical *Asinus aureus* was one of the most famous Latin works in prose, imply this, but Vives also referred to prose in spelling out the seventh condition. Moreover, condition five stressed that everything concerning moral life was free ground for writers, and the text singled out comedy, apology, and dialogue as suitable genres to enhance moral improvement.[96] Thus, although *Veritas fucata* set out to discuss the limits of poetry, it ended up building a scheme within which the union of truth and humanist literary studies was both morally acceptable and useful for the enhancement of virtue. The reason for this was that, in the current state of affairs, truth could not reveal itself without disguise because humans would simply not accept it.

Rather than offering a theory of dissimulation in the Erasmian mould, *Veritas fucata* participated in the defence of humanist literary studies in an academic debate on poetry and humanist learning. While the issue had gained new relevance in the humanist-scholastic dispute, it was part of an age-old academic debate over the possibilities and threats of poetical and rhetorical licence (*licentia*) which had been fought within academic circles throughout the Middle Ages. It had long surfaced in many of the rebuttals of Plato's condemnation of poetry such as in Macrobius's commentary on the *Somnium Scipionis*.[97] Still, it is noteworthy that Vives's intervention coincided with Erasmus's growing interest in the *decorum* of truth, and its argument that humans were not able to look truth directly in the eyes was strikingly close to Erasmus's own views of the time. Quite significantly, the members of the delegation of Error comprised of Homer, Lucian, Apuleius, and Hesiod are – except for Hesiod – mentioned as representatives of the satirical tradition within which Erasmus placed his *Praise of Folly* (*Moriae*) in his dedication letter to Thomas More.[98]

There are more similarities. Erasmus himself was quite capable of referring to the traditional commonplace about the nakedness of truth in his discussions on the necessity of rhetorical dissimulation and *decorum*. In a defence of the union of rhetoric and truth in his famous letter to Dorp, Erasmus, drawing on the authority of Augustine, claimed that 'the Gospel truth slips into our minds more agreeably, and takes root there more decisively, when it has charms of this kind to commend it than if it were produced naked'.[99] Another way of discussing the moulding of truth to the contextual requirements of the situation was the relationship between Greek and Roman philosophies. In the famous dialogue between a sailor named Raphael Hythloday and Thomas More on the possibilities of counselling in the first book of More's *Utopia*, the respective views of the two interlocutors were discussed as a debate between Greek philosophy, which dealt with truth, and the Roman rhetorical model, which adjusted itself to different contexts. In a similar spirit, Erasmus, in a preface to an edition of the *Tusculanae Quaestiones*, offered Cicero a place in the development of philosophy from its Greek origins as someone who brought philosophy 'onto the stage', and taught it to speak 'in such a fashion that even a miscellaneous audience can applaud'.[100] Vives agreed. In his *Somnium et vigilia* (printed in 1520), which served as an introduction to and commentary on Cicero's *Somnium Scipionis*, a part of *De republica* that had survived thanks to Macrobius's widely disseminated commentaries, Vives made a fictional Cicero explain that his *De republica* had extensively drawn on Plato's work but with the difference that he, unlike Plato, had taken into account the great variety of natural talent (*ingenia*) among humans in enhancing virtue.[101] In short, while different discussions had different reference points, they all stressed the importance of communicating truth through literary means that would adjust it to the audience.

Transformative Rhetoric and the Ideal Prince

While the immediate context of *Veritas fucata* was that of an academic debate at Louvain, Vives's interest in the decorous adjustment of truth took place at a moment when he was engaged in a life of *negotium* and counselling. Now the discussions on the contextual adaptation of truth were certainly relevant for civic rhetoric since the possibilities of counselling were intrinsically linked to speech in the minds of the group of friends around Erasmus. As they well knew, dealing with the powerful in the civic realm required a decorous understanding of the different registers of the *ars oratoria*. Some of these ways could fit in with the paradigm of *philosophia Christi* that aspired to transformative speech capable of restoring Christianity to a life befitting Christians on all levels of human association. Erasmus surely included the reformation of princes as a vital part of this project. In a letter to Budé, he defended the usefulness of his work, claiming that in his book on the 'Christian Prince I lay down principles on which no theologian dares lay a finger'.[102] In his *Institutio Principis Christiani*, Erasmus drew on the ancient genre of mirror-for-princes, epitomised by Seneca's *De clementia* that, through an epideictic praise of an ideal ruler and vituperation of a tyrant, sought to produce self-reflection in the ruler that could lead to his self-transformation.[103] As he claimed in his preface to the work, he hoped that Charles V, to whom the work was dedicated, would try to improve himself by imitating 'the picture of a true and upright Christian prince'.[104]

Erasmus also thought of his less famous and more oratorical *Panegyricus* (printed in 1504), a laudation of Archduke Philip (1478–1506), as a companion piece to the *Institutio Principis Christiani* with which it was often printed.[105] While according to some of his critics, the *Panegyricus* bordered on flattery, Erasmus never ceased to explain that its laudatory element (or false praise) enabled character transformation. As he maintained, his text was 'not so much praise as precept', and that there was 'surely no more effective method of reforming princes than to present them with a pattern of a good prince under the guise of praising them'.[106] He further claimed that, under the semblance of flattery, the work could 'reform bad rulers', and 'improve the good', and that this manner of exhorting 'rulers to honourable action under the cover of compliment' was definitely better than approaching the king with 'the repellent teachings of Stoicism and the barking of the Cynics'.[107] The promise of transformative rhetoric, epitomised by the power of the gospels, was part of a broader theory of cure which metaphorically likened an orator to a physician of the soul.[108]

Vives could also refer to the transformative potential of the image of a perfect ruler. His *Somnium et vigilia*, built around Cicero's *Somnium Scipionis*, which recounted the dream encounter of Scipio Aemilianus with his dead grandfather Scipio Africanus, greatly underlined the transformative dimension of Cicero's text. Although Macrobius's famous commentaries on *Somnium Scipionis*, with their Neoplatonic undertones, emphasised various elements of the text such as its relevance to cosmography and the theory of dreams, Macrobius had already pointed out that the fundamental principles of good government should be communicated to readers through different literary devices that would instil in humans the will to do good works.[109] In his dedication letter to Érard de la Marck (1472–1538), the prince-bishop of Liège, Vives primarily stressed the political dimension of the text as an exercise in the self-reflection of the prince. He claimed that the work was about 'the instruction and formation of the perfect and complete prince' and added that 'nothing in all philosophy is more excellent' than the formation of the ruler.[110] The *Somnium*, and Vives's fictional commentary on, or amplification of, it entitled *Vigilia*, depicted the cosmic journey of the young Scipio, whose ascent to the heavens and across the cosmos enhanced his awareness of the eternal rules governing the universe. This adoption of a cosmic view on the nature of things and on one's position within the bigger scheme of things was a preparation for ethical self-transformation and thus for a truthful judgment of earthly matters. What is more, in his *Vigilia*, Vives amplified at length the Erasmian moral code that followed from this cosmic awareness, focusing especially on the judgment of the pettiness of merely human things. In this moral code, justice, just like in classical thought, was described as the 'the bond of human partnership', but it had to be supported by piety and charity towards one's parents, friends, and fatherland. Other virtues demanded of a ruler were self-control (*continentia*), equity (*aequitas*), moderation (*moderatio*), and fortitude (*fortitudo*).[111]

Rhetoric and Political Counsel

Despite the emphasis put on transformative rhetoric, humanist correspondence often revealed a much more realistic view of the character of the rulers of their time. As James Tracy has argued, Erasmus's praise of Charles was always coupled with a suspicion about his actual political measures, and the less than perfect nature of rulers was frequently discussed in his correspondence.[112] Many of his actual political texts also hinted that rulers fell short of the standards required of a self-governed prince. In *Querela Pacis* (*On the Complaint of Peace*, 1517), Erasmus suggested that 'princes are powerful rather than learned, and moved more by their desires than by rational judgment'.[113] This view of the reality of the rulers of the time was incorporated into practical rhetorical advice. Just as in other domains of life, Erasmus arguably knew that not all political rhetoric aspired to complete transformation, and his detailed advice on the use of rhetoric in works such as his letter-writing manual, *De conscribendis epistolis,* revealed a more varied and subtle understanding of the possibilities of different rhetorical genres. In *De conscribendis epistolis*, he recommended yet again false praise as a way of criticising or advising 'a ruler or a king [...] whose ears will not tolerate any criticism at all'.[114] Although Erasmus was primarily describing advice that aimed at correcting a particular fault in the ruler rather than suggesting a certain course of action, his recommendation presupposed the less-than-perfect nature of the prince as a starting point of advice.

It was, however, in the first book of Thomas More's *Utopia*, printed in Louvain and recommended by Vives as one of the political texts worth reading in his 1531 *De disciplinis*, that counselling was discussed in a strikingly non-utopian way as a practice that, instead of transforming the ruler, sought to guide him within existing possibilities.[115] While *Utopia* has been the object of myriad interpretations on an infinite number of issues (e.g., the relationship between books One and Two or the extent to which More the character in the dialogue represented More's thought), there is agreement that one of the two major themes of Book One (the other is poverty) concerned the relative merits of a life of *otium* and *negotium* with a specific focus on counsel.[116] In the discussion, the very presupposition was that in addressing the ruler one could not take for granted that the formation of his character had been successful. In this context, *Utopia* discussed the problem of counselling, not that of tutoring or character formation.

The first part depicted a conversation between a sailor, Raphael Hythloday, who had first-hand knowledge of the island of *Utopia*, Pieter Gillis, and Thomas More himself. After a detour to questions of theft, poverty, and private ownership, Thomas More and Hythloday came back to the original theme of the dialogue which was started by Gillis's initial remark that Raphael should put his knowledge at the service of a prince as a counsellor. This suggestion was ironically rejected by Hythloday since 'the difference [between service and servitude] is only a matter of one syllable'.[117]

In the ensuing debate, Hythloday, who argued for the impossibility of expedient counselling and for the merits of a contemplative life, made the first move by presenting two hypothetical situations of counselling. In the first, a discussion on French foreign policy was portrayed, in which counsellors sought methods for broadening the power and the territory of the French king through cunning and perfect domination of methods of *realpolitik*. Here Hythloday, instead of answering the original question, tried to reframe it by arguing that it was not expedient to enlarge territory and power in the first place and that all effort should be focused on governing the territory given to the prince in question. In the second example, reminiscent of the first one, Raphael was forced to argue against a herd of counsellors on the possibilities of filling the treasury of the king through manipulation of existing laws, the value of money, make-believe wars, legislation, and the interpretation of laws to the prince's advantage. Against counsellors who agreed on the principle that the king should maximise his treasury, Hythloday would have to argue that these policies are both dishonourable and ruinous to the king, whose duty lay in perfecting his people and guarding their pursuit of a good life.[118] He concluded by suggesting, in a form of a question, that he likely would not be successful since his listeners 'would turn deaf ears to me'.[119]

Thomas More, the character in the dialogue, answered by arguing for the rhetorical philosophy of Cicero: 'There is another philosophy, better suited for the role of a citizen, that takes its cue, adapts itself to the drama in hand and acts its part neatly and appropriately'.[120] In doing so, More restricted rhetorical philosophy to the incomplete world: he was ready to grant that it was impossible to make everything good in a corrupt world, but the rejection of the ideal of complete transformation should not make the humanist abandon the commonwealth since he could try to make things as little bad as possible. Hythloday, however, was not convinced. According to him, either one spoke the truth or adjusted one's methods to the way people already understood the world, which was to confirm the error. There was simply no way to reform people who persisted in their corrupted nature through any kind of indirect rhetorical approach.[121] The debate mirrored one of the fundamental problems of all rhetorical theory stemming from the tension between the obligation to teach and argue for an honourable cause, on the one hand, and the fact that teaching was possible only if one could ground it in the opinions the audience would accept as valid premises, on the other. If these premises were wrong, one could argue that there was no way to perform the duties of a counsellor (the position of Hytholday) or that these premises, as wrong as they might be, could be used for one's cause if one mastered the rhetorical philosophy of Cicero (the position of More).

Adjusting Deliberative Rhetoric to Princely Counsel: Vives's *De Consultatione*

The tensions inherent in *Utopia* are, I would argue, apparent in Vives's views on counsel as it was outlined in *De consultatione*. In the last part of the chapter, dedicated to a close reading of *De consultatione*, the aim is to uncover the ways in which counselling was supposed to work in practice and to compare this to the idealised interpretation of the prince normally associated with Vives and more generally, Erasmian political theory.

Vives's relationship to the princes of his time is somewhat complex. On the one hand, in his early 1520s correspondence one can find praise of Henry VIII whose favour he was seeking. In a 1523 letter to Cranevelt he described his experience in England in favourable terms declaring that in his current state 'you cannot imagine anything that would please me more than the princes'.[122] On the other hand, in his commentaries on Augustine he could claim that 'in this world all kings are afraid of having a person with whom to share their power'.[123] This idea was much closer to how Vives conceived of princes both in his rhetorical and political literature, and his suspicion grew even stronger during the 1520s as he came to fully understand the endemic nature of dynastic warfare. The fact that the rulers of his time were driven by a hunger for power and were prone to warfare and destructive passions was visible in *De consultatione* and in his political interventions of the 1520s (Chapter 3).

De consultatione, Vives's only work on deliberative rhetoric, revealed serious problems with princely counsel. The work – written in 1523 and dedicated to Louis of Flanders (1488–1555), the Habsburg ambassador at Tudor court – was a painstakingly technical presentation on rhetorical invention (*inventio*) that adjusted the precepts of deliberative rhetoric to political counsel.[124] In other words, it was meant to offer headings through which an orator could come up with material and strategies when addressing a ruler. The manual can, of course, be viewed as a deliberate appropriation of classical theory into a new, princely context within the internal history of rhetoric, but its interpretation of the ruler as an object of persuasion also provides a highly significant take on Vives's view of the princes of the time and the possibilities of actual political counsel. Indeed, *De consultatione* closely mirrored broader discussions on princes and princely rhetoric, by and large affirming what *Utopia* had suggested and what a long tradition of classical and medieval writers operating under monarchs had known: that addressing those in power was a delicate matter in which the price of a wrong course of action was not merely rhetorical inefficiency but one's own position and possibly even life.[125] Although the work was printed only in 1532 together with Vives's main opus on rhetorical theory, *De ratione dicendi*, it has been argued that many aspects of the work suggest that its overall structure coincides with the 1523 manuscript.[126]

Scholarship, scant in quantity, has given an ambivalent view of the work because of the conflict between Erasmian (or Christian) humanism and the highly technical tone of *De consultatione* that presented the use of words as an instrumental question of persuasion.[127] However, if the work is situated within the broader humanist theory of decorous rhetoric, we can see that it did not necessarily serve as a denial of pious Erasmian humanism but as a continuation of humanist aspirations to make a difference through varied linguistic means. Although it was a technical exposition of tools of persuasion, this was nothing new within Northern humanist rhetoric; many rhetorical manuals presented rhetorical theory as an internal question of artistic persuasion and had relatively little to say about how the link between one's ethical character and ability to persuade fed into rhetorical practice. Furthermore, despite its instrumental tone, some aspects of the work admittedly united it with Erasmian and Christian themes. In a traditional vein, the handbook stressed that a counsellor should be a man of prudence and introduced Christian concepts into the topics of prudence (e.g. piety) which, given the intertextual purpose of topics to lead one to existing materials and commonplaces, should guide the counsellor to Christian *sententiae*.[128]

Vives himself thought of the work as more than a compilation of classical precepts. He boldly claimed that the topics of argumentation should be 'exposed according to a reliable and new method', implying that classical precepts would not fulfil the requirements of present-day deliberations.[129] While some of the treatment was standard, such as his assertion that deliberations concerned possible actions in the future, the claim about originality was not just an empty *topos* in itself.[130] With respect to classical handbooks which often underlined the strictly political nature of the themes debated, Vives gave a more open description of possible themes arguing that 'we deliberate on everything that is in our control', implying that they could concern potentially anything.[131] In a Renaissance vein, Vives's focus on rhetorical invention and his complete omission of memory (*memoria*) and delivery (*pronunciatio*) – two of the traditional five parts of classical oratory – indicate that he was thinking about contexts that were not merely oral but literary, and the publication of *De consultatione* with the later *De ratione dicendi* – which treated purely literary genres at length – further foregrounded the possible uses of its precepts in writing. Ultimately, however, by far the most significant element of Vives's *De consultatione* was its choice of focus. In classical accounts of deliberative rhetoric on which Renaissance manuals drew, the focus was standardly on the presentation of topics that enabled the orator to argue for the honourable (*honestum*) and expedient (*utile*) nature of any course of action proposed in a debate on political issues.[132] In a stark contrast to this tradition, the description of *inventio* in *De consultatione* was pronouncedly attuned to the analysis of the qualities and relations of persons involved and had relatively little to say about the analysis of the question deliberated. As Vives put it, 'before everything else we should consider who is the person we are counselling, next, who we are, then, who are the other counsellors'.[133] In other words, *De consultatione* told more about how to find the right tone and strategy to persuade a specific person than about how to invent convincing arguments. This was undoubtedly motivated by the fact that *De consultatione* dealt with situations which addressed those above the speaker.

Topics from Persons and the Authority of the Speaker

The core of *De consultatione* was structured on topics from persons that were eclectically appropriated from classical rhetoric. More specifically, Vives drew on the topics found in Cicero's *De inventione*, much of which had already been incorporated into Erasmus's *De conscribendis epistolis*.[134] In *De inventione*, Cicero introduced these topics in the treatment of disposition (*dispositio*) and claimed that the arguments drawn from the attributes of persons could be used in the confirmation (*confirmatio*) of one's argument which sought to lend credibility and authority to one's case.[135] In Vives's treatment, the link to disposition was lost and the topics from persons were presented as a storehouse of material for deliberations. They were situated under three general topics that Vives could have adopted from the exposition of demonstrative rhetoric in the *Ad Herennium* but also from other sources.[136] These described a person on the basis of what was in his/her soul (*in animo*), in his/her body (*in corpore*), and what was external to him/her (*externa*), which provided a way of collecting all the material one possessed on oneself, the deliberator, and other possible counsellors. Under the topic of the soul, one could find a list of sub-headings with which one could extract material in order to analyse one's natural capacities, what one had acquired through learning (*habitus*), and one's emotional dispositions; bodily topics helped to gather information on one's physical constitution such as age; externals referred, for example, to one's goods, lineage, and family relations.[137]

It hardly comes as a surprise that Vives drew on Cicero, Quintilian, and the *Ad Herennium* since much of classical rhetoric exhibited an acute awareness of the importance of mastering the character of the persons involved in a rhetorical situation for the successful exposition of one's case. The control of character delineation and biographies could serve different purposes. In demonstrative rhetoric dedicated to praise (*laudatio*) and blame (*vituperatio*), character description was the subject matter through which the object of praise could be described as someone epitomising virtue in his/her actions. In judicial rhetoric, the crafting of characters could affect not only the way in which the accused and potential witnesses were perceived and assessed but also contributed to the credibility of the narration by attributing motives and causes of action to the accused that were in line with his/her character. Furthermore, in different rhetorical genres, an examination of the audience could shed light on how to build one's case so that it was in accordance with one's assessment of the expectations and qualities of those addressed. Finally, one's *ethos* was closely linked to the mastering of one's own character and biography as they were outlined in a speech.[138]

Although the information extracted from personal topics served a range of purposes in *De consultatione*, the topics that were employed in judicial rhetoric to scrutinise the character of the accused and the witnesses were, in the work, mainly used to get information on the qualities of the deliberator; they are essentially a way to build a close analysis of the person the orator is addressing and to assess one's personal relation with him/her. This had not been as central to the rhetorical tradition. Roman theory could occasionally suggest a closer analysis of the person of the deliberator in speeches before rulers; Quintilian's *Institutio oratoria* not only underscored the value of the *ethos* of the speaker in deliberations in a general sense but also claimed that when we were trying to convince just one person, 'it is his character that will make the biggest difference'.[139] Still, classical and Renaissance treatises on deliberative rhetoric, with their focus on the question debated, did not incorporate the person of the deliberator into their subject matter in any systematic way. The standard distinction was between learned and unlearned audiences, who preferred honesty and expediency respectively, and it was voiced in works such as the widely diffused encyclopaedia *Margarita philosophica* (1503) and several others, but the emphasis was overwhelmingly on presenting the argumentative possibilities of topics for the investigation of the question.[140]

These personal topics drawn from the deliberator could serve a variety of functions. They could provide support for a suggested course of action since they supplied information about what was becoming according to one's specific duties as a prince or what was possible considering one's external instruments. One could, for instance, appeal to the noble lineage of the deliberator and argue that his/her actions should not disgrace his/her ancestors: 'since you are from a most noble background, it is just not to be disgraceful to your ancestors'. Conversely, if one could not draw on the examples of a noble family, one should tell the deliberator that 'you have to pursue nobility by yourself'.[141] Material drawn from the personal attributes of the deliberator could thus be used when one wanted to show that a proposed course of action was in line with his/her person, family, specific duties of the office, and a range of other things.

Equally importantly, one could draw on personal topics in the construction of one's own *ethos*. Part of *ethos* certainly referred to one's ethical qualities and moral reputation. In *De consultatione*, Vives claimed that one's *ethos* stemmed from the opinion the audience had of one's prudence (*prudentia*), honesty (*probitas*), and friendship (*amicitia*), which loosely corresponded to Aristotle's tripartite division of the sources of *ethos*.[142] However, unlike in

Aristotle's *Rhetoric*, where these qualities were exhibited in a speech, Vives underlined one's life that preceded the rhetorical situation as a source of authority in itself. While not stressed by Aristotle, this was nothing new. Roman rhetorical tradition had pointed out the relevance of one's general reputation to one's authority, and Christian adaptations of classical theory, most notably Augustine's *De doctrina Christiana*, had portrayed one's ethical nature as it was revealed in the totality of one's life as the principal source of authority.[143] Moreover, Erasmus's own rhetoric, epitomised by his *Paraclesis*, often asserted the virtuous nature of the speaker as a precondition of a truly transformative rhetoric. This union was incarnated in Christ. Vives had clearly absorbed the idea that one's life was an important source of ethical authority by the early 1520s. He had added to his 1519 reprint of the 1514 *Clipeus* a passage which portrayed the life of St Paul as a source of his persuasive authority.[144] In *De consultatione*, Vives stated that honesty stemmed from the great persuasive potential of one's way of living which consisted in an 'honest and saintly' life, and from the agreement between one's life and words.[145] The adoption of the Augustinian and Christian description of one's ethical authority under the heading 'honesty' (*probitas*) in *De consultatione* thus surely referred to the broader Erasmian union of ethics and rhetoric.

But even though Vives could point to one's ethical life as a source of authority, *De consultatione* made perfectly clear that one's authority and *ethos* needed adjustment according to the specific requirements of the situation. Most revealingly, Vives claimed that Quintilian's emblematic definition of the orator as a 'good man skilled in speaking' (*vir bonus dicendi peritus*) referred, among other things, to the fact that he 'would not persuade if he was not believed to be good'.[146] This implied that we should not only be virtuous but that our reputation for virtuous character should be recognised by the audience, which linked *ethos* to social recognition.[147] Equally importantly, this was why the exposition of *ethos* in a speech or piece of writing had to be geared to meet the expectations of the audience. In this task, all information about the deliberator and one's relationship to him/her were of some relevance. 'Love' (*amor*), Vives sustained, could be exhibited 'more openly' (*apertius*) since everyone tended to think themselves worthy of love, but if the 'trust' (*fides*) resulting from love was questioned through 'envy' (*invidia*), we might have to strengthen it by reminding the deliberator of our ties with him/her. In the exhibition of the intellectual quality of prudence we should, instead, be extremely careful not to seem arrogant.[148]

Throughout the discourse, Vives wrote, we should speak in a manner that did not 'diminish the general opinion of honesty, friendship, and prudence, and that rather aspires to augment it'.[149] One of the factors we should take into account was our relationship to the person we were addressing, as well as his/her personal attributes. Vives claimed that we could speak 'more openly' (*apertius*) with a friend and 'humanely' (*humane*) with an inferior, and he presented different ways of choosing a tone of speech based on a categorisation of the person we were addressing according to his/her 'habits' (*mores*), 'natural talent' (*ingenium*) and other contextual factors. In deciding the correct tone, we should assess our authority in the eyes of the deliberator, which depended on issues such as age, education, and familiarity with him/her.[150]

Although many of the precepts could be employed in all contexts in which one was advising anyone superior to oneself, the discussion focused on princes and Vives recommended *De consultatione* especially to the counsellors of rulers.[151] Here the reader was explicitly encouraged to diverge from a direct and open approach. One was told to address the prince with 'modesty and reverence', not as someone who was 'ignorant' (*imperitus*), and when discussing 'issues of his kingdom', one should speak to him as if he was a man of 'great prudence and sane judgment'.[152] One should also be well aware that the rhetorical situation was distinctively different from the republican debates of antiquity that were central to classical rhetorical theory: 'in the senate of a city, where everyone is nearly equal to one another [...] there is more liberty than in front of a prince'.[153] In a similar spirit, in a later section, Vives argued more generally that one had to accommodate the tone to one's audience, arguing that one should understand what was appropriate and convenient to say in specific situations; for instance, speaking 'under tyranny' (*sub tyrannide*) was different than when one spoke 'in liberty' (*in libertate*).[154] The majesty of the prince drove one towards modesty, and if one dissimulated or kept silent on some matters, he would interpret it as respect for his presence.[155] If the prince 'did not understand' what we were trying to say, it was possible to 'remind him lightly', but we should avoid the perception that we were reproaching him.[156] The impossibility of open speech, *parrhesia*, was related to the importance of keeping the ties of *ethos* with the prince, love in particular, intact. As Vives explained, one should always respond to the love offered to oneself, and especially so with the powerful and with the prince, 'whose friendship can be of great profit, and whose hatred can cause harm'.[157] It was even better to call him 'very stupid' (*stultissimus*) than not to show love, which was judged to be dangerous.[158] One should opt for an open attack only against other counsellors, provided that they were 'parasites, flatterers, the ruin of princes' and posed a threat to 'public opinion' (*existimatio*), 'public expediency' (*publica utilitas*), and the 'defence of honesty' (*tutela honesti*).[159]

Many of the themes of *De consultatione* were, of course, familiar from the Erasmian discourse of counselling. The stress put on friendship (*amicitia*) is a case in point. Several Erasmian texts, most notably Erasmus's *Institutio principis*, described the relationship between the prince and his counsellors primarily as one of friendship which, in contrast to the corrupt practice of flattery, implied mutual love and truthful speech.[160] Erasmus's (1516) political compendium, built around his *Institutio principis Christiani*, went as far as to include Plutarch's *De discrimine adulatoris & amici* (*How to Tell a Flatterer from a Friend*) in its corpus. Plutarch's work showed how a ruler could recognise a flatterer by his outward appearance which, for Erasmus, served as a potential remedy against untrustworthy flatterers. But, although Vives discussed counselling in *De consultatione* as a form of friendship, the account of friendship occurred largely in a rhetorical framework in which it was described as an instrument or form of *ethos* that enabled one to persuade or cure the prince. In fact, in the absence of the possibility of oratorical *parrhesia*, the description of counsel as a form of friendship came close to suggesting that the rules of deliberative rhetoric should be incorporated into a form of familiar discussion or conversation (*sermo*). Referring to the distinction between public speaking and private counsel, Vives explicitly maintained that with 'a multitude' (*multitudo*) one could rely on ornaments and 'a more full oration' (*oratio plenior*), but with just 'one person' (*apud unum*) this would be 'ridiculous' (*ridiculus*).[161] This might be read as a particularly political manifestation of an Erasmian tendency to blur the boundaries between oration and conversation by incorporating oratorical advice into forms of *sermo* in letter writing and other linguistic practices. In a letter to Budé, Erasmus compared his own conversational style to Budé's grand eloquence. He reminded Budé that an effective style did not have to 'compel admiration' as Quintilian had thought, but it had to treat any subject persuasively and effectively. It was often important to avoid a grand rhetorical style. As he maintained, 'since much of the art lies in concealing art, because any suggestion of artifice makes the speaker less credible, I do not see how a style can be effective which parades itself and shows off'.[162]

Within this scheme, the central presupposition was that the prince was not the self-governed ruler envisioned in Erasmian educational plans but rather an instrument of power whose actions should be directed to the good by the counsellor in specific debates. The prince's world of ideas and expectations were not taken as expressions of a sovereign will that should be listened to, but they were analysed as a point of departure for rhetorical composition with the question of how he could be persuaded, brought to reason, and prevented from sinking into tyranny looming in the background. This reversed intellectual power relation that was inherent in the writing of *De consultatione* was described in Vives's later *De pacificatione* (1529) and *De anima* by an analogy already found in the Middle Ages that likened the prince to will (*voluntas*) and the counsellor to reason (*ratio*).[163] In *De consultatione*, Vives explicitly discussed deliberations as a way of directing the will of the one we were counselling towards what was truly good.[164]

Emotions and Passions

This inversed power hierarchy was built into Vives's discussion of emotions. One might argue that some parts of *De consultatione* could be interpreted through the typical metaphor of moral philosophy as medicine of the mind that, rather than using existing emotional dispositions for persuasion in concrete matters, strove to produce more long-standing reflection in the prince.

Vives put forward several arguments throughout *De consultatione* that were meant to counter the instantaneous and passionate nature of rhetoric. He claimed that counsel should ideally be valid not only when addressing a specific person but true 'in all similar deliberations' (*in omni* [...] *deliberatione consimili*), recommended that speeches should be written down since improvised speeches made 'prudent' (*cordatus*) and 'skilful' (*callidus*) men utter stupid words, and maintained that the empire of the Spartans was more long lasting than that of the Athenians, which was based on swift deliberations.[165]

Closely linked to his suspicion of a merely passionate response, Vives underlined that these well-pondered orations should not focus on evoking strong passions. Hesitantly, he stated that 'passions of the soul should not [...] be excited and thrown into disorder', admitting only that they could be 'pinched' by 'things themselves'.[166] He further declared that a counsellor should not 'light up those passions but calm and appease them. Persuasion is not worth so much that in order to achieve it, you would want to be a bad person'.[167] Here he referred to the dichotomy between good, ethical emotions and disturbing passions that Roman rhetorical writers, especially Quintilian, had developed on the basis of Aristotle's *ethos* and *pathos*. Vives's distrust of strong passions was, naturally, in stark contrast to much of the Roman theory that described elaborate ways of using them, with Quintilian lavishly praising the force of passions to dominate the judges in legal cases by making them abandon all enquiries 'into truth'.[168] In contrast to Quintilian, Vives did not want to throw the deliberator into a state where he was dominated by his/her instantaneous passions and affirmed that 'a dispassionate soul should not be used'.[169]

Despite this suspicious attitude, emotions and passions were central for provoking reflection and, consequently, for persuasion in *De consultatione*. The most fundamental technique of emotional persuasion concerned the redescription of the ends the person deliberating had set himself. As an example of a twisted understanding of the ends of political action, Vives portrayed a man who had set himself the goal of gaining power and who would do everything in order to reach that objective even if it implied the destruction of humankind.[170] If one wanted to redescribe the ends, one had to show that the goal set had to be understood through negative evaluative terms. According to Vives, one should argue in these and other cases that what the prince had set as his final aim was 'not magnanimity but cruelty, not glory but vanity, not honour but an empty shadow, not magnificence but madness, not justice but injustice, not liberality but profusion, not fortitude but foolhardiness, not a dispute but a brawl, not erudition but fraud'.[171] Here Vives activated the resources of the rhetorical theory of neighbouring concepts according to which one could always find an opposite concept that could be employed to describe the same action but with a different normative value. Since neighbouring positive and negative evaluative terms competed for the description of exactly the same set of actions, normative terms could be used flexibly to argue one's case.[172]

The redescription of the ends of a specific action was not, however, the only technique proposed. Drawing on a theory of passions that emphasised their interrelations and the possibility of countering one passion with another, Vives stated that 'strong passions should be countered with another passion considered of no less importance by the one deliberating', and offered some examples.[173] This effectively showed the proposed action in a novel light; one could, for instance, evoke the emotional disposition of the person advised in order to show that what he/she was seeking was threatening to some other passion of his/hers; a man 'inspired by ambition' could be persuaded to refrain from a given action by referring to a 'loss of personal property'.[174]

The first way of dealing with emotions could perhaps be linked to the curing of the mind. Just as the vice of falsehood in *Veritas fucata* was primarily an erroneous labelling of things, a rhetorical redescription could be understood as a truthful description; the prince should understand that what he was searching for was madness and not in line with virtue and reason. The second method, however, was clearly different. Appealing to the possible loss of one's private possessions when advising someone who was ambitious was not overcoming his/her ambition but rather countering it in the context of a specific course of action by appealing to a threat. This method implied that erroneous passionate impulses, rather than being cured, could be countered.

But what ultimately made it difficult to think of *De consultatione* as a simple exercise in the curing of the prince was that the precepts were set out to facilitate persuasion in the context of a specific debate on a course of action to be taken. Unlike epideictic rhetoric, which did not have a temporally set goal, deliberative rhetoric was by definition limited to a specific question and a moment in which that question had to be treated. Both ways of using emotions and passions in deliberations had been exemplified in Vives's *Declamationes Syllanae*. In arguing for Sulla's abdication and countering an argument about power as a source of glory, Fonteius claimed that remaining in power was not an act of glory but a burden and that true glory came from being considered worthy of office (redescription of ends: power is not glory but a burden, true glory comes from being worthy of office).[175] In countering Sulla's fear of post-abdication revenge with a fear of losing glory, Fonteius argued that the true fear should be that Sulla's reign might become an example of perpetual kingship which would not only be disastrous for a Republican culture but ultimately strip Sulla of glory (countering fear of revenge with a fear of being a bad example unworthy of glory).[176] This more instrumental view was also apparent in *De consultatione* when Vives wrote that 'another *ingenium*' could either be 'drawn or forced', and whereas drawing could use the categories of honesty, religion, and law, force had to be partly based on charm, so that 'an ambitious man can be seduced through honour'.[177]

The last idea presupposed a deliberator who was still seduced by honour and who thus failed to embody the qualities of a truly Erasmian prince.

These motivating principles had been rejected in many texts and with special vigour in Vives's *Vigilia*, primarily a *speculum principis*, which had turned the yearning for honour and mundane glory into one of its major themes. The *Vigilia* amplified at length a paragraph of Cicero's *Somnium* that discussed the insignificance of a merely human glory which, due to its temporal and spatial limits, was never universal or immortal. In Vives's *Vigilia*, Africanus reminded young Scipio that, in his ascent to higher matters, his yearning for glory, the most seductive of vices even for men of talent (*ingenium*), would be difficult to shake off.[178] Africanus elaborated at length on the imaginary nature of glory based on the erroneous judgment of the multitude, contrasting it with true glory that followed virtue like a shadow follows a body.[179] Despite the link between virtue and glory, one should cultivate an indifferent and disdainful attitude towards glory.[180] In the end, an eternal judgment which assessed everything according to its true measure would attribute true glory to the virtuous. In the actual world it was the judgment of the wise, few in number, that came closest to correct standards and should thus be preferred to the opinion of the multitude.[181]

In place of the idealised picture of the *Vigilia*, the point of departure of *De consultatione* was closer to Erasmus's advice to Vives's pupil, Cardinal Croy. In a discussion on virtue, Croy had defended a Stoic line according to which happiness resided only in virtue. In condemning the staunch Stoic position, Erasmus had reminded Croy that the Peripatetic tradition was more in tune with common life and experience since it did not completely overlook gifts of nature or worldly advantages such as fame, power, or riches. Although one should not actively search for worldly goods, they should not be dismissed since they possessed great potential for the enhancement of the virtue of others.[182] In deliberations, the counsellor harnessed his worldly attributes (influence, reputation, authority) to ensure that the worldly goods and gifts of nature possessed by a less-than-perfect prince (power, resources, wealth) were employed for good purposes.

As we will see in the next chapter, Vives, when he himself took the role of a counsellor in the 1520s, had interiorised much of what was stated in *De consultatione*. He not only employed some of the technical precepts of *De consultatione*, but he clearly also activated his worldly attributes, such as reputation, in order to direct the power of rulers to the enhancement of peace and concord.

Notes

1. Allen 2:12 (Ep. 304, Dorp to Erasmus. CWE 3:18).
2. Allen 2:127 (Ep. 347, Dorp to Erasmus. CWE 3:155).
3. Allen 2:127 (Ep. 347, Dorp to Erasmus. CWE 3:156).
4. Allen 2:274 (Ep. 435, Budé to Erasmus. CWE 3:331). See also Budé to Erasmus, Allen 403, 120–37.
5. Allen 2:364 (Ep. 480, Erasmus to Budé. CWE 4:105).

88 *Conversation and the rhetoric of counsel*

6. Allen 4:165 (Ep. 1061, Lee to Erasmus); Latomus, 1519, Ci^v: 'Non scribendum adversus hominem'.
7. Allen 4:164 (Ep. 1061, Lee to Erasmus. CWE 7:177).
8. Erasmus, LB IX:91D (*Apologia*. CWE 71:57–8).
9. For invective as an argumentative practice among humanists, see Laureys – Simons – Becker, 2013.
10. The nature of the humanist-scholastic debate has been extensively discussed. James Overfield has claimed that there never was a European-wide humanism-scholasticism debate and that the Reuchlin affair was primarily about anti-Semitism. Rummel, on the other hand, stated that in the early sixteenth century, the humanism-scholasticism debate was the primary intellectual debate of Europe. Nauert has adopted a middle position, although he seems to be somewhat closer to Rummel. See Overfield, 1984, 329-30; Rummel, 2002; Rummel, 2008; Nauert, 1998, 428; Ménager, 2008, 45–54.
11. Perreiah, 1982, 11–2. Perreiah claims that Valla and Vives engage with the system *in toto* but in the case of Vives that seems to be an overstatement. In no text that I know of does Vives make an explicit connection between different aspects of scholastic theory, that is *summae, suppositio, consequentia, probatio*, etc.
12. Vives, 1979, 92–3.
13. Vives, 1979, 88–9: '... ex Cimmeriis tenebris in lucem egressus sum, uidique quae essent illae disciplinae, quae homine dignae ac subinde humanae dicuntur'. See also 26–31, 86–94. The Cimmerians were a nomadic people who were described in Homer's *Odyssey* as living in a city 'where horrid night is spread over wretched mortals', Homer, 1919, 401 (11.13–9). Edward George has also argued that *In pseudodialecticos* is not an internal critique of dialectic but instead focuses primarily on social issues. See George, 1992, 131.
14. The information is taken from the Universal Short Title Catalogue (https://www.ustc.ac.uk/).
15. For the importance of Erasmus to his printers, see Vanautgaerden, 2014, 105–14; Pettegree, 2010, 65–90; Eisenstein, 1983; Crousaz, 2005. Erasmus was very aware of the commercial side of printing as well as of how it could affect the form of the book. See Allen 5:612 (Ep. 1531, Erasmus to Vives).
16. Allen 1:344–5 (Ep. 145, Erasmus to Anna van Borssele); Allen 1:432 (Ep. 201, Erasmus to Jan Obrecht). For a more detailed description of this process; see Grendler, 2006, II, 42–64. Erasmus's formal qualification as a doctor of theology was not considered very highly by his scholastic adversaries.
17. Jardine, 1993. The 1516 edition was entitled *Epistolae aliquot illustrium virorum ad Erasmum Roterodamum et huius ad illos* (Louvain: Thierry Martens, 1516). For a description of different editions; see Ferguson in CWE 1:xix–xxiii. For a complete list of all Erasmus's works; see Vanautgaerden, 2008, 501–27.
18. A reader of Erasmus's monumental *Farrago* (1519) would find a list of his most significant correspondents in the page following the title page. The list included most of the prominent humanists of England, France, the Low Countries, and Germany such as More, Budé, Luther, Melanchthon, and many others; Erasmus, 1519, 2. Erasmus most likely adopted the custom from Italian humanists. Giovanni Pico della Mirandola's letters (*Aurae epistolae*) were especially widely circulated among the European humanist community in the early sixteenth century.
19. The term was coined in *quattrocento* Italy, but Erasmus and some of his friends were the first ones to use it more or less systematically, see Waquet, 1989.
20. Aristotle, 1934, 460–5 (1156b); Cicero, 1971, 126, 130, 140–2 (5.18, 6.20–1, 9.29–31). For exclusive Christian friendship, see Lochman – López, 2011, 3–9. Erasmus makes the distinction between Christian *caritas* and particular *amicitia* in a

1531 colloquy entitled *Amicitia*; Erasmus, ASD I/3, 709 (*Colloquia*). Vives also presents a very traditional view of intimate, exclusive friendship (he employs both *amicus* and *familiaris*) in his *Introductio ad Sapientiam*, a didactic book on wisdom for schoolboys; see Vives, 1527a, 26^v-26^r. For a treatment of Erasmus's conception of friendship as consisting of *aequalitas, similitudo, benevolentia, officia*, and *admonitio*, see Charlier, 1977.

21. Cicero, 1939b, 350–3 (19.62–4); Cicero, 1913, 134–9 (1.37.132–1.38.136); Cicero, 2009, 62–3 (2.4.7–8).
22. Vives, 2013, 479.
23. Tournoy – Mund-Dopchie, 2015, 114–5 (Ep. 7, Budé to Vives): '… aequum est hominem amari ingenio, doctrina, urbanitate, lepore suavique sermocinationis usu praeditum …'.
24. Charlier, 1977, 60–4; Furey, 2006, 4–5, 23–4, 141–5.
25. Havu, 2019; Garanderie, 1967, 13–5; Charlier, 1977, 205–8.
26. Allen 4:163 (Ep. 1061, Lee to Erasmus).
27. Some aspects of this process are discussed in Jardine, 1993, 16–20.
28. Allen 3:492–3 (Ep. 917, Erasmus to Juan de la Parra. CWE 6:251–2).
29. Allen 4:189 (Ep. 1066, Erasmus to Budé. CWE 7:206).
30. Allen 4:209 (Ep. 1082, Erasmus to Count Hermann. CWE 7:229).
31. Allen 4:267 (Ep. 1106, More to Erasmus. CWE 7:291).
32. Allen 4:209 (Ep. 1082, Erasmus to Count Hermann CWE 7:229).
33. Allen 4:268 (Ep. 1106, More to Erasmus. CWE 7:291–4).
34. Allen 3:616 (Ep. 987, Budé to Erasmus. CWE 6:401).
35. Allen 4:36 (Ep.1004, Erasmus to Budé. The letter is in Greek, CWE 7:39).
36. Allen 4:272 (Ep. 1108, Vives to Erasmus. CWE 7:298).
37. Allen 4:272 (Ep. 1108, Vives to Erasmus. CWE 7:300).
38. Allen 4:273 (Ep. 1108, Vives to Erasmus. CWE 7:302).
39. Vives, 1522, aa3^r-aa6^r.
40. Vives, 1522, 41 (i.vii), 53 (i.xvii): 'Quo uiro Gallia acutiore ingenio, acriore iudicio, exactiore diligentia, maiore eruditione nullum unquam produxit: hac uero aetate nec Italia quidem'.
41. De Vocht, 1928, 32 (Ep. 13, Vives to Cranevelt).
42. Allen 5:11 (Ep. 1256, Vives to Erasmus. CWE 9:17). The combination of friendship and an asymmetrical relationship was already a possibility in the classical discourse; Aristotle, 1934, 477–9 (1158b–1159a).
43. IJsewijn, 1992–1995, 41:55 (Ep. 20, Vives to Cranevelt), 41:72–3 (Ep. 26, Vives to Cranevelt): 'mea non refert'.
44. Vives's introduction discusses Erasmus and his theology at length; see Vives, 1522, aa3^r-aa6^r. See also González González, 2008, 53–5; Noreña, 1970, 132–7.
45. He was interested in it at the time; see IJsewijn, 1992–1995, 41:24–7 (Ep. 7, Vives to Cranevelt), 41:55–8 (Ep. 20, Vives to Cranevelt), 41:73 (Ep. 26, Vives to Cranevelt).
46. Tournoy – Mund-Dopchie, 2015, 82–5 (Ep. 5, Budé to Vives).
47. For his dissatisfaction with teaching, see IJsewijn, 1992–1995, 42:50–1 (Ep. 55, Vives to Cranevelt), 43:25 (Ep. 61, Vives to Cranevelt); Allen 5:113 (Ep. 1306, Vives to Erasmus). For the importance of teaching among Erasmus's generation of humanists in the Low Countries, see Maas, 2011, 49–50.
48. *Clarorum Hispanensium epistolae ineditae*, 1901, 247–8 (Vergara to Vives); *Clarorum Hispanensium epistolae ineditae*, 1901, 260–1 (University of Alcalá to Vives). Vives was also at some point offered the post of the tutor of the Duke of Alba's children. On Vives's possible economic interest as a member of a family of merchants; Sinz, 1963, 80.
49. De Vocht, 1934, 1–12; De Vocht, 1928, 197–9 (Ep. 80, Vives to Cranevelt), 355 (Ep. 130, Fevyn to Cranevelt).

50. Vives, 1526e.
51. Vives was already widely known and read in the 1520s, although his prestige grew even greater in the 1530s; González González, 1987, 43; González González, 2007, 66–7, 103–11; Fantazzi, 2014, 156–7.
52. About the process of printing Augustine's *De civitate Dei* and how Froben and Erasmus were actively pushing Vives to finish the project; see Allen 4:551 (Ep. 1222, Vives to Erasmus); Allen 5:11–2 (Ep. 1256, Vives to Erasmus); Allen 5:38 (Ep. 1271, Vives to Erasmus); Allen 5:61 (Ep. 1281, Vives to Erasmus); Allen 5:98 (Ep. 1303, Vives to Erasmus); Allen 5:112–3 (Ep. 1306, Vives to Erasmus); Allen 5:281 (Ep. 1362, Vives to Erasmus); Allen 6:173 (Ep. 1613, Vives to Erasmus); De Vocht, 1928, 12–3 (Ep. 5, Vives to Cranevelt), 15–6 (Ep. 6, Vives to Cranevelt), 18 (Ep. 8, Vives to Cranevelt). For an analysis of the correspondence between Vives and Erasmus; see Fantazzi, 2014.
53. Allen 6:476 (Ep. 1792, Vives to Erasmus).
54. Allen 7:470 (Ep. 2040, Erasmus to Vives); Allen 7:512–3 (Ep. 2061, Vives to Erasmus). After Vives gently complained about this to Erasmus, he was eventually included in the second edition; see Erasmus, 1529, 175.
55. There are some cases when, despite heavy editing, Vives did not change the date of his dedicatory letters. These are definitely staged letters in the sense that they do not reproduce the original one. Probably the most glaring example is the *Declamationes* in the 1538 edition, the original dedication letter is substantially altered, yet the date remains 1520.
56. For Vives and the printing world, see Tournoy, 1994.
57. Tournoy – Mund-Dopchie, 2015, 84–5 (Ep. 5, Budé to Vives).
58. Ménager, 2008, 45–54. The importance of Lucian and Lucianic satire for Erasmus and several other humanists is well known; see Margolin, 1999, 224–5, 233; Fumaroli, 1980, 94; Geri, 2011. Erasmus also translated Lucian. For Thomas More and Lucian, see Baker-Smith, 2009, 168–9.
59. Bietenholz, 1975. For Erasmus's analysis of these problems; see his own *Lingua*.
60. In his immediate reception, he was known as a man of judgment; Moreno Gallego, 2006, 67–79. It should be noted that there are some satirical elements in some of his 1520s dialogues, such as *De Europae dissidiis et bello Turcico*; yet satire is not a dominant genre in his 1520s work.
61. Vives, 1527b, 43ᵛ (55); González González, 1998, 81.
62. Allen 6:374 (Ep. 1732, Vives to Erasmus. CWE 12:268). See also Allen 5:10 (Ep. 1256, Vives to Erasmus); Allen 5:281 (Ep. 1362, Vives to Erasmus).
63. Marlow – Drewery, 1969, 2; Luther, 1908, 600–1; Allen 4:329 (Ep. 1135, von Hutten to Erasmus); von Hutten's *Expostulatio* elaborates on the matter. See, for example, von Hutten, 1523, b[i]ʳ.
64. Mayans 5:247 (*De concordia*): 'invectivae, criminationes, recriminationes, epigrammata, apologiae, antapologiae, epistolae, dialogi; advocatur tota facultas dicendi, intenduntur oratoriae artis nervi …'.
65. Vives, 2013, 475–80, 484–90. He had already made some of these points in his private correspondence; Allen 6:374–5 (Ep. 1732, Vives to Erasmus), 9–39.
66. As a classical genre, *diatribe* referred to a popular version of a philosophical dialogue and was hence closely linked to the tradition of *sermo*; Remer, 1996, 92–3.
67. O'Rourke Boyle, 1983, 6–9. Erasmus praised this attitude towards discussion over the definitions of the scholastics in his apology against Latomus; Erasmus, LB IX:100D-101C (*Apologia*).
68. Vives, 1526a, IXᵛ: 'de iis solis & inquiratur & statuatur rebus, quae ad summam pietatis spectant, ad sanctos mores'.
69. Chomarat, 1981, 1:16–24.

Conversation and the rhetoric of counsel 91

70. Hoffmann, 1994, 4–5.
71. Erasmus, LB V:137E (*Paraclesis*): 'At ego sane si quid huiusmodi uotis proficitur, tantisper dum mortales omneis, ad sanctissimum ac saluberrimum Christianae philosophiae studium adhortor, ac ueluti classicum canens euoco, uehementer optarim eloquentiam mihi dari, longe aliam quam fuerit Ciceroni. Si minus picturatam quam fuit illius, certe multo magis efficacem'.
72. Erasmus, LB IX:89E-90B (*Apologia*. CWE 71:55).
73. Erasmus, LB IX:93F-94B: 'Deinde distinguit Theologiam qua sapimus deum, & qua docemus deum, ex una duas faciens'. He is criticising Latomus here for making a distinction between theological reasoning and teaching.
74. Bietenholz, 2009, 141–2.
75. Cicero, 1939b, 356–61 (21.69–22.74). The central content of *decorum* is mentioned, for instance, in ASD I/2: 222–3 (*De conscribendis epistolis*).
76. For *decorum* as a hermeneutic principle, see Eden, 1997.
77. Bietenholz, 2009, 142–7; Zagorin, 1990, 34–5.
78. Allen 4:374 (Ep. 1156, Erasmus to Peutinger); Allen 4:404 (Ep. 1167, Erasmus to Lorenzo Campeggi).
79. Allen 4:487 (Ep. 1202, Erasmus to Justus Jonas. CWE 8:203).
80. Allen 4:488 (Ep. 1202, Erasmus to Justus Jonas. CWE 8:203). Erasmus is here turning around Augustine's words in *Contra Faustum Manichaeum*, according to which Jesus did not adjust his words to the audience; Augustine, 1886, 338–9 (XVI.32).
81. Allen 4:488 (Ep. 1202, Erasmus to Justus Jonas. CWE 8:204).
82. Allen 4:402 (Ep. 1167, Erasmus to Lorenzo Campeggi. CWE 8:110).
83. Erasmus, ASD II/1-9, 5:160–4 (*Adagia*); Erasmus ASD IV/3, 67–70 (*Moriae encomium*); Snyder, 2009, 52.
84. See also Hoffman, 1990, 109–10.
85. Allen 3:359 (Ep. 856, Erasmus to Pirckheimer); Allen 3:439 (Ep. 899, Erasmus to Maarten Lips); Allen 3:552 (Ep. 950, Erasmus to Jan Slechta). At times Erasmus raises his conscience above the judgment of his supporters, but even then, he reminds them that the judgment of the good agrees with his conscience; Allen 3:534 (Ep. 942, Erasmus to Draco).
86. Allen 2:12–4 (Ep. 304, Dorp to Erasmus). Vives also referred to the judgment of Erasmus's conscience that, while misunderstood by the opponents, would be rightly understood by posterity; Allen 5:39–40 (Ep. 1271, Vives to Erasmus).
87. Vives, 1991d, 114–7: '... modo suaui sed efficaci'.
88. Mayans 7:100 (Vives to Crommas): '... ut juvenes quosdam, vanae et spurcae poësi deditos, ad sanctiores musas disciplinasque pleniores et fructus et pudicitiae revocarem ...'.
89. Mayans 1:164 (Vives to Croy): 'non uni sensui Spiritus sancti verba esse alligata: sacras litteras idcirco agrum appellari semper vernantissimum, feracissimum, uberrimum, quod sensus in eis sint plures, admirabiles, et veri tamen omnes, idque in eodem spiritu qui illas dictavit'. Vives is referring here to his own rhetorical exercises that drew on the *Penitential Psalms*. This genre was completely different from Erasmus's attempt, in his paraphrases, to reconstruct the literal sense of the Bible. It is not quite clear whether Vives's point here is to underscore the literal ambiguity of the Bible that produces different interpretations or to stress the rhetorical accommodation of an originally unambiguous message. For the background of these problems, see Ossa-Richardson, 2019, 163–5.
90. Vergara was Vives's closest Spanish friend at the court of Charles V in the early 1520s. He had served as secretary to Cardinal Jiménez, one of the most influential people in Spain, in 1516–1517, and he was sent to the Low Countries in 1520 to inform Cardinal Croy about the state of affairs in Toledo, thus meet-

92 Conversation and the rhetoric of counsel

ing Vives's protector. In January 1521, he became Charles V's court chaplain and during the 1520s, after some initial problems with Erasmus on the Zùñiga affair, he became the most important advocate of Erasmus's cause in Spain. See Bietenholz, 1985–7, 3:384–7; Bataillon, 1991a, 127–34, 167–8, 256–7.

91. Mayans 2:518 (*Veritas fucata*): 'ego tibi simpliciter et ex usu vulgari hominum loquor'.
92. Mayans 2:519–20 (*Veritas fucata*): '... omnes aliena induebant nomina rejectis propriis, ita mendacium vocabatur negligentia, perjurium asseveratio veritatis, astutia prudentia ...'.
93. Mayans 2:520 (*Veritas fucata*): 'Cuncta erant in porticu *Veritatis* contraria, nam illic nuda erant omnia, aperta, simplicia, certa, solida, et, quo maxime veritati similia, vera ...'.
94. Mayans 2:522–7 (*Veritas fucata*).
95. Mayans 2:525 (*Veritas fucata*): '*Veritas* se libentius nudam acturam respondit'; 'Homerus se non dubitare ita esse quae *Veritas* diceret, ait, ceterum nosse se mores, et ingenia sui populi'.
96. Mayans 2:528–9 (*Veritas fucata*): '... quaecunque vel ad mores spectabant, vel ad aliquem vitae usum, libera relinquntur scriptoribus ...'.
97. Macrobius, 1994, 1–8 (1.1–1.2). See Kempshall, 2011, 445–8.
98. Erasmus, ASD IV/3, 68 (*Moriae encomium*).
99. Erasmus to Dorp, 337, 111–3: 'Et iucundius illabitur et acrius insidit in animos evangelica veritas huismodi lenociniis commendata, quam si nuda producetur ...'.
100. Allen 5:339 (Ep. 1390, Erasmus to Johann von Vlatten. CWE 10:97); More, 1965, 48–50. 86, 98, 102.
101. Vives, 1521, 51: 'Multo tamen quam ille aliam meae ciuitati clausulam addici, alia etiam hominum respectans ingenia'. Vives wanted to lecture on *Somnium Scipionis* at Louvain; IJsewijn, 1992–1995, 41:13 (Ep. 2, Vives to Cranevelt), 41:25–6 (Ep. 7, Vives to Cranevelt), 41:29 (Ep. 8, Vives to Cranevelt).
102. Allen 2:254 (Ep. 421, Erasmus to Budé).
103. For Seneca; see Stacey, 2007, 30–57.
104. Erasmus, ASD IV/1, 135 (*Institutio principis Christiani*. CWE 27:204).
105. Allen 2:93 (Ep. 337, Erasmus to Dorp).
106. Allen 1:397 (Ep. 179, Erasmus to Nicholas Ruistre. CWE 2:79).
107. Allen 1:399 (Ep. 180, Erasmus to Jean Desmarais. CWE 2:81).
108. Allen 1:397 (Ep. 179, Erasmus to Nicholas Ruistre); Allen 5:314–22 (Ep. 1381, Erasmus to Henry VIII).
109. Stahl, 1990, 12–3; Macrobius, 1994, 1–8 (1.1–1.2).
110. Vives, 1521, 5: '... quo libello perfectus & absolutus in republica princeps instituitur, atque formatur. Nullumque est in tota philosophia praestabilius opus, atque diuinius'.
111. Vives, 1521, 99–100: 'Iusticia nodus humana societatis'. See also 92–4, 143–4, 149–50, 153–4; Cicero, 1913, 21 (1.7.20). The idea that the contemplation of the universe could show the insignificance of merely human affairs was typical of classical philosophies; Hadot, 2002, 53–4.
112. Tracy, 1978, 88–107. On how Erasmus linked taxation and warfare in his belief that a group of mercenaries was a plot of the central government to get funding for war, see Allen 2:494–5 (Ep. 543, Erasmus to More).
113. Erasmus, ASD IV/2, 66 (*Querela pacis*. CWE 27:297).
114. Erasmus, ASD I/2, 488 (*De conscribendis epistolis*. CWE 25:189).
115. Vives, 2013, 457–8. See also Vives, 1527c, 56ʳ.
116. What More might have intended to say in work has been debated for centuries. See Skinner, 1987; Bradshaw, 1981; Hexter, 1952; Surtz – Hexter, 1965; Fenlon, 1975, Curtis, 2006.

117. More, 1965, 54 (All translations from *Utopia* are from More, 2002; More, 2002, 13).
118. More, 1965, 86–96.
119. More, 1965, 96 (More, 2002, 34).
120. More, 1965, 98 (More, 2002, 34–5). The adaptation to the drama at hand and the use of a theatrical metaphor can be found in Cicero's *De officiis*, Cicero, 1913, 116 (1.36.114–5). For a discussion of *Utopia* in the tradition of deliberative rhetoric, see Logan, 1994.
121. More, 1965, 98–102.
122. De Vocht, 1928, 197 (Ep. 80, Vives to Cranevelt): 'nihil concipi potest quod mihi arrideat magis, quam Principes'.
123. Vives, 1522, 171 (v.xxiiii): 'Hic in mundo reges omnes timent habere consortem'.
124. For Louis of Flanders, Lord of Praet, see Bietenholz, 1985–7, 2:41–2.
125. For the Middle Ages, see Kempshall, 2011, 29–32.
126. Vives never made an effort to merge its precepts together with his 1530s literature on rhetorical theory. Differently from his 1530s writings, *De consultatione* focuses almost exclusively on rhetorical *inventio*, not on *elocutio*. For opinions on the problem, see George, 1992; 142–3; van der Poel, 1991; Rodríguez Peregrina, 1996, 350–1.
127. Mack has described the ethical tone of the treatise as awkward since Vives, while emphasizing the spontaneous persuasiveness of ethical life, gives detailed information on how to construct an appearance of it in speech or in writing; Mack, 2008, 253. Noreña does not analyse *De consultatione* in depth even though he calls it 'an important political treatise on diplomacy and negotiations'; see Noreña, 1970, 86. George also comments on the movement between descriptive and normative points; see George, 1992, 142. Rodríguez Peregrina does not rate the work very highly and considers it a transitory work; see Rodríguez Peregrina, 2000, LVIII-LX. This view is echoed in David Walker; Walker, 2017, 15. Adams interprets it as setting forward Vives's 'ideas on conciliation between princes'; see Adams, 1962, 235. For a more positive assessment, see van der Poel, 1991.
128. Vives, 1536, 241, 243. See also 258–9 on using Christian examples. The Christian dimension is emphasised in van der Poel, 1991, 808–10.
129. Vives, 1536, 233: '... inventio tota [...] certa quadam & nova ratione proponendi ...'.
130. Vives, 1536, 238; Aristotle, 1926, 23, 39 (1357a, 1359a). In *Ad Herennium* the fact that deliberative rhetoric is about choosing the right course of action is mentioned, *Ad Herennium*, 156–7 (3.2.2); Quintilian, 2001, 2:126–7 (3.8.22–3).
131. Vives, 1536, 239: 'Ergo de omnibus quaecunque sunt in nostra potestate consultamus'. Aristotle famously declared that the most important topics of deliberations were ways and means, war and peace, defence of the country, imports and exports and legislation, Aristotle, 1926, 41 (1359b). In the *Ad Herennium* and *De inventione* it is taken for granted that the range of deliberative rhetoric is the treatment of these issues in the Senate. See, for instance, *Ad Herennium*, 158–61 (3.2.2).
132. See, for instance, *Ad Herennium*, 156–73 (3.2.2–3.5.9); Cicero, 1960a, 322–43 (2.51.155–2.58.175).
133. Vives, 1536, 234: 'Ante omnia considerandum qui sit, cui consulimus: tum qui nos: deinde qui alii consultores'.
134. Cicero, 1960a, 68–83 (1.24.34–1.28.43); Erasmus, ASD I/2 (*De conscribendis epistolis*), 385–6. Erasmus most likely took his list from George of Trebizond; Mack, 2011, 94.
135. Cicero, 1960a, 68–71 (1.24.34).

94 *Conversation and the rhetoric of counsel*

136. *Ad Herennium*, 178–83 (3.7.13–4). These three topics were fairly standard in renaissance manuals on demonstrative rhetoric; see, e.g., Celtis, 1532, [A6]r.
137. Vives, 1536, 234–6. Some of these topics could be employed in the analysis of a question. Vives builds an analogy between man and a political community (*republica, civitas*) through which one can find material on the internal and external qualities and possessions of a *civitas*. See Vives, 1536, 237–8.
138. Quintilian, 2001 2:102–17, 3:184–217 (3.7, 7.2); *Ad Herennium*, 72–5, 172–85, 386–95 (2.6.9, 3.6.10–3.8.15, 4.50.63–4.51.65); Cicero, 1960a, 44–7 (1.16.22).
139. Quintilian, 2001, 2:134–5 (3.8.38): '… sed mores praecipue discrimen dabunt'.
140. Reisch, 1503, [Dvii]r-[Dviii]v.
141. Vives, 1536, 256: 'nam quum sis nobilissimus, aequum est te non dedecori esse tuis maioribus: aut quum sis ignobilis, debes incipere nobilitatem a te ipso'.
142. Vives, 1536, 244: 'Duo sunt in consiliis potentissima ad persuadendum, opinio probitatis, & opinio prudentiae'. Vives, at times, seems to place *amicitia* under the heading of *probitas*. However, he also enumerates all three side by side; see Vives, 1536, 247. In Aristotle, a correct display of one's virtue was based on: prudence (*phronesis/prudentia*), an intellectual quality that guaranteed one could form correct opinions; virtue (*arete/virtus*), a moral quality referring to the moral purpose of the orator; and goodwill (*eunoia/benevolentia*), which emphasised the specific relationship between the speaker and the audience; see Aristotle, 1926, 17 (1356a), 171 (1378a).
143. Augustine, 1962, 163–7 (4.27.59–4.31.64); Cicero, 1942, 1:150–2, 1:308–10, 1:450 (1.49.214-5, 2.37.154-56, 2.81.333).
144. Vives, 1991d, 114–7.
145. Vives, 1536, 244: 'Existimatio probitatis duabus potissimum rebus uel paratur, uel confirmatur. Parabitur primum si honeste & sancte vivas, ac consulas […] Nec est quod perinde auertat homines a persuasione, quam si uitam dictis uideant dissentire'. Plutarch's *De discrimine adulatoris & amici*, suggested by Erasmus to rulers, underlines the inconsistency of one's life and *persona* as a central sign of flattery; Plutarch, 1516, Q[1]r-Q2r.
146. Vives, 1536, 244–5: 'Caput est apud Quintilianum […] non posse oratorem nisi uirum bonum esse […] quod non persuadebit, nisi credatur talis'.
147. For the link between authority and the Republic of Letters; see Havu, 2019.
148. Vives, 1536, 245–6.
149. Vives, 1536, 247: 'Ergo tota oratione danda opera est, ne quid dicas, quod opinionem uel probitatis, uel amicitiae, uel prudentiae imminuat: augeat potius quantum licebit'.
150. Vives, 1536, 248–50.
151. Vives, 1536, 233: '… quod tibi & tui similibus, qui frequenter de rebus magnis cum Princibus consultatis, nihil est perinde necessarium, ut consilii expediendi modus & facultas'.
152. Vives, 1536, 248: 'Quippe ad principem ita loquendum, tanquam praeditus eo sit, quod est maxime principis, magna prudentia, et iudicio rebus sano'.
153. Vives, 1536, 250: 'In senatu civitatis, ubi omnes fere sunt pares […] maior liber[t]as, quam apud principem'.
154. Vives, 1536, 270.
155. Vives, 1536, 250.
156. Vives, 1536, 250–1: '… si non intelligat, potest […] summoneri leuiter …'.
157. Vives, 1536, 251: 'cuius amicitia tantopere prodesse potest, & obesse odium'.
158. Vives, 1536, 251.
159. Vives, 1536, 253: 'parasiti, assentatores, pernicies principum'.
160. Erasmus, ASD IV/I, 175–82 (*Institutio principis Christiani*).
161. Vives, 1536, 269–70.

162. Allen 2:464–5 (Ep. 531, Erasmus to Budé. CWE 4:230). On relating his courteous style to persuasive effect; see Allen 4:100 (Ep. 1033, Erasmus to Albert of Brandenburg).
163. Vives, 1959, 99–100; Mayans 5:420 (*De pacificatone*).
164. Vives, 1536, 239, 240: 'Tractantur haec perpensa uoluntate & facultate, nam qui & potest, & uult, faciet, utique non facturus si alterum desit'; '... quoniam omnia ad voluntatem deliberantis referuntur'; '... quae ad iudicia nostra referuntur magis, quam ad ueritatem rerum'.
165. Vives, 1536, 247, 261, 264–5: 'Athenienses quod ea celeritate uterentur, non diu imperium tenuisse [...] diutius & maius cunctatores Lacedaemonios habuisse imperium'. The dichotomy between Sparta and Athens can also be found in *De disciplinis*; Vives, 2013, 173.
166. Vives, 1536, 259: 'Affectus non sunt [...] concitandi & perturbandi [...] Vellicantur [...] ex rebus ipsis'.
167. Vives, 1536, 259: 'Verum sancti consultoris erit, non accendere hos affectus, sed sedare ac placare, nec est tanti persuasio, ut uir malus esse ob eam uelis'. In another passage, Vives, 1536, 251 (erroneously numbered as 252): 'Nemo est qui non malit sibi caetera omnia, quam iudicium aut prudentiam detrahi ...'.
168. Quintilian, 2001, 3:46–9 (6.2.6–7).
169. Vives, 1536, 260: '... sic nec animo utendum commoto ...'.
170. Vives, 1536, 259: 'qui ad potentiam, uel per stragem cuncti generis humani conitetur peruadere'.
171. Vives, 1536, 260: '... non esse eam magnanimitatem, sed crudelitatem: non gloriam, sed vanitatem: non honorem, sed inanem umbram: non magnificentiam, sed uecordiam: non iustitiam, sed iniuriam: non liberalitatem, sed profusionem: temeritatem, non fortitudinem: rixas, non disputationem: captiones, non eruditionem ...'.
172. This aspect of rhetoric is described well in Skinner, 1996, 138–52; Skinner, 2007.
173. Vives, 1536, 260: 'Opponendum percussae affectioni, aliam affectionem apud ipsum non minorem ...'.
174. Vives, 1536, 260: '... incitato ambitione, iacturam rei familiaris'.
175. Vives, 1989b, 68–73.
176. Vives, 1989b, 62–3.
177. Vives, 1536, 264: 'Alienum ingenium corpusque; uel allicitur, vel cogitur. Allicimus aut recta ratione ostensa, ut honesto, pio, legibus: aut affectu eius capto. Id sit partim rationis uiribus, partim dolo, qui illectamento aliquo tegitur: ut auarus pecunia capitur uelut esca, uoluptate delitiosus, honore ambitiosus ...'. In a letter to Cranevelt, he writes that he would rather live with lions than with drunkards since lions can be controlled by using their instincts. Thus, bestiality, while not cured, could be controlled; De Vocht, 1928, 82 (Ep. 30, Vives to Cranevelt).
178. Vives, 1521, 126: '... non facile possis excutere & repudiare, ambitionem illam & gloriae cupiditatem'.
179. Vives, 1521, 126–7: 'Neque enim gloria de vitiis unquam nascitur, neque gloria est quod imperita multitudo stulta & levis plebes iudicat, vel non iudicat potius'; 'Vera namque gloria virtutem semper tanquam umbra corpus consequitur, sermonibusque et voce constat, eorum qui optime de summis virtutibus iudicant'.
180. Vives, 1521, 127: 'Sed profecto illud est plane perfecti & consumati viri etiam ipsam gloriam cum caeteris humanis despicere, aut certe negligere'.
181. Vives, 1521, 134, 138–9: 'Gloria inter optimos viros optima'; 'Gloria qualis in caelo'.

182. Allen 3:562 (Ep. 957, Erasmus to Croy); Allen 3:569–72 (Ep. 959, Erasmus to Croy). Erasmus argued in his *Institutio principis Christiani* that certain imperfections of a prince such as ambition should not be suppressed since they could be turned to good use; see Erasmus, ASD IV/I, 140 (*Institutio principis Christiani*). He made a similar point in his *De conscribendis epistolis* in discussing how an ambitious man could be motivated by evoking honour; see Erasmus, ASD I/2 (*De conscribendis epistolis*), 325–6.

3 Managing Discord
Vives on Politics (1523–1529)

Vives's Political Texts

In the years 1519–1529, Vives's published literature witnessed a remarkable interest in a wide range of political and social questions. The varying stylistic and thematic choices of the works reflected the different contexts in which they were composed. The first set of texts from 1519–1522 were predominantly fictional writings destined for the academic milieu of Louvain of which *Praefatio in Leges Ciceronis* (an altered version of a text that had appeared in 1514 under the name *Praelectio in Leges Ciceronis*), *Aedes legum*, and *Pompeius fugiens* were printed in the edition of his *Opuscula varia* that came out in 1519. In 1520, *Argumentum Somnium Scipionis Ciceroniani* appeared both on its own (Thierry Martens, Louvain), and together with Vives's *Somnium et Vigilia* (J. Thibault Gorneens, Antwerp), and in 1521 Froben published an edition of *Argumentum Somnium Scipionis*, which comprised Vives's *Somnium et Vigilia* together with Cicero's original treatment of Scipio's dream in Book Six of Cicero's *De re publica* (*The Republic*). The set of school texts incorporating Roman political thought into a pedagogical context was completed with *Declamationes Syllanae quinque*. In 1522, Vives's commented edition of Augustine's *De civitate Dei*, commissioned by Erasmus, appeared from Froben's printing house in Basel. Despite its theological, philological, and encyclopaedic aims, the comments presented a number of extensive reflections on themes such freedom of the will that, while not overtly political, were to condition the discussion on ecclesiastical and political life throughout the 1520s.

Vives's academic endeavours were followed by a set of political, often deliberative texts on current issues such as a Church council and dynastic warfare. The composition of these coincided with his political activity at the Tudor and Habsburg courts at a moment of great political and religious tumult. His political compendium of 1526 entitled *De Europae dissidiis & Republica* (De Croock, Bruges 1526) comprised deliberative letters to powerful men (Pope Adrian of Utrecht, Henry VIII, Bishop John Longland, d.1547), translations of Isocrates's speeches, and a fictional dialogue on warfare and recent political history (*De Europae dissidiis et bello turcico*).

DOI: 10.4324/9781003240457-4

98 *Managing discord*

All these texts combined a demand to end the political and religious strife within Europe with a call for a unified war or defence against the Ottoman Empire. Vives's output of political and social literature reached its apex with the publication of the famous *De subventione pauperum* in 1526 (De Croock, Bruges) on relief for the poor, and, finally, with a grandiose compendium entitled *De concordia & discordia in humano genere* (1529). Although the overall message of the 1529 compendium was in consonance with Vives's earlier writings, it was arguably the only treatise in which he offered an in-depth look into the political problems bedevilling the Europe of his time.

In this chapter, the purpose is to clarify Vives's political thought and activity in these years by looking at three issues. First, through an analysis of the concept of *epikeia* (reasonableness), I offer an account of Vives's distinctively ethical understanding of politics, which is crucial for understanding his political thought. Secondly, I show how Vives, as a member of a broader humanist network, activated his interpretation of *epikeia* and other political commonplaces in order to criticise the rulers of his time for futile and destructive warfare especially in his 1526 compendium. Third, I discuss *De concordia* as a specific interpretation of ethical politics in which the moral self-government of individuals was largely analysed as being dependent on several external circumstances such as the cultural and material environment in which one's character was formed.

All three are of decisive importance for understanding how Vives conceptualised the relationship between rhetoric and politics. The interaction between his ethical conception of politics and rhetoric shows that, while Vives arguably had a deep-rooted conviction about the ethical nature of politics, he could employ the resources of the *ars rhetorica* in flexible ways in communicating his overall message about peace and concord to diverse audiences. The interaction between ethical self-government and external factors, for its part, provides a basis for Vives's views on rhetoric as they are outlined in Chapters 4 and 5, where I argue that he grounded much of classical rhetoric into non-confrontational genres. When Vives's redefinition of rhetoric is read in the context of *De concordia*, it becomes clear that non-confrontational rhetoric, which did not divide people, contributed to the ethical self-government of individual people since it suppressed open discord which, in Vives's view, tended to bread further discord not only in language but in all human interaction.

Law, *Epikeia*, and Self-control

While Vives was not a legal scholar by training, he had discussed jurisprudence and especially the relationship between law and politics in his 1519 *Opuscula*. In *Opuscula*, and throughout his career, he often underscored the centrality of the Aristotelian concept of *epikeia*. In his 1519 *Aedes legum*, a fictional dialogue, Vives presented a lengthy description and eulogy of *epikeia*, much of which drew on Budé's 1508 *Annotationes in Pandectarum libros* in which the French humanist praised the concept and emphasised its equivalence with the Latin term *aequitas* (equity).[1] Both Budé and Vives built a dichotomy between rigorous or written law (*ius*) and *epikeia*, and Vives defined *epikeia* as 'the interpretation (*interpretatio*) and correction (*emendatio*) of law' in particular cases.[2] Aristotle, in the *Nicomachean Ethics*, had described *epikeia* precisely as 'a rectification of legal justice' which was necessary since there were cases that could not be covered 'in a general statement'. *Epikeia* was thus needed in order to correct law 'where law is defective because of its generality'.[3] Both Vives and Budé drew on Aristotle's claims that general laws could never cover the infinite number of individual cases satisfyingly and that the inability of universal statements to cater to all particular cases was not accidental but part of the basic problem of law. They both referred to Aristotle's description of the Lesbian rule according to which indefinite things could not be fit into definite standards, and Vives notably evoked the Aristotelian idea that one could envision the possible solution to any case by imagining the answer the lawgiver would give to the question if he/she was present.[4]

Budé's claim, echoed by Vives, that *epikeia* was a synonym of the Latin *aequitas*, was becoming a commonplace in the early sixteenth century, not least because of Budé's *Annotationes*. The likening of *epikeia* to *aequitas*, and especially to the Ulpian definition of jurisprudence as the science of the equitable and the good (*aequum et bonum*), had the consequence that it further increased the already great semantic polyvalence of the original Aristotelian concept.[5] While Aristotle's treatment of *epikeia* had accentuated the myriad and undefinable nature of legal cases embracing the difference of individual circumstances that could not be covered with universal statements, in Cicero's writings and Roman law, *aequitas* had been used primarily as a technical term denoting justice, which underlined the similar treatment of similar cases. Rather than focusing on the differences between cases, the Ciceronian interpretation served as a way of suppressing particularity.[6] Still, in a rather different key, Cicero had also defined *aequitas* in opposition to the strictness of law, giving birth to the famous commonplace, often quoted by medieval and early modern writers including Vives, according to which a merely technical application of law represented the greatest injustice (*summum ius, summa iniuria*).[7] During the Middle Ages, the Ciceronian definition was frequently associated with Christian virtues such as charity (*caritas*) or mercy that moderated the strictness of law. At the same time, in the Christian tradition, *epikeia* or *aequitas* was increasingly discussed in the context of natural law. This meant that the correction or completion of positive law happened through a connection with the eternal law instituted by God.[8] Thus, what had been primarily a problem within legal interpretation and civic prudence in antiquity was linked to participation in divine providence through Christian natural law.

In Vives's *Aedes legum*, and in his other texts on jurisprudence, *epikeia* or *aequitas* was not a technical term of jurisprudence but rather implied the broadest possible understanding of the nature of law and legal justice. In *Aedes legum*, *epikeia* did not overrule law but rather brought it to its perfection since, according to Vives, only an interpretation of law in individual cases undertaken in the spirit of *epikeia* could guarantee the just nature of legal judgment. What was presupposed throughout *Aedes legum* was that the laws which *epikeia* interpreted or brought to completion were good in themselves, an element that was built into the claim that *epikeia* could refer to those intentions or judgments of the lawgiver that were thought to be reasonable. As Vives claimed, *epikeia* was a way to follow the 'norm of nature', according to which all laws were formed in the first place.[9] That *epikeia* was intrinsically linked to natural law was further reinforced, albeit in a slightly different sense, in Vives's later texts, where the Latin equivalent *aequitas* was frequently discussed as a synonym of justice or natural law. In his commentaries on Augustine's *De civitate Dei*, Vives likened equity to natural and divine law, and in his monumental *De disciplinis*, he devised a history of law where *aequitas*, rather than being a virtue that complemented existing law, was synonymous with justice and served as the natural fount of all positive law, the source from which it was derived.[10] In *De disciplinis* he wrote that *aequitas* 'is a certain universal quality; law a derivation and subdivision'.[11] Thus, *aequitas*, as a form of universal justice, could serve both as a correction or completion of existing laws and as their source.

For Vives, the treatment of *epikeia/aequitas* was closely connected to fundamental questions of political philosophy. While some humanists, most notably Thomas More in his *Utopia*, were suspicious of the possibilities of using *epikeia* to twist laws to the ruler's advantage, Vives's positive interpretation of its political and legal potential was by no means exceptional in the humanist circles around him.[12] Indeed, in a literature that took as its starting point the princely nature of rule across transalpine Europe, the mirror-of-princes genre frequently described rulers, in a somewhat Stoic or Senecan vein, both as lawgivers and judges, whose central virtue was justice.[13] Both Erasmus's *Institutio Principis Christiani* and Budé's *L'institution du Prince* (1519) partook in a genre and a discourse that did not primarily come up with a legal definition of the office of the prince but instead offered a description of the internal and external dimension of ethical self-government that enabled good rule according to right reason. In this tradition, the performance of justice or *aequitas/epikeia* was considered inseparable from the cultivation of the ethical *persona* of the ruler.[14]

Budé's *L'institution*, which frequently likened princes to judges and described them as guardians of justice and equity, offered Francis I (1494–1547) and other potential readers the story of the Persian king Artaxerxes as an example of just and equitable behaviour. In evoking a Christian interpretation of equity as clemency, Budé described how Artaxerxes had opted for clemency in tempering an old and severe law that had ordered capital punishment for those who had failed in public offices such as governors or generals.[15] Erasmus, who did not discuss the Aristotelian concept of *epikeia* in any of his works, referred sporadically to its Latin counterpart *aequitas* in *Institutio principis Christiani*. For Erasmus too *aequitas* served as an ethical concept, a counterpart of justice that, through the ethical self-government of the ruler, guaranteed the spirit of the laws. He claimed that the method of 'making a city or kingdom prosperous is to have the best of laws under the best of princes', that the king should obey laws 'provided that these conform to the ideals of justice (*aequitas*) and honour', and that the prince is 'a sort of embodiment of the law'.[16]

Vives agreed that the practice of justice, *epikeia*, and *aequitas* was not a question of merely juridical prudence but of civic virtue that was inseparable from one's ethical self-government. In *Aedes legum*, Vives called *aequum et bonum* the 'way, norm, reason, law, mind, sense, spirit, soul, and life' of laws, and claimed that only men of great *ingenium* were able to interpret law through equity.[17] He further insisted that a happy political community (*civitas*) was secured by a 'good man' rather than by a 'good law', implying the ethical nature of the guarantor of laws as a key to their correct interpretation.[18] The ethical and spirited description of the law and its guardians could function in a close analogy to Erasmian theology. If in Erasmus's ethical theology one's inner transformation in Christ served as a precondition for a truly Christian life, in Vives's description of law one's internalisation of natural law was tied together with one's self-control, which could then be externalised in a virtuous practice of *epikeia* and *aequitas*. Revealingly, Vives's guardians and practitioners of *aequitas* could be likened to priests, whose inner spirituality was a *topos* in Erasmian parlance; in *De concordia* Vives asked, 'what else are jurists than [...] priests of the good and the just ...?'.[19]

The analogy between Erasmian theology and Vives's perception of law was further reinforced by the fact that they both thought that law should primarily contribute to the moral improvement of humans. In this way the prince, in giving and interpreting laws, should function as a doctor of the social body who strove for the perfection of its individual parts. This view of law was in accordance with a whole tradition of Dominican political thought spearheaded by Thomas Aquinas (1225–1274) and Albertus Magnus (1193–1280) that, unlike Neo-Augustinians who concentrated on the punitive element of jurisprudence, had emphasised the didactic dimension of positive law as a possibility to instruct citizens in natural life under the guidance of reason.[20] Many Erasmian humanists agreed with this ideal. Erasmus, in his *Institutio principis Christiani*, pictured the Christian ruler as a doctor of a political body and argued that laws should, above all, be persuasive and contribute to the perfecting of citizens. He maintained that a prince should 'promote the kind of laws which not only prescribe punishment for the guilty but also dissuade men from breaking the law'.[21]

Vives stressed this point throughout his career and made it with special vigour in his *In Leges Ciceronis praefatio*. In this short text, Vives argued that a lawgiver or a judge should be primarily a philosopher since the fundamental questions of law, such as man's ultimate *telos* and the means to arrive there, belonged to the subject matter of philosophy. In line with the

Thomistic tradition, he claimed that natural law manifested itself in natural inclinations such as sociability (*congressus ac humanae communicationis appetitus*), the cult of Gods (*veneratio Deorum*), the sense of vice (*male actae vitae conscientia*) or the respect of one's superiors. Although humans could agree on the *telos* of life that consisted in a 'living according to one's nature', and although there was an agreement that humans were created with an aptitude for 'felicity' (*beatitudo*), differences of opinion emerged on what that state consisted of, which resulted in the emergence of the different philosophical schools of Antiquity.[22] Since laws were invented to contribute to a virtuous life, the legislator should be a specialist in understanding natural law, in living according to its precepts, and in its contextual implementation according to the community and places one lived in.[23] Once again, this linked the ethical nature of the lawgiver and interpreter to his capacity to serve as an authority in natural and positive law in perfecting others.

As has been noted in the scholarly literature, Vives's strongly ethical interpretation of law and jurisprudence largely omitted the nuanced semantic distinctions between natural, divine, and positive law or fundamental terms such as justice (*ius*, also law and right) and law (*lex*).[24] Like Erasmus in his criticism of scholastic theology, Vives stressed that detailed specialist discussions conducted in the discourse of law, instead of solving problems, distanced law from its original simplicity. Moreover, in his critique of the interpretative tradition that had twisted the meaning of Roman Law, Vives grouped all scholastic jurists, irrespective of their positions on fundamental questions of law and politics, together as representatives of a flawed understanding of law. Consequently, Bartolus de Saxoferrato (1313–1357), one of the most famous legal writers on tyranny, was coupled with Accursius (c.1182–1263), a known enemy of popular sovereignty. This somewhat diverged from the more refined assessments of professional jurists such as Budé.[25] Despite this, Vives developed his philosophical understanding of jurisprudence in close connection with certain specific themes.

First, Vives's views were meant to be a critique of both the commentary tradition and the practice of Roman Law. As Constant Matheeussen has shown, the theme and composition of *Aedes legum* and *In Leges Ciceronis praefatio* was closely related to the academic disputes between humanists and scholastics in Louvain. In this debate, the evocation of the philosophical nature of law was one of the strategies employed by humanists for bringing law into the remit of humanist textual criticism and philology and freeing it from the confines of the traditional specialists of Roman Law working in the *mos italicus*.[26] This, for Vives, was tied together with the second point he frequently underscored with regard to Roman law. In referring to the ethical simplicity of law, protected by the lawgiver, Vives engaged in a critique not only of specific interpretations of certain legal points but also of the very practice of legal litigation, based, according to him, on argumentative manipulation that twisted the original spirit of the laws and distanced them from justice.[27] This critique, for its part, was linked to Vives's third point which was that the technical nature of Roman Law, rather than serving as a guarantee against arbitrary power, functioned primarily as a legitimatizing practice of the arbitrary actions of the powerful. Quite bombastically, he quoted in his commentaries on Augustine Thrasymachus's twisted understanding of law, as presented in Plato's *Republic*, according to which law was nothing other than what was 'expedient for the one who has power' and claimed that this was the understanding of justice that 'we use in our cities nowadays'.[28] To argue that legal practice went hand in hand with the private interest of the powerful was to maintain that it served precisely the cause from which it was supposed to protect the weak.

The claim that a merely technical interpretation of the law made it the handmaiden of the powerful was further linked to Vives's fourth theme, which was his inclination to associate the simplicity of law with customary law to the detriment of the interpretive tradition of Roman law. In his commentaries on Augustine, he described the customs and the supposed concord of the old Hispanic peoples and stated that each of the peoples was governed by magistrates who were men of great 'learning' (*eruditio*) and 'uprightness' (*probitas*), and 'things were settled by equity and benevolence, not by the quantity of laws'.[29] In *De disciplinis*, Vives called for a 'science of justice' (*ars iustitiae*) which would not be based on the elaboration of written law but on simple principles that would be easily understandable to all.[30]

It is particularly telling that Vives's call for a return to the simplicity of laws happened precisely at the moment when the role of specialist jurists was growing both in the central administration of the Habsburgs as well as in regional councils.[31] Furthermore, his plea for legal simplicity, based on the internalisation of the principles of justice and equity, reflected the ideally consensus-based political culture of the Low Countries between the prince and the provinces. This reciprocal culture of *consuetudo* was manifested by the *joyeuses entrées* of the Burgundian princes, which served as a symbolic demonstration of the respect for the ancient rights and privileges of towns on the part of their rulers.[32] In discussions between towns and the central power, the prevalent discourse had long been framed by the normative ideal that the duty of the princes was to act in accordance with the common good, which meant the active performance of virtues such as justice and equity.[33] Vives's ideas on jurisprudence, based on the correct interpretation of a few laws, could have resonated especially well in his home province Flanders, since its relationship to the count, Charles, was essentially moderated through a simple culture of *consensus*, not based on written documents.[34]

When Vives himself engaged in an equitable interpretation of Roman Law, he systematically argued that power was not a legal prerogative but that it was instituted in an exemplary individual for the enhancement of the common good. In several writings he took up the famous idea found in *Decretum* that rulers were free from law (*legibus solutus*). In *De disciplinis*, Vives wrote that this freedom was initially granted to wise and prudent rulers by the people precisely because of their virtuous nature, yet the fact that this 'custom' (*mos*) had been turned almost into a 'right' (*ius*) or a 'law' (*lex*) was profoundly questionable since it essentially sanctioned the use of power by those blinded by their passions.[35] In *De pacificatione*, Vives made an even more explicit constitutionalist argument. He claimed that kings were originally instituted for the maintenance of peace, concord, and tranquillity; that a king, a prince, and a magistrate 'was elected by the people to uphold justice, to be the protector and defender of laws, the bond of civil concord'; and that princes, in taking power, 'swear' (*jurat*) allegiance to the law.[36] The development of this constitutional idea was in sharp contradiction to the discourse of universal monarchy that was gaining popularity in Charles V's court and that tried to broaden the legitimacy of imperial power.[37] Already in his letters to Cranevelt in the early 1520s, Vives frequently complained about lawyers and at times coupled his ridicule of jurists with a criticism of their ability to discuss the universal aspect of the emperor's power.[38] In his commentaries on Augustine's *De civitate Dei*, Vives wrote in a particularly telling passage that it was 'stupid to declare that the Emperor of the Romans has authority over the whole world' and that the princes were 'inflamed by these fictitious titles, which are nothing else than torches for the earth and a plague for all human kind'.[39] The concept of universal monarchy violated the idea that absolute power was not a legal prerogative but the severest of burdens, a duty to work for the common good in accordance with natural law.

In defending the system of *consuetudo* and criticizing lawyers for their support of the power of rulers, Vives relied on the basic message of the most widely printed Northern humanist work on princely rule: Erasmus's *Institutio principis Christiani*.[40] Drawing on the New Testament and classical (often Stoic) sources, Erasmus's *Institutio* painted a fresco of a virtuous ruler (epitomised by Christ himself), to whom power was a burden, a duty to work for the common good, not a prerogative or licence to do as he wanted, as an erroneous classical legal vocabulary (*imperium, auctoritas, potentia*) might suggest.[41] The Erasmian conceptual scheme of ethical self-cultivation comprised a specific interpretation of what exterior signs testified to an ethical rule, the most important of which was the upholding of the old Low Countries culture of *consuetudo* between princes, provinces, and towns. As James Tracy has argued, the external signs of self-restraint in the *Institutio* actually reproduced an outcome favourable to the point of view of towns that had traditionally been wary of the power of the princes.[42] Erasmus took up several issues that would have resonated well in the context of the Low Countries. He not only reminded Charles that he ruled over free citizens, not slaves, and that there was a mutual responsibility between the ruler and his subjects, but he also favoured a constitutionalist form of mixed government.[43] Like Vives in *De pacificatione*, Erasmus in the *Institutio* claimed that originally 'kings were appointed, by popular agreement, because of their exceptional qualities'. However, although a perfect monarchy was the best form of government because it mirrored the rule of God, in the current state of affairs, 'monarchy should preferably be checked and diluted with a mixture of aristocracy and democracy to prevent it ever breaking into tyranny'.[44] Ultimately, Erasmus was much keener to tell the ruler what not to do than what to do; a good ruler should live in the country and uphold justice, but he should avoid warfare, know the customs and habits of his people, tax lightly, legislate sparsely, and avoid all innovation in his dealings with the towns and provinces.[45] The avoidance of warfare, in particular, was central to Erasmus's message to rulers. As he stressed in *Institutio* (but also in other contemporary works such as *Querela pacis*), a ruler should always focus on the just administration of his lands, not on expanding them.[46]

This ethical conception of law had implications across the spectrum of Vives's thought. It not only conceptually framed his political interventions, but it also implied that the answer to political questions did not lie in an autonomous legal discourse but in moral and civic philosophy. Interestingly, Vives's own reluctance to delineate legal answers to the political problems of his time was in contradiction to a tradition of legal and moral casuistry that sought to expand the language of law to the treatment of ever more social or political questions and disputes.[47] Vives's ethical politics was centred on the virtue and dispositions of the agent, not on providing a normative and legal description of specific actions. Consequently, Vives's views on law opened up a door to a range of ethical, critical, rhetorical, and formative discourses that tried to guarantee that the supreme lawgiver and interpreter of the law, the prince, would be a man of virtue capable of judging and ruling according to natural law.[48] Still, while his interventions were often framed as a critical reproof of those in power, they never resulted in a delineation of any kind of right to resist existing secular authorities. They were an attempt to defend political peace and religious concord within the existing system of *consuetudo* and recognised hierarchies, not an attempt to change them.

The Project of Peace

Erasmus's and Vives's arguments about the avoidance of dynastic warfare and about respect for the culture of *consuetudo* were closely interlinked since the warfare of Habsburg princes was financed by towns and provinces.[49] In 1477, Mary of Burgundy (1457–1482) married Archduke Maximilian of Austria (1459–1519), who would be elected emperor in 1493, and after Mary's death in 1482, the Burgundian Netherlands came under the rule of Habsburg princes. Partly due to the Great Privilege of 1477 that reconfirmed old privileges and rights of provinces and partly because Maximilian could not inherit Mary's lands, the Habsburgian rule in the Low Countries remained weak by European standards. By the early sixteenth century, many towns and provinces had developed a distinctive civic consciousness and identity, and their relationship with the princes was based on a culture of mutual consensus confirmed in the famous *joyeuses entrées*. One of the manifestations of this culture was that not only taxes but also questions related to warfare that legally pertained to the prince were constantly negotiated with the towns represented by the General Estates.[50] The towns were extremely well aware that the warfare of Habsburgian princes with France and with the Duchy of Guelders, as well as Charles's Spanish and European plans after he became the ruler of Spain (1516) and emperor (1519), were ultimately dependent on their will and ability to finance wars. In addition to the fiscal burden, the development of commerce based on international connections and products, especially English cloth, did not encourage aggressive international policies.[51]

The project of peace was not, however, merely a Low Countries phenomenon; the idea of peace as an external manifestation of princely self-government was firmly grounded in the self-interpretation of the transnational circle of friends around Erasmus. Guillaume Budé, for instance, not only drew on the discourse of peace but even associated the Republic of Letters with its maintenance when, in a 1517 letter to Thomas More, he argued that humanist correspondence could be likened to embassies that conserved peace between allied monarchs.[52] This dream was transformed into actual projects. The last years of the 1510s represented the culmination of pacifist humanist plans that had been developed and propagated in London, Mechelen, Brussels, and Paris after a series of wars that had taken place mainly on the Italian peninsula between France and the League of Cambrai led by the Holy Roman Empire and England.[53] In 1518, the Treaty of London designed by Cardinal Wolsey, the Lord Chancellor of England, was signed by the ambassadors of all European powers. According to the solemn treaty, all major European nations agreed, among other issues, to a non-aggression pact that also required them all to fight any party that broke the agreement.[54] In 1520, a series of talks between European princes took place on the continent, culminating in a flamboyant meeting between Henry VIII and Francis I on the Field of the Cloth of Gold, where the intention was to end warfare for all time, no less.[55] While some humanists expected the dawning of a new age, the dream was, however, quickly shattered in the early 1520s when European monarchs embarked on a new series of wars that dominated the decade.[56]

Vives was one of those striving for peace, and the idea was shared by his main humanist contacts in the Netherlands, such as Erasmus and Franciscus Cranevelt. He could also discuss peace and the horrors of warfare with Budé, a member of Francis's court, to whom he sent a copy of his 1529 treatise on peace (*De concordia*).[57] With his departure to England, Vives activated Erasmus's and his own contacts with a powerful humanist faction at the Tudor court comprised of Richard Pace (c.1482–1536), Cuthbert Tunstall (1474–1559), Bishop Fisher (1469–1535), and Thomas More.[58] This group had been influential in the politics of the late 1510s that had led to the Universal Peace of 1518 and still strove for a European peace under the protection of the Emperor Charles V at a moment in which the powerful Cardinal

Wolsey, the architect of the Peace of London, had adopted a more belligerent attitude to European politics.[59] In England, Vives also became closely connected with the Spanish queen Catherine of Aragon, a member of the Habsburg family and patron of English humanists.[60] During the divorce (or annulment) negotiations, which lasted from the mid-1520s to the early 1530s and pitted the English peace faction and the Habsburg family against Cardinal Wolsey, Vives acted as a counsellor for the queen. He encouraged Catherine to refrain from her own defence in a trial that he regarded as mere theatre; but this strategy did not appeal to the queen, and in 1528 Vives left England for good.[61]

Throughout the 1520s, Vives also maintained close ties with powerful members of the Spanish court. He was well connected to a faction of Spanish Erasmian humanists composed of Archbishop Alonso de Fonseca (1475–1534, archbishop from 1523), the inquisitor general Alonso Manrique (1471–1538), the Benedictine friar Alonso de Virués (1493–1545), and especially Juan de Vergara, whom he had met in the early 1520s in the Netherlands and who served as the secretary to Fonseca from 1524 onwards. In addition to Vergara's and Manrique's personal familiarity with humanist circles in the Low Countries, the unifying bond between his Spanish links was undoubtedly their support for and propagation of Erasmian humanism in Spain, which was manifest in the 1527 Valladolid debate on Erasmus's works. As a matter of fact, some of them took a markedly different stance on political questions compared to Vives in the aftermath of Francis I's release from his captivity in Spain in 1526. In the late 1520s, Archbishop Fonseca supported Chancellor Mercurino di Gattinara's (1465–1530) aggressive line in the council of state and Manrique defended Alfonso de Valdés's (c.1490–1532) defence of the Sack of Rome against the papal nuncio Baldassare Castiglione (1478–1529).[62]

Although peace was popular in the learned circle around Erasmus, the Republic of Letters should not be thought of as merely a consortium of autonomous intellectuals who called for peace at different courts for purely theoretical reasons. The project of peace articulated broader concerns within the society of the time, and many humanists worked to achieve issues of significance for their more local allegiances as well as for their networks of patronage. Erasmus is a case in point. His *Institutio principis Christiani*, *Querela pacis*, and other texts from around 1515 that outline the project of peace were written at a moment when a group of pro-French aristocrats led by Jean le Sauvage (1455–1518) and Guillaume de Croy, Lord of Chièvres, were fighting for control of Charles's future policies against the pro-English faction led by Charles's aunt, Margaret of Austria. Both Sauvage and Chièvres served as Erasmus's protectors and supported his yearning for peaceful policies, especially with France.[63] When Charles's court and entourage adopted a more international and above all Spanish outlook in the late 1510s and 1520s, the faction representing the high aristocracy of the

108 *Managing discord*

Burgundian Low Countries, some of whom were vassals of the French king, continued to push for peace with France.[64]

The young Guillaume de Croy, whom Vives tutored until early 1521, was the nephew of the powerful Lord of Chièvres, which meant that Vives was part of the clientelist networks of the Chièvres family. After the death of young Croy and his uncle in 1521, Vives's contacts with the political aristocracy of the Low Countries did not come to a halt. In the 1520s, Vives was in contact with both Louis of Flanders, Lord of Praet, who had served Charles as a counsellor, ambassador, and bailiff of Ghent and Bruges, and Joris van Halewijn (c.1470–1536), a member of the court and an ambassador who was well known for his favourable attitude towards humanist studies and humanists.[65] The project of peace could not only benefit the cause of much of the aristocracy of the Burgundian Low Countries, but it was also firmly in agreement with the will of the towns and provinces that were represented in the General Estates. Vives, who married into the Bruges merchant family of Valdaura in 1524, called himself a citizen of Bruges in his *De subventione pauperum* and was well connected to the intellectual and commercial elites of the great town of Flanders, was no doubt very aware of this dimension.[66] Considering this, it is evident that his work for a project of peace in different courtly environments was in accordance with the interests of his adopted hometown Bruges.[67]

In this complex picture where different agendas for peace intersected in the 1520s, I agree with Cathy Curtis that Vives strove to adopt the role of a relatively independent counsellor.[68] In assessing his activities, the possibilities and limitations of advising rulers should be borne in mind. Within the traditional scholarship on state-building, the early sixteenth century has been seen as a moment of institutionalisation of practices of counselling manifest in the establishment of more or less stable councils with specific functions in different European polities. Lately, various scholars have seen this not merely as the emergence of more effective forms of government but have increasingly emphasised councils and institutionalised forms of counselling as places where broader concerns and demands were articulated by the representatives of different factions within the society.[69] At the same time, a growing focus on practices of counselling instead of institutional history has revealed the fluctuating nature of councils, the functioning and composition of which was not separable from the will of the ruler. In practice, power continued to be inseparable from personal relations with the prince, and in the case of Charles V, for instance, one can perceive a certain change not only with regard to the persons close to him who disposed of power but also with respect to the specific functions officially embodied by these people in the court and in the administration.[70]

Although Vives was connected to networks of counsel, he never achieved a position in the emerging councils at the Tudor and Habsburg courts, which were reserved for the high nobility or jurists, nor did he obtain a formal position within the state bureaucracy as a secretary. While he played a role in the peace project of the late 1510s as a speechwriter (in the context of the peace negotiations of Cambrai in 1517) and was in the divorce negotiations between Henry and Catherine, his direct influence within European courts and institutionalised forms of counselling remained modest compared to someone like Thomas More.[71] Still, Vives certainly pushed for peace by using his scholarly authority in dealing with his contacts. Indeed, he most likely worked for the project of peace in different courtly environments as an intellectual friend (of Halewijn), as a tutor (of Croy), or as a man of scholarly authority who composed deliberative letters to the most powerful men of the time (Henry VIII, Pope Adrian of Utrecht, Charles V).

It seems to be clear, however, that Vives did not think that counselling was restricted to direct forms of political counsel or princely education. In addition to tutoring and counselling in the context of the court, both orally and through letters, Vives, like Erasmus, was quite eager to turn the supposedly private discourse of princely self-government into a public political language of counsel. This further element implied that although princely literature addressed the ruler himself and emphasised his character formation, many humanists sought a wide readership for their works on princely conduct and rule. Erasmus's *Institutio principis Christiani* (and other works), Vives's 1526 political compendium *De Europae dissidiis & Republica* (1526), and his *De concordia* (1529) were all printed, which meant that the self-government of the prince was not thought to be merely a private matter between the ruler and his conscience, but that a somewhat broader audience was invited to witness the results of the ethical transformation of the prince.

According to both Erasmus and Vives, the powerful should always remember that all their actions were watched. Although conceptually this was linked to the claim that the example of the powerful had transformative potential with regard to citizens and subjects, it also reminded them of the expectations the people might have for the correct performance of princely duties.[72] As Vives claimed in a printed letter to Henry VIII, 'darkness of solitude' do not 'prevent what the monarch does from being communicated to the people', and that he should think of himself as being 'in a theatre full of people, where neither his acts nor his words remain hidden'.[73] In a letter to Vives's pupil, Cardinal Guillaume de Croy, Erasmus claimed that he should think of himself as being 'in a vast theatre, with the eyes of the whole world bent on him alone', and that he should remember that the powerful have the 'responsibility to answer the world's expectations'.[74] By disseminating the discourse of self-government, humanists clearly tried to set the discourse within which the actions of the ruler could and would be judged. Echoing a recurrent humanist yearning for freedom of expression, Erasmus expressed the hope in his *Lingua* (*The Double-Edged Tongue*, 1525) that kings would 'bear tolerantly advice and open criticism given in published writings provided that there is no disloyal abuse'.[75] The language of self-government, the external sign of which were peace and respect for a culture of *consensus*,

110 *Managing discord*

would have resonated quite well with the Netherlandish reading public that had long expected these from their prince. Furthermore, these ideals had been amply inscribed in Erasmian educational works through which new generations were being acclimatised to them (Chapter 1).

The Rhetoric of Criticism: *De Europae dissidiis & Republica*

The discourse of ethical self-government was actualised in Vives's interventions in the political and religious debates of the time. In fall 1526, his first political compendium, entitled *De Europae dissidiis & Republica*, appeared in print in Bruges. The work included a 1522 letter *Ad Adrianum VI Pontificem de tumultibus Europae* to Pope Adrian of Utrecht – favourably disposed towards Erasmian humanism – on princely warfare and on a possible Church council. This letter was accompanied by Vives's Latin translations of Isocrates's orations *Areopagitica* and *Ad Nicocles*, dedicated to Cardinal Wolsey in 1523, two letters to Henry VIII from 1525, entitled *De Rege Galliae capto* and *De regni administratione, bello, & pace*, as well as a letter to Bishop John Longland, Henry's confessor. The edition was rounded out with a fictional dialogue, *De Europae dissidiis et bello turcico*. In the scholarly literature, it has sometimes been argued that while the 1529 compendium was fully dedicated to peace, the 1526 one had a more political flavour. This shift in emphasis between 1526 and 1529 seems, however, to concern the selection of genres rather than the overall message, since the overwhelmingly chief concern of the 1526 compendium was peace in its different forms (ecclesiastical concord and political peace).[76]

The printing of the compendium in fall 1526 coincided with a critical moment for the project of peace. In 1525, the Battle of Pavia and the ensuing imprisonment of Francis I had provisionally ended the Italian wars between the Habsburgs (allied with England) and the French. However, in May 1526, Francis, after having been released from his imprisonment in Spain, formed the League of Cognac together with the Pope, Milan, Venice, and Florence – openly challenging the emperor and nullifying the content of the Treaty of Madrid.[77] Besides the threat of a renewed war between European dynasties, in August 1526, a Christian army was defeated by the Ottomans, leading to a partition of Hungary and to a growing fear that the Turks might enter the heart of Europe.[78] What is more, during 1526, Vives personally experienced the cooling down in Anglo-Habsburg relations at the English court.[79] All this meant that European peace was threatened both within and without (the Turks).

Vives's decision to publish private letters in order to sustain the overall argument about the importance of civic and religious concord is worth noting. Although this was partly motivated by the urgency of voicing an opinion at a critical moment, it conditioned the generic choices of the compendium. It strengthened the notion of actively presenting deliberations to the most powerful figures of Europe, which lent them an air of immediacy and personal commitment. It also enabled Vives to approach peace from different angles even though the question treated in the original letter had ceased to be relevant, as was the case of Vives's address to Pope Adrian, who was already dead.[80] Ultimately, the compendium included political and religious deliberations (*De rege Galliae capto* to Henry VIII and *De tumultibus Europae* to Adrian), mirrors-for-princes (*De regni adminstratione, bello, & pace* to Henry VIII), discussions on good government (Isocrates's speeches and Vives's dedication letter to Wolsey), arguments for inner peace as a precondition of social harmony (Vives to Longland[81] and *De regni adminstratione, bello, & pace* to Henry VIII), and a fictional dialogue which combined assessments of past actions with a future-oriented deliberation (*De Europae dissidiis et bello turcico*). Thus, the compendium did not engage in a conceptual clarification of peace but in a rhetorical exercise where humanist commonplaces were moulded to the specific requirements of individual texts (audience, specific question treated).

The compendium also struck a balance between strident criticism and respect for authority and *status quo*. On the one hand, it reinforced the idea that the discord besetting Europe had to be dealt with within the existing system of *officia* and hierarchies. On the other hand, it not only presupposed the failure of the powerful to act according to the duties and virtues of their positions, but it also engaged in a sweeping criticism of their past deeds, which was supposed to frame expectations for correct future action. Since powerful positions (*officia*) were instituted solely for the enhancement of common good, the compendium hinted throughout that, should the powerful fail in the performance of their office, they would amount to a corrupted version of their position, which, in the case of princes, implied tyranny. Moreover, despite Vives's ties with the Habsburg and Tudor courts, the compendium was quite symmetrical in its attribution of blame for discord, with Francis and Charles getting their fair share in the dialogue *De Europae dissidiis et bello Turcico*.

Vives's basic strategy of connecting the discourse on virtues and duties with a critique of discord was most clearly discernible in his longer letters to Adrian and Henry. In addressing the new Pope Adrian, who was favourable to some of Erasmus's ideas, Vives knew that he voiced a more general concern within Erasmian circles. In fact, his letter closely developed certain points Erasmus had made in his prefatory letter to *Commentarii in Psalmos* destined for Adrian.[82] The first part of Vives's letter presented a eulogy of Adrian's papacy, celebrating that, after a sequence of bad popes, virtue had finally been rewarded with his election. He had been chosen 'solely for the innocence of his life' and because of the 'life of previous popes your [Adrian's] person seemed to embellish the most prestigious earthly distinction'.[83] This praise, however, served only as a device that strengthened Vives's demand for Adrian to take the right course of action. He stressed that the pope has been given 'the occasion to show, or to put it more aptly, to exercise your uprightness and prudence' at a moment in which things were falling apart.[84] In an argument that drew on the link of Adrian's virtuous *persona* with the successful performance of his office, Vives went as far as to claim that his 'earlier life' had created 'such expectations for the future' that he cannot act differently from 'what everyone expects' and what 'universal consensus had sacredly promised to everyone in your name'.[85]

In his defence of a European concord, united in the body of Christ against division, Vives naturally presented the Erasmian call for a Church council that would focus on the stabilisation of a few essential points of faith and leave questions of non-essentials open for debate.[86] By drawing on the historical role of popes as arbitrators of wars between Christian rulers and on Adrian's personal history as one of Charles's main advisers, Vives, however, discussed papacy also as a politically significant office.[87] As a part of a thorough critique of princes who 'laugh at the misfortunes of their subjects that they do not understand' and who, misled by 'ambition and avarice', cause great havoc and destruction because of a small dispute, Vives called for Adrian to serve as a supreme advisor with the authority of the pope.[88] Activating the commonplace about law and the concept of just war as masks of violence and private advantage, he reminded the pope that men close to princes encouraged them to think that any war that was pleasing to them was a just one. Against these precepts Adrian should teach princes and their advisers that war between Christians, brothers, and members of the same body was 'unjust, wicked, against divine law, against what is pious'.[89]

Vives's longer letter to Henry VIII (*De regni adminstratione, bello, & pace*) linked the project of peace to the transformative rhetoric of the mirror-for-princes tradition. He connected public salvation to the judgment of princes (who are what a soul is to a body), built a dichotomy between a good, durable government based on love and a bad government based on fear, and claimed that the princes should primarily try to 'make themselves and their people good', linking this claim to education.[90] In the shorter piece addressed to Henry (*De rege Galliae capto*), clemency against France was recommended: in the present situation, in which France was without its king, Henry could conquer the minds of the French people best by showing princely virtue towards them.[91] Seeking to enliven his argument in *De regni administratione*, Vives painted a verbal picture, full of rhetorical *enargeia*, of the harm of warfare, which depicted the sufferings of the people and the disastrous effects of war on commerce and the cultivation of letters. He described how it was 'a diversion in warfare to plunder houses, pillage sanctuaries, snatch virgins, to burn entire cities and towns'.[92]

These humanist commonplaces on princely virtue supported the central demand of the letter which was the cessation of warfare.[93] In doing so, the text made a somewhat circular argument that the only true peace resided in inner self-government, yet inner concord was made possible only in a world where the exterior peace was secured. The cessation of warfare was backed up by two arguments drawn from the office of the prince. The first was that the people had a right to expect peaceful actions from princes since it was simply their duty to guarantee it. Vives wrote that 'all the people expect and demand from you as their right [...] that you complete it [peace]', and, in another part, he reminded the ruler that a prince who failed to perform his duty satisfactorily would be laughed at and despised just like a failed 'painter, shepherd, shoemaker, or workman'.[94] This demand for princes to perform according to the requirements of their duty was, however, tempered with a promise of wealth and especially glory that resided in peaceful actions rather than in warfare. This promise, following the precepts of *De consultatione*, appealed to the ambitious and selfish side of princes. As Vives stated, 'a righteous and peaceful prince rightly attains all these things: the praise of men of letters who owe the prince their *otium*. Augustus was most illustrious and praised by writers of every genre to whom he had provided the possibility of leisure with his prosperous peace extended to the whole globe, thus obtaining a glory that is very rare among men'.[95]

Whereas the letters hinted at the failures of the powerful, the central piece of the compendium, the dialogue entitled *De Europae dissidiis et bello Turcico*, made this blatantly apparent. In the dialogue, the shades of the already dead Minos, Tiresias, Basilius Colax, Polypragmon, and Scipio discussed worldly affairs in a conversation which was partly sparked off by Minos's observation that so many souls had lately arrived in the afterlife.[96] The ensuing discussion evolved into an account of discord and warfare which, largely through an extended analysis of European history from the fifteenth century up to Vives's day, expanded on the irresponsible and erroneous actions of princes and popes, especially in the context of the Italian wars. This history served a multiplicity of functions within the text. First, it linked a critique of the responses of the princes of the time, especially Charles and Francis, to the problems that they had inherited from the past as representatives of their dynasties.[97] In this way, their shortcomings were not just direct outcomes of their *personae*; instead, the mutual hatred between Charles and Francis was shown in the light of a broader dynastic conflict, partly stemming from juridical claims to the same geographical areas, within which they had been raised and in the context of which they attributed meanings to individual political objectives and to accomplishments that would bring about glory.[98] Vives elaborated on their competition in Italy and in the imperial elections of 1519 'through bribes' (*largitionibus*),[99] and quite openly likened their political behaviour to that of children bereft of self-control and ruled by their passions. In discussing whether or not the Treaty of Madrid was just, it was pointed out that the conditions were considered just by the imperials and unjust by the French, who did not respect them, which, according to Tiresias, was a typically childish reaction from both parties. As he put it, 'this used to happen to my kids when they played with each other; nobody ever did injustice but always suffered it'.[100]

Second, the meticulous reconstruction of history demonstrated that warfare was a realm ruled by fortune (*fortuna*), devoid of any rationality, and that it that never brought forth any sustained advantages. Already in his

114 *Managing discord*

shorter letter to Henry VIII (*De rege Galliae capto*) Vives had made this point as part of his argument against the invasion of France in the aftermath of the capture of Francis I. By drawing on the unpredictable nature of war as a realm of fortune where the winner could well have been the loser, by reversing the potential outcomes of past battles, and by reminding Henry that the roles could change in the future, Vives had underlined the extent to which warfare always escaped the control of its actors.[101] In the dialogue, the idea that a sequence of wars only led to new warfare was summed up by Polypragmon. To Minos's enquiry about 'which part has been made wealthier or is in a betted condition' on account of warfare, Polypragmon answered that it had brought absolutely nothing positive: 'both [Charles and Francis], together with all their allies, are exhausted, kingdoms are pillaged, the nobility is weak and impaired, cities that once flourished are levelled to ground, fields are plundered and abandoned'.[102] Ultimately, the power game camouflaged as a defence of one's rights was not honest (*honestum*) nor expedient (*utile*) to any of the parties.

Although the dialogue undoubtedly carried some deliberative weight against warfare, it introduced a further twist which was of more than coincidental significance. This concerned the inclusion of the Turkish threat in the dialogue, more aggravated after the Christian loss at Mohács (1526), which was said to have been facilitated by the discord and warfare between Christians. Tiresias, an Erasmian voice within the dialogue, had already hinted at what was to come when he claimed that peace between Francis and Charles would make their forces and troops 'very threatening to the Turk'.[103] What was implied here and in other places in the dialogue was given maximum centrality in the longest speech of the dialogue in which Scipio Africanus, one of the rare military heroes of Erasmian circles, defended a joint war against the Turks.

In his deliberative speech, Scipio started by aligning himself with the critique of the princes blinded by their anger and discord before moving on to argue that it would be both more advantageous and more honourable to wage war on the Turk. He argued that if one wanted money, riches, or land, then Asia was the best option because of its immeasurable wealth and its large territory. Much of the argument centred on a detailed analysis of the weaknesses of the Turkish army and military structure and on the use of historical examples to prove that a victory could be achieved since Europeans were by their very nature stronger than Asians, as their military history had shown since the Greek-Persian wars. In the end, if 'the wind changed direction a little and you directed your hatred and anger against the Turk, you would learn to know the spirit of the Asians'.[104] After this long speech by Scipio, Tiresias did not condemn his ideas but somehow incorporated them into his own position. In an Erasmian vein, Tiresias stated that Europe's strongest defence lied in Christ, who guaranteed mutual love and concord. Yet he continued by claiming that if the princes still 'wish to augment their land, it would be better if they fought against a stranger and

Managing discord 115

an enemy of piety and not someone they are united with through blood and initiation to shared mysteries [Christ]'. In a later paragraph, he went on to plead for a common defence of Germany.[105]

The meaning of this passage is of central importance in a broader discussion as to whether the dialogue can be read as a Christian pacifist demand for peace or as a political deliberation calling for a common European war against the Turks.[106] In some ways, the dialogue form enabled Vives to make these two, mutually exclusive, points simultaneously.[107] There clearly was a conceptual hierarchy between the two options; Scipio argued that a war against the Turks was not necessarily pleasing to the Christ, that it was a lesser evil than warfare between Christians, and framed his argument as advice to princes 'blinded by their mutual hatred' and motivated by wealth and military glory, which the philosophy of Christ, as propounded by Tiresias, strictly condemned.[108]

Yet, despite being presented as the second-best option, Scipio's speech emerged as quite a tempting piece of advice, the main content of which was never really denounced. Indeed, in *De consultatione* Vives had already offered advice on how to argue for a defence of Cyprus against the Turks, which included the question 'what would be better for Europe than to direct the weapons of its princes from internal wars against the Asians'?[109] To leave it as a serious alternative for the reader must have been Vives's intention in a compendium that, in many of its texts, linked European discord with the Turkish threat. But even if war was seen merely as a lesser evil, the speech was quite disturbing. Not only was it at odds with the philosophy of ethical self-government but it also implied that warfare was not a world of unpredictability ruled by the caprice of fortune. By referencing history, Scipio established a set of historical constants such as the natural strength of Asians and Europeans that were supposed to frame possible outcomes in future wars.[110] Suddenly warfare could emerge as a practice on which rational deliberation was possible and in which one could anticipate future outcomes and achieve goals, at least when fighting against non-Christians. The conflict between two alternative deliberations was, however, just one instance of the rhetorical plurivocity of the compendium that often transcended classical rhetorical precepts that were primarily centred on an analysis of an individual speech with a clearly defined purpose. Another example was that the individual *ethea* of different texts, which were composed for different audiences, were never harmonised. The result was that some texts showed great *decorum* in the criticism of princes (letters to Henry) while others, such as the dialogue, revealed a strikingly licentious treatment of the rulers of the time.

Nonetheless, all the texts communicated similar ideas. With regard to the Turks, Vives conveyed that warfare, although not the ideal solution, was an acceptable possibility given the urgency of the situation. In doing this, he was walking a tightrope between two conflicting opinions. On the one hand, through Tiresias, he could align himself with Erasmus, who, in *Dulce bellum*

116 *Managing discord*

inexpertis, had claimed that 'the best way to subdue the Turk' was through heavenly teaching coupled together with a Christian life that accords with it.[111] Similarly to Erasmus, Vives, in works such as *De concordia*, extended his trust in rhetoric as a non-violent solution to discord to cover the Turks to whom the word of Christ should be revealed in the right spirit.[112] In this Erasmian tradition, 'holy war' and crusading spirit were systematically condemned and only a defensive war against Turkish aggression was allowed, as Erasmus himself had stated in *Dulce bellum inexpertis*.[113] On the other hand, the official policy of the Catholic Church, since the Fifth Lateran Council (1515–1517), had called for a crusade against the Turks. This call, often delineated in aggressive rhetoric, was the context of Scipio's speech, in which war was presented as a viable option given the nature of rulers and the recent success of the Turks. Indeed, towards the late 1530s other critiques of the crusading spirit were moving in the same direction. Luther, who had considered the Turks an instrument of God's wrath in the 1510s, came to consider a defensive war against them a necessity in his *On War Against the Turk* (1529). Erasmus himself, while primarily pleading for a peaceful conversion of the Turks, accepted war in the case of necessity in his *Utilissima consultatio de bello Turcis inferendo* (*A Most Useful Discussion Concerning Proposals for War against the Turks*, 1530).[114]

Although the call for aggression was an answer to a specific political problem Europeans were facing with the Ottoman Empire, it still reveals a deeper dimension of Vives's notions of peace and concord in his 1526 and 1529 political compendia. In contrast to some scholars, most notably Alain Guy, who have underlined the universal dimension of Vives's pacifism, I believe that concord and peace cannot be disentangled from a Christian worldview.[115] Since political peace was perfected by an inner transformation in Christ, on the one hand, and since its significance was to enable a truly Christian life for Europeans, on the other, it was not primarily a political or legal concept but inseparable from the success of a Christian life based on charity, benevolence, and other socially constructive emotions. Vives often pointed out that a true peace in and between souls would never be a possibility under Turkish rule, which, according to him, was essentially tyranny built on fear.[116]

In arguing his case for a European peace and a collective defence or military expedition against the Turks, Vives, employing the full arsenal of rhetorical strategies, called for the powerful to fulfil the duties demanded by their *officia*. This is what they were instituted for and this is what would bring them true glory, both human and divine.

The Immediate Context of *De concordia* (1529)

Whereas the 1526 compendium had called for peace in the aftermath of Francis's capture at Pavia and the Christian defeat at Mohács, the 1529 compendium, comprising *De concordia*, *De pacificatione*, and *De conditione vitae sub turca*, appeared in a different political and personal climate. Personally, Vives's active career at the Tudor court in the service of the Queen was over, and, at the turn of the 1530s, he increasingly sought the attention of Charles V, to whom *De concordia* was dedicated.[117] Politically, the war between Charles V and the League of Cognac had greatly disappointed Vives's expectations for the Treaty of Madrid, and in his private correspondence he expressed annoyance at Francis's decision to break the treaty.[118] The problem was further aggravated by the military success of the Turks, who, under the leadership of Suleiman the Magnificent (1494–1566), were approaching Vienna, which further contributed to the urgency of putting an end to religious and political discord within Europe. In a delicate moment, Vives raised his voice to defend peace against a powerful faction at the Habsburg court, led by Chancellor Mercurino di Gattinara, which had objected to the Treaty of Madrid, pushed for aggressive military policies, and legitimised Charles's imperial plans by portraying him as a universal monarch and supreme ruler of the world.

The idea of universal monarchy has been extensively debated by historians, and the extent to which it influenced Charles's specific decisions and interpretation of imperial policies remains unsettled.[119] Although it seems clear that many of Charles's actions can be understood through the logic of dynastic warfare and that some of his advisors who used this discourse – such as Gattinara – conceived of current political problems primarily in legal terms, a somewhat eclectic notion of universal monarchy served as a political language through which the actions of the emperor were justified in the official imperial propaganda of the late 1520s.[120] Works such as *Pro divo Carolo* (1527) and Alfonso de Valdés's *Diálogo de las cosas acaecidas en Roma* (1528), the latter of which tried to justify the Sack of Rome, drew extensively on an imperial discourse which was an eclectic mixture of eschatological promises of divine rule, legal arguments, and aggressive ideas of divine authority. In addition, the promoters of imperial propaganda often claimed that the description of a universal monarch as a guardian of Christendom was compatible with the Christian monarch as depicted in Erasmian works. Gattinara even asked Erasmus to prepare a printed edition of Dante's (c.1261–1321) *Monarchy* (1313), which, he reckoned, 'would be helpful to the emperor's cause'.[121] This manoeuvre showed not only an acute awareness of the most widely available discourses needed for the justification of imperial policies but also a recognition of the authority that Erasmus, the leading theoretician of the self-governed prince, could give to the project. In the hands of Charles's counsellors, the Erasmian pacifist prince was turned into a ruler who, as an instrument of God, had to fight for Christian values against those representing vice, a category that included the opponents of the emperor and especially the Medici Pope Clement VII (1478–1534).[122]

In his classical study, Carlos Noreña wrote that Vives 'became briefly but intensely involved in the Erasmian messianism of Charles V's Court'.

Yet I believe, as Edward George has hinted, that this is an illusion created by what might be called false praise and that Vives, with his ethical and constitutional understanding of law, detested the idea of universal monarchy.[123] Indeed, his complaints about warfare were throughout the 1520s in agreement with a faction of predominantly Flemish counsellors at the court that had opposed Gattinara, pushed for the Treaty of Madrid and, after its failure, had increasingly lost their role in the management of Charles's politics.[124] But in a further twist, Gattinara's powerful faction had, in the new climate unfavourable to Charles, envisioned a solution to the war with the League of Cognac which was well in line with Vives's goals. This consisted of a peace among princes (the peace negotiations began in Summer 1529 and led to the Treaty of Cambrai) and a concord based on a Church council. Vives was clearly aware of this. In a demonstration of rhetorical flexibility and in order to advance his own agenda, Vives's dedicatory letter to Charles in *De concordia* embedded a defence of political peace and a Church council in the language of universal monarchy dominant at the time in the official propaganda.

In the early parts of the letter, Vives resorted to a language that was not very far from Gattinara's own assessment of the emperor's success as described in the *Autobiografia*. Vives expanded on Charles's rise to the imperial throne and his military success against the Pope and Francis I, who, even after forming the League of Cognac with 'great words and horrible conditions' for those unwilling to participate, were once again defeated.[125] Ultimately, it was evident to everyone that Charles's 'success was not the result of human, but divine forces'.[126] Throughout, Vives's knowledge of imperial discussions and decision making seemed to be good. In direct opposition to Alfonso de Valdés's depiction of imperial policies in the Sack of Rome as an instrument of divine vengeance, Vives wrote that Charles should demonstrate that he was not the agent of God's 'wrath' (*ira*) for our 'vices' (*scelera*), but an instrument of divine 'clemency' (*clementia*).[127] In a reference to Gattinara's sceptical position vis-à-vis the Madrid Treaty of 1526, the peace negotiations of 1527 and the Sack of Rome, Vives claimed that Charles had demonstrated the will of a pacifier even when he was criticised for forgiving the French king and the Pope when they had been at Charles's mercy.[128]

Moreover, in accordance with the precepts of *De consultatione*, the praise of Charles's demonstrations of power, military success, and virtue served merely as a prelude to a demand for the emperor to promote the cause of political peace and ecclesiastical concord. As Vives maintained, 'we demand nothing from unknown virtue as an obligation; from manifest virtue we demand everything'.[129] Precisely because of his power and virtuous actions, Vives argued, people expected from Charles as 'their right' (*iure suo*) and saw it as 'a duty' (*officium*) or as 'a debt' (*debitum*) to them that he assumed the role of a pacifier; and in a later part of the letter he promised glory, both human and divine, if Charles were to direct his powers to the building of concord and peace. In a creation of pictorial *enargeia*, Vives suggested that the pillars of Hercules in Charles's coat of arms might mean that he, just like Hercules, could serve as a substitute for Atlas, who had to carry the world on his shoulders.[130] Ultimately, through the language of universal monarchy and power, Vives reproduced the Erasmian idea of power as a burden and demanded that Charles must act as a self-governed prince for the common good. His divinity and power were nothing more than instruments for serving the people, not prerogatives of authority.

As it turns out, all the works following the dedicatory letter, *De concordia*, *De pacificatione* or *De conditione vitae Christianorum sub Turca*, dissociated themselves from the idea of universal monarchy. Just like the 1526 compendium, they were extremely harsh on the princes of the time, portraying them as failing in their basic duties and implying that their actions could be seen as tyrannical. In a reference to Charles and Francis in Book Three, Vives described how 'today two princes possess what more than 100 years ago belonged to twenty rulers'. Linking their actions to the immensity of their empires and kingdoms, he stated that they did not construct but destroyed, made no contribution to studies and education, and, ultimately, taxed people immoderately to sustain their wars and lifestyle.[131] But this direct critique was complemented with an attempt to generalise the particular problems confronting Europe. Thus, *De concordia* was not primarily a political deliberation on a specific issue but an analysis of the causes of whatever problems on which one might be asked to deliberate.

The Dynamics of Concord and Discord in the Context of the Reformation

De concordia was essentially an investigation of the causes and consequences of concord and discord. In order to fully appreciate what Vives was doing in the treatise, we have to first unravel Vives's peculiar interpretation of concord as the result of passional and emotional impulses and then to discuss its implications in the framework of some of the most pressing debates of the time concerning the role of natural sociability, free will, and, ultimately, the very possibilities of concord. These questions had emerged with some force in the context of the Reformation, when Erasmus and other Catholic humanists had to defend an optimistic interpretation of man's ethical nature against Luther and his followers, who, in a more Augustinian spirit, stressed man's sinfulness as an inevitable component of earthly concord.

Closely following Erasmus's *Querela pacis*, the most widely printed work on peace at the time, Vives opened *De concordia* by affirming the natural sociability (*societas, communitas*) between humans, typical of the Aristotelian and Thomistic traditions, on which different forms of human associations from family ties to political and ecclesiastical communities were built.[132] He claimed that humans were 'made, formed, equipped, and inclined to peace, tranquillity, concord, love, and friendship'.[133] He extensively elaborated on the natural, pre-political gifts humans were endowed with for political life, such as free will, reason, memory, speech, and physiological qualities like the face, smile, tears, laughter, which testified to their social and benevolent nature. In addition, their bodily weakness showed that humans were not self-sufficient but greatly dependent on the help of others throughout their life.[134] On account of all this, what triggered the main part of the text was Vives's bewilderment as to the reasons that had resulted in 'so much dissension, discord, enmity, hatred', and that had separated humans from their true nature.[135] Indeed, Vives's primary purpose in *De concordia* was to analyse the causes, consequences, and remedies for this separation, also touched upon by Erasmus in *Querela pacis*.[136]

While Vives discussed the dichotomy of concord and discord as a battle between God and the Devil, his main line of argument traced humans' separation from their true nature back to the loss of their self-government through passions, above all, self-love (*amor sui*) and pride (*superbia*).[137] Although Erasmus's *Querela pacis* had hinted on numerous occasions that passions were the reason why human beings had degenerated from their original nature, Vives's analysis exceeded Erasmus's and pointed towards a broader medieval legacy.[138] The stress put on pride was common in the Christian tradition. Already in Augustine's *De civitate Dei*, which Vives knew well, pride served as the origin of the free will that led Adam and Eve, in defiance of Divine will, to the first transgression of their own God-like humanity.[139] Thomas Aquinas, whom Vives referred to on the subject of pride in his commentaries on Augustine, described pride as excessive self-love that was not merely one of the seven capital sins (its role was given to vainglory), but the queen of all vices, a frame of mind from which all other vices arose.[140] In *De concordia*, other vices were the result of pride, and they conditioned humankind's passional responses to and judgments on the phenomena surrounding it. As Vives wrote, 'pride attacks with two javelins: envy and wrath', which produce a twisted and malicious interpretation of the actions of others and which both were 'armed with the will to hurt'.[141] Ultimately Vives considered vice, interpreted as passional responses, as the primary source of discord and disorder.

In emphasizing a pre-political scheme of vices and passions, Vives mostly focused on how these manifested themselves in all forms of human association (family, church, politics) without clearly distinguishing between them. There was no discussion on politics as an autonomous field with its distinct problems; political concord was not predicated on the right constitution of government but was rather analysed as just one manifestation of our natural charity, benevolence, and friendship.[142] While different duties (*officia*) were discussed, concord was largely a package deal in which harmony in one form of social life bred concord in other areas. Throughout the work, Vives could employ the medieval metaphor of a social body to imply an organic yet hierarchical interdependence of all the parts that worked towards a common goal, and its malfunctions could be understood in terms of disease and cure.

To argue for an overarching model of concord, based on the external manifestation of self-government and threatened by unrestrained passions, was to go against some classical and Christian models with which Vives was familiar. Although he occasionally could draw on the examples of classical empires whose concord was not premised on Christian self-government, Vives strongly denounced models of concord built merely on self-interest. In Book Four, in which the road to concord was set out, he discussed 'pirates and robbers' who 'maintain a certain peace and concord among themselves' despite the violent and destructive nature of their activities.[143] As he must have known, this was a reference to Augustine's *De civitate Dei*, in which the community of robbers and pirates was used to describe an association devoid of justice and, hence, not worthy of the name of a truly political community.[144] Augustine had strongly implied that the Roman Republic had been nothing more than a community of robbers since it had always lacked true justice, a claim that denied the very concept – justice – through which Roman political self-interpretation had taken place in writers like Cicero. In dismissing Roman models of concord such as the *concordia ordinum*, based on the harmony of dissonant voices which implied managed conflict as a source of concord, Augustine claimed that justice implied just control over one's body and passions and that if there was no justice in individual persons, there could be no true justice in the community composed of them.[145]

Yet Augustine himself did not provide Vives with a model of concord either. Augustine had discussed at length the separation of human beings from their true nature following the Fall, which had resulted in a turmoil and division not only between the City of God and the Earthly City, but, at least to a certain extent, within the will of all humans. In Book 19 of the *De civitate Dei*, Augustine delineated three models of peace: eternal peace, peace of the inhabitants of the City of God, and peace in the Earthly City. While eternal peace was unattainable to humans in this life, the peace in the City of God could be grounded in love and charity. Yet, since the inhabitants of the City of God had to live in the midst of the Earthly City, bereft of faith and spiritual self-governance, political concord was merely a common agreement among humans on the administration of things necessary for bodily life such as health and safety and, although it created useful bodily conditions for the practice of faith for the City of God, its primary contribution was the censure of sin and vice through putative measures, not the enhancement of virtue.[146]

The Augustinian idea of political authority as a remedy against the sin that inevitably formed part of the temporal world was widely taken up in the discussions on secular authority within Reformed circles in the 1520s. The most famous exponent of this approach was Martin Luther. Although Luther's position on the exact relationship between secular and ecclesiastical authorities varied across the 1520s and 1530s, in accordance with the development of his attitude to the papacy and to secular authorities, he certainly contributed to the revival of an Augustinian understanding of secular power and peace. While in his *Appeal to the Christian Nobility* (1520), Luther had claimed that temporal authority should punish spiritual authority because it was divinely ordained to deal with evil (represented in the current situation by the Pope), in his *On Temporal Authority and the Limitations in Obeying It* (1523), he defended a radical separation of the mandates of spiritual and temporal authorities.[147] In outlining his idea of two kingdoms, Luther maintained that it was 'God's will that the temporal sword and law be used for the punishment of the wicked and the protection of the upright', yet emphasised that its role dealt exclusively with life, property, civic peace, punishment, and other external matters on earth.[148] Although a spiritual community of Christians could live without law in a state of grace, in the real world Christians were expected to follow the divinely ordained secular authority whose work was necessary for the containment of sin and the upholding of a peaceful existence among humans. In this model, secular authority appeared as a necessary post-lapsarian answer to sin, not a cure for it.[149]

The discussion of whether secular government enhanced virtue or served as a remedy for vice was connected to the view that was taken on human possibilities under the guidance of reason and free will. As a matter of fact, it was precisely in the discussion of free will that the separation of Erasmus and Luther became clear. As is known, the debate between Erasmus and Luther (1524–1526) chiefly concerned the possibilities of reaching justification and salvation by the use of man's free will and not on the social implications of that question.[150] Luther insisted that humans were justified only through grace and that their free will was utterly incompatible with God's foreknowledge and omnipotence in matters of salvation.[151] In his *De libero aribitrio* (*Of Free Will*, 1524) and *Hyperaspistes* (1526–1527), Erasmus disagreed on various grounds and defended a traditional model between Pelagianism and Augustinianism according to which grace and free will cooperated in the attainment of salvation. Despite the strictly theological resonance of the debate, he was always clear that the question had implications for the performance of ethical acts in this world. He claimed that those who 'attributed much to free will' wanted to 'spur men on to hope and moral endeavour'.[152] Drawing on medieval theology, Erasmus maintained that even before sanctification or justification, grace was operative on earth in the natural gifts given to all alike (natural grace) and in particular grace (*gratia peculiaris*) through which individual human beings, although still in a state of sin, could behave 'as a candidate for the highest kind of grace'.[153] He was relatively optimistic both about the possibility of human beings using their free will for morally good acts within the limits of these preparatory graces, as well as about their role in justification: through these graces, human beings could begin to lead a Christian life, which could contribute to their salvation. By trying to be good, humans could become good.

In his commentaries on *De civitate Dei*, Vives had little to say about Augustine's classification of different forms of concord and peace. Instead, he expounded at length on free will. In his commentaries on Book Five, Vives provided a strong defence of the freedom of the will, stating that God had made our will free. In a somewhat Augustinian fashion, he argued that God's foreknowledge was compatible with free will since, while God saw human history in his/her timeless existence (*nunc stans*), the history perceived by him/her was realised through the voluntary actions of humans. He continued by claiming that there were 'many things that could occur but never occur' and that we can freely choose between two options.[154] According to Vives, Augustin stated simply that 'man does not sin because God foreknows that he is going to sin', moving on to quote Chrysostom who stressed that it was human being who willingly sinned.[155] He elaborated on the ability of making free moral choices in his discussion of destiny (*fatum*), central to Peripatetic and Stoic philosophy. Although he was well informed about several understandings of fate – such as the Stoic interpretation of fate as a determined sequence of causes – he preferred a natural theory of destiny defended by the Aristotelian commentator Alexander of Aphrodisias against the Stoics. Vives wrote that according to this theory things that happened through choice or haphazardly were not part of destiny. In a later passage in his commentaries of the Chapter X of the Book V of *De civitate Dei*, Vives further argued that the Stoics did not, in the end, maintain that fate implied necessity with regard to those things humans made choices about. Just like Alexander of Aphrodisias, Vives was explicit about the ethical dimension of the question. He claimed that if those who were bad were so on account of destiny, then castigation or exhortation to virtue would make no sense or difference. Emphatically, he insisted that the good deserved praise and commendation and the bad castigation and vituperation since 'the one who did good and the one who did bad acted on their free will under God's gaze, not by his/her commandment'.[156]

From Discord to Concord

Despite Vives's defence of free will on moral grounds, it was not exactly clear what humans, both individually and collectively, could achieve freely in their current post-lapsarian state. Scholarship has typically underscored the optimism of *De concordia*. Already Noreña's classic study, while acknowledging a tension between Stoic ideals of moral perfection and the Augustinian idea of the Fall, nevertheless maintained that *De concordia* 'lacks the truly Augustinian insistence on the powerlessness of man, on the total reliance of man on God's grace and assistance'.[157] In a similar vein, Fernández-Santamaría has emphasised the temporal possibilities of humans for building an earthly society of *bonitas* as a gateway to divine *felicitas* in *De concordia*. According to this view, questioned by others as a somewhat Pelagian reading of *De concordia*, human chances of creating a society of concord are rated quite high.[158]

Still, there were several elements that somewhat complicate an optimistic reading of *De concordia*'s reliance on the possibilities of earthly concord. Vives quite consistently underscored that the separation between man's true nature and the current state of discord was such that humans could hardly rely on their natural capacities for reaching concord. In Book Four, Vives underlined how, in the current state of humankind, a victory of concord was a nearly impossible task with human wisdom alone and without divine help.[159] Equally, in his letters towards the late 1520s, he was very pessimistic about reaching immediate political peace or religious concord. As he repeatedly pointed out, those who were supposed to solve current problems through the correct performance of their duties (*officia*) were controlled by their passions to such an extent that they could scarcely be counted on to bring about concord. In 1528, he wrote to Cranevelt that 'without the peace of Christ nothing will be sufficiently tranquil; and we are unworthy of that peace'.[160] Yet this scepticism typically concerned immediate religious and political harmony and did not rule out the possibility of reaching some form of concord in a more remote future. In what follows, I would like to argue that *De concordia* can best be seen as outlining a path to an imperfect concord and relative perfection according to post-lapsarian realities, which, in turn, served as a preparation for the perfect concord achieved through Divine grace.

The move from discord even to an imperfect concord was, undoubtedly, an arduous task since in *De concordia* there were no existing communities, not even among the scholarly elite, that could provide an example of concord for others to imitate. Instead, the work employed a markedly personal language that emphasised the inner peace of individuals as a precondition of social concord. This was expressed most clearly in Book Four of the treatise, which described a movement starting from the Socratic ideal of 'know thyself', towards the true peace perfected by Christ and Divine aid.[161] In the process of increasing self-knowledge that prepared one to ask for final freedom in the spirit of humility, one should come to understand one's God-like nature, the gifts with which humans were endowed, the hierarchy of soul and body, the dynamics of reason and emotion, and one's current limitations in the post-lapsarian state.[162] A similar path from self-knowledge to an active life in the service of others was presented in the highly popular *Introductio ad Sapientiam* (1524) in the form of maxims and short precepts that could be memorised by the reader.[163] These precepts can be seen as part of a broader Erasmian culture of self-government that comprised an array of practices such as affective meditation, prayer, or more reflective forms of self-cure.[164]

In addition to advice on self-cultivation, the structure of *De concordia* comprised a strong rhetorical element aimed at enhancing self-reflection and self-transformation. Its focus on the descent of humans from their nature and on what this implied for the performance of specific *officia*, a point that was elaborated in *De pacificatione*, was always coupled with visual language that painted a picture of the outcomes of concord and discord, respectively. In one of the many visual passages of Book three of *De concordia*, Vives stated:

> Discord produces men who are dispersed and gone astray, full of terror and fear, with no trust in any place or man. They are like a foot wounded recently by a thorn which does not walk with confidence. Assemblies and associations sanctioned by law are broken up; the covenants of concord are destroyed; buildings, farms, towns demolished; whatever was fastened permanently to the ground was torn out; discord also produces hunger, plague, scarcity in all things, ignorance, idleness, bad morals, and skilful and vigorous mercenaries out of soldiers who are thrown out of their armies.[165]

In addition, *De conditione vitae sub turca* was essentially an exercise in demonstrating and visualising what would follow if one really lived under Ottoman rule; it was clearly meant to provoke deliberation about a hypothetical future and the causes and reasons that would bring it about (e.g. moral weakness, false yearn for liberty from current princes).[166]

The recourse to *enargeia* as a rhetorical device through which one could address and activate the fantasy of the reader was common to Northern humanist ethical and political language of the time. Vives himself had used it as part of his letter to Henry VIII (*De bello & pace*), and Cuthbert Tunstall, among others, had treated peace and warfare through a visual language that amplified their consequences in his speech on the occasion of the engagement of Francis I's son (also Francis) to Henry VIII's daughter Mary.[167] In creating a visual presence, *Deregni adminstratione, concordia* aspired to make individual readers, regardless of their positions within the existing hierarchy, reflect on the causes and consequences of their own actions.

Yet *De concordia* did not merely argue that social concord was the result of a sequence of transformative experiences on the individual level but that the cultivation of one's character itself was tied together with social life. Unlike in contemplative monastic traditions, in Vives and Erasmian humanism more broadly, the philosophy of self-government was meant for a broad lay population whose life was deeply embedded in social and political circumstances. Naturally, the very fact that works such as *Introductio ad Sapientiam* and its counterpart *Satellitium animi* (1524) were written for school purposes testifies to how self-government was forged in the classroom.[168] But more importantly, *De concordia* sustained that economic circumstances, peace, and right material conditions were not just signs of self-government but an important context for self-cultivation.[169]

Vives, in *De concordia*, wrote about those who 'sustained themselves through manual labour', but were forced to dedicate themselves to 'robbery' (*latrocinium*) against their natural *ingenium*.[170] In emphasizing economic and material conditions, *De concordia* could draw from a broader interest in these issues. The idea that individual character, the spring of actions, was greatly shaped by politics had been a main thesis in Thomas More's *Utopia*, where Raphael Hythloday defended it fiercely. In a famous passage, Hythloday argued that the enclosure of common land and other erroneous political and legal measures had driven many to poverty and theft, which meant that a merely legal response to their crimes would be like punishing those who you let 'to be badly brought up' and whose characters you allowed to become corrupt.[171] Likewise, Vives's earlier and more famous *De subventione pauperum*, in its call for a communal welfare system for Bruges, had established a close link between economic and social circumstances and character cultivation. In a broad interpretation of the Greek word *eleemosune* (alms), *De subventione pauperum* claimed that all acts that enhanced the virtue of citizens/subjects were acts of virtue and mercy on the part of the city fathers. He maintained that 'whoever therefore needs the help of other people, is poor and in need of compassion [...], which does not only consist of money, as the multitude believes, but in all actions which alleviate human needs'.[172] One could indeed help with 'prayers, advise, prudence, precepts for life [...] words, strength, effort, care [...] dignity, authority, favour, friendships, money'.[173] Vives thus maintained that poverty was the consequence of erroneous policies rather than bad individual choices and that concord, both individually and socially, was largely dependent on the reform of circumstances that nurtured exclusion and discord.

Equally as importantly, Vives thought that individual judgments were closely related to the ways in which assessments were embedded in the culture surrounding us (e.g. educational patterns, books, modality of discussion, material culture). Because of this, a major thread of *De concordia* was to explain how discord had corrupted the collective signs of sociability such as language and images (collective memory) that should enhance concord. As he wrote in Book Two, 'everything ought to serve discord [...] we turn speech, and tears, and friendship – which God's generosity gave us for mutual help – to our mutual destruction'.[174] Again, he was not alone. This had been absolutely central in the *Institutio principis Christiani* in which Erasmus had described at length the significance of the material culture and honorific titles surrounding the monarch, discussing the flattery of portraits, statues, and inscriptions, and providing examples of how to portray a ruler engaged in state business rather than in leisure pursuits or as a figure of military power. Honorific names were also depicted as an opportunity for reflecting on the duties of good government.[175]

Vives also described how emotional interpretations of individual events were socialised and turned into the collective memory of families, neighbourhoods, and political communities. In Book One of *De concordia*, he complained that in order to celebrate warmongers, 'poems and histories were written, arches erected, statues with beautiful inscriptions were mounted in the most frequented places of towns'.[176] He continued by declaring that if these criminal acts had not been rewarded in this way, 'perhaps we would have had less belligerent princes', and that in recent times 'admiration for the deeds of Alexander the Great drove Charles of Burgundy [1433–1477] to become involved in wars in which he himself perished and which put the whole of Belgium in extreme danger'.[177] In Book Three, he elaborated on the theme. He complained that, in wars, both sides 'erect trophies against the other' and wrote that signs of victory tended to 'incite souls of both parties' and to aggravate enmities.[178] This quasi-sociological element implied that any attempt to build a society of concord would have to go through a renewal of the material and rhetorical culture that currently sustained the discord of individuals and habituated them to it.

There were naturally specific themes and targets that were singled out in *De concordia*. Its depiction of military glory was a far-reaching critique of very concrete cultural practices, the clearest example of which was the strong chivalric *ethos* of Burgundy that idolised warfare and that had attracted Charles in his youth.[179] Vives also denounced the growing aesthetic culture of luxury and ostentation of the nobles and the commercial elite, the public, rhetorical discord of the learned circles that contributed to social and religious tumult, and lawyers and counsellors for justifying and legitimizing warfare.[180]

But, as argued, these complaints were grounded in a more ambitious interpretation on the role of culture in the habituation of passions that sustained discord. This framework helps us to comprehend better Vives's publications of the 1530s, most of which were started in the 1520s, as an essential contribution to the possibilities of concord. The pedagogical treatise *De disciplinis* can be seen as an attempt to purify education, and *De ratione dicendi*, on rhetoric, made a plea for a rhetoric of *decorum* that would contribute to social concord by hiding open confrontation. Finally, *De anima*, on the soul and emotions, was meant to ground Aristotelian moral philosophy (ethics, politics, and economics) and rhetoric in knowledge of the soul. They continued a trend, already apparent in *De concordia*, of analysing the consequences of the passions, led by pride, which had burst onto the scene at the Fall. In this project, concord was not predicated on a return to a pre-lapsarian state but rather on the ability of humans to come to grips and to live with the impulses that were natural to them in their current state. In this picture, *De concordia*, and Vives's later works, defended reform in education, morals, and manners within the existing institutional setting as a way to achieve the only concord available for humankind. This concord could be a preparation – or a way of asking – for the true concord that could come about only through Divine grace, but it had to be grounded on post-lapsarian realities.

This was indicative of a marked trend within Vives's political reflections in the 1520s and 1530s to condemn the attempts of Radical reformers to base political associations on mere spirit and spontaneous charity. When, in the mid-1520s, in the aftermath of the Peasant Revolt, the followers of Thomas Müntzer (c.1489–1525) and other pamphleteers had turned the Christian plea for spirituality and equality into a defiance of the existing secular order, Vives argued that this was to use the Bible for political ends, a way 'to assure the Gospel with three hundred thousand soldiers, destroying everything, and sowing calamity and death wherever they enter'.[181] Similarly, when a radical Anabaptist sect tried to turn the city of Münster into a new Jerusalem in 1534–1535, Vives was quick to condemn this in his *De communione rerum* (1535) as part of a wider reaction within Catholic and Protestant circles against the events.[182] He claimed that their violence was a result of a divergence of opinions and a questioning of age-old truths, that the Anabaptists turned the personal imperative of giving based on charity (*caritas*) into the violent appropriation of others' possessions, and that a spiritual and communal way of living was only possible when the blood of Christ had still reigned in the hearts of true Christians.[183] As a cure for a social body ruled by the most powerful and not by the best, Vives recommended a mixture of tolerance and punishment. Whereas most of the followers were ignorant victims of a hoax, which a Christian flock could be protected against through education and rhetoric, the leaders should be severely punished.[184] What he proposed as a solution to a particular case in *De communione* was given a wider application in the 1531 *De disciplinis*, in which Vives argued that, in the absence of love as the glue of a political community (*civitas*), justice, strengthened with power and force, had to take its place.[185]

The call for punitive measures and the stress put on obedience was, of course, not alien to Erasmian ways of thinking especially in the late 1520s and 1530s, when ecclesiastical and political discord was quite apparent. Still, while all explicit discord had to be avoided because it bred further discord, the theory of concord incorporated knowledge and practices through which it could be forged within the post-lapsarian reality. In the absence of a perfect Christian spirit, that was the only solution. In this post-lapsarian world, one of the most central issues was to the purification of language from its divisive elements, and it is to that question that we will turn in Chapters 4 and 5.

Notes

1. Budé's treatment of *epikeia* was very influential in the early sixteenth century; see Haas, 1997, 12–3, 36. Vives recognized his debt to Budé's text; see Vives, 1522, 52–3 (ii.xvii).
2. Vives, 1984b, 28: '*epikeia* [...] dicit non id ius esse [...] sed legis emendationem atque interpretationem'.
3. Aristotle, 1934, 313–7 (1137a–1138a).
4. Vives, 1984b, 28–9; Budé, 1508, fols. I^r–II^r.
5. For instance, in Bade's Latin edition of the *Nicomachean Ethics*, *epikeia* is translated with the word pair *aequitas* and *bonitas*: Aristotle, 1530, fols. lxxxix^r–xc^r. See Kelley, 1991, 77.

6. Cicero, 1960b, 396 (3.23); Watson, 1974, 173–4. For the differences between the Aristotelian *epikeia* and Roman *aequitas*, see Majeske, 2006, 3, 18–20.
7. Cicero, 1913, 34–5 (1.10.33); Majeske, 2006, 19–20; Vives, 1984b, 29.
8. Gerson, 1960–1973, 3:189 (*De vita spirituali animae*), 9:95–6 (*Regulae mandatorum*), 9:152–3 (*De quattuor virtutibus cardinalibus*); Thomas Aquinas, 1962, 2:546–8 (*Summa Theologiae* IIaIIae 120); Pascoe, 1973, 66–8; Haas, 1997, 17–31; Majeske, 2006, 20–7.
9. Vives, 1984b, 29: 'neque velit semper ius summum sequi, quae saepissime summa iniuria est, sed ipsi naturae normae (ad quam, ut dixisti, leges omnes conditae, directae ac formatae, sunt) sese accommodet'. Vives's introductory lecture to the *Laws* of Cicero expounds at length on the emanation of all positive law from natural law; see Vives, 1984a, 2–3.
10. Vives, 1522, 660 (xix.xxi); Vives, 2013, 252: 'sed fontem illum [*aequitas*] uberrimum non quiuerunt totum in tam angusti aluei limites corriuare: ex eo in ciuitatem deduxerunt quantum quidem uidebatur illi congregationi opus esse, easque leges nominarunt'. See also 251–2, 458–60.
11. Vives, 2013, 252: 'Aequitas uniuersalitas est quaedam, lex deductio et species'.
12. More, 1965, 90–4. More's views were most likely linked to the growing power of the Chancery court controlled by Lord Chancellors in practising equity in the English context; Majeske, 2006, 31–4. For equity in *Utopia*, see Karlin – Teti, 2017.
13. Portraying rulers first and foremost as judges was common in the Middle Ages; see Dumolyn, 2006, 7.
14. Already in Aristotle *epikeia* is described as an ethical disposition; Aristotle, 1934, 317 (1138a).
15. Budé, 1547, 85^v–87^r.
16. Erasmus, ASD IV/1, 194 (*Institutio principis Christiani*. CWE 27:264). See also 186, 202, 204, 212. For the proverb 'Summum ius, summa iniuria', see Erasmus, ASD II/2 (*Adagia*), 432–4.
17. Vives, 1984b, 29: '… legum viam, normam, rationem, legem, mentem, sensum, spiritum, animum, vitam'; '… cum non nisi magnorum maximeque praestantium ingeniorum sit illam iuris aequitatem invenire'.
18. Vives, 1984b, 39: 'atque hoc quidem est quod Aristoteles in libris de republica sentit, cum gubernari felicius ciuitatem ait ab optimo uiro, quam ab optima lege'.
19. Vives, 2013, 459; Vives, 1984b, 26; Mayans 5:310 (*De concordia*): 'Juris prudentia ex hac ipsa est disciplina [Moral philosophy] genita: ¿Quid aliud sunt jurisconsulti, quam (sicut Ulpianus ex Celso dicit) sacerdotes boni, aequi, antistites justitiae, praesides legum patroni juris?'
20. Coleman, 2006, 6–9.
21. Erasmus, ASD IV/1, 195–6 (*Institutio principis Christiani*. CWE 27:265). See also 164–5, 172, 196, 205.
22. Vives, 1984a, 2–4: '… vivere secundum naturam hominis …'.
23. Vives, 1984a, 6: 'perquirit siquidem naturalium cognitor rerum sitne lex secundum naturam: an loco temporique, an etiam universis quibus fertur satis congruat commodaque sit: an uni solum parti bona, reliquis veo iniqua sit; an obtineri possit quod iubet, quod vetat; quam utilis, quam necessaria, quam rebus praesentibus, quam futuris apta atque conveniens'. See also Vives, 1521, 93–4, 150.
24. Monzón i Arazo, 1992, 315–6.
25. Monzón i Arazo, 1992, 308–9. Vives's criticism of Roman Law always concerned its interpretative tradition rather than Roman Law *per se*, which, interpreted simply and in the spirit of *epikeia*, provided the best written basis for a legal tradition; see Vives, 2013, 465.

26. Matheeussen, 1982, 97. On the historical background of the debates between jurists and moralists; see Coleman, 2011, 190
27. Vives, 1984b, 29: 'sunt enim innumerarum litium incitamenta et fomites, non solum orationatim ac dictionatim, sed syllabatim etiam litteratimque (ut quidam faciunt) persequi ac mordicus tenere leges velle'; Vives, 2013, 464–5. Law as discord and feud was contrasted to the simplicity of Ulpian's *epikeia* by other writers in Erasmian circles; see Pace, 1517, 48.
28. Vives, 1522, 660 (xix.xxi): 'Id esse ius quod ei qui plus potest utile est'; 'haud dubie tale est maxima ex parte ius, quo nunc in ciuitatibus utimur'. See also Vives, 1984b, 26: 'eae sunt aranei telulae, quae minutula irretiunt animalia, maioribus cedunt; neque vero iis solis, sed levibus quoque, cum maioribus libet'; Plato, 2013, 1:48–51, 68–73 (338c–339a, 343a–344c).
29. Vives, 1522, 244 (viii.ix): 'aequo & bono transigebantur res, non legum numero'.
30. Vives, 2013, 458–66.
31. Damen, 2003, 51–2, 4.297–8; Ridder-Symoens, 1981, 293–6; Ridder-Symoens, 1996.
32. For a history of the development of the civic culture of the Low Countries, see Koenigsberger, 2001; Van Gelderen, 1992, 13–30.
33. Dumolyn, 2006, 1–10; Vanderjagt, 1981, 45–74.
34. Erasmus made very similar points in *Institutio*; Erasmus, ASD IV/1 (*Institutio principis Christiani*), 203–4. For Erasmus and the culture of *consuetudo*, see Tracy, 1978; 1996, 94–7.
35. Vives, 2013, 253–4. He was also very harsh with the idea that the prince can do whatever pleases him (*principi licere quicquid libeat*). His description of the rise of political power in *De subventione pauperum*, destined for the city of Bruges, was even more critical of the emergence of the power of princes. Here the power of kings does not arise from their ethical qualities but is an outcome of their ambition; see Mayans 4:424 (*De subventione pauperum*).
36. Mayans 5:418 (*De pacificatione*): 'Regem, Principem, Magistratum elegit populus, ut adsit justitiae, ut patronus sit ac propugnator legum, ut vinculum concordiae civilis'. See also Vives, 1522 (iv.vi), 114.
37. The idea of the emperor as the ruler (*dominus*) of the whole world could be found in the medieval lawyer Bartolus, and it became increasingly dear to Charles's lawyers; see Galasso, 2001, 101.
38. Vives describes the defence of the universal power of the emperor by an incompetent French lawyer, Gallus Sulpitius, in a Louvain dispute; Ijsewijn, 1992–1995, 41:26–7 (Ep. 7, Vives to Cranevelt). Somewhat more vaguely, Vives writes satirically in another letter that Louvain is full of people who seem to know everything about war and peace; Ijsewijn, 1992–1995, 43:67 (Ep. 85, Vives to Cranevelt).
39. Vives, 1522, 172 (v.xxv): 'Stultum est affirmare imperatorem Romanum ius habere in totum orbem terrarum …'; 'Accenduntur principes istis fictitiis titulis, qui aliud nihil sunt, quam faces orbis terrarum, pestiisque totius generis humani'.
40. In Vives's *De disciplinis,* Erasmus's *Institutio principis Christiani* is one of the few contemporary works recommended; Vives, 2013, 458. See also Vives, 1989b, 94–5; Vives, 1527c, 56ʳ.
41. Erasmus, ASD IV/1 (*Institutio principis Christiani*), 150–64, esp. 152, 164.
42. Tracy, 1978, 125.
43. Erasmus, ASD IV/1 (*Institutio principis Christiani*), 163–4, 165–6, 167. For a particularly strong interpretation of Erasmus as an anti-monarchical thinker based on his *Adages*, see Mann Phillips, 1964, 109.
44. Erasmus, ASD IV/1, 162–3 (*Institutio principis Christiani*. CWE 27:231).

45. Erasmus, ASD IV/1, 166, 182–91 (*Institutio principis Christiani*).
46. Erasmus, ASD IV/1, 182, 213–9 (*Institutio principis Christiani*); Erasmus, ASD IV/2, 88 (*Querela pacis*).
47. Leites, 1988, 119–20; Stone, 2004; Jonsen – Toulmin, 1988, 88–142.
48. For the Italian background of this idea, see Hankins, 2019.
49. Erasmus made the link between warfare and taxation in *Institutio*; Erasmus, ASD IV/1 (*Institutio principis Christiani*), 184–5.
50. Tracy, 1990; 2002, 70–2; Cools, 2001, 317. On Erasmus and Geldenhouwer and the culture of joyous entries; see Vermeir, 2014.
51. Loades, 2001, 247–9; Koenigsberger, 2001, 93–122.
52. Gadoffre, 1997, 344–5.
53. Tracy, 1978, 49–51. The peace treaty of 1514 was between France and England. In 1516, Charles, as Count of Flanders, signed the Peace of Noyon with Francis I. In 1517, the Emperor Maximilian and Francis signed the Treaty of Brussels. In 1517, Vives was involved in the peace negotiations; see González González, 2008, 43. Flanders, in particular, had close ties with England, though this did not mean that they were anti-French – quite the contrary; Koenigsberger, 2001, 93–5.
54. The project was influenced by the currents of Erasmian thinking in the English court; Gwyn, 1990, 98–102; Adams, 1962, 160–1, 178.
55. Tracy, 1978, 49–69, 109–12, 1990, 1–89.
56. Knecht, 2001, 93–4, 117–28; Gwyn, 1990, 378.
57. Mayans 7:219 (Vives to Budé); Allen 6:260 (Ep. 1665, Vives to Erasmus); De Vocht, 1928, 458 (Ep. 167, Vives to Cranevelt), 315 (Ep. 115, More to Cranevelt), 355 (Ep. 130, Fevyn to Cranevelt).
58. Adams, 1962, 188–203; Curtis, 2008, 127–32. Vives also mentions others; De Vocht, 1928, 197–8 (Ep. 80, Vives to Cranevelt).
59. Curtis, 2008, 127–32.
60. De Vocht, 1928, 232–3 (Ep. 90, Vives to Cranevelt).
61. Curtis, 2008, 130–2; Adams, 1962, 270–2.
62. Bietenholz, 1985–1987, 2:42–3, 2:373–5, 3:384–6.
63. Martínez Millán, 2012, 111–2; *Querela pacis* was written at the request of Jean le Sauvage, Radice in CWE 27:290; Bietenholz, 1985–7, 2.326.
64. Martínez Millán, 2012, 121–4; Martínez Millán – Rivero Rodríguez, 2001, 131–44.
65. Bietenholz, 1985–7, 2.41–2, 2.158–9; De Vocht, 1928, 142 (Ep. 56, Vives to Cranevelt); Mayans 7:146–8 (two letters from Vives to Halewijn). While Vives knew Praet well and even dedicated his *De consultatione* to him, Praet did not agree with Vives on all political matters. In 1525, Praet supported an aggression against France, which was directly opposed to Vives's peaceful plans.
66. Mayans 4:420 (*De subventione pauperum*): '... meque pro cive ejus duco...'.
67. His trips to different courts could have practical purposes; we know that his sojourn in England had also a commercial dimension that was linked to the activities of his Bruges family. Noreña, 1970, 77, 94; De Vocht, 1934, 19.
68. Curtis, 2008, 114.
69. Martínez Millán, 1992, 11–24; Vermeir, 2009; Blockmans, 2002, 127–36; Richardson, 2002, 113–4; Martínez Millán, 2012, 109; Michon, 2011, 2012, 9–13.
70. Headley, 1983, 31, 38.
71. González González, 2008, 43–4.
72. For prince as an example, see Erasmus, ASD IV/1 (*Institutio principis Christiani*), 142, 150–2; De Bom, 2016, 115.
73. Vives, 1526c, XIII^r–XIIII^v: 'Sic Princeps affectus suos omnes in ciuitatem transfundit, & ad eius exemplum tota sese comparat multitudo. Quocirca illud est optimo Principi curandum, & in quae tantum nomen merito competat, vt

talem ipse se & publice, & privatim praebeat, quales velit subditos habere, positumque sese arbitretur in refertissimo theatro, ubi nullum eius factum, vel dictum occultum sit. Nec tenebrae, aut solitudo obstat, quominus in vulgus dimanet, quicquid agat'.
74. Allen 3:563–4 (Ep. 957, Erasmus to Croy. CWE 6:338).
75. Erasmus, ASD IV/1, 322 (*Lingua.* CWE 29:355).
76. Calero, 1999, 13–21. Karl Kohut agrees that peace as the main theme of both compendia, Kohut, 2014, 562.
77. Knecht, 2001, 125–8; Mallet – Shaw, 2012, 155.
78. Blockmans, 2002, 40.
79. Curtis, 2008, 130–1; De Vocht, 1928, 495 (Ep. 185, Vives to Cranevelt), 509 (Ep. 193, Vives to Cranevelt).
80. The original deliberative context of *De rege Galliae capto* to Henry VIII had likewise ceased to exist. The letter was composed directly after the news of the Battle of Pavia had reached England, and it argued that England should not take advantage of the situation. This had become irrelevant in autumn 1526 when Francis I was not only free but had already formed the League of Cognac.
81. Vives, 1526f, LXX^r, LXXII^r. John Longland was the Bishop of Lincoln, Henry's confessor and an influential figure at the Tudor court.
82. Allen 5:107–8 (Ep. 1304, Erasmus to Adrian).
83. Vives, 1526a, II^r: '... sola vita innocentissime acta ...'; 'superiorum Pontificum vita effecit, vt maximum in terris ornamentum ipse ornasse videaris'.
84. Vives, 1526a, III^{v-r}: 'Tum etiam datam tibi occasionem ostendendae, seu vt aptius dicam, exercendae probitatis, & prudentiae tuae'.
85. Vives, 1526a, IIII^r: 'Commovit anteacta vita tua hanc de futuris expectationem, vt intergum iam tibi non sit, aliter agere, quam quod omnes sperant, quam quod vniuersis consensus pro te publicus spopondit'.
86. Vives, 1526a, VIII^v–IX^v.
87. Vives, 1526a, VII^v–VII^r. Pope Alexander VI had served as an arbitrator in the disputes between Portugal and Spain in the 1490s on the division of new-found territories; see Hale, 1995, 131.
88. Vives, 1526a, V^r: 'nati, & educati inter regias opes, indulgentissima semper vsi fortuna, calamitates ciuium quia non intelligunt, rident. Ita pro nihilo habent propter suam vel rixulam, vel ambitionem, vel avariciam ...'.
89. Vives, 1526a, VII^v–VII^r: '... bellum hoc inter fratres, et quod plus est, initiatos eodem baptismate, iniquum, sceleratum esse, contra fas, contra pium ...'.
90. Vives, 1526c, XIII^r, XVI^v: 'Principibus laborandum [...] ut ipsi boni, suos quoque bonos faciant'.
91. Vives, 1526b.
92. Vives, 1526c, XVIII^r: '... [locus &] ludus sunt in militia domos diripere, fana spoliare, virgines rapere, solidas urbes atque oppida incendere ...'.
93. Vives, 1526c, XVIII^v.
94. Vives, 1526c, XXII^r, XX^r: 'Gentes omneis [...] a te expectare, ac prope suo iure exigere, vt qui pacis initia & spem mundo ostendisti, eam tu idem absoluas ...'; 'Quippe siue pictorem, siue pastorem, siue caligarium, siue fabrum, aut alium quaecumque nemo non tum ridet, tum etiam odit, qui explere munus suspectum non queat'.
95. Vives, 1526c, XX^v: 'Idcirco probum et quietum Principem iure haec omnia consequuntur, laus a litteratis, quam suum illi ocium debent, quo nomine clarissimus fuit Augustus Caesar concelebtarusque ab omni scriptorum genere, quibus ille festa pace toto orbe diffusa altissima fecerat ocia, nactusque est eam gloriam, quam est per gentes rarissima ...'.
96. Vives, 1526d, XXIII^r.

97. Vives, 1526d, XXVI^v–XXXIII^v.
98. For a particularly strong criticism of legal claims to specific geographical areas by Tiresias, see Vives, 1526d, XXXVIII^v: 'Nam ista vetera iura, quod aliud sunt, quam viviradices, unde alia ex aliis succrescunt bella …'.
99. Vives, 1526d, XXIX^v.
100. Vives, 1526d, XXX^r: 'sic vsv veniebat filiis meis colludentibus, nullus unquam faciebat iniuriam, accipiebat semper'.
101. Vives, 1526b. The idea of fortune as referring to outcomes that do not fall into the teleological design of the agent was theorized in Vives's commentaries on Augustine; Vives, 1522, 145–6 (v.i). It is worth mentioning that some of the same vocabulary is evoked in Vives's understanding of deliberative rhetoric that deals with future oriented choices. As he argues in his *De consultatione*, deliberation is never about necessities since there is no point of debating about something that is already settled; see Vives, 1536, 238.
102. Vives, 1526d, XXXI^r-XXXII^v: 'vtra pars facta est ditior, aut meliore est conditione?'; 'vtrique […] & socii eorum omnes exhausti, regna compilata, nobiltas fracta et accisa, florentes olim vrbes solo acquatae, agri exinaniti, deserti …'.
103. Vives, 1526d, XXXII^v: 'tunc Christiani orbis firmiores opes, copiae, vires, & Turcis impense formidabiles'.
104. Vives, 1526d, XLII^r: 'Paulum si reflarent venti & odia atque iras vestras in illum transferretis, agnosceretis illico Asianos animos'.
105. Vives, 1526d, XLIII^r-XLIIII^v: '… aut si regnum liberet augere, alienissimum potius & pietatis hostem bello impeterent, quam vicinum, sanguine et mysteriorum initiatione coniunctum'.
106. Margolin, 1982, 130–1; Calero, 1999, 14–5.
107. Zappala, 1991, 830. Zappala perhaps emphasizes the openness of Vives's understanding of the dialogue form too much. Instead, as part of the 1526 compendium, the dialogue is caught in a tension between a pacifist *ethos* and a call for a common defence against the Turks.
108. Vives, 1526d, XXXVIII^r: 'Si Europae Principes odio inter se caeci, discordia furentes arma a Christianis vellent in Turcam conuertere, omnia quae expetunt, prolixius assequerentur, & copiosius'. In its condemnation of military glory, it diverged from much of Italian *quattrocento* humanism, where it was regarded as a display of virtue. See for instance Vergerio, 2002, 66–9, 72.
109. Vives, 1536, 263: 'quid enim Europae optabilius, quam conuerti Principum eius arma in Asianos, a bellis intestinis?'.
110. Vives, 1526d, XLI^r.
111. Erasmus, ASD (*Dulce bellum inexpertis*), II/7, 38 (CWE 35:431).
112. For a call for conversion, see Mayans 5:390 (*De concordia*). See also Erasmus, LB V:140C (*Paraclesis*).
113. Erasmus, ASD (*Dulce bellum inexpertis*), II/7, 40.
114. Erasmus, ASD (*De bello turcico*), V/3, 78: 'His ita respondendum arbitror, nec mihi placere bellum adversus Turcas, nisi huc adigat ineuitabilis necessitas'. See Pippidi, 2013, 69–83.
115. Guy, 1972, 122. For a distinction between absolute pacifism within Christianity and Vives's attitude towards the Turks; see Calero, 1999, 44–8, Noreña, 1970, 225.
116. Mayans 5:454–7, 460 (*De conditione vitae sub turca*).
117. See Mayans 7:137 (Vives to the Lord of Praet); Mayans 7:140 (Vives to Honorato Juan); *Clarorum Hispanensium epistolae ineditae*, 1901, 253: 'Is [Charles] de te praedicatione mea magnifice sentit'.
118. De Vocht, 1928, 533 (Ep. 202, Vives to Cranevelt), 567–8 (Ep. 217, Vives to Cranevelt).

134 *Managing discord*

119. Menéndez Pidal, 1946, 10–25; Brandi, 1959, 74–8; Blockmans, 2001, 179–89; García Cárcel, 2003, 31–3; D'Amico, 2010, 73–4, 83–94.
120. Martínez Millán – Rivero Rodríguez, 2001; Headley, 2001.
121. Allen 6:420–1 (Ep. 1757, Gattinara to Erasmus); Allen 6:470–1 (Ep. 1790a, Gattinara to Erasmus). For imperial propaganda, see Rummel, 1997; Headley, 1983.
122. Gattinara's autobiography mixes legal, dynastic, and universal notions of monarchy in many places. What is more, he discusses their importance in the context of legitimating specific actions, as in the case of the appropriate reaction in the aftermath of the Sack of Rome; see Gattinara, 1991, 164–5.
123. Noreña, 1970, 146; George, 1997, 254.
124. Martínez Millán – Rivero Rodríguez, 2001, 135–44.
125. Mayans 5:188 (*De concordia*): 'Conspirarunt tot Reges ac nationes, coierunt metuendam societatem potentiae, conflarunt foedus grandibus verbis, et horribilibus conditionibus, iis qui eo foedere non comprehenderentur'.
126. Mayans 5:188 (*De concordia*): 'hos tantos, tamque admirandos successus, non humanarum esse virium, sed divinarum ...'.
127. Mayans 5:189 (*De concordia*); Valdés, 1956, 14–5. For the differences between Vives and Valdés, see Fernández-Santamaría, 1977, 38–57. Other works that drew on the idea of universal monarchy included Miguel de Ulzurrun's's *Catholicum opus imperial regiminis mundi* and Pedro Mexía's much later *Historia imperial y cesárea*.
128. Mayans 5:188 (*De concordia*); Gattinara, 1991, 120–6, 171–7.
129. Mayans 5:189 (*De concordia*): 'ab incognita virtute nihil velut debitum reposcimus, a cognita omnia'.
130. Mayans 5:189, 191–2 (*De concordia*).
131. Mayans 5:264 (*De concordia*): 'habent hodie duo Principes quod ante centum annos habuerunt viginti ...'; 'non aedificant, immo diruunt; non locupletant sodalitia, immo spoliant; alunt paucos et magna ex parte inutiles, ne quid dicam pejus; ab omnibus auferunt, nemini dant, nisi maligne ac sordide'.
132. Erasmus, ASD IV/2 (*Querela Pacis*), 61–6.
133. Mayans 5:201 (*De concordia*): 'Expositus est nobis homo a natura ipsa, id est a Deo, rerum omnium parente ac principe factus, instructus, ornatus, appositus ac pacem, quietem, concordiam, amorem, amicitiam, ad ea ipsa edoctus a filio Dei, et Deo ipso'.
134. Mayans 5:196–201 (*De concordia*).
135. Mayans 5:201 (*De concordia*): 'unde ergo tantum per universum hominum genus dissidiorum, tantum discordiarum, inimicitiarum, odiorum ...'.
136. Erasmus, ASD IV/2 (*Querela pacis*), 64: 'Tot argumentis natura docuit pacem concordiamque ...'.
137. Mayans 5:196, 204–5, 208–9 (*De concordia*).
138. Erasmus, ASD IV/2 (*Querela pacis*), passim., especially 82–8.
139. Augustine, 1522, 429–30 (xiiii.xiii).
140. Aquinas, 1962, 2:711 (*Summa Theologiae* IIaIIae 162.8). Thomas also claimed that pride was man's first sin; Aquinas, 1962, 2:712–3 (*Summa Theologiae* IIaIIae 163.1); Vives, 1522, 366 (xii.vi).
141. Mayans 5:204 (*De concordia*): 'impetit superbia duobus jaculis invidia et ira [...] utraque et invidentia et ira voluntate malefaciendi est armata'. See also 229–30.
142. Mayans 5:227 (*De concordia*).
143. Mayans 5:331 (*De concordia*): 'piratas et latrones [...] tamen inter se pacem quandam et concordiam conservant ...'.
144. Both employ the term *latrocinia* or *latrocinii societas*; Augustine, 1522, 112–3 (iiii.iiii); Mayans 5:331 (*De concordia*).

145. Augustine, 1522, 57–9 (ii.xxi), 659–60 (xix.xxi). In his commentaries, Vives presented his interpretation of law as participation in Stoic-Christian natural law; Vives, 1522, 660 (xix.xxi).
146. Augustine, 1522, 649–57 (xix.xi–xix.xvii), 659 (xix.xx). For Augustine and politics, see Weithman, 2001, 237–40.
147. Luther, 1980, 126–37, 164–8.
148. Luther, 1966, 87, 105.
149. Luther, 1966, 89–92. Luther did not represent all mainstream Reformed though. Some, most notably Zwingli, stressed more the positive effects of secular government for religious renewal; Baylor, 2011, 236.
150. Luther, 1908, 661–4; Erasmus, LB IX:1220F–1221A (*De libero arbitrio*).
151. Luther, 1908, 753–4, 771–2, 786.
152. Erasmus, LB IX:1222F (*De libero arbitrio*. CWE 76:27).
153. Erasmus, LB IX:1223D–1224B (*De libero arbitrio*. CWE 76:31–2).
154. Vives, 1522, 155 (v.ix): 'Creauit deus uoluntates nostras liberas, quae ideo liberae sunt, quia ille uoluit, & utrumlibet possunt facere ex contrariis [...] Certum est enim fieri pleraque posse, quae nunquam fient ...'.
155. Vives, 1522, 157 (v.x): 'Quid erat tricis illis & uerborum laqueis opus, nisi simpliciter loqui, ut hic Augustinus non ideo peccare hominem, quod deus praesciuit eum peccaturum, qui si nolit potest omnino non peccare, idque si faciat, hoc praesciuit deus ...'.
156. Vives, 1522, 145–6 (v.i), 157 (v.x): 'Nos uero, & bonis paratum praemium parata merito est laus, malis vituperium, poenaque quod libera uoluntate & ille bene fecit, & hic male, idque spectante deo non cogente'.
157. Noreña, 1989, 48–9.
158. This is one of the main arguments of Fernández-Santamaría, see especially Fernández-Santamaría, 1998, viii–ix. His interpretation has been criticized for turning Vives into a Pelagian and forgetting the role of grace; see Pabel, 1999, 488; George, 1999, 1158. Despite this, Fernández-Santamaría captures the optimistic implications of Vives's framework for social thinking more clearly than his predecessors.
159. Mayans 5:377 (*De concordia*): 'Profecto homini, hoc rerum statu, sine divina ope impossibilis est'.
160. De Vocht, 1928, 680, (Ep. 266, Vives to Cranevelt): 'Sine pace Christi nihil erit satis pacatum; et hac sumus indignj!'. See also 673 (Ep. 261, Vives to Cranevelt), Allen 7:513 (Ep. 2061, Vives to Erasmus); Mayans 7:150 (Vives to Vergara).
161. Mayans 5:338 (*De concordia*).
162. This is the main point of Book Four; see esp. Mayans 5:338, 391 (*De concordia*).
163. Vives, 1527a, 2^r–3^v (1–11), 11^r–12^v (208).
164. An example of this tradition is Vives's own compilation of texts which included *Sacrum diurnum de sudore*; *Jesu Christi, concio de nostro & Christi sudore*; *Meditatio de passione Christi in psalmum XXXVII* (1529).
165. Mayans 5:321 (*De concordia*): 'ex discordia relinquuntur dispersi ac dispalati homines, pleni terrore ac formidine, nulli se loco, nulli hominum credentes, ut pes ab spina recens laesus vestigium secure non figit, dissipati conventus et congregationes sublatis legibus, rupto concordiae foedere; aedificia, villae, urbes dirutae, quidquid solo affixum erat evulsum, fames, pestis, inopia rerum omnium, imperitia, inertia, pessimi mores, et ex militibus exauctoratis, peritissimi ac strenui latrones'.
166. For an in-depth rhetorical analysis of *De conditione*, see George, 2014.
167. Tunstall, 1519, 15–6. See also Curtis, 2008, 118–23; Curtis, 2011, 32.
168. González González, 2007, 70–1.
169. This dimension is emphasized in Dust, 1987, 10–1, 180,
170. Mayans 5:263 (*De concordia*): '... qui se manuum labore sustentabant ...'.

136 *Managing discord*

171. More, 1965, 64–71. See also Vives, 1526c, XVIII[r]–XIX[v]. The link between English humanism and Vives on poverty was underlined already by Noreña; see Noreña, 1970, 96.
172. Mayans 4:426 (*De subventione pauperum*): 'quisquis ergo aliena ope indiget, pauper est, et ei misericordia est opus, quae Graece eleemosina dicitur, non in sola pecuniae erogatione sita, ut vulgus putat, sed in omni opere, quo humana indigentia sublevatur'. Fantazzi has also stressed this; see Fantazzi, 2008, 97–8. For analysis of the work, see especially Matheeussen, 1986; 1993; 1998, Fantazzi, 2008.
173. Mayans 4:430 (*De subventione pauperum*): 'benefaciendum [...] votis, consilio, prudentia, praeceptis vitae [...] verbis, viribus, labore, procuratione [...] dignitate, auctoritate, gratia, amicitiis, pecuniae'.
174. Mayans 5:235 (*De concordia*): 'omnia oportet discordiae servire [...] sermonem, et lacrimas, et amicitias, quas ad mutuum auxilium ex Dei munificentia acceperamus, in mutuam perniciem convertimus …'.
175. Erasmus, ASD IV/1 (*Institutio principis Christiani*), 177–8. For the importance of social custom for error in Erasmus and More, see Baker-Smith, 2009, 168–9.
176. Mayans 5:214 (*De concordia*): '… poëmata, et historiae consriptae, erecti arcus, positae statuae in celeberrimis urbium locis cum praeclaris inscriptionibus …'.
177. Mayans 5:214–5 (*De concordia*), 'Quod si rei omnium scelestissimae non tanta fuisset merces proposita, minus fortasse habuissemus Principes bellaces'; 'nuper Carolum Burgundiae ducem admiratio gestorum Alexandri coegit iis se bellis intricare, in quibus ipse periit, et in extremum discrimen universam Belgicam adduxit …'.
178. Mayans 5:288 (*De concordia*): 'Utrique se non raro pro victoribus habent, et gerunt, et trophaea in sua quisque regione de altero statuit, ut bellis Peloponnesiacis Athenienses et Lacedaemonii; quae signa victoriae, ad diuturnitatem impressa, dici non potest quantum incitant utrorumque animos, et veteres jam ac prope obliteratas inimicitias revocant et exacerbant, unde multa et olim nuper ea sola de causa reparata esse bella novimus …'.
179. Blockmans, 2002, 14–6.
180. Mayans 5:205, 246–54, 310, 313 (*De concordia*).
181. De Vocht, 1928, 434 (Ep. 157, Vives to Cranevelt): 'Hoc demum est asserere Evangelium, trecentis milibus armatorum militum late omnia popularj, & quacumque ingrediantur, clades ac strages dare!'. The condemnation of the Peasant Revolt among the learned elite was almost unanimous irrespective of their religious alignment. Luther himself was a fierce critic of the radical Reformation; see Hillerbrand, 2007, 145–6.
182. Vives may have reacted because the events in Münster were connected to social disorder radiating from the Anabaptist sect in the Low Countries. See Hillebrand, 2007, 119–23; Duke, 1990; 58–9, 85–8; Tracy, 1990, 160–70; Stayer, 1991, 123–38.
183. Mayans 5:465, 468–9, 471 (*De communione rerum*).
184. Mayans 5:466–7 (*De communione rerum*).
185. Vives, 2013, 456: 'Verum ubi charitas abest, iustitiae officium in eius locum succedit, non illius blandae ac inermis, sed armatae potestate ac uiribus, quae fraenos concitationi animorum iniiciat'. In the Low Countries, this was precisely what many town fathers had not done. Only in 1535 did harsh measures begin to be taken against the strong Anabaptist community in some Dutch towns. Duke, 1990, 88, 106.

4 Redefining Rhetoric in *De disciplinis* (1530–1531)

The Background of *De disciplinis*

Vives's most important contribution to education and pedagogy, *De disciplinis*, appeared in 1531. *De disciplinis* was perhaps his most ambitious treatise, yet it seemed like the work of a solitary figure in comparison to his publications at the turn of the 1520s which were framed as Erasmian interventions. Gone are laudatory introductions from other humanists, gone are eulogies from the printer, and gone are promotional campaigns undertaken in other humanist works. Traditionally, as in Noreña's classic study, the 1530s have been seen as a moment of almost complete isolation not only from the activities of the Republic of Letters but also from the world of politics.[1] Recently, new findings have somewhat altered the traditional interpretation and we now know that Vives continued to be in touch with the imperial court; in 1531 he was granted a pension by Charles V, to whom he had dedicated his *De concordia*, and, throughout the 1530s he wrote to the emperor on themes such as the education of young Prince Philip.[2]

Despite this, *De disciplinis* appeared at a moment of certain disillusionment. Vives's career in day-to-day politics was largely over and there were few traces of optimism concerning the holders of powerful *officia* of the time in his works of the 1530s. Despite the Peace Treaty of Cambrai in 1529 between Charles and Francis and the conciliatory attempts in ecclesiastical issues at the Diet of Augsburg in 1530, Vives's 1530s *oeuvre* did not display belief in European secular and religious rulers bringing about lasting political or ecclesiastical concord. Simultaneously with his personal experiences, the optimism of the Northern humanist movement about cultivating spiritual and political renewal personified in Erasmus had suffered severe blows, not only because of the persistence of political and religious discord but also because of the growing dominance of Reformed materials and pamphlets in the public discussion. In this climate, the dissolution of the Erasmian Republic of Letters as a public project was becoming ever more evident, with the protagonists of the movement taking differing paths. Erasmus's struggle with Catholic and Reformed theologians and his call for tolerance as the only possible solution to religious dissent was in stark

DOI: 10.4324/9781003240457-5

contrast to the violent anti-Protestant policy in England of More (who became the Lord Chancellor in 1529) in the name of the consensus of all Christians represented by the Catholic Church.[3] Vives, whose relationship with Erasmus remained distant, dedicated the 1530s to the publication of extensive treatises concerning education (*De disciplinis*), rhetoric (*De ratione dicendi, De conscribendis epistolis*), and the soul (*De anima*), removed from day-to-day politics.

Even though *De disciplinis* appeared in 1531, it was the product of a longer project, which had most likely started at least in the mid-1520s.[4] Unlike many pedagogical texts of the time, *De disciplinis* was not connected to a project of reforming an old institution or establishing a new one. Rather than presenting a simple programme of study, Vives framed it as an encyclopaedic treatment that drew on and combined different genres of writing.[5] What the reader finds in *De disciplinis* is a critical assessment of the corruption of all arts (*De causis corruptarum artium*), a constructive proposal for the teaching of arts that assesses exercises, literature, placement of schools, relevance of knowledge, and a number of thematic questions (*De tradendis disciplinis*), and, finally, a treatment of metaphysics and dialectic that puts forward a humanist alternative to or reading of Aristotle's *Organon* in Eight separate books.[6]

While the prominent place of *De disciplinis* within humanist theories of education is a commonplace, its importance within Vives's work and the broader humanist tradition remains somewhat open. Since the nineteenth century, the treatise has frequently been described, sometimes in exalted tones, as a foundational work of modern pedagogy, but these interpretations, often focusing on how it anticipated specific traits of modernity, have hardly ever aimed at historical precision.[7] In a reassessment of a broad historiography that has understood *De disciplinis* primarily as a pedagogical work, Valerio Del Nero has more recently interpreted it as a significant humanist attempt to ground pedagogy in a philosophy of language that, unlike the formalism of the Middle Ages, underscored the historical, contextual, and inventive nature of speech.[8] In a more explicit attempt to interpret *De disciplinis* as the culmination of Vives's social and political philosophy outlined in *De concordia*, Fernández-Santamaría has depicted the work as the realization of humanity's journey to earthly and social *bonitas*. In his view, *De disciplinis* bridged the gap between man's capacity for the *ars vivendi*, based on the natural ability of all humans to recognize good (*synderesis*), and a social world of happiness realized through the precepts of expedient arts.[9]

What both interpretations share with a long tradition of Vives scholarship is an understanding of *De disciplinis* as a constructive and relatively optimistic humanist alternative to what can be broadly described as the scholastic culture.[10] No doubt one of the principal objects of censure in *De disciplinis* was the tradition of late-medieval learning, which was criticized for its method, contemplative aspirations, excessive focus on disputations, and a number of other issues. But Vives was equally clear that classical and humanist knowledge too had to be subjected to critical judgment, since arts and sciences had never been perfect in a post-lapsarian world. As István Bejczy has argued, the historical narrative Vives was trying to convey to the reader was not about the one-dimensional corruption of a perfect classical antiquity; rather, he emphasized that the seeds of corruption had been there in all post-lapsarian human history.[11]

This was more than an empty programmatic statement since Vives effectively engaged in a critique of classical and humanist learning throughout the work. Interestingly, although much of the discussion was driven by an urge to harmonize classical learning and piety, so dear to Northern humanists, many of his points mirrored only in part the tension between Christianity and paganism.[12] Vives's treatment of rhetoric and the *trivium* was indicative of this since he did not primarily attempt to appropriate classical rhetoric into a Christian context as Erasmus would do in his 1535 *Ecclesiastes*, dedicated to the art of preaching. Rather, Vives, who had very little to say about preaching or a distinctly Christian rhetoric, adjusted adversarial classical rhetoric in *De disciplinis* and other 1530s works into new, often asymmetrical and literary contexts, in which overtly adversarial tactics should be repressed. While in this process the suppression of emotion enhanced one's self-control, so important for a pious Christian speaker (the speaker and the audience were not overwhelmed by harmful passions), and served as a remedy against the vices of the tongue such as loquacity, Vives, at the same time, depicted the conditions in which rhetoric could regain its power to move and persuade in a variety of practical environments which were only indirectly linked to Christian piety (e.g. the court, counsel, letter writing).

In this chapter, I intend to explain what forms this redefinition took in different parts of *De disciplinis*, which have usually been analysed as separate, largely unrelated discussions. More specifically, I show that Vives's treatment of the history, teaching, and the technical side of rhetoric were intrinsically linked to the same problem of re-evaluating the place of rhetoric in a Christian and monarchic world in which some post-lapsarian limitations had to be taken seriously. Indeed, both the description of the corruption of arts (*De causis*) and the constructive proposal of *De tradendis* contributed to this project since they spelled out problems inherent in adversarial rhetorical culture, redefined the proper scope of rhetoric, and reassessed the place of rhetoric in the educational path. The main argument of this chapter is that throughout these interventions, Vives wanted to accentuate the role of rhetoric as the glue of political and religious communities, while simultaneously reminding his readers that open verbal confrontation, rather than enabling political and ecclesiastical concord, posed a serious threat to harmonious collective life.

The History of Rhetoric

Vives's account of the history of rhetoric drew on the conceptual framework that he used in his analysis of the universal history of arts and disciplines in the opening section of the Book One. Indeed, already this general treatment of the arts amply confirmed the critical element of the work, which aspired to purify the inherited tradition within which the culture of his time had to operate. The historical analysis was focused on the extent to which natural human talent or force of mind (*ingenium*) had, with the help of diligence (*diligentia*), been able to overcome its limitations and to bring about advancement in arts and disciplines.[13] *Ingenium* and *diligentia* were familiar from the analysis of the talent of individual students in classical and humanist educational literature, but here Vives employed them in a much broader sense to investigate the collective history of arts and disciplines.[14] While there was an optimistic undertone about the possibilities of *ingenium* to cater for human necessities and intellectual needs, Vives's description of *ingenium* was ambivalent since, according to him, from *ingenium* 'were born all human inventions, both expedient and harmful, good and bad'.[15] This ambivalence was due to the fact that *ingenium* operated in a post-lapsarian world, so its powers were tainted by corruption. Moreover, diligence (*diligentia*), which motivated and directed *ingenium*, was not only driven by necessity (*necessitas*), enjoyment (*delectatio*), and the admiration of the magnitude and beauty of things, but also by 'some desire of honour and money', which, for Vives, were part of the post-lapsarian reality.[16]

In his depiction of how arts and disciplines answered the necessities of the body and, in a later stage, of the soul (wisdom), Vives frequently pointed out the ability of honour to motivate *ingenium* in its investigative endeavours. Ultimately, in discussing the reasons why the arts had never in their entire history reached perfection, Vives argued that this was mainly due to 'the blindness and weakness of the arrogant soul', which was conceptually associated with a desire for glory and honour.[17] Thus, although the reader was told that the respective ends of the different arts were brought together in a union with God, which gave them an ontological and providential design, the arts had always fallen short of their true *telos* since in the post-lapsarian state they had been motivated by precisely those passions that could blind human judgment.[18] Furthermore, there was no promise of overcoming these post-lapsarian limitations. Vives predicted instead that there would only be a constant struggle for betterment: 'All this progress has been achieved with the force of arms against the current of a river as it were, and as soon as the arms began to lose their force, the arts fell back into their earlier state'.[19]

The same forces were also operative in the evolution of particular arts. Vives's history of the corruption of rhetoric was an example of how these motivating principles were put into play in a way that distinguished his narrative from the more laudatory accounts of classical rhetoric typical of the time and exemplified, for instance, by Johannes Sturm's *De amissa dicendi ratione* (1539). While Sturm did not put forward a history of rhetoric, he lamented the deformation and corruption of Roman rhetoric and yearned for men who would 'show us the structure and method in learning that would be most like the art of the ancient Romans and Greeks'.[20] For Vives, regaining the rhetorical tradition was appropriating it since the classical tradition had serious problems. As in his other texts, Vives began by reminding the reader that 'there are two things that above all bind and keep human associations together: justice and language'.[21] Drawing on classical works such as Cicero's *Brutus*, he outlined a history of rhetoric that started with a depiction of how the art of eloquence was born out of the necessity to regain property in Sicily.[22] From its forensic use, rhetoric was extended into politics so that 'just like it had moved judges, it would move the souls in popular assemblies, the senate in the curia, and finally all those who had influence in the Republic, in whose hands and control the faith of the whole city was placed'.[23]

Vives made it clear that, whereas in monarchies the tongues of orators were tied by fear, in free republics they enjoyed even greater power than those who were just. Especially in those republics in which one addressed 'a restless, ambitious mob, gifted with sharp *ingenium* and swelled with the aura of liberty' – such as Athens, Rhodes, Sicily, and Rome – 'the orator imposed his dominion'.[24] This rhetorical culture in which men eager for 'honours, riches, fortunes, dignity, and power' made use of rhetoric to speak to the people was, however, partly responsible for its decay since in republican contexts orators who wanted to receive praise for their speeches did not cultivate rhetoric with knowledge-based ends.[25] While Vives admitted that in the 'well-governed commonwealths' (*in bene constitutis civitatibus*) of Crete and Sparta, famous for their mixed constitutions, oratory did not become tyrannical, his description of republican rhetoric, driven by praise and power based on the judgment of the multitude, was thus a negative one. Republican regimes were the natural habitat of rhetoric and had produced great speakers, but these had ultimately contributed to the destabilization of the political community. Indeed, with some clear allusions to Tacitus, such as Vives's point about Sparta and Crete as well-governed commonwealths, the historical sketch had echoes of the *Dialogus de oratoribus*, in which Tacitus had argued that eloquence was 'a foster-child of licence, which foolish men called liberty, an associate of sedition, a goad for the unbridled populace'.[26]

Vives's description of the changes in rhetoric in later times was not, however, more positive. His intention here was to unite the decadence of rhetoric with a change in the political outlook of Rome, and not with the internal tensions of rhetoric in the flourishing republican context. The harmful effect of the empire on eloquence and the practice of oratory was already established in classical antiquity and amply presented in Italian humanist descriptions of the history of humanist eloquence.[27] In this spirit, Vives maintained that in the political environment of the imperial era, rhetoric degenerated in the forum, in the courtroom, and in the senate. In the senate, claimed Vives, 'opinions were not expressed freely as before, but in order to flatter established power, they were more eulogies of princes than deliberations on public good'.[28] In the same vein, rhetoric in other contexts evolved into mere amusement, and a new political situation brought with it a separation of rhetoric from its social and political role. The decline of rhetoric as a means to glory led to a simultaneous decline in the diligence that was put into its study: 'when all benefits were removed, they considered the dedication to effort worthless'.[29]

If the depiction of republican rhetoric, with its ability to incite emotion, was a negative one, these changes did not take rhetoric in the right direction either, as Vives's language clearly revealed. Mere amusement, for instance, was described as the ultimate flaw of rhetoric in the later *De ratione dicendi*, where he proposed, in referring to one of the three duties of an orator (*docere, delectare, movere*), that instead of delighting (*delectare*), one should talk about keeping people's attention (*detinere*).[30] What is more, in describing the move in deliberative rhetoric from considerations of public good to the flattery of existing power, Vives was using a language every reader of humanist texts would have recognized as a serious shortcoming.[31] Moreover, he linked the decline of oratory to the rise of specialists in law in political matters which, in Vives's *oeuvre*, appeared as a major contemporary concern.[32]

What was notable about Vives's account of the history of rhetoric in *De disciplinis* was that there was an almost exclusive focus on rhetoric as a civic practice, and that he did not claim that the problems of rhetoric were solved by Christian orators. Vives's short depiction of the birth of Christian rhetoric stressed that, although religious orators surpassed classical rhetoricians in their knowledge of things (*res*), 'we [Christian orators] are inferior in all parts of eloquence, the force of persuasion, maxims, arguments, the disposition of the speech, words, oratorical genres, delivery'.[33] The historical account was in accordance with the classical and civic flavour of his reassessment of the art of eloquence in other parts of *De disciplinis*.

The Criticism of Classical Rhetorical Theory

In the spirit of the motives of *De causis* to engage with the history of arts, the historical narrative was closely interwoven with a critical assessment of some classic ways of interpreting the relationship of rhetoric to philosophy, dialectic, and ethics. As Don Abbott argued already some time ago, *De causis* took for granted that classical rhetoric was tied together with specific political circumstances, which offered the possibility for a critical re-evaluation.[34] Indeed, the historical narrative effectively opened a space for a criticism of several issues that were built into the rhetorical tradition. Regarding ethics, Vives notably challenged Quintilian's famous definition of the orator as a 'good man skilled in speaking' (*vir bonus dicendi peritus*) and wrote that, in attempting to present Cicero and Demosthenes, the most revered orators, as good men, Quintilian not only failed to accomplish what he set out to do, but also sought 'to unite things that were by nature distinct' (rhetorical ability and moral goodness).[35] In fact, Quintilian's definition, originally attributed to Cato, had been wrongly interpreted to refer to the morally good man envisioned by Socrates and the Stoics, whereas in common usage, it merely referred to 'men who are not notorious for any infamous action'.[36] Vives's notion of the relationship of rhetoric to philosophy also challenged Quintilian. Vives wanted to prove that Quintilian's attempt to incorporate all knowledge, most notably moral and political philosophy, into the scope of rhetoric was an erroneous one. In different parts of his *Institutio*, Quintilian had contended that the subject matter of rhetoric potentially concerned all things and that ethics especially, wrongly reserved for philosophers, belonged to the orator.[37] Arguing against Quintilian and others who defended the omnipotence of rhetoric (such as Crassus in Cicero's *De oratore*), Vives maintained that, while a rhetorician could express things better, the authority in different arts belonged to specialists. As he instructed the reader, even Aristotle's *Rhetoric* introduced moral philosophy unsystematically and only in so far as it was useful for an orator who adjusted it to 'the capacities of the people'.[38] This point was also made with vigour in the description of the corruption of moral philosophy. Here Vives warned of those who took their understanding of virtue from rhetorical figures and sophisms and thought that what was 'beautifully' (*belle*) said was also 'well' (*bene*) said.[39]

This discussion was embedded in Vives's reassessment of the five parts of oratory: invention, disposition, style, delivery, and memory (*inventio, dispositio, elocutio, pronuciatio, memoria*). Mirroring his condemnation of the omnipotence of rhetoric, Vives claimed that invention belonged to each and every science in its proper subject matter and to dialectical procedures, not specifically to the orator.[40] Emphasizing prudence to the detriment of precepts in the accommodation of rhetorical invention to specific contexts, Vives equally denounced the very possibility of condensing rhetorical disposition to predetermined formulas. At the same time, the tradition of working through specific commonplaces (*ratiunculas*) designed for different legal cases or parts of the oration was likened to the wisdom and language of children, and described as an attempt to steer the immensity of an ocean into the narrow confines of a river.[41] With a focus on rhetoric that contained written expression, delivery was said to be an ornate addition to rhetoric instead of a part of it, and memory was described as an independent art that provided help for other arts and sciences.[42] Style, according to Vives, was a proper part of rhetoric, although it had been obscurely treated by the classical tradition. His critique of figures and tropes as a heterogeneous collection of expressions was coupled with the observation that the traditional division into three styles (*imus, summus, mediocris*) failed to capture the infinity not only of possible but also of actually employed stylistic variations.[43] A similar criticism was levelled at the conventional tripartite classification of rhetorical genres (judicial, deliberative, and demonstrative), which was based on 'use' or 'custom' (*consuetudo*) rather than 'the nature of the thing' (*rei natura*) and did not do justice to the presence of rhetoric in all human communication. This, Vives wrote, was partly because classical theorists such as Cicero and Quintilian, while aware of the possibility of a broader spectrum of genres, had thought that others could be 'derived' (*deriuari*) from these three. But it was equally related to the specific context within which classical orators earned the favour of the people.[44]

Vives's views on the relationship of rhetoric to philosophy and ethics, which were amplified throughout the chapter, were condensed into a brief discussion, drawn from Quintilian, on the proper definition of rhetoric. Although he did not come up with a definition of his own, he brushed aside those that linked it to ethics (rhetoric as virtue) or philosophy (rhetoric as wisdom, rhetoric as a science of things) and favoured a view of rhetoric as an art of words disconnected from s*cientia* and virtue. He equally agreed with Cicero's description of rhetoric as a power or force (*vis*) in *De oratore* but was less than satisfied with his other attempts in the same work to refer to it as a science that brings together the arts of thinking and speaking. As Vives maintained, Cicero 'mixes things that are absolutely separate and believes that thinking and speaking well belong to rhetoric. This is reasonable and I hope he would persuade people of it, but it is equally not true'.[45]

The Criticism of Contemporary Rhetorical Theory

Although the criticism was framed as a discussion with classical authorities, most notably Quintilian, the motive for Vives's reassessment of Roman and Greek precepts derived precisely from the authoritative position of classical writers within contemporary rhetorical theory. His critical examination of the tradition was thus simultaneously a dialogue with the rhetorical principles that were still dominant. To fully appreciate this aspect of *De disciplinis*, we need to make a little detour to the rhetorical theory of the time.

Not only did the *genera*, parts, and stylistic divisions inherited from the past form the basis of most manuals on rhetorical theory, but the humanist discourse on eloquence often continued to underline its union with ethics and philosophy. Quintilian's ethical definition of the orator, while often challenged in the late sixteenth century and effectively discarded by Petrus Ramus (1515–1572), was frequently echoed in rhetorical literature and in reflections on rhetoric.[46] We find it in Gregor Reisch's (c.1467–1525) encyclopaedic and often printed *Margarita Philosophica*, and Johannes Murmellius (c.1480–1517), in his *De artibus tum liberalibus tum mechanicis* (1510), presented Quintilian's definition, together with that of Socrates and a few others, as authoritative.[47] The most widely disseminated commentary apparatus around Quintilian's *Institutio oratoria* did little to challenge this view. Raphael Regius's (c.1440–1520) popular commentaries on the *Institutio oratoria*, printed by Bade in 1515, not only described Quintilian's perfect orator as an 'earthly God' but also emphasized that Virgil, in his call for a 'man honoured for noble character and service' (*pietate gravem ac meritis si forte virum*), confirmed this view.[48]

The idea that moral and political questions (*quaestiones civiles*) especially belonged to the subject matter of oratorical invention was frequently voiced in rhetorical manuals, as in Konrad Celtis's (1459–1508) *Epitome in rhetoricam Ciceronis* (1532).[49] In a more ambitious vein, Quintilian's idea of extending rhetoric into philosophy had already been welcomed by Italian *quattrocento* writers. In the context of his translation of Aristotle's *Nicomachean Ethics*, Leonardo Bruni (c.1370–1444) had debated with Alfonso de Cartagena (1384–1456) over the extent to which rhetoricians could treat the subject matter of specific arts and disciplines, which was linked to the relationship of dialectical and rhetorical principles in philosophical translation.[50] What is more, while there were attempts to promote reformed dialectic to the detriment of rhetoric in the invention of arguments, another strand subordinated dialectic to rhetoric.[51] The omnipotent nature of rhetoric was defended most famously in Lorenzo Valla's polemical *Repastinatio*, which claimed that dialectic, the traditional art of truth, was merely a part of rhetorical invention.[52] In Vives's *De disciplinis*, Valla was actually denounced, among other things, for his views on grammar (excessive admiration for Quintilian and Cicero) and dialectic, which, according to Vives, were mostly wrong.[53] One implication, already present in Quintilian, of the extension of rhetoric to dialectical invention and philosophy was that all studies could be subjected to the organizational structures and persuasive ends of oratory. Already in Italian educational handbooks, the acquisition of moral philosophy could be incorporated into a rhetorical framework which underscored its importance not primarily for the cultivation of character but for material abundance. In discussing oratorical training based on Cicero and Quintilian, Battista Guarino's *De ordine docendi et studendi*, well known to Vives, reminded the reader that one should also consult Cicero's other books which were 'full of moral philosophy [...] which for orators [...] is a vital subject'.[54]

An extensive and ethically optimistic understanding of rhetoric and rhetorical training was also built into the very self-interpretation of early sixteenth-century humanist culture. Unlike Vives, who was sceptical about the possibilities of turning rhetoric into a science, many works defined rhetoric as the science (*scientia*) of speaking well. This definition could be found as one possible option, for instance, in Johannes Murmellius's description of the liberal arts in *De artibus tum liberalibus tum mechanicis*.[55] But more importantly, not only was the link between humanist studies and the cultivation of morals (*mores*) based on a literary education within which rhetoric was central but rhetoric or eloquence was also elevated into its main component. Christoph Hegendorf (1500–1540), one of the most frequently printed writers on rhetoric and literary education in the early sixteenth century, underlined the significance of eloquence in the clearest of terms in his *De instituenda vita, et moribus corrigendis juventutis* (1529). In an exhortation to literary studies (*paraeneses*), Hegendorf promoted the study of eloquence, which, for him, was not merely a knowledge of words but an encyclopaedic knowledge of all things: 'when I say eloquence [...] I include in it the whole encyclopaedia, that is, the circle of all good arts'. Hegendorf, an admirer of Erasmus, further placed his identification of rhetoric with encyclopaedia in a tradition spearheaded by Quintilian and Erasmus, in which the organizing principles of rhetorical topics were a leading factor in the acquisition and classification of knowledge.[56]

The reference to Erasmus was not random since the Dutch humanist had stressed the union of eloquence, ethics, and wisdom in different ways. As seen, the Erasmian project of rhetorical theology was dependent on the close link between eloquence, the virtue of the speaker, and his/her acquisition of truth (Chapter 2). In his educational writings, Erasmus not only argued that eloquence and wisdom should ideally be united but also, since things and words were irreducibly bound together, that eloquence was practically inseparable from wisdom and knowledge. He could of course distinguish between knowledge of words (*verba*) and knowledge of things (*res*). Yet, in his criticism of the scholastic curriculum and its focus on dialectic, formulated in his *De ratione studii* and *De pueris instituendis* (*On Education for Children*, 1516), he repeatedly stated that the study of languages and linguistic expression was not merely an accessory to the knowledge of things but actually contributed to it. In *De ratione studii*, Erasmus reminded the reader that, while knowledge of things and words were separate issues, 'a person who is not skilled in the force of language is, of necessity, short-sighted, deluded, and unbalanced in his judgment of things as well'.[57] Moreover, his insistence that the wisdom of classical and Christian authors could only be captured through grammatical and rhetorical methods established a close relationship between the study of languages and rhetoric, on the one hand, and wisdom, on the other. In his *De pueris instituendis*, Erasmus maintained that 'neglect of language has certainly led to the decline and destruction of all sciences'.[58] Further emphasizing the contribution of liberal arts to the acquisition of eloquent wisdom, Erasmus depicted famous men who were 'distinguished [...] by both learning and eloquence' because 'they acquired [...] the art of refined speech and obtained [...] an excellent grounding in the liberal arts'.[59] This argument was further supported by a more practical attempt to ground the acquisition and communication of knowledge in rhetoric and grammar, the methods and topics of which became the main way to store and categorize knowledge.

We do find a similar claim that eloquence and wisdom were not only ideally linked to each other but that the study of rhetoric contributed to wisdom in other contemporary attempts to turn literary studies into the cornerstone of education. In *Encomium eloquentiae* (*The Praise of Eloquence*, 1523), Philipp Melanchthon (1497–1560), the father of Protestant humanist education and one of the authorities in rhetoric in *De disciplinis*, stressed the usefulness of speech in all human communication: in politics, business, and private matters.[60] Like Erasmus, Melanchthon argued that eloquence was not a superfluous cosmetic feature but instead an art that made truth apparent and without which we could not 'explain what we ourselves want, or understand correctly the extant writings of our ancestors'.[61] But even more importantly, Melanchthon wrote that 'by practicing those arts that compose eloquence, one's natural abilities are stimulated and developed, so that one comes to consider all human affairs with greater prudence'. With the clearest of tones, he argued that 'our ancestors saw that [...] the art of speaking well and the faculty of judgment, harmonized with each other by nature'.[62] He gave two reasons why prudential judgment was trained by the study of rhetoric: first, because it brought students in touch with writers who exhibited prudence and, second, because it made them think about what aspects of their writings they should admire and imitate.[63] Melanchthon also emphasized the significance of rhetorical studies for theology.

Thus, different writers whom Vives knew well and many of whom were cited as authoritative in *De disciplinis* had in manifold ways not only embraced Quintilian's definition of oratory as an ethical and encyclopaedic practice but, in promoting liberal studies, had often portrayed rhetoric as conducive to wisdom, prudence, and judgment. Therefore, in challenging Quintilian, Vives was struggling against an optimistic and all-encompassing understanding of rhetoric, conceived as an encyclopaedic art that introduced one to all knowledge through commonplaces, as the heart of the humanist *trivium*.

The Ambivalence of Rhetoric

Despite the predominantly optimistic view of rhetoric, some concerns about its destructive possibilities had been raised by numerous promoters of rhetorical education, including Erasmus and Melanchthon. Indeed, it seems clear that the traumatic experiences of the violent 1520s had raised awareness about the threat of uncontrolled rhetoric by the time of the composition of *De disciplinis*. Consequently, in analysing the widespread social tumult of the time, several writers connected religious and political division increasingly to the ability of rhetoric to divide humans.

The *vituperatio* of rhetoric's claims to morality, truth, and wisdom had been the bread and butter of all attacks on rhetoric since Plato's denunciation of the art of eloquence laid out most famously in the *Gorgias*. These attacks were well known to the humanist tradition in the form of Giovanni Pico's satirical letter to Ermolao Barbaro, and Cornelius Agrippa's (1486–1535) widely disseminated portrayal of rhetoric in *De incertitudine et vanitate scientiarum et artium* (1530), which largely echoed the traditional criticism of the art of eloquence. Agrippa wrote that rhetoric was 'nothing other than an art of flattery, adulation, and [...] lying' and that one had to resort to its deceitful speech only if the truth of one's case was not persuasive.[64] Agrippa further argued that rather than engendering prudence, rhetoric was extremely dangerous to political life 'since it produces prevaricators, shifty tricksters, perverts of the law, sycophants, and all kinds of men with wicked tongues'.[65] In a passage that resembled Vives's own youthful depiction of rhetoric as a form of cognitive power in his introductory lecture to the *Ad Herennium*, Agrippa explained how rhetoric, with its immense powers to persuade and move emotions, played a decisive role in political matters. But whereas Vives had used his description of the power of Cicero and Demosthenes as an exhortation to the study of rhetoric, Agrippa, for his part, warned against the ability of rhetoric to lead the audience 'into the prison of error while perverting the sense of truth'.[66]

Agrippa was quite an exceptional figure, but the overly optimistic depiction of rhetoric so typical of humanist texts in the 1510s and early 1520s was becoming more and more problematized even by two of the leading proponents of humanist studies: Erasmus and Melanchthon. Erasmus formulated his view on the disastrous possibilities of the vices of the tongue for all aspects of human life most clearly in his 1525 *Lingua*. He painted a highly ambivalent picture of the use of the tongue both as a 'deadly poison and life-giving remedy', and argued that 'nothing is more destructive than an evil tongue, and yet nothing is more healing if a man use it rightly'.[67] In the dedicatory letter, Erasmus further claimed that 'so great is the force of the onslaught that it threatens the total ruin and destruction of the liberal arts, good morals, civic harmony, and the authority of the leaders of the church and the princes of the realm alike'.[68]

These destructive possibilities were not primarily associated with the rigidity of scholastic language but rather with the excesses of loquacity that were threatening precisely because of their persuasiveness. In certain passages, the vices of an unbridled tongue could be connected to the corruption of liberal arts, brought about not by the scholastic curriculum but instead by 'the loquacity of the declamatory schools' which has 'ruined eloquence'.[69] Yet, Erasmus's main argumentative thread did not engage in a critical assessment of eloquence. Rather, its structure, drawn from classical texts such as Aulus Gellius's *Noctes Atticae*, was built on a dichotomy between the stupidity of loquacity and the good sense of eloquence, or, in other words, the vices of the tongue and the virtues of speech represented by true oratory. He explicitly maintained that 'eloquence is never found without sense, and equally loquacity is always combined with stupidity'.[70] In this way, the ambivalence concerned the organ (tongue), not the art of good speech, which was described precisely as the appropriate remedy against the vices of tongue and the political and social discord plaguing Europe. Thus, despite his awareness of the ambivalent possibilities of the use of speech, Erasmus did not condemn rhetoric as such and even in the culmination of his theological work, *Ecclesiastes* (1535), continued to model the preacher on a Christianized version of Quintilian's orator. In *Ecclesiastes*, Erasmus still insisted that 'by imparting these disciplines soundly and exercising them appropriately, one acquires a certain mental dexterity both for sound judgment and for ease in speaking'.[71]

Melanchthon, for his part, modified his views on the art of rhetoric and especially its relationship to dialectic. Somewhat similarly to his *Oratio*, in the dedication letter to his *De rhetorica libri tres* (1519), he looked back at antiquity when students proceeded from grammar to rhetoric, which was a truly universal art that taught about all matters, and regretted that in later times the role of rhetoricians was taken over by 'disordered' (*inconditus*) dialecticians. Although the dedicatory letter aimed at a union of rhetoric and dialectic, *De rhetorica* incorporated some procedures, such as the didactic genre, into a rhetorical framework.[72] In the third major rhetorical treatise that Melanchthon composed, *Elementorum rhetorices libri duo* (1531), the situation was decidedly different. While he discussed rhetoric mainly, although not exclusively, as a practice of reading and judgment rather than as a merely productive art, he strongly argued for the interdependence of dialectic and rhetoric, and described his rhetorical treatise as complementary to his work on dialectic (*De dialectica libri quattuor*, 1529).[73] Furthermore, in a section that clarified the relationship between dialectic and rhetoric, he portrayed rhetoric primarily as an art of style that was of relevance when we wanted to move the audience by addressing their emotions. He claimed that teaching (*docere*) was part of dialectic, showed how general questions (what is virtue?) belonged to the subject matter of dialectic, and underlined that one's ability to speak well and with wisdom was dependent on one's knowledge of those arts.[74] In short, Melanchthon had become increasingly sensitive to the importance of uniting rhetoric with knowledge of substantive matter (separate sciences) and with knowledge of dialectical argumentative procedures in textual analysis and production.[75]

Now there were doubtless different reasons for problematizing rhetoric in the works of Erasmus and Melanchthon. Melanchthon's pronounced emphasis on dialectic in the cultivation of judgment in reading might have been a way to instruct pupils on how to turn rhetorical displays into clear argumentative patterns which, in a Europe beleaguered by religious discord, would encourage a more analytical attitude towards the divisiveness of language. Erasmus's personal experience with scholastic theologians, Reformed writers, and other scholarly opponents had left him exceedingly frustrated by the mid-1520s, when his rhetorical and transformative *philosophia Christi* was being threatened by the Reformation or coupled with it by his conservative opponents.

Still, different problematizations of rhetoric clearly mirrored a broader concern among European humanists about religious and political discord. Erasmus's *Lingua* had united the vices of the tongue with the current state of political and ecclesiastical discord and maintained that this was partly due to the emerging pamphlet culture which facilitated the publication of anonymous and scandalous accusations. Erasmus argued that 'it has now become a regular practice to publish scandalous pamphlets under false names' and that 'the laws now turn a blind eye to these abominable crimes'.[76] Agrippa's attack on rhetoric also engaged with current issues. He asked, 'aren't the authors of these heresies the most articulate men, who possess both verbal eloquence and an elegant writing style?'[77]

Vives's case was somewhat different from those of Erasmus and Melanchthon since he had emphasized the centrality of dialectic already in *In pseudodialecticos*, which placed him in the avant-garde of humanist dialectic in the 1510s. Still, Vives's constructive proposal for dialectic in *De disciplinis* occurred in a moment in which he was clearly thinking about the threat of adversarial rhetorical culture to political and religious concord. In his correspondence, he complained that printers and book sellers were more interested in making money from trifling dialogues and pamphlets than advancing scholarship.[78] In *De concordia*, Vives had elaborated on how the natural gifts that were given to humans for a harmonious social life, including speech, had been turned into instruments of division which was apparent in political, ecclesiastical, and scholarly discussions. Later, in his *De comunione rerum* (1535), he argued that 'from discord in opinion we came to disagreements in life' and people moved from verbal battles to fight with 'spears, swords, cannons'.[79] This established a close link between adversarial writing and social and political violence.

Ciceronianism and the Relevance of Rhetoric

Despite his reservations about the rhetorical culture of the time, Vives did not want to condemn eloquence but improve it so that it could successfully perform its role in religious and political life. In criticizing an inclusive understanding of rhetoric, Vives did not claim that rhetoric should not ideally be united with ethics and wisdom, but rather that one should not think that there was a natural bond between these issues. In fact, his discussion of contemporary rhetoric, just like his portrayal of the history of eloquence, made abundantly clear that he was primarily striving for a rhetoric that regained its proper role as an ethical practice and as the glue of political and social life.

This can perhaps be best observed in Vives's critique of contemporary rhetorical education as merely literary and irrelevant rather than destructive. Unlike classical orators, who were experts in rhetorical practice, theoretical knowledge, and the guiding of souls, modern orators, according to Vives, did not know what emotions were, were ignorant of how to adapt words and genres to different themes, came up with lifeless maxims (*sententia*), based their arguments on trivial school rhetoric, and did not pay attention to the rules of disposition and rhetorical presentation.[80] He also bluntly stated that 'up to now, no one has practised the art of declamation, at least not in argumentative matters, as it were in a contest or a wrestling-school'. Contemporary rhetoric, Vives argued, either focused on discourses without an opponent (demonstrative exercises of praise and blame) or, in cases where there was an opponent, on a fierce battle based merely on insults.[81] While the second accusation was, as well as other things, a comment on the reality of rhetorical culture among religious sects and scholars, the first alluded to a rhetoric of mere *delectatio*.

Vives associated this rhetoric of *delectatio* with the vice of Ciceronianism that Erasmus, in his famous dialogue *Ciceronianus*, had ridiculed. Vives's lengthy complaint about Ciceronianism was practically a summary of Erasmus's book (it is mentioned by Vives) which, for its part, drew on earlier disputes between Angelo Poliziano and Paolo Cortesi (1465–1510) and, more recently, Giovanni Francesco Pico della Mirandola (1470–1533) and Pietro Bembo (1470–1547). In the *Ciceronianus*, Erasmus had embarked on a fierce critique of a distinct humanist strand, composed mostly of Italian humanists or admirers of Italian humanism (most importantly Christophe de Longueil, 1490–1522), who, in crafting their own literary style, had adopted Cicero as their sole source of imitation.[82] In the dialogue, Bulephorus, the voice of reason, engaged in a healing exercise of a Ciceronian, Nosoponus, who had dedicated his life in monastic fashion to the imitation of Cicero, composing long handbooks and lexicons based solely on his writings.[83] Harnessing a wide range of arguments to present his case, Erasmus both debunked the myth of Cicero as a perfect writer (e.g. recalling his errors, his limited abilities in poetry, and the loss of some of his works) and redescribed the very practice of imitation.[84]

While Erasmus, in addition to the geographic tension between Italy and transalpine Europe, framed the discussion mainly as a contest between the pagan Antiquity and the Christian present, most of his arguments were elaborated into deep insights into proper modes of imitation.[85] Bulephorus suggested an eclectic approach to imitation that drew on the specific virtues of each writer and recalled that Cicero's true greatness was never based primarily on the specific technical and verbal choices he made, but rather on his ability to speak according to his inner talent (*ingenium*) and with a sound grasp of appropriateness (*decorum, apte dicere*), which took into account various contextual elements such as the theme, the audience and one's *persona*.[86] Thus, true imitation of Cicero, which avoided being an empty and inanimate reproduction of the Roman orator, entailed emulating his knowledge of things, his contextual *decorum*, and his success in speaking in accordance with his natural talent. Only by flexibly adapting Cicero's model to a changed, Christian context could rhetoric be useful and not mere amusement.[87]

Vives had already referred to the debate and defended Erasmus's main points in a letter to Galcerano Cepello and he further elaborated on Ciceronianism in *De disciplinis*. He censured the rigorous imitation of Cicero's words and sentences by pointing out his stylistic limitations, the fact that he had not treated all subjects, and, most importantly, that the end result of linguistic imitation was a scattered mosaic of bits and pieces which failed to do justice to the theme treated and, what was worse, was rhetorically ineffective. Vives also claimed that true emulation should focus on 'his knowledge of present and past things, examination of philosophical schools, handling of the human soul, sharpness in bringing things together. With these virtues he persuaded better the senate, the people, and the judges than with his verbal and stylistic resources'.[88] However, within a very similar argumentative structure on imitation and *decorum,* there was a pronounced difference from Erasmus's work. Whereas Erasmus, already in the dedication letter, focused on the appropriation of Cicero into a Christian world, Vives did not mention Christ and there was only one brief allusion to Christianity.[89] Rather, he described the rhetoric of Ciceronians as 'useless' (*inutilis*) and 'inefficient' (*inefficax*), which for Vives was a grave sin, since rhetoric was a form of 'battle' (*pugna*) that aimed at 'persuasion' (*persuasio*) and 'victory' (*victoria*): furthermore, he referred to the classical idea, very present in Cicero's *De inventione*, that rhetoric was part of a civil science in pointing out that it did not just deal with everything, but it had to 'speak especially about public and civil matters'.[90] What was presented to the reader was thus not only an exhortation to a proper mode of emulation that encompassed all fields in which rhetoric could be used, but a more pronounced emphasis on the power of rhetoric to get things done in civic matters.

The constructive proposal of the proper imitation of Cicero can be seen as an answer to the vices of contemporary rhetoric (mere *delectatio* – ranting) and to those of classical rhetoric (*delectatio*/flattery – oratorical licence and omnipotence). Since rhetoric was a technical skill or a force, Vives's stress on general issues (*persona*, prudence, subject matter) in the imitation of Cicero implied that, for a healthy oratorical culture to emerge, emulation had to be extended beyond his style (rhetoric in the strict sense) to his virtue, knowledge of different disciplines, contextual adaptation, and dialectic. Throughout *De disicplinis*, rhetoric appears as a highly ambivalent popular art, a force that speaks to the passions of the multitude who did not partake in truth. For it to perform its social function, its relationship to other arts had to be reassessed.

Dialectic and *Inventio*

A central part of the reassessment of rhetoric dealt with the scope and nature of dialectic. Similar to *In pseudodialecticos*, Vives continued to condemn scholastic dialectic and engaged in a purification of the Aristotelian *Organon*. He found fault with Aristotelian essential definitions, modal logic, medieval ideas on hypothetical arguments, the medieval theory of supposition, medieval attempts to extend dialectic into metaphysics and other disciplines (which decided on the truthfulness of their propositions), and the separation of dialectic from ordinary language analysis.[91]

To be sure, Vives's views on dialectic were not only in line with an ever-growing tradition of humanist dialectical works but engaged in the critical evaluation of a rapidly transforming scholastic culture. Numerous signs indicate that in the universities directly related to Vives's life, the actual education in faculties of arts had already changed or was about to change.[92] In 1530, the theological faculty of Paris complained that the Faculty of Arts was teaching more Agricola than Aristotle.[93] Louvain, the university to which Vives had been closely connected, was experimenting with the work of Agricola, as witnessed by the 1535 edition of Aristotle's *Organon* that drew heavily on the Dutch humanist.[94] In English universities, similar developments were taking place, as indicated by the statutes of the Faculty of Arts in Cambridge that put forward the names of Aristotle, Agricola, Melanchthon, and Trebizond as authorities in dialectic.[95] Indeed, it has even been suggested that by 1530 writing on dialectic in the purely scholastic tradition had almost completely ceased.[96]

Even though Agricola had gained a reputation as the torch bearer of the new dialectical learning, much had happened since the publication of *In pseudodialecticos*. Several humanist works had emerged in the field, spearheaded by Melanchthon's *Compendiaria dialectices ratio* (1520) and Johannes Caesarius's (c.1468–1550) *Dialectica* (1526), both of which enjoyed great success in the printing world. Older humanist treatises were successful as well. Trebizond's *Isagoge dialectica* was published 14 times between 1515 and 1530, and Agricola's classic *De inventione dialectica* had been woven more closely into the emerging humanist tradition through the commentary of Phrissemus and through Bartolomeus Latomus's (1485–1566) *Epitome*, which first appeared in 1530.[97] Latomus's own *Summa totius rationis disserendi et dialecticas et rhetoricas partes complectens* (1527) had also established a close link between dialectic and rhetoric by showing how the analysis of speech (*ratio dicendi*) was focused on the oration (*oratio*), which could be investigated through dialectical and rhetorical topics. This effectively highlighted the interdependence of rhetorical and dialectical methods.

Vives's constructive proposal was part of this tradition and it focused almost exclusively on dialectical invention and the topics. In describing the causes of the corruption of dialectic, he had already argued that judgment (*iudicium*) of truth and error, one of the two traditional parts of dialectic, belonged to separate arts in their respective subject matter since dialectic could not judge the factual veracity of propositions.[98] Vives asserted that dialectic was an 'instrument of invention' (*instrumentum inveniendi*) and that there were no separate methods of invention for rhetoric and dialectic, but there was 'just one [method of invention], and it belongs rather to dialectic than to rhetoric'.[99] Vives sustained that it was precisely the inability of dialecticians to understand the proper scope of their art that had led to the invasion of rhetoricians into the field of invention. Because dialecticians 'ignore what is the goal of dialectic, what belongs to it and what does not [...] rhetoricians seized all that part that deals with the invention of arguments'.[100]

In place of rhetorical invention based on ready-made locutions designed for specific purposes (parts of speech, specific questions treated), Vives suggested throughout *De disciplinis* a set of general, dialectical topics that could be used in the analysis of all terms proposed.[101] Now, the exact nature of Vives's dialectical topics has raised some questions in the literature, partly because they seem to take a central place both within scientific enquiry into the order of things and in rhetorical composition. Within different scholarly traditions the extent to which Vives's epistemology was reflective or constitutive of reality has been debated, and recently Lodi Nauta has presented dialectical topics as a 'reflection of the ontological order and as such an instrument and heuristic aid for the human mind'.[102] Nauta's account retains the ambiguity of Vives's topics as reflective of Aristotelian essences yet, because of the epistemological limitations of the post-lapsarian state, elucidates how the only knowledge possible for humans was based on categorizations of things dependent on topical similarities and dissimilarities. As Nauta has noted, this brought topical descriptions of individual things to the centre of attention.[103] This interpretation does justice to Vives's insistence in the third part of *De disciplinis* that there was a fixed order of things and Aristotelian essences to be known, but that, in our current epistemological state, they were out of our reach, which, effectively, paved the way for a knowledge based on a broad range of dialectical topics.

However, while Nauta is perfectly aware of the persuasive dimension of language, his focus is on topics as mediators between reality and cognition. But within Vives's peculiar claim that the same set of topics was to be used in scientific enquiry (general questions) and rhetorical production (particular questions), he gave considerable attention to the ability of the topics, with their access to things (*res*), to provide abundant material for an orator. In this sense, the topics were an index that did not provide entry to a readily categorized order of things but to all possible ways in which, in light of authoritative literature, a thing could be analysed or placed in relation to other things.

Now it is likely that, for Vives, the scientific dimension of topics was meant to guarantee that a rhetorician, in the invention of material, was given access to the most universal and truthful knowledge available to humans which, for its part, was supplied by individual arts and sciences. At the same time, the rhetorical aspect of topics implied that all rhetorical flexibility was built into their use. Vives stressed their flexibility to a great degree. He was clear, for instance, that Boethius's search for maximal propositions, which were supposed to test the validity of interference in dialectic, was a harmful and useless attempt to condense the infinity of topics into overly narrow limits.[104] What is more, in addition to Aristotle, in the second part of *De disciplinis* he mentioned Giorgio Valla (1447–1500), Melanchthon, George of Trebizond and, at a more advanced level, Agricola, the fifth book of Quintilian's *Institutio oratoria*, Boethius, and, Cicero's *Topica* and *De inventione* as authoritative works in dialectic. He even claimed that it was Cicero, especially in his *De inventione*, not Aristotle, who made dialectic useful.[105] This was a list that not only relied on humanist dialectic but also introduced influential books of classical rhetoric, such as Quintilian, with no dialectical aspirations.

But even more importantly, this mélange of rhetorical and dialectical traditions was apparent in the topics themselves. Take, for example, the category of definition, which had a long history in both the rhetorical and the dialectical tradition. In the dialectical tradition, it was one of the key concepts in Aristotle's *Posterior Analytics* – part of his *Organon*. In the work, the principal task of definition was to state what something *is* in its essence. For Aristotle, definition had a particular form, and was always composed of a *genus*, showing a general category of sameness, and *differentia*, establishing a difference called *species* in relation to all other substances of a certain *genus*. The famous definition of human beings as rational animals, for instance, was composed of what is defined (*homo*), the *genus* under which it falls (*animal*) and the difference (*differentia*) that defined its species (*ratio*). Moreover, some of the works used in the teaching of dialectic – such as Boethius's *Topics* – were specifically designed to test the essential nature of possible definitions.[106] In definitions pointing towards categories, one saw, thus, the most essential way something *was* something, and how it was related to all other beings through sameness and difference.

Yet definition was also a rhetorical concept. Already in Aristotle's *Rhetoric* definition was said to be one of the topics that could help one gather material. It was very much present in the Roman tradition as well: the *Ad Herennium*, for instance, used it as a potential conflict in arguments and as a topic of invention.[107] The merging of the two notions of definition – essential and rhetorical – could be observed in the most widely read humanist books on dialectic, Agricola's *De inventione dialectica,* Trebizond's *Isagoge dialectica,* Bartolomeus Latomus's *Summa totius rationis disserendi et dialecticas et rhetoricas partes complectens* and Caesarius's *Dialectica*. Agricola, for instance, opened up space for non-essential definitions by arguing that proper *differentia* were hard to find. This was an assertion that led him to a demonstration of the method of division that could use other properties in its search for suitable definitions.[108] Trebizond, for his part, was clear that what he called a substantial definition was just one of four possible genera, and presented the rhetorical possibilities inherent in definition at length.[109]

Vives admitted the existence of essential definitions, but proceeded in an Agricolan vein to argue that they were hard to find, and, because of this, 'essential definitions teach us very little, and are of very little use to us, and for this reason I think they are rare'.[110] Following this line of thought, his main constructive aim was to show how one could build or invent definitions using division, which took as its point of departure an appropriate working definition of a thing, drawn from authoritative texts, and divided it to a point where its particular nature was revealed.[111] By quoting Agricola, Vives worked through the word *ius* (law, also right or justice) moving from an initial claim that '*ius* contains a certain power of force and order', to a definition that captured its particular nature, and differentiated it from everything else. This definition was: '*ius* is a decree of a higher power for the preservation of the state of the city (*civitas*), established according to equity and good'.[112] After the presentation of definition and division, Vives described how, through a number of dialectical topics, one could gather material and draw definitions from, e.g. interpretation, etymology, metaphor, and analogy.

The flexibility in drawing definitions was coupled with an explicit call for rhetorical *decorum* in using them. In the closing section of *De explanatione cuiusque essentiae*, Vives not only taught us that the relative merits of short and long definitions were dependent on the *ingenia* of the audience, but also that Cicero and Quintilian underscored that definitions had to 'agree' (*congruere*) with the situation one was handling. As he maintained, 'Cicero defines glory in one way in thanking Cesar for letting Marcellus to return from exile, namely popularly to the multitude; and in another way in the philosophical discussions among the few in the *Tusculan Disputations*'.[113] In this way, the employment of definitions was placed in the context of the rhetorical distinction between learned and popular audiences.

For Vives, topics and especially definitions certainly connected the orator to the true knowledge of different arts and sciences through dialectic. Consequently, they exercised a potentially controlling effect on the orator since they brought him into contact with the commonly accepted truths of separate sciences. As a matter of fact, Vives filled his section on definitions with a number of examples that would have pleased most Northern humanists: 'erudition is acquired through exercise, study, and doctrine'; 'a city (*civitas*) without justice is a reservoir of thieves'; 'the greatness of a commonwealth comprises the dignity and importance of its body of citizens'; 'honour in the eyes of the people is a place of esteem to which blind chance has elevated some without purpose'; and 'a good prince is one who does not look after his own interests but those of the people'.[114]

Yet, dialectical topics were also a generative tool that fulfilled the old Ciceronian dream of uniting wisdom with eloquence. In showing how rhetorical questions could be connected to dialectical invention, the orator was offered a method for universalizing particular questions and, consequently, more comprehensive and analytical argumentative tools. This knowledge enabled a wide spectrum of argumentative possibilities that could be called upon according to the circumstantial requirements of the situation.

Teaching, Character, and Adversarial Speech

Some of the cautions regarding rhetoric in *De causis* was also built into Vives's practical suggestions for education in the second part of *De disciplinis*. While the part, centred on educational practices and materials, engaged with an entirely different genre of writing compared to *De causis*, it did, as we will see, partake in its concern with the propensity of language to divide humans by activating destructive passions. More specifically, while

De tradendis disciplinis greatly emphasized that studies needed to have a practical, often rhetorical application in different aspects of a life of *negotium*, Vives was suspicious of a tradition that, by encouraging argumentative confrontation, had tried to train schoolboys for a life of active engagement. At the heart of this suspicion was the question as to what extent the ability of adversarial rhetoric (or dialectic) or verbal rivalry contributed positively to one's character. Did it nurture the kind of abilities that were needed in the world of *negotium* or did it perhaps cultivate the kind of passions that, while enabling powerful rhetoric, were ultimately detrimental to the self-government of the speaker and to collective life at large? As will become clear, with regards to elementary education, Vives leaned towards the latter option.

In *De tradendis*, Vives firmly aligned himself with the humanist ideal of presenting an extensive education as a major part of reforming and improving people's moral, social, and political lives. At the time he was writing *De disciplinis*, the Netherlands, together with many other parts of Europe, was experiencing an expansion of the schooling system, and the high level of literacy and learning was widely recognized by sixteenth-century contemporaries.[115] The Netherlands boasted different educational institutions for elementary schooling, such as private, more practically oriented vernacular schools for merchants; however, Latin schools, which were more and more frequently publicly administered, formed the cornerstone of the system of education.[116] In the course of the sixteenth century, humanist learning gradually crept into the curricula of grammar and Latin schools, and, at least in some cases, the process was fostered by local humanist circles.[117]

Many Latin schools also had increasingly structured learning paths based on classes or grades. The famous schools in Deventer and Zwolle both had nine classes, the first two of which were dedicated to very elementary exercises. From class seven to three (the numbering ran downwards), pupils were educated in Latin through different grammar exercises, and introduced to the basics of the *quadrivium*, dialectic, philosophy, and increasingly to the *ars eloquentiae* together with some instruction in Greek. In classes two and one, found only in a minority of educational institutions, they were further instructed in philosophy, and possibly law, geometry, and in some cases even theology. These two higher classes already partly coincided with the kind of education one would acquire in the faculties of arts at the university level.[118] Johannes Sturm, in his *De literarum ludis recte aperiendis* (1538), based his model of different classes essentially on his experience in the schooling system of the Low Countries. In a truly humanist vein, he gave pronounced importance to the study of classics, and especially to the art of rhetoric.[119]

While Louvain was the only university in the Netherlands, the universities of Cologne, Italy, Paris, as well as Orleans in the case of legal studies, were regularly frequented by students from the Low Countries.[120] Although a person with a university education could make a career in a variety of institutions, ranging from the Catholic Church to academic and scholarly settings, many of those employed in the highest echelons of civic life were university graduates, and in regional councils, for example, people with a university education were becoming increasingly numerous. This can be seen in the Councils of Brabant and Flanders where most of those employed were experts in law – a career that became, in some cases, a formal requirement for certain offices.[121] Thus, universities were catering the people in charge of politics, spiritual life, and education in the Burgundian Netherlands, as well as in its central and regional administrations.[122]

The expansion of schooling and university education and its significance for career evolution, was, as is well known, greatly promoted by most humanists. Erasmus, in his *De pueris instituendis*, was referring to a potentially large audience when, in the opening sentence, he encouraged the reader to educate/her his children in the liberal arts: 'if you follow my advice [...] you will see to it that your infant son makes his first acquaintance with a liberal education immediately'.[123] Although *De pueris* was framed as a treatise for 'philosophers and statesmen', Erasmus still insisted that, even though not everyone became a prince, everyone 'should be educated for that end'.[124] The ideal of extensive education was at the heart of Vives's *De disciplinis*, which called for a school to be established in every town, and a university to be founded in every province.[125]

For Erasmian humanists, as well as for the earlier humanist and scholastic traditions, the promotion of studies was premised on the ability of education to form the character of students and turn them into civilized creatures.[126] The very first sentence of the preface of *De disciplinis* stated that the training or discipline (*disciplina*) of the mind 'is what separates us from the manners and habits of the beasts, what restores us to our humanity and lifts us up to God himself/herself'.[127] Despite agreement on the importance of character, there were, however, different views as to the exact nature of the character that was ideally to be formed. Because of this, educational writers – with varying degrees of emphasis on the relationship of education to piety, religion, and civic life – had ascribed centrality to different materials and pedagogical methods in the formation of character.[128]

It is well known that Erasmian educational reformers, including Vives, were decidedly critical of late scholastic pedagogy, which, according to humanists, was focused on external constraints rather than on practices that would bring about an internal propensity for virtue. In *De pueris instituendis*, Erasmus had formulated a strong critique of the scholastic model of education, based on fear and corporal punishment, and underscored the contribution of enjoyment for learning; and Vives, although not completely forbidding corporal punishment, stressed the impact of playfulness on encouraging the student to be diligent in his studies.[129] Both Erasmus and Vives also banned the discipline and rigour of the scholastic tradition sometimes associated with the Parisian college of Montaigu, which, while avowing to promote the cultivation of virtue, humility, apostolic spirit, and inner piety so dear to Erasmus and Vives, relied on strict daily routine, organized religious exercise, public confessions, and students exercising surveillance over the morality of one another.[130] As part of their critique, they also routinely denounced formalized adversarial disputations that, as shown in Chapter 1, had been at the very heart of medieval pedagogy and investigation of truth.[131]

In *De disciplinis*, Vives did not, however, only express concern about scholasticism, but also engaged in a criticism of a prevalent humanist practice to develop character through adversarial practices. It has been often argued that in Italian *quattrocento* manuals, the cultivation of virtue and morals was placed, at least ideally, in the context of a civic ideal of an active life (*negotium*), the successful performance of which was rewarded with honour. Pier Paolo Vergerio's (1370–1444) *De ingenuis moribus ac liberalibus studiis* (1402), a popular presentation of liberal studies, insisted that these were a way to 'seek honor and glory, which for the wise man are the principal rewards of virtue'.[132] Vergerio also argued that both letters and arms should be studied, cited examples of princes of old, and claimed that liberal studies were useful both for a life of *otium* and of *negotium*.[133] Erasmus's exhortation to liberal studies in *De pueris* was not only framed as a guidebook for the navigator of the commonwealth but also declared that 'nothing' was 'more conducive to wealth, social status, influence and even good health [...] than moral and intellectual excellence', which were achieved through such studies.[134] The acquisition of active virtue could be linked with rhetorical exercises that were distinctively different from medieval disputations but that still encouraged rivalry between students for honour and victory. In Erasmus's often printed *De ratione studii*, a curriculum for John Colet's (1466/1467–1519) St Paul's school, an rhetorical training based on the development of truly oratorical themes was suggested and the teacher was told to 'stimulate the pupils' spirits by starting with comparison among them, thereby arousing a state of mutual rivalry'.[135]

The critique of scholastic and of humanist cultures both incorporated a reassessment of their ideas of adversarial speech and writing. Throughout all three parts of *De discilinis*, the most obvious reservations were reserved for the practice of disputations. In the first part on the corruption of arts, Vives argued that in pristine times, they cultivated the force of the mind of the students (*vigor animi*) and clarified truth. But when praise and riches accompanied a win in disputations, they lost their pedagogical and epistemological meaning: 'a distorted desire for glory and money invaded the souls of the debaters so that, like in a fight, only a victory was sought with no concern for the elucidation of truth'.[136] In their degenerated form, they provoked intellectual factions, verbal discord, and, eventually, violence, since they had turned into a theatre, where, instead of truth, the approval of the multitude was pursued. Through scholarly exercises, students were socialized into an environment that praised, not the acceptance of their own errors, but victory in disputes, which falsely excited their self-esteem and pride.[137]

Yet Vives did not ban disputations but rather aspired to restore them to their former splendour. This was in accordance with a broad humanist tradition that had criticized scholastic disputations (often eristic ones that served as a way to teach dialectical inference; the theory of *obligationes* was developed for this purpose) yet incorporated them into education.[138] As seen, *De disciplinis* partook in a trend to replace scholastic materials with humanist textbooks, where formal validity was of secondary importance.[139] Furthermore, although disputations were normally associated with the culture of universities, some form of grammatical or rhetorical disputations played a part throughout the student's educational path. For instance, in Johannes Sturm's curriculum for Latin schools, disputations were described at length, with Sturm denouncing 'the piling up of propositions', suggesting brevity, recommending brief and polished epilogues to disputations, and even claiming that 'a free discussion is what best suits this assembly'.[140]

Vives's constructive idea of disputations as clarificatory exercises in truth (at times, they are described almost as conversations) was put forward in the third part of *De disciplinis* in a book called *De disputatione*. Here he distinguished between a form of internal disputation,[141] which served as a test of propositions and arguments, and exterior disputations where the passion for glory of the disputants had to be countered with two remedies: first, that the disputants grasped 'what the issue of the controversy is' and, second, that the respondent 'clearly understands the nature of everything that is discussed'. This enables him to separate it from other issues clearly and to define and divide everything 'correctly' (*recte*).[142] Disputation thus appears as a Socratic practice of clarifying truth and the nature of a problem cooperatively in a spirit where victory was not sought.

Elementary Education and the Absence of Confrontation

Whereas the denouncing of scholastic disputation was quite apparent, Vives's engagement with rhetorical confrontation was more subtle and built into his educational proposals, which covered the entire gamut of education from Latin schools to various university faculties. In elementary education, traditional ideas about classical and Christian character development shook hands with an overwhelmingly classical syllabus. The typically Erasmian union of piety and learning was presented to pupils through works such as Vives's own *Introductio ad Sapientiam*; the humanist tradition of surveying the natural talent of pupils was suggested; the significance of all social ties (e.g. family) for shaping character through habituation was affirmed; and, finally, the contribution of some disciplines – most importantly moral philosophy and history (purified from the cult of warfare) – to the pupil's prudential character was underlined.[143] These were mostly traditional ideas. The sensitivity to individual talent had been, since Quintilian, a way to secure the suitability of studies to individual developments and to protect the arts from those unsuitable for their study. The role of moral maxims and history in character building had been foregrounded in popular treatises such as Isocrates's *Epistola ad Demonicum* and Vergerio.[144]

While Vives's educational endeavours have sometimes been placed within a tradition of religious educational treatises,[145] the curriculum and practical description of Latin schools was markedly classical, focused on the arts of prudence, and almost completely based on the reading of pagan authors. Vives offered an impressive list of classical authors, which was not meant as an exhaustive reading list but rather as a critical overview of the literature that could be of use at this level.[146] He also described the pedagogical path from the acquisition of linguistic skills to more demanding oral and written exercises such as translation, elementary letters, tales, amplification of examples or proverbs, and rewriting poems without following metrical rules.[147] In all this, Vives, in a humanist vein, maintained that at this elementary level, the contact with classical authors brought knowledge (Latin is the seat of knowledge) and, eventually, enabled the acquisition of a personal style.[148] Throughout the description, the confrontation between students was carefully controlled. Disputations (described as *concertatiunculae*) among students could be a way to incite the interest of very young pupils through 'praise and little rewards' (*laude et praemiolis*), but with time these disputations should develop into a 'comparison of studies' (*collatio studiorum*). The themes were merely grammatical and concerned the comparison of norms with use in linguistic expression, the explanation of obscure passages, sentences, apothegms, fables, histories, or parables, and the clarification of the meanings and etymologies of words.[149] For Vives, the education of Latin schools, covering the years between seven and fifteen, was philological in nature, prepared one to 'engage with those things in life that are common to all', and left higher disciplines (e.g. medicine, law) for universities.[150] Although he wrote that pupils should gradually move towards larger themes that included the city (*ciuitas*) and the commonwealth (*republica*), these were not treated in an oratorical framework.[151]

The non-oratorical and mostly grammatical or philological treatment of political themes is apparent in Vives's own *Exercitatio linguae latinae*, published in 1538, which included exercises on just these themes.[152] The work, which belonged to a tradition that included, e.g. Petrus Mosellanus's *Paedagogia in puerorum usum conscripta* (1518) and Christoph Hegendorf's *Dialogi pueriles* (1520), contained a collection of 25 dialogues on a variety of themes ranging from everyday situations to questions of princely rule, focusing on a conscious development of vocabulary together with the teaching of virtuous manners, viewpoints, and *sententiae* through short descriptions based on humanist commonplaces. They also wove simple ideas on the commonwealth and good government into the structure of a schoolbook.

Especially in dialogues *Regia* and *Princeps puer*, Vives offered an account on good government, counsel, and ethical demands of self-governance of those in power. In these dialogues, the defence of the reasonable point of view was usually given to one of the characters.[153] Consequently, there were no conflicting opinions and the mode of discussion was consensual; it taught, defused emotion, and nurtured concord.[154] The final dialogue on precepts of education (*Praecepta educationis*) between Budé and Grympherantes was quite revealing. Grympherantes embodied what a schoolboy should have learnt in school and was questioned by the famous French humanist. Adopting a serious tone, Grympherantes presented the fruits of education, emphasizing manners and obedience to authority in response to Budé's questions. When Budé implied that 'unworthy men' (*homines indignissimi*) occupy important offices and asked if they should be honoured, Grympherantes answered that children of his age were not allowed to pronounce judgment on the matter because they had not acquired sufficient wisdom.[155] Under further enquiry about what happened to obedience, 'if laws and customs are bad, unjust, and tyrannical', Grympherantes reiterated his earlier position that schoolboys should not judge the matter.[156]

Both the dialogues and *De disciplinis* show that, for Vives, elementary education was primarily geared to produce a large pool of people with good Latin skills who were introduced to wisdom through maxims and commonplaces but who were not expected to write political or religious texts. Their wisdom and familiarity with basic political themes were perhaps an antidote against bad rhetoric since they potentially constituted an audience capable of proper judgment and reason.[157] But they were clearly not encouraged to be part of these discussions. As Vives wrote, those who did not ascend higher in their studies due to lack of ability or desire, would have linguistic skills enabling them to pursue a life of *negotium* in the role of 'a public scribe, undertake less eminent office holding, or partake in embassies'.[158] Although they had a polished style (*eloquentia* in this narrow sense) that could be used in a practical life of lay affairs, their training was not oratorical.

This can be contrasted to the markedly oratorical flavour of Erasmus's *De ratione studii* and also that of Sturm's *De literarum ludis recte aperiendis*, which promoted liberal studies by depicting how those trained in liberal arts were capable of defending the commonwealth.[159] In Erasmus's *De ratione studii*, we find advice for training in the three genres of rhetoric (judicial, deliberative, demonstrative), the invention and arrangement of arguments and propositions, amplification and the use of emotions, and, finally, the development of truly oratorical themes.[160] Erasmus's *De conscribendis epistolis* also embraced the development of themes on both sides of the matter with little consideration for truth, so important for Vives in his denunciation of disputations. Erasmus recommended the defence of dubious things, such as tyranny, and explicitly maintained that 'nothing is so inherently good that it cannot be made to seem bad by a gifted speaker'.[161] Likewise, Johannes Sturm's suggestions for higher grades were primarily structured around rhetorical training which ultimately led to apt, decorous speech, 'worthy of a free man, and appropriate to the occasion and the person'.[162]

Rhetoric, Dialectic, and a Life of *Negotium*

It was only after the elementary stage that liberal arts received a full treatment and oratorical, conflictual speech was dealt with. The second stage

Redefining rhetoric in De disciplinis 163

covered by *De tradendis* stretched until the youngster was approximately 25 years old, as Vives stated.[163] This meant that he was describing here a syllabus roughly equivalent to the faculty of arts in the universities of Northern Europe. In this part, Vives dedicated significant attention to dialectic, rhetoric, physics, first philosophy (metaphysics), and mathematical subjects, and it was here that, according to him, there was a move from language acquisition to the arts and disciplines.[164] It is also in this phase in the chronology of the learning of different skills that the integral union of dialectic and rhetoric entered the picture since the whole basis of these studies lay in the *trivium*.

In dialectic and rhetoric, the first step belonged to dialectical judgment, which was trained to decern truth through reformed disputations, the more precise description of which was included in a separate book of *De disciplinis* entitled *De censura veri*. While Vives offered some advice that seemed to concur with the formal aspirations of medieval disputations, he by and large downplayed the role of the art of obligations (it was not really an art in itself) and described the questions of disputations as 'Socratic'. 'By employing divisions and definitions', these questions gradually drew the opponent to one's side and they were 'most useful to many things: to the testing of truth, sharpening the *ingenium*, and refuting the one who opposes us'.[165] In the part on dialectical invention, Vives, drawing on humanist treatises and Cicero, presented ways of examining the arguments of authoritative texts and portrayed the way in which topical invention should be exercised in analysing terms and themes on both sides (*ad partem utramque excogitabuntur argumenta*).[166] In discussing dialectical judgment and invention, he advised that the exercise in dialectic should not be 'quarrelsome' (*rixosa*); since quarrelling was built into the nature of dialectic and rhetoric, this could turn the pupil into someone 'thorny, quarrelsome, deceitful', and the study of these disciplines should be reserved for those with the right kind of natural talent (*ingenium*).[167]

Dialectical invention, firmly in line with humanist ideas, offered ways of investigating terms and, through them, themes, but it lacked an emotional and contextual component. This belonged to rhetoric which was first foremost about emotions and contextuality. In an emphatic fashion, Vives highlighted the immense, even tyrannical powers of rhetoric, which was 'the cause of the greatest goods and evils'.[168] Despite its destructive possibilities, it was precisely in the current corrupt state of things that its dominion over emotions and the will should not be disregarded: 'certainly, the more corrupt human souls are, the more carefully its study should be taken up by prudent and honourable men'.[169] The oratorical training, based on a large variety of classical and contemporary authors, taught students the *officia* of rhetoric (here teach, persuade, and move) and, as repeatedly underlined by Vives, the understanding of the contextual element in rhetoric (the speaker, audience, place, time, the case).

In practical exercises, students progressed from the treatment, amplification, and synthesis of non-controversial questions to the practice of other duties of rhetoric (teaching, *docere*, and delighting, *delectare*), to the analysis of controversial questions, and finally, with controversial questions, to the moving of emotions.[170] While Vives reiterated that one should never speak against truth and that true eloquence should always defend piety, the good, and justice, the pinnacle of oratorical training was an exercise in which arguments from multiple viewpoints were standardly presented: the declamation. Unlike in Antiquity, where 'they declaimed on those things in school that never happened in life', modern students 'should declaim on those matters that could be of use in later life'.[171] They should take time in preparing their written declamations and read Seneca the Elder's *Controversies*, and the teacher should regularly explain declamations to them putting a lot of emphasis on the contextual aptness of arguments: 'first, he [the teacher] should consider the subject matter. After this, he should move to the speaker, the time, and the audience'.[172]

What should we make of the role of declamations in *De disciplinis*? Declamation undoubtedly comprised the whole spectrum of oratory where arguments on specific issues were tailored for the emotional dispositions of the audience. Furthermore, declamation was in its essence about arguing things from both sides, which created a potential tension with the yearn for truth. In his youthful *Declamationes Syllanae*, Vives had not only exemplified the genre, but, as seen, also underlined that the criterium for one's saying should be primarily persuasion.[173] Similarly, he had criticized Ciceronianism, among other things, for its lack of efficiency to persuade and to win a debate. Vives seemed to be fully aware of the tension between declamations and truth, and I believe that the way in which oratory was framed by the educational path in *De disciplinis* was, for Vives, essentially a way to control its ambivalence. Unlike in Erasmus, who discarded dialectic almost completely in his educational manuals, oratory followed a course in dialectic where one was introduced to non-contextual, and general truth in an environment that excluded verbal confrontation. Oratory was the culmination of language education, but it could only enter the picture at an advanced stage once the pupil had supposedly familiarized himself with truth.

This rhetorical ability was undoubtedly essential to Vives's educated and prudent man, and it was more attuned to civic contexts than to religious oratory. The examples of topical invention were often political (the prince, the republic), the Senecan *Controversies* which Vives suggested included the only classical example of political declamations (*suasoria*), and Vives's own declamations composed in and for a school context were decidedly political, as we have seen. Moreover, in *De disciplinis*, as in his *De ratione studii puerilis* (1523) on elementary education, he recommended political texts such as More's *Utopia* and Erasmus's *Institutio principis Christiani* for students.[174] Interestingly, in a 1538 Basel edition (Robert Winter), Vives's declamations were printed together with a selection of his political texts, which accentuated the link between declamatory exercises and contemporary concerns.[175]

The political element was further supported by the fact that the authors he advised students to imitate included not only moralists (Seneca and Plutarch) but also some of the most famous political orators (e.g. Cicero, Demosthenes, Isocrates, and the orations of Livy's history).[176]

The description in Book Five of *De tradendis* of the other arts in which students should be educated also expanded at length on the studies (history, moral philosophy, political philosophy, law) that were meant to be put into practice in a civic life of *negotium*. Even the dedicatory letter of *De disciplinis*, composed for the Portuguese King Joâo III (1502–1557), flamboyantly underscored the close bond between knowledge and power. Here Vives elaborated on the 'agreement' (*consensio*) between princes and the learned who contributed to the commonwealth through counsel.[177] Thus, while Vives's educational project incorporated the ideal of pious self-cultivation, it was primarily tailored to a practical and civic education for the realization of a life of *negotium* in various *officia*.

In this life of *negotium*, rhetoric was not of course necessarily performed in the classical *fora* of political oratory. This, as we will see, was apparent in Vives's adaptation of rhetorical theory to different contexts (see Chapter 5) and in his incorporation of different rhetorical tools into *De tradendis* (such as *sermo* or Socratic questions). It was equally clear in Vives's depiction of the prudent, educated man. In his *De vita et moribus eruditi*, the culmination of *De tradendis*, Vives demonstrated that all studies were judged solely by their usefulness to other people. Common good should be the yardstick of both his studies and *negotium*. In a life of study, the investigative work of the scholar should, according to Vives, always be undertaken with the goal of furthering the arts and the common good – something to which his own projects aspired. In a life of *negotium,* the prudent man should act as a doctor of the soul either of princes and, if that turned out to be impossible, of the people. As he pointed out, 'the hearts of most princes are corrupt and intoxicated with the magnitude of their fortune to such an extent that no art is able to make them better' in which case 'we should direct our attention to the people who are more manageable'.[178]

Vives's wise man was strikingly different from such classical models as Quintilian's ideal orator, to which *De disciplinis* was compared by Foster Watson.[179] While Quintilian's orator used his knowledge, 'to guide the counsels of the senate, or lead an erring people into better ways', he was ever ready to bend truth if the cause required this, and he overcame shyness and fear through self-confidence. For Vives's learned man, a life of *negotium* was a battle against vice in a world of discord where the purity of his character was threatened and had to be cultivated incessantly in times of *otium*. He contemplated death, feared his own passions, recognized the potentially dreadful consequences of eloquence, and saw the world as one of profound and threatening discord.[180] Furthermore, unlike Roman orators, to whom the context of the common good to be defended in political orations was the good of the state, Vives's orator was a Christian or Stoic mediator of cosmic reason which, in more practical terms, often implied the necessity to denounce the reason of the state or the narrow interest of political constellations.[181] He was also strikingly different from the kind of a courtier that Italian manuals were beginning to portray. He was not the man of *sprezzatura* and aesthetic *decorum* depicted by Castiglione, capable of securing his place in the court by interiorizing and mastering its manners, ways of speaking, and culture. While this ideal was pronouncedly Italian, it had echoes in works such as Thomas Elyot's (c.1490–1536) *The Boke named the Governour* (1531), which described practices such as hunting, hawking, and dancing in a positive light. In contrast, Vives stressed that a prudent man had to keep his distance from these exercises, which were mentioned only once, and in very suspicious terms, in *De disciplinis*.[182]

Nor was Vives's wise man a specialist in law or a participant in the vernacular rhetorical culture represented in the Low Countries by the Chambers of Rhetoric.[183] Rather, as an ideal type, he is perhaps best described as an erudite man of the Republic of Letters with a firm grounding in Latin but with a schizophrenic relationship to an active life since, on the one hand, it was a world of discord that easily corrupted one's soul and, on the other, it was where his skills should be put into practice in a range of reforming projects. He was a scholar who criticized power slightly removed from the court, not a courtier who engaged with all the supposedly corrupting tendencies of an active life. It was this Latin-speaking actively engaged humanist whom Vives offered an educational ideal in *De disciplinis*. As we will find out in Chapter 5, he, in tune with the treatment of declamations in *De disciplinis*, also provided this ideal type with all possible knowledge of rhetoric and emotions without which he simply could not make a difference in the world of corruption and discord.

Notes

1. Noreña, 1970, 105–20.
2. González González, 2008, 60–1.
3. Guy, 2000, 106–22; Tracy, 1997, 49–55.
4. Del Nero, 1991, 12; Vigliano, 2013, lvi–lx; Sinz, 1963, 83–6. In his letters to Cranevelt there are some hints at the work in the summer and autumn of 1525; De Vocht, 1928, 457 (Ep. 167, Vives to Cranevelt). In another letter to Cranevelt, he clearly refers to *De disciplinis*; De Vocht, 1928, 478–9 (Ep. 175, Vives to Cranevelt). In early 1527, Juan de Vergara wanted to know more about the project: *Clarorum Hispanensium epistolae ineditae*, 1901, 254 (Vergara to Vives).
5. In this sense, it is unique within humanist literature; see Vigliano, 2013, lxviii, xc. Examples of pedagogical texts that are written as curricula for an institution include Erasmus's *De ratione studii* and Johannes Sturm's *De literarum ludis recte aperiendis* (1538).
6. These three parts were thought of as a unity in the sixteenth century, but the third part was left out already in the seventeenth century and, consequently, the unity of the work is lost in Mayans' edition of Vives's works; Del Nero, 1991, 16–9; González González, 2007, 90–1.

Redefining rhetoric in De disciplinis   167

7. Lange, 1887, 76–777, 809–33. In the English-speaking world, it was the work of Foster Watson that disseminated this view; Watson, 1913, xvii–xxi, ci–ciii. For classical interpretations of *De disciplinis* as a cornerstone in the history of pedagogy, see González González, 2007, 291–309.
8. Del Nero, 2008a, 179–80; Del Nero, 1991, 11–2.
9. Fernández-Santamaría, 1998, 83–144. Noreña writes about a Pelagian faith in the perfectibility of the individual; see Noreña, 1970, 178.
10. Del Nero, 1991, 40–8, 95–106; Del Nero, 2008a, 178–85; Fernández-Santamaría, 1998, viii–ix. Some classical interpretations have noted Vives's willingness to question not only scholasticism but also the Renaissance; see Ortega y Gasset, 1961, 63.
11. Bejczy, 2003, 70–1. Tracy makes the same observation, Tracy, 1996, 65–6.
12. See, e.g., Erasmus, ASD V/4 (*Ecclesiastes*), 35–8; Budé, 1535. For the importance of *pietas*, see Del Nero, 1991, 32–4. Vives's denunciation of Aristotle's earthly happiness (*eudaimonia*) is an example of a Christian critique; Vives, 2013, 237–42. The second part is also entitled *De tradendis disciplinis seu de institutione Christiana*, which accentuates the Christian flavour. For rhetoric in *De disciplinis*, see George, 1992, 145–54; Rodríguez Peregrina, 1995.
13. Vives, 2013, 9–19, 273.
14. *Diligentia* and *ingenium* are employed frequently in humanist literature; see Agricola, 1532, 14. They are also employed in this sense in the second part of *De disciplinis*.
15. Vives, 2013, 9: 'Hinc sunt nata inuenta hominum omnia, utilia, noxia, proba, improba'.
16. Vives, 2013, 16: '… cupiditate aliqua excitatur decoris et pecuniae'. See also 17–8.
17. Vives, 2013, 18: 'Nunquam ergo uel perfectae fuerunt artes uel purae, ne in sua quidem origine: ea est superbissimi animi caecitas atque imbecillitas'.
18. This point is made with special vigour in the first book of *De tradendis*, which reiterates many of the arguments made in *De causis*: see Vives, 2013, 278–80. However, in *De causis* we are told that the corruption of arts is bound together with an erroneous interpretation of their *telos*; ibid. 79 (2013).
19. Vives, 2013, 18: 'Haec omnia quasi brachiorum ui aliquo usque progressa tanquam aduerso flumine, ubi primum coeperunt brachia remitti, relapsa sunt'.
20. Sturm, 1538a, iii^v-[iiii]^r (Translation from Sturm, 1995b, 122): '… nobis ordinem uiamque illam in discendo ostendant, quae ueterum Romanorum Graecorumque rationi sit maxime consentanea'.
21. Vives, 2013, 171: 'Humanae omnes societates duabus potissimum rebus uinciuntur ac continentur: iustitia et sermone'. This same assertion is repeated in *De ratione dicendi*; see Vives, 2000, 3: 'Qui humanae consociationis uinculum dixerunt esse iustitiam et sermonem, hi nimirum acute inspexerunt vim ingenii humani …'.
22. The story about the birth of rhetoric in Sicily for judicial purposes was a common one in classical antiquity; see Cicero, 1939a, 48–9 (12.45–6).
23. Vives, 2013, 172–3: '… translatum est instrumentum, ut quemadmodum mouerant iudices, mouerent etiam animos in concione populi, senatus in curia, denique eorum omnium qui plurimum possent in republica, et in quorum manu atque arbitrio fortuna esset omnis posita ciuitatis …'.
24. Vives, 2013, 173: '… dominatus est orator, ubi eloquentia inuenit turbas acumine ingenii praeditas, inquietas, ambiciosas, et libertatis quadam aura tumefactas'.
25. Vives, 2013, 172: '… quando homines proclivitate naturae ad honores feruntut, ad opes, ad fortunas, dignitatem, potentiam, perlumti studuerunt ut optime ad conciones ciuium dicerent …'.

26. Tacitus, 1913, 342–3 (40.2): '... eloquentia alumna licentiae, quam stulti libertatem vocabant, comes seditionum, effrenati populi incitamentum, seine obsequio, sine severitate'.
27. Baker, 2015, 107.
28. Vives, 2013, 189: 'in senatu sententiae dicebantur non libere ut antea, sed in adulationem potentiae compositae, erantque magis encomia principum quam deliberationes de publicis utilitatibus'.
29. Vives, 2013, 190: 'Inane uero censuerunt laborem aliquem fructu omni adempto suscipi'.
30. Vives, 2000, 97–100. He might have been influenced by Augustine's hesitant exposition of *delectare*; see Augustine, 1962, 136–7 (4.13.29).
31. Vives makes the connection clear in the early part on the corruption of rhetoric; Vives, 2013, 171–2. Monarchy is explicitly interpreted as tyranny in Vives, 2013, 189.
32. Vives, 2013, 190.
33. Vives, 2013, 191: 'nam quanto illos superamus rebus, tanto partibus omnibus eloquentiae, tota ui persuadendi, sententiis, argumentis, dispositione, uerbis, genere orationis, actione inferiores sumus'.
34. Abbott, 1986, 195.
35. Vives, 2013, 177: '... res tam diuersas natura uoluerit coniungere'.
36. Vives, 2013, 177–8: '... uiri boni et nominantur et habentur qui nullo sunt probro infames'.
37. Vives, 2013, 175–7, 180–2; Quintilian, 2001, 1:408–9 (2.21.4); Cicero, 1942, 2:62–5 (3.21.78–81); Cicero, 1960a, 14–7 (1.5.7); Vickers, 1988, 169–70. He also argues against Aristotle's definition of rhetoric as an art that sees what is probable in each thing, see Vives, 2013, 174.
38. Vives, 2013, 175: '... ad captum popularem'.
39. Vives, 2013, 237.
40. Vives, 2013, 180–2.
41. Vives, 2013, 181.
42. Vives, 2013, 179–80.
43. Vives, 2013, 182–3.
44. Vives, 2013, 178–9; Quintilian, 2001, 2:34–7 (3.4.12–6).
45. Vives, 2013, 177–8: 'confundit quae sunt discretissima; atque eiusdem esse artis retur bene sentire et bene dicere, utiliter sane – atque utinam id hominibus persuaderet! – sed non perinde uere ...'.
46. On Ramus and Cicero, see Judith Rice Henderson, 1999.
47. Reisch, 1503, [Dvii]ᵛ; Murmellius, 1515, Biiᵛ. See also Ringelberg, 1538, 307; Bade, 1510b, Aiiʳ.
48. Regius, 1515, fol. IIIʳ: 'Nam perfectus orator: quem se velle instituere proponit: est tanquam Deus quidam terrenus [...] Quam quidem definitionem Virgilius quoque approbare videtur: cum inquit. Tum pietate gravem: ac meritis si forte virum quae Conspexere ...'; Virgil, 1999–2000, 1:272–3 (1.150–2).
49. Celtis, 1532, A5ʳ.
50. Hankins, 2003–2004, 1:200–7; Copenhaver, 1990, 90.
51. We find, however, other attempts to delineate the proper fields of dialectic and rhetoric on the basis of invention. Johannes Murmellius, for instance, claimed that dialectic was responsible for the invention of things (*res*) whereas the invention of words belonged to rhetoric; Murmellius, 1515, Biiʳ-Ciᵛ: 'Dialectica ad inueniendas res acutior, rhetorica ad inuendas dicendas facundior'.
52. Valla, 1982, 175–7.
53. Vives, 2013, 89, 170.
54. Guarino, 1514, Xʳ (Translation from Guarino, 2002, 292–3).
55. Murmellius, 1515, Biiᵛ.

56. Hegendorf, 1529, [A7]^r: '... cum eloquentiam dico [...] totam Enciclopaediam, id est, orbem illum artium optimarum comprehendo'.
57. Erasmus, ASD I/2, 113 (*De ratione studii*. CWE 24:666).
58. Erasmus, ASD I/2, 49 (*De pueris*. CWE 26:320).
59. Erasmus, ASD I/2, 76 (*De pueris*. CWE 26:344).
60. Melanchthon, 1523, Aiiii^v-Aiiii^r. For Melanchthon in *De disciplinis*, see Vives, 2013, 364, 382, 388, 401.
61. Melanchthon, 1523, Av^r (Translation from Rebhorn, 2000, 101).
62. Melanchthon, 1523, [Avi]^r (Translation from Rebhorn, 2000, 102).
63. Melanchthon, 1523, [Avii]^v-[Avii]^r.
64. Agrippa, 1531, Fol. XXV^v (Translation from Rebhorn, 2000, 77): '... constat totam illam ac omnem Rhetoricae disciplinam, nihil aliud esse quam adsentationis adulationisque, & [...] mentiendi ariticium'.
65. Agrippa, 1531, Fol. XXV^r (Translation from Rebhorn, 2000, 79): 'Ni hoc artificio nihil periculosius ciuilibus officiis, ab hoc, praeuaricatores, tergiuersatores, calmuniantes, sycophantae, & caetera huiusmodi sceleratae linguae hominum nomina descendunt'.
66. Agrippa, 1531, Fol. XXVI^v (Rebhorn, 2000, 80): '... ducentem in captiuitatem erroris, peruertendo sensum ueritatis'.
67. Erasmus, ASD IV/1, 238 (*Lingua*. CWE 29:262).
68. Erasmus, ASD IV/1, 235–6 (*Lingua*. CWE 29:259–60).
69. Erasmus, ASD IV/1, 262 (*Lingua*. CWE 29:286).
70. Erasmus, ASD IV/1, 248 (*Lingua*. CWE 29:272); Gellius, 1927, 1:72–81 (1.15).
71. Erasmus, ASD V/4, 249 (*Ecclesiastes*. CWE 68:469–70).
72. Melanchthon, 2017b, 37–44, 48–82.
73. Melanchthon, 2017a, 271–3.
74. Melanchthon, 2017a, 273, 275–8.
75. See also Weaver, 2017, xliii-xlv.
76. Erasmus, ASD IV/1, 288 (*Lingua*. CWE 29:316). See also 316.
77. Agrippa, 1531, XXVII^v (erroneously XVVII. Translation from Rebhorn, 2000, 81): 'nonne auctores illorum homines disertissimi, linguae eloquentia, & calami elegantia instructi?'
78. IJsewijn, 1992–1995, 43:27 (Ep. 61, Vives to Cranevelt); Allen 5:281–3 (Ep. 1362, Vives to Erasmus).
79. Mayans 5:465 (*De communione rerum*): 'Ex dissensione opinionum ventum est ad dissidium vitae [...] coeptum est [...] certari [...] hastis, gladiis, bombardis'.
80. Vives, 2013, 191.
81. Vives, 2013, 192: 'Hactenus nemo declamauit, utique in materia argumentosa et quasi in certamine et palaestra'.
82. For the historical background of the Ciceronian debate, see Knott in CWE 28.
83. Erasmus, ASD I/2 (*Ciceronianus*), 606–15.
84. For debunking the myth of Cicero, see Erasmus, ASD I/2 (*Ciceronianus*), 617–21.
85. For the adaptation of classical rhetoric to a Christian world, see especially Erasmus, ASD I/2 (*Ciceronianus*), 600, 636–47.
86. Erasmus, ASD I/2 (*Ciceronianus*), 634–6, 647–9.
87. Erasmus, ASD I/2 (*Ciceronianus*), 626, 649–50.
88. Vives, 2013, 196: '... imitentur potius rerum praesentium et praeteritarum cognitionem, scrutationem sectatorum sapientiae, tractationem humani animi, colligendi acumen, quibus potius uirtutibus omnia senatui et populo et iudicibus persuaserit, quam facultate uerborum et dictionis!'. See also 197–8; Vives, 1978, 506–8 (Ep. 139, Vives to Cepello).
89. Vives, 2013, 198: 'Quid loquentur de nostro foro, de nostris legibus, institutis, moribus, de pietate nostra per omnia Ciceroniani?'

170 *Redefining rhetoric in* De disciplinis

90. Vives, 2013, 201: '... Rhetoricam aiunt, quum de rebus aliis omnibus, potissimum de publicis ac ciuilibus dicturam'. For civil science and eloquence in the Renaissance, see Skinner, 1996, 19–40, 66–110.
91. Vives, 2013, 128–9, 134–5, 147–8, 155–64.
92. Nauert, 1990.
93. Mack, 1993, 265. In Paris, humanism entered especially through colleges; Rosa di Simone, 1996, 290.
94. Mack, 1993, 269–70; Papy, 1999, 182–5.
95. Jardine, 1974, 51.
96. Ashworth, 1988, 76.
97. Vives was explicitly placed in this tradition already in the 1530s; González González, 2007, 92–3.
98. Vives, 2013, 123–4. The argument that rhetoric concerned civic questions and did not touch upon the subject matter of separate arts was made with force in Sulpitius Victor's *De arte oratoria*, which was printed by Froben in 1521; Sulpitius Victor, 1521, 83–4. For a discussion of this, see Caesarius, 1535, C^v-C^r.
99. Vives, 2013, 123, 143: '... sit una [inventio] tantum, eaque magis dialectici iuris quam rhetorici'.
100. Vives, 2013, 145–6: 'quorsum pertineat dialectica ignorat, quae sua, quae aliena [...] totam eam partem quae est de argumentis inueniendis occuparunt rhetores ...'.
101. There is a separate book dedicated to dialectical invention in the third part entitled *De instrumento probabilitatis*.
102. Nauta, 2015, 339. See also Waswo, 1987, 113–33; Coseriu, 1971.
103. Nauta, 2015, 343–5.
104. Vives, 2013, 145: 'quod aliud non fuit quam infinitam possessionem locorum contrahere in magnas angustias'. This idea was possibly taken from Agricola; Mack, 1993, 142.
105. Vives, 2013, 144, 387–8, 401–2.
106. Aristotle, 1960a, 181 (90b); Aristotle, 1960b, 281–3 (102a), 560–1 (139a); Aristotle, 1933, 321–7 (1029b–1030b); Jardine, 1974, 35–42.
107. Aristotle, 1926, 305 (1398a); *Ad Herennium*, 86–9, 130–3 (2.12.17, 2.26.41).
108. Agricola, 1992, 36–44 (1.V). For Agricola and definition, see Mack, 1993, 151–6.
109. Trebizond, 1509, DVii$^{v\text{-}r}$. See also Valla, 1519, 24–6.
110. Vives, 1532, 519–20: '... quo sit ut essentiae diffinitiones parum nos doceant, minimeque sint nobis utiles, ac ea de causa, ut puto, rarae'. The idea that it is hard to achieve certainty on essences also links Vives to a Ciceronian tradition of academic scepticism; Casini, 2009.
111. Vives, 1532, 521: 'Quapropter ad recte diffiniendum, sumendum est de principio non tam genus, quam superius quiddam accomodatum experimendae rei, siue id essentiae sit, siue adhaerentis, sive etiam metaphorae: tum concinnandum, & coarctandum adiunctione inferiorum, dum illud totum quadret, ac fiat proprium ...'.
112. Vives follows Agricola almost word for word here. See Agricola, 1992, 40–2 (1.V); Vives, 1532, 521–2: 'Invenimus primum ius uim quondam in se habere cogendi, & iussum [...] Ius est decretum maioris potestatis ad tuendum ciuitatis statum ex aequo & bono institutum'.
113. Vives, 1532, 528: 'aliterque gloriam finit Cicero agens Caesari gratias pro Marcello restituto, nempe ad populum populariter, quam in Tusculanis quaestionibus Philosophice disserens apud paucos'.
114. Vives, 1532, 524–6: '... eruditio paratur usu, paratur studio, paratur doctrina'; 'honor popularis est locus dignitatis, quo caeca sors sine delectu evehit'; 'civitas sine iustitia est receptaculum latronum'; 'Maiestas reipublicae est in qua continetur dignitas & amplitudo civitatis'; 'bonus princeps est, qui non in cogitatione suorum commodorum, sed publicorum est cunctus'.

115. Goudriaan – van Moolenbroek – Tervoort, 2003, 3–4; Vickers, 1988, 257; Huppert, 1977, 61–5. Despite this, the prevalence of Latin education should not be exaggerated; it has been estimated that Latin schools were destined only for about 5–7.5 per cent of the youth; Maas, 2011, 44–5.
116. Goudriaan – van Moolenbroek – Tervoort, 2003, 3–5; Tervoort, 2005, 32–4. For the Brethren of Common life and schooling, see Post, 1968, 553–65.
117. Goudriaan, 2003, 168–72; Post, 1968, 553–67; Koenigsberger, 2001, 19–22, 132–40.
118. Post, 1968, 561–3.
119. Sturm, 1538b, 12^r-13^v, 18^v-25^v, 28^r-29^v. See also Sturm, 1995a, 61–63. For Sturm and the influence of his education in Liège on his educational model, see Post, 1968, 558–60.
120. Tervoort, 2005.
121. Damen, 2003, 51–2; Ridder-Symoens, 1981, 293–6; Ridder-Symoens, 1996; Zijlstra, 2003, 297–8.
122. For the careers of those who studied in Italy, see Tervoort, 2005, 381–407.
123. Erasmus, ASD I/2, 23 (*De pueris*. CWE 26 :297).
124. Erasmus, ASD I/2, 52, 64 (*De pueris*. CWE 26 :323, 334).
125. Vives, 2013, 306, 319: 'Statuatur in unaquaque prouincia Academia communis illius ...'; 'Constituatur in quaque ciuitate ludus literarius'.
126. This point is made in Erasmus's *De pueris instituendis*; Erasmus, ASD I/2 (*De pueris*), 31–2.
127. Vives, 2013, 5: '[cultus ingeniorum/disciplinas] ... nos a ferarum ritu et more separat, humanitati restituit, et ad Deum extollit ipsum ...'.
128. The fiercest debates on the relationship between the humanist and scholastic models of education concerned Italy. A tradition going back to Eugenio Garin has emphasized the innovative nature of humanist educational paradigms that stressed the cultivation of the character of a man of *negotium* through a focus on eloquence. Another tradition, deriving from Anthony Grafton's and Lisa Jardine's *From Humanism to the Humanities* (1986), underscored continuity, pictured the humanist ideal of *negotium* as false and unattainable through their pedagogical tools, and stressed that humanism, rather than nurturing civic participation, paved the way for a curriculum of obedience; Garin, 1968; Grafton – Jardine, 1986; Grendler, 1991, 404–5; Black, 2001, 10–11, 366, 368; Carlsmith, 2010, 15–8; Karant-Nunn, 1990.
129. Vives, 2013, 355–8; Erasmus, ASD I/2 (*De pueris*), 61–3.
130. Erasmus, ASD I/3 (*Colloquia*), 531–3. Erasmus's friend Aurelius also complained of this in 1524; see Tilmans, 1992, 13–4.
131. See also Weijers, 2013, 71–176.
132. Vergerio, 2002, 28–9. For the questioning of this ideal, see n. 128 above.
133. Vergerio, 2002, 36–9.
134. Erasmus, ASD I/2, 29 (*De pueris*. CWE 26:302).
135. Erasmus, ASD I/2, 132–5, 136 (*De ratione studii*. CWE 24:682).
136. Vives, 2013, 55: '... praua uel honoris uel pecuniae cupiditas animos disputantium inuasit, ut tanquam in pugna sola spectaretur uictoria, non elucidatio ueritatis ...'.
137. Vives, 2013, 54–63.
138. Weijers, 2013, 177–207.
139. Périgot, 2005, 306–7.
140. Sturm, 1538b, 33^v, 33^r (Translation from Sturm, 1995c, 115): 'Liberalis decet hunc coetum disquisitio'; 'Suspecta est enim propositionum conglobation ...'.
141. The idea of disputation as a faculty or mental discourse as opposed to an active exercise was already developed by medieval thinkers; see Périgot, 2005, 295–8; Vives, 1532, 609–18.

172 *Redefining rhetoric in* De disciplinis

142. Vives, 1532, 619: 'quid positum sit in controuersia'; 'respondens perspectam illorum omnium habeat naturam, de quibus agitur'. See also 618, 620. On the importance of truth in theological disputations, see Vives, 2013, 479–80. For rheological disputations and university education, see Weijers, 2013, 180–2.
143. Vives, 2013, 313–4, 320–33. 435–40, 450–5.
144. Quintilian, 2001, 1:96–103 (1.3); Vergerio, 2002, 8–14, 49; Isocrates, 1508: the first four pages. Vives's *De ratione studii* also mentions these kinds of short sentences (*sententiolae*) as an antidote to changing fortunes and poisonous things; see Vives, 1527c, 54^v: '... antidota aduersus venenum, & prosperae fortunae, & iniquae'.
145. IJsewijn, 1988, 198. IJsewijn is not, however, referring here primarily to Vives's *De disciplinis*. Marcel Bataillon has described *De disciplinis* as an attempt to purify education morally and socially; see Bataillon, 1991b, 330. As Bataillon has demonstrated, at least some people, most importantly the poet André Resende, understood Vives as a moralist with little sympathy for poetry.
146. Vives's critical assessment of authors was widely referenced in the sixteenth century; see González González, 2007, 90.
147. Vives, 2013, 352: 'Scribent epistolam facilem aut fabellam. Dilatabunt exemplum, apophthegma, sententiolam, prouerbium. Soluent et diffundent carmen numeris astrictum, atque eadem efferent absque numeris ...'.
148. For language as a gateway to wisdom, see Vives, 2013, 387.
149. Vives, 2013, 353–4.
150. Vives, 2013, 366: 'Magis uersabitur in iis quae sunt uitae communia ...'. For the philological emphasis, see Vives, 2013, 380. It is worth noting that in most cases one teacher was responsible for the curriculum of one grade and specialized teachers may have been used in grades two and one; see Post, 1968, 559–62.
151. Vives, 2013, 365–6. Earlier, in referring to the themes of elementary education, Vives had also made similar remarks; see Vives, 2013, 340.
152. For the significance of the dialogues and their reception history, see González González –Rodríguez, 1999.
153. In dialogue 19, it is Sofronius and in dialogue 20 Sofobolus, Vives, 1539, 83–94.
154. The reception of the dialogues in the sixteenth century stressed their moral nature; see Mahlmann-Bauer, 2008, 356–60.
155. Vives, 1539, 123.
156. Vives, 1539, 125: 'Quid si sunt leges aut mores praui, iniqui, tyrannici?'
157. Vives's history of rhetoric already linked the outlook of rhetorical culture to the *ingenium* of the audience; see Vives, 2013, 172–3.
158. Vives, 2013, 379: 'Huius porro ad uitam usus fuerit, ut sit scriba ciuitatis publicus, capessat minores magistratus, fungatur legationibus'.
159. Sturm, 1538b, 3^v.
160. Erasmus, ASD I/2 (*De ratione studii*), 130–6.
161. Erasmus, ASD I/2, 429 (*De conscribendis epistolis*. CWE 25:145–6).
162. Sturm, 1538b, 25^v (Translation from Sturm, 1995c, 103): 'Aptum appello quodcunque literatum est, & doctrina illuminatum, & liberale, & rebus personisque accomodatum'.
163. Vives, 2013, 419: 'Hoc est adolescentiae curriculum ad quintum et vicesimum annum, aut eo circiter'.
164. Vives, 2013, 387: 'Hactenus cognitioni linguarum uacauimus, quae fores sunt disciplinarum omnium atque artium, earum certe quae monumentis magnorum ingeniorum sunt proditae'. Here Vives also stated that one could start the acquisition of arts already when one was finishing one's linguistic studies. But generally speaking, *De disciplinis* did disentangle grammar and language acquisition from rhetoric and dialectic.

165. Vives, 2013, 388: 'Socracticae interrogatiunculae [...] diuisionibus ac diffinitionibus, uehementer sunt ad multa conducibiles: ad uerum experimendum, ad exacuendum ingenium, et ad reuincendum eum qui contra tendit'.
166. Vives, 2013, 399.
167. Vives, 2013, 388, 397–8: 'reddunt enim spinosos, rixosos, fraudulentos'.
168. Vives, 2013, 400: 'is est maximorum et bonorum et malorum caussa'. For a classical formulation of this idea, see Cicero, 1942, 2:42–5 (3.14.55).
169. Vives, 2013, 400: '... certe quo sunt corruptiores animi hominum, eo ars haec accuratius deberet a prudentibus et probis uiris suscipi ...'.
170. Vives, 2013, 402–3.
171. Vives, 2013, 404: '... de iis rebus dicebant in schola, quae nunquam in uita contigerent ...'; 'Declament iuuenes [...] de iis argumentis quorum aliquis sit deinceps usus in uita ...'.
172. Vives, 2013, 404: 'Consyderabit primum qua de re dicatur. Hinc quis, quo tempore, ad quos fingatur dicere'.
173. Vives, 1989b, 110–1. See p. 55.
174. Vives, 2013, 404–5, 457–8; Vives, 1527c, 46^r.
175. These texts were his letter to the Pope Adrian (*De tumultibus Europae*), two letters to Henry VIII (*De Francisco Galliae Rege a Caesare capto* and *De pace*) and *De bello turcico*. In addition to these, Quintilian's *Paries palmatus*, along with Vives's response to Quintilian, and his translations of Isocrates's orations *Areopagitica* and *Nicocles* appeared in the edition.
176. Vives, 2013, 408–9.
177. Vives, 2013, 3–4.
178. Vives, 2013, 471: 'Corda uero plerorumque principum adeo sunt corrupta et magnitudine illa fortunae ebria, ut nulla arte refingi queant in melius [...] curam nostram traducamus in populum magis tractabilem ...'. See also 472, 474. The idea that a life of *otium* and *negotium* are closely connected could be found, for instance, in Plutach's *De liberis educandis* (*On the education of children*); Plutarch, 1966, 34–7 (7F-8B).
179. Watson, 1913, ci–cii.
180. Vives, 2013, 466–90. Quintilian, 2001, 5:210–1 (12.1.25–7): '... cum regenda senatus consilia et popularis error ad meliora ducendus'.
181. The idea of a narrow interest of the state in Roman thought was criticized by the Younger Seneca, who stressed the participation of the prince in the commonwealth of reason as a precondition of good rule; Tuck, 1990, 44–5; see Seneca, 1965, 186–9 (4.1–2); Stacey, 2007, 29–30. In his *Praefatio in Leges Ciceronis*, Vives claimed that a prince, as a lawgiver, should be a citizen of the cosmic commonwealth of reason; see Vives, 1984a, 6: '... is etiam, tamquam optimus civis huius universae civitatis, quae totum genus humanum capit, quid inventa sua publicos in usus in medium reponit'. His *De consultatione* made perfectly clear that whereas the Romans thought of the *patria* as the context of what is honest (*honestum*), we should remember that the true measure was religion; Vives, 1536, 254. More generally, for freedom as freedom from ignorance, see Vives, 2013, 479.
182. Vives, 2013, 477; Elyot, 1531, 70; Castiglione, 1556, 41–5; Kristeller, 1988, 291–2. For a comparison between the two although with a particular focus on style, see Kennedy, 1996. For Castigilione's *sprezzatura*, see also Rebhorn, 1993; Berger, 2000; Kolsky, 2003.
183. Dixhoorn, 2008, 136–41; Spies, 1999, 57–8.

5 Rhetorical *Decorum* and the Functioning of the Soul (1532–1540)

Vives's Last Years

Vives's life in the years after completing *De disciplinis* is something of an enigma. On the one hand, his fame as a leading humanist rose to new heights with the publication of some of his most ambitious and widely diffused writings. His prominence is reflected in the number of printed editions of his works (around 70 different editions during the 1530s) and in his new popularity among the prestigious Basel printers in the aftermath of Erasmus's death.[1] On the other hand, we know little about Vives's life in this period, partly due to the lack of a source comparable to his letters to Cranevelt and partly because of his decision to avoid public disputes and political life. There were admittedly some signs of regular contacts with the powerful of the time. In addition to his correspondence with the Emperor, he spent some time (at least in 1537–1538) in Breda as the private tutor of a Valencian lady Doña Mencía de Mendoza, the wife of Count Nassau.[2] Despite this, his scholarly fame was not really accompanied by a realisation of that reputation in a visible life of *negotium*. In the last decade of his life, Vives clearly thought that a life of study in Bruges was best for himself and, possibly, the best way to contribute to the long-term reformation of a continent whose current situation he considered hopeless given the nature of its rulers and the severity of its discord.

When one looks at Vives's intellectual preoccupations, rhetoric and the functioning of the soul were central. While some of his published literature dealt with the immediate problems of the time (*De communione rerum* against the Anabaptists) and with specific educational goals (*Exercitatio linguae latinae* on the teaching of Latin at the elementary level), his most extensive treatises of the 1530s were *De ratione dicendi* on rhetoric and *De anima* on the soul. These works were complemented by *De conscribendis epistolis* on the application of rhetorical precepts to the extremely popular genre of letter writing. Vives himself thought of *De disciplinis*, *De ratione dicendi*, and *De anima* as closely connected in their subject matter. In point of fact, in *De disciplinis* he made references to *De ratione dicendi* and *De anima* – both of which were most likely ongoing projects already in 1531 – as

DOI: 10.4324/9781003240457-6

extensions of specific themes such as the order to be used in the teaching of the arts (*De ratione dicendi*) or the workings of interior discourse (*De anima*).[3]

In this chapter, I analyse Vives's last works as the culmination of his thought on rhetoric and political philosophy. My aim is to uncover how *De ratione dicendi*, with its pronounced stress on non-confrontational *decorum*, can be seen as a mature attempt to adapt the precepts of classical rhetoric into less openly antagonistic genres of speech. I also argue that Vives's interest in the audience as the key to rhetorical production partly explains why he emphasised that rhetorical theory was ultimately dependent on knowledge of the emotions. In this spirit, *De anima* will be interpreted as a continuation of Vives's concern with the rhetorical arousal of emotions and as the apex of his political philosophy based on ethical self-government. As we will see, the extension of rhetorical theory to the knowledge of emotions not only reintroduced emotions, especially those of the audience, into the centre of rhetorical theory, but it also provided an explanation for the persuasive potential of a rhetoric of *decorum*.

De ratione dicendi

De ratione dicendi was Vives's most exhaustive and ambitious treatment of rhetorical theory. Yet it is not very well known because it never gained the popularity of the much simpler *De conscribendis epistolis*. As has been pointed out, one of the reasons for the lack of following might well have been the originality of the book, which purposely broke down many of the standard categorisations of rhetorical theory and mostly avoided schematic presentations of rhetorical precepts.[4] This originality, which often drew and expanded on the critical points he had made in *De disciplinis*, manifested itself in various forms. The treatise was not structured around the three traditional genres of rhetoric (judicial, deliberative, epideictic) or around the five parts of oratory (invention, disposition, style, delivery, memory), all of which were absent as separate topics. Despite the reorganisation of the structure, the focus was on the subject matter that would have traditionally fallen under style and on the decorous adaptation of one's message to particular situations. Issues pertaining to rhetorical invention, such as the topics and argumentative forms, were discussed only sporadically and in a non-systematic way. This was in line with Vives's claim in *De disciplinis* that invention and judgment belonged to dialectic.

While many classical precepts found their way into *De ratione dicendi*, they were situated within a scheme that endorsed rhetorical flexibility and promoted new genres of mostly literary rhetoric important for the sixteenth-century context. These genres taught about things (*res:* description, probable narration, history, apologues, fables, and poetic fictions) and about words (*verba:* paraphrase, epitome, explication, commentary, and translation).[5] Some of these, such as description and narration, were not necessarily independent genres but skills that could serve in different rhetorical tasks, whereas others, such as fables, were closely connected to the kind of exercises that trained schoolboys in eloquence.[6] Commentary and translation were indispensable for humanist philology, whereas history was of great significance in the early sixteenth-century princely context, as epitomised by Thomas More's *History of King Richard III* (1519), a fierce critique of tyranny.[7] *De ratione dicendi* also expanded the category of style from tropes and figures to a broader treatment of style and, most importantly, claimed that the key to rhetoric did not lie in any system of formulaic precepts but in an understanding of the contextual requirements of any situation, which, for its part, fell under *decorum*.

The rethinking of many issues of rhetorical theory and the self-proclaimed originality of *De ratione dicendi* did not necessarily mean that Vives thought all other materials on rhetorical training were outdated and irrelevant.[8] Mayans y Siscar and Bonilla already noted that the work was not meant as an elementary introduction to rhetoric.[9] Rather, *De ratione dicendi* is best understood as a more advanced treatment that could break with existing categories because it presupposed familiarity with them. Indeed, Vives's *De disciplinis,* despite its criticism of all existing rhetorical theory, introduced classical works into its syllabus, which implied that traditional handbooks could serve as an elementary introduction to the art in the school context. While this solution might have been a practical one motivated by the absence of suitable contemporary handbooks, Vives clearly expected the reader of *De ratione dicendi* to be familiar with existing rhetorical theory, which allowed for greater originality and complexity.

The Rhetoric of *Decorum* and the Importance of the Audience in *De ratione dicendi*

In what follows, I focus on what I take to be the essential feature of the work: its pronounced stress on *decorum* as the essence of rhetoric. While others, most notably Peter Mack, have emphasised that Vives's *De ratione dicendi* contained the most extensive treatment of rhetorical *decorum* since classical antiquity, the reasons motivating Vives's interest in it remain largely unknown.[10] In my view, Vives's fascination with *decorum* was an attempt to ground socially, politically, and religiously meaningful rhetoric in appropriateness in an increasingly literary, monarchical, and religiously sensitive context.[11] In this environment, passionate and openly adversarial rhetoric would only aggravate religious discord and division by nurturing destructive emotions and, politically, fail to guide rulers to work for the common good. Because of this, rhetorical theory was embedded in civil or non-adversarial language that did not shatter the appearance of concord yet aimed at persuasion by overcoming the emotional and cognitive resistance of the audience. Unlike in some Italian manuals, *decorum* did not primarily function within a courtly milieu; it did not imply a move from oratory to non-passionate polite conversation that aspired to be pleasing, as was typical of some Italian manuals such as Castiglione's *Il cortegiano* (1528), but appropriated the civic duties of oratory to persuade and enhance common good in a more classical spirit across an array of oratorical genres.

As Vives forcefully argued in the dedicatory letter to the work (addressed to Francisco de Mendoza y Bobadilla), the power of language had to be tied together with *decorum* for rhetoric to retain its socially constructive role. In the letter, firmly in accordance with *De disciplinis*, we are told that two things formed the bonds of societies: 'justice' (*iustitia*) and 'language' (*sermo*). We are also shown that 'of the two, language is certainly stronger and more powerful among men' because, unlike justice that had power only over those who were 'rightly' (*recte*) and 'virtuously' (*probe*) instructed, it 'draws the minds of men to itself and dominates the emotions', which wield power over all humans.[12] 'Well trained and educated language' was very useful for social life, but there was nothing more 'destructive' or 'inconvenient' than speech that was not accommodated to 'places, times, and persons'.[13] We are also told that to speak 'suitably' (*apte dicere*) was important for a prudent man and that *decorum* was 'the foundation' (*caput*) of the art of rhetoric.[14] Part of this call for apt and educated speech was Vives's insistence, already familiar from *De disciplinis*, that true eloquence was unattainable for the young and inexperienced and should be reserved for those who were experienced, prudent, and familiar with the other arts, especially dialectic.[15]

In the treatise proper, Vives, just like in *De disciplinis*, linked this ambivalent power of rhetoric to the maintenance of social life (*societas*) and its history to the republican conditions of Antiquity.[16] He maintained that 'there is indeed no other instrument that is as suitable for human association'.[17] He also argued that 'the one who is most skilful in speaking clearly reigns among men', and in republics in which liberty was valued and where it led to great rewards, it flourished.[18] Vives wanted to recover rhetoric, but, as he put it, 'we do not renew the rhetoric of the ancients as it was, but we teach a completely new one'.[19] While this claim referred to several issues, such as the change in the contexts in which rhetoric was performed – Vives wanted to extend rhetoric from judicial and deliberative rhetoric to numerous other genres – it certainly was related to the centrality of *decorum*.

The stress put on *decorum* was both conventional and exceptional. It was conventional in referring to a concept that was strongly present in classical theories of art, poetry, ethics, and rhetoric, where it referred both to a principle and a disposition to act and speak appropriately.[20] In the rhetorical tradition, *decorum* (or its Greek approximation *prepon*) could be found in Greek treatises on rhetoric such as Aristotle's *Rhetoric*; yet the most frequently cited passages in the Renaissance were taken from Roman writers, above all, Cicero and Quintilian. It has been argued that in Cicero's rhetorical writings *decorum* carried the meanings of the Greek concepts of *prepon* (propriety, appropriateness) and *kairos* (occasion, right time to do something).[21] This mélange implied that propriety in rhetoric could be

178 *Rhetorical* decorum

linked to the right occasion, to the contextual requirements of a situation. The list of these requirements usually included things such as the characteristic features of a speaker, subject, audience, occasion, and place. Yet the implications of *decorum* are quite diverse depending on which terms of the list were emphasised. In Cicero's theoretical writings, the relationship between style, subject matter, and the speaker was usually dominant, which underscored more the general rules of suitability in the spirit of *prepon* than adaptation to particularities. In *De oratore*, the main point was the connection between subject matter and style, although other aspects were also mentioned.[22] In *Orator*, the list of contextual issues was included but the focus in the examples offered was on how to choose *sententiae* (thoughts) and words (*verba*) in accordance with one's rank, age, and social position.[23]

In Quintilian's *Institutio oratoria*, *decorum* was more explicitly associated with the possibilities of persuasion in a concrete case. This shifted the balance towards *kairos* or, more importantly for Quintilian, to a more meticulous analysis of one's audience (most importantly a judge in legal cases).[24] Quintilian tells us that a speech that lacks *decorum* not only fails 'to lend distinction to the oratory but will ruin it and make the facts work against us'. The words we use should not only be elegant but also they must 'accord with the views towards which we wish the judge to be guided and influenced'. Indeed, we should 'first of all know what is appropriate for winning over, instructing, and emotionally affecting the judge, and what our object is in the different parts of the speech'.[25] This persuasive framework is the context in which Quintilian's thorough analysis of the speaker, subject matter, audience, time, and place takes place. Furthermore, Quintilian was absolutely clear that *decorum* was not just about words but more generally about the ways in which we present our case persuasively. As he put it, 'all this question of appropriateness of speech is not solely a matter of Elocution, but shares ground with Invention; if even words can make such a crucial difference, how much more can the content do so'.[26] Both Quintilian's explicit analysis of *decorum* within the persuasive duties of rhetoric in concrete cases and his insistence that *decorum* was not merely a question of style but also possessed argumentative relevance (how to present one's case in front of a specific audience) were, although not directly appropriated form Quintilian, central in Vives in *De ratione dicendi*.

There are other classical traditions that Vives could have drawn on. An important current that emphasised rhetorical appropriateness and that was becoming increasingly available in the 1520s and 1530s was the Hermogenian strand of eloquence. Hermogenes, in *On Types of Style*, discussed the force of language (*deinotes*) as a form of *prepon*, a general category according to which all other considerations of style were moulded to meet the contextual requirement of the situation. Hermogenes argued that the orator who masters the adaptation of his style to different situations, themes, and audiences would be 'the most forceful of orators' and would 'surpass all others'.[27] Hermogenes's views on *deinotes* had been included in George of Trebizond's

Rhetorica's lengthy discussion on gravity (*gravitas*), in which true gravity (*vera gravitas*) was seen essentially as a form of judgment or an ability to adapt one's style to the situation.[28] By the early 1530s, Vives was familiar with Trebizond's *Rhetorica* and Hermogenes's rhetorical works and, in *De disciplinis*, he included both in his curriculum, describing Hermogenes as a suitable authority on forms of diction.[29] While Vives's examples of *decorum* in *De ratione dicendi* were not taken directly from Hermogenes and Trebizond, the portrayal of *decorum* as a standard of adaptation could have been reinforced by his familiarity with these authors.

Decorum described as a list of contextual requirements (speaker, audience, place, time, etc.) was frequently mentioned in medieval treatises of applied rhetoric such as poetry or the *ars dictaminis*, but it was seldom presented as a main issue.[30] This same trend to presuppose *decorum*'s importance yet omit a large treatment of it was evident in late fifteenth- and early sixteenth-century humanist treatises of rhetoric, letter writing, and style. None of the following works portrayed *decorum* as a central category of analysis that demanded a separate treatment under its own heading: Erasmus's *De copia* and *De conscribendis epistolis,* Rudolph Agricola's *De inventione dialectica*, Giorgio Valla's rhetorical works, Despauterius's *De figuris* (1519), Alberto Mancinelli's (1451–1505) *Carmen de figuris* (1489), Joachim Ringelberg's (c.1499–c.1531) short *Rhetorica* (1530), Philipp Melanchthon's *De rhetorica libri tres*, Johannes Caesarius's *De rhetorica* (1534), Konrad Celtis's *Epitome in rhetoricam Ciceronis, & non inutile scribendarum epistolarum compendium*, Bartolomeus Latomus's *Summa totius rationis disserendi*, or Geraldus Bucoldianus's *De Inventione et Amplificatione oratoria* (1534).[31] When *decorum* appeared as a separate topic, as in Johannes Rivius's (1500–1553) *De rhetorica libri II* (1539), it was often short and emphasised very general rules of suitability rather than the persuasive element of the concept. Rivius's account offered a lengthy quotation from Cicero's most famous passage on *decorum* in *Orator,* but his own exposition merely stated that *decorum* was first and foremost about the adaptation of words (*verba*) to correct themes (*res*), which, rather than underscoring the temporal or persuasive aspects of *decorum* as finding the right tools for a specific occasion, focused on the adaptability of verbal ornaments to different thematic issues.[32]

In this context, Vives's *De ratione dicendi* appeared as quite exceptional since, in the midst of rhetorical handbooks that did not give *decorum* much centrality, it argued that *decorum* was the most important component of the art or, more boldly, that rhetoric was essentially an art of *decorum*. Highly significantly, Vives's interpretation of *decorum* shifted the perspective from theme and speaker to the audience to an extent rarely found in other Renaissance treatises.

The stress on the audience did not mean that other issues were absent from Vives's account of rhetorical *decorum*. Even in rhetorical treatments of *decorum*, such as Cicero's *Orator*, a distinctively rhetorical *decorum* could be compared to the *decorum* of one's life.[33] This idea drew on Cicero's account of *decorum* in *De officiis*, where he underscored that, while *decorum* was an aesthetic concept and dependent on the gaze of others, it was inseparable from what was right (*honestum*).[34] This ethical interpretation, according to which *decorum* consisted in the externalisation of one's virtue in speech, manners, and courtesy, had been incorporated into Renaissance thought. In Erasmus's hugely influential *De civilitate morum puerorum* (1530), *decorum* was a fundamental term denoting the proper performance of virtue in polite manners. Although Erasmus claimed that external *decorum* is a 'crude part of philosophy' compared to the knowledge of piety, liberal arts, or duties, it was still useful because 'in the present climate of opinion it was very conducive to winning good will and to commending those illustrious gifts of the intellect to the eyes of men'.[35] Vives certainly took the ethical nature of *decorum* for granted. It is also likely that his understanding of rhetorical *decorum* presupposed a wider field of decorous conduct in politeness and manners but *De ratione dicendi* did not expand on it as such and Vives never employed the concept to set forth a code of behaviour.[36]

Decorous speech also demanded considerations of the subject and the person of the speaker as Cicero had amply demonstrated. In *De ratione dicendi*, we find stylistic precepts designed for speaking about God, heaven, nature, and morality.[37] Regarding one's person, Vives provided detailed advice on how to speak in accordance with one's age (young men/old men), profession (artisans, philosophers, political men), and dignity or office (magistrate, prince).[38]

The analysis of other aspects of *decorum* still paled in comparison with Vives's nuanced treatment of the audience. The audience had naturally been one of the factors in discussions on the possibilities of rhetorical persuasion. With its tendency to simplification, classical rhetoric had, however, mostly concentrated on the differences between a popular and a learned audience in conditioning rhetorical choices.[39] On a different note, the discussion of the *exordium* under arrangement (*dispositio*) had standardly divided the audience into those who were favourable to one's cause and/or *persona* and those who were not, which conditioned the way in which the *exordium* – traditionally described as the place where the goodwill of the audience had to be secured – was constructed.[40] However, once these categorisations were taken into account and applied to certain aspects of the speech, there was no need to examine the particularities of a specific audience in any detail. It was mostly in the *Institutio oratoria* that the consideration of particularities was suggested, with Quintilian, in dealing with judicial speaking, inviting the speaker to be aware of contextual issues such as the general climate of opinion and the view that the judge had of the matter.[41]

These categories (learned-unlearned, favourable-opposed) were frequently taken up in early modern materials (see p. 81). But sometimes, additional factors important for the contemporary context could be included. For instance, in Lorenzo Traversagni's (1425–1503) late fifteenth-century *Margarita eloquentiae castigatae* (1478), the categories of those who were learned (*scholasticos*) and the people (*populus*) were joined by an analysis of the prince.[42] Perhaps more pertinently for Vives, some writers that he knew well explored the audience in more detail. Antonio de Nebrija's *Artis rhetoricae compendiosa coaptatio, ex Aristotele, Cicerone et Quintiliano* (1515) offered, in the part on the deliberative genre, detailed advice on how to analyse the audience. Nebrija not only made the classical distinction between an educated and a popular audience (for example *senatus – populus*), but he also distinguished between individuals who were convinced by honesty (Cato) and those who were not (Marius), and invited his readers to consider the sex (*sexus*), merit (*dignitas*), age (*aetas*) and the manners (*mores*) of the deliberator.[43]

The dichotomy between learned and unlearned audiences was naturally present in Vives. He distinguished private instances of speaking from a speech destined for the people (*populus*), and we are reminded, in accordance with classical theory, that popular audience was the mother and nurse (*nutrix*) of oratory. 'Private conversation' (*collocutio, sermo*), for its part, 'has to be simple' (*simplex debet esse*) and mimic the style of Cicero's letters to Atticus.[44] Yet, like Nebrija, he was keenly interested in a more detailed examination of the audience for which he employed five main topics: talent (*ingenium*), learning (*eruditio*), memory (*memoria*), age (*aetas*), and habits (*mores*). These headings were familiar from many rhetorical manuals as possibilities for investigating persons, yet they had not been primarily linked to the analysis of one's audience but mainly to other issues such as the character of an object of a demonstrative speech.[45] Under *ingenium*, those of 'acute mind' (*acuto ingenio*) were distinguished from the 'dull' (*hebeti*); under *eruditio*, the learned were juxtaposed with those who were unlearned; under *memoria*, specific advice was given about speeches designed for those who did not understand or remember well; and under age, it was stated that people preferred to listen to speeches that would be suitable for them as speakers on account of their age. Finally, concerning habits (*mores*), we are told that the variety of different character types made it impossible to provide detailed advice, but as a general rule one should design the oration for different character types (e.g. the suspicious, the capricious, the haughty).[46] The inclusion of these topics in *De ratione dicendi* was not just a multiplication of attributes one could give to learned and popular audiences respectively but an attempt to devise categories for thinking about the more particular qualities of a given audience. In fact, most of the categories did not directly reflect social hierarchies but pointed instead to individual capacities under categories that were systematically expounded in Vives's other works such as *De disciplinis* or *De anima*.

Vives's interest in the audience was extended to cover the specific relationship between the speaker and the audience. Indeed, the very criteria of *decorum* were connected with the point of view of the audience. Vives told his readers to consider carefully the relationship (*relatio*) between all the people involved (speaker, audience, persons spoken about) and regarding different aspects of life (family, erudition, virtue, age, strength, office, rank, riches). Here the standard for judging whether we are inferior, superior, or equal to our audience can vary greatly (is rank more important than wisdom?), but we should always use as our yardstick the opinions of the audience. We must 'study what is the judgment of those we address' and adopt this as our starting point.[47] If we addressed someone inferior to us, we could concentrate on the matter and forget about other issues concerning *decorum*; but when we spoke to a person who was on our level, let alone superior to us, we had to proceed more carefully and 'precisely' (*accuratius*). Especially when speaking to someone above us, care for the majesty of the person addressed (*reverentia maiestatis*) should be apparent in speech.[48] In categorising 'friends' (*amicus*) or 'enemies' (*inimicus*), the decisive factor was yet again the point of view of the person you addressed: 'I do not call an enemy a person you hate, but a person who hates you; for when you hate him/her and he/she esteems you – which is very rare – you consider him/her a friend and you speak to him/her just like when you both like each other'.[49]

Considering the decisive role of the *exordium* and the peroration in emotional arousal in classical theory, it is not a great surprise that Vives's most extensive discussion of disposition was presented under *decorum*.[50] But once again, and despite describing the *exordium/proemium* as a suitable place for winning the goodwill (*benevolentia*) and attention (*attentio*) of the audience, his stress was not on giving formulaic precepts but on the issues one should think about throughout the speech.[51] The reader was told that 'everything should refer to the final end' (*finis*) the orator had set himself, that the order of arguments should always be decided with a victory in mind (that is, persuasion), and that one should try to figure out the things to which the audience attributed meaning.[52] Achieving one's ends in a speech was greatly dependent on being able to overcome all the impediments to success posed by our audience on account of 'their attention, natural talent, emotions'.[53] In addition to the *exordium*, Vives strongly argued that all impediments had to be removed 'not only in the beginning, but all parts of the oration', which is why orations on 'civil issues' (*causa civilis*) were full of intermediary *exordia* that continuously mediated the orator's relationship with the audience.[54]

Despite his insistence throughout the work that the analysis of emotions belonged to *De anima*, he offered a short analysis of problematic emotions in the section on *decorum* since the main impediment to persuasion resided in the emotional dispositions of the audience towards us or the theme spoken about. First, there were 'mild' (*mansueti*) emotions such as 'the hope of gain' (*spes lucri*) which did not pose great problems and could be controlled through right medicines. Second, there were 'ignoble' (*degeneres*) emotions such as 'fear' (*metus*) or 'the contempt of self' (*contemptus sui*), the cause of which should be 'secretly removed from the soul' (*causam ex animi subtrahere*). Finally, there were 'impetuous' (*praeferoces*) and 'very swift' (*praerapidi*) affections such as 'hatred' (*odium*), 'anger' (*ira*), 'indignation' (*indignatio*), and 'envy' (*invidentia*). These were most problematic, and they must be 'attacked indirectly by us when they arise against the speaker or the subject matter'.[55] What *decorum* and disposition enable us to do is precisely the management, suppression, countering, and use of these emotions. Highlighting this dimension, Vives described emotions as affections that incited humans to follow the good and to avoid the bad, and instructed his reader to turn to his work on the soul (*anima*) for a more thorough treatment.[56]

Precisely in the context of emotions, one finds perhaps the best example of how an invention starting from the audience should operate: an orator/a writer should reconstruct the emotional dispositions and specific preferences of his/her audience by entering their mind through the imagination:

> Before all else we should consider who we are and who are the people whose emotions we are trying to kindle or calm – what is their opinion about matters to which they attach the greatest or only a little importance, to which feelings they are susceptible and to which feelings they are averse, from which feelings they easily pass owing to their temperament, convictions, habits, age, sex, state of health, physical makeup and personal circumstances; the time, the place, and lastly all those things which I explained in my treatise The Instrument of Probability [In *De disciplinis*). We should adopt their frame of mind, and their whole temperament, while we work out what is in our interests. We should put ourselves in their position and carefully consider, supposing we were them, and shared the same convictions as them, by what means our emotions would be aroused or assuaged in the present matter.[57]

This method leads to familiar advice. Quite in the spirit of *decorum*, one should hide (*dissimulare*) one's art in using emotions: 'if in persuasion art should be dissimulated, more so should it be in moving the emotions, which is a more delicate matter'.[58] Open battle was not encouraged; one should instead draw out emotions 'in secret' (*latenter*). Only once emotions had begun to appear was it possible to fight with 'more powerful arms' (*fortioribus armis*).[59] In yet another section on persuasion (*De persuasione*), the orator was invited to accommodate his speech to different audiences. Vives employed the metaphor of a battle against the resistance of the audience, but at the same time, he warned the speaker to avoid the appearance of a fight in most cases. If the fight was overt, the human soul, mostly because of arrogance, did not want to be beaten or defeated, which is why an ordinary speech (*ratio loquendi commune/sermo*) was often more expedient than undisguised oratory.[60] Throughout *De ratione dicendi* he is essentially giving flesh to the idea that rhetoric is about fight and persuasion but that this should rarely be made apparent.

When the centrality of *decorum* has been highlighted, as in Don Abbott's work, it has been standardly linked to style and elocution.[61] While elocution is no doubt central in *De ratione dicendi*, the concept was, however, clearly meant to guide most of the choices of rhetorical disposition and invention too. It is of course true that Vives thought that the invention of arguments belonged to dialectic, whereas rhetoric, rather than analysing particular questions (*quaestio*), dealt instead with the adaptation of one's message to contextual circumstances. But part of this adaptation certainly dealt with inventive tasks since to adapt one's message to the judgments of the audience was also to emphasise those dimensions of the theme that spoke to their opinions and emotional dispositions. The argumentative element had been unquestionably part of his rhetorical *De consultatione* and it was also included in the description of *decorum* as the adaptation of the theme to the emotions and expectations of the audience. This meant that the scope of rhetoric exceeded mere questions of style. Vives himself openly stated that his treatise dealt with 'the adaptation of both words and meaning to different ends'.[62]

De ratione dicendi was undeniably an innovative work. Yet it was perhaps somewhat baffling for most contemporaries in that it entailed reorganising the structure of a rhetorical handbook, omitting most formulaic precepts, offering relatively few examples, and, finally, claiming that the success of rhetoric was dependent on so many contextual factors that it was an art of prudence and *decorum* which could not be squeezed into precepts.

Decorum in Other Genres of Rhetoric

While the focus on *decorum* interpreted primarily through a correct assessment of the audience was quite original, it introduced a variety of issues which had been discussed by Erasmus and Vives for decades. It clearly incorporated earlier ideas about the necessity of self-hiding, dissimulation, and the avoidance of strong passions as integral components of persuasive rhetoric (see Chapter 2). Perhaps most importantly, it gathered under the concept of *decorum* a determined attempt to go beyond the formulaic approach to rhetoric found in Erasmus's and Vives's earlier work.

This approach certainly had precedents. The centrality of the audience was already noticeable in Agricola's *De inventione dialectica*, which connected *decorum*, in the few passages dedicated to the concept, to an analysis of the audience. In the part on the emotions, the reader was told that *decorum* meant the accommodation of the colour of the speech to the person of the speaker based on the estimation made of the audience and the theme one was talking about.[63] To a greater degree than in classical works on rhetoric, Agricola stressed that the *exordium* and peroration were more concerned with the audience than with the thing spoken about, and connected the level of argumentation needed to the disposition of the audience towards the subject and the speaker.[64] Agricola also highlighted that someone who could survey (*pervidere*) the opinion of the audience about the person of the speaker and the subject of the speech, would be well prepared to win its good will and to be successful in speaking more generally.[65]

The attempt to rethink rhetorical theory was also evident in more reflective discussions on the adaptation of classical rhetoric to contemporary concerns. Already in *Lingua*, Erasmus pointed out that the 'first merit of speech is that it should be appropriate, taking into account the case, circumstances, place, and people involved'.[66] Perhaps the most in-depth discussion took place in the context of a debate on the correct manner of imitating Cicero in *Ciceronianus*. Here Erasmus, speaking through the mouth of Bulephorus, expanded in the clearest of terms on the lack of *decorum* of those who aimed at a direct imitation of Cicero in the contemporary world. Although Cicero's language, because of its magnificence, could be compared to the art of Phidias, the merely artistic dimension of oratory was irrelevant since rhetoric aspired to persuasion and not to delight. As Bulephorus bluntly stated, while Ciceronian speech could be of some ceremonial use for a diplomat addressing an Italian audience (preferably in Rome), it was irrelevant for sermons, for addressing the multitude, and for the conduct of serious political affairs which was 'dealt with in private, through letters and conversations in French'.[67] In another passage, Erasmus claimed the following:

> There is nothing to stop a person speaking in a manner that is both Christian and Ciceronian, if you allow a person to be Ciceronian when he speaks clearly, richly, and appropriately, in keeping with the nature of his subject and with the circumstances of the times and of the persons involved.[68]

Here *decorum*, rather than a dynamic principle that mediated between rhetorical precepts and the contextual requirements of a particular situation, referred to the accommodation of classical rhetoric to contemporary concerns. It was the standard by which Cicero should be judged. Vives, in *De disciplinis*, largely agreed. In the discussion on Ciceronianism, he had denounced a speech that was 'of a beautiful appearance' yet inefficient in persuasion partly on account of lack of *decorum*.[69]

Vives's insistence on the importance of *decorum* could also be interpreted as a particular instance of his tendency to see several disciplines as guided by prudential judgment rather than fixed precepts. As we have seen, in Vives's understanding of law, *epikeia* served as a mediator between universal rules and particular situations that could never be covered by a systematised legal code. Just like *epikeia*, *decorum* was described as a form of prudence that mediated between general standards and particular situations. In the part of *De disciplinis* on rhetoric, Vives had restricted rhetorical invention to prudence, 'the counsellor and governess of all issues', which decided what to say, where to say it, on what occasion, and in front of what audiences.[70] *Decorum* could thus be seen as part of prudence, which adopted general precepts to specific situations.

Although Vives's proposal in *De ratione dicendi* was motivated by a broader interest in particularity across all possible actualisations of rhetoric, the great stress he put on *decorum* clearly mirrored more historically specific issues in adapting classical rhetoric to contemporary concerns. In omitting the traditional three genres of rhetoric (deliberative, forensic, demonstrative), *De ratione dicendi* did not systematically connect its precepts on *decorum* to specific genres of speaking or writing. Vives's other rhetorical works were, however, best understood as applications of the ideals of *decorum* to practical concerns. His *De consultatione* was an early adaptation of the primacy of *decorum* and contextual analysis to the practice of counselling (Chapter 2). His highly popular *De conscribendis epistolis* elaborated on the potential of decorous speech in letter writing, especially when one addressed those in power.

In the epistolary genre, Vives's approach was markedly different from the prevalent tendency to offer formulaic precepts. The schematic approach was apparent in those works that were most often printed with Vives's treatise: Christoph Hegendorf's *Methodus scribendi epistolas* (1527), Konrad Celtis's *Methodus conficiendarum epistolarum* (1537), and Erasmus's youthful *Formula conficiendarum epistolarum* (printed in 1520). Celtis's *Methodus* introduced a five-fold structure of the letter (*principium, caussa, narratio, enumeratio, character*), in which the *principium* was divided into the salutation and the *exordium*. In this division, the *exordium* served as the place in which the recipient was turned into an attentive (*attentus*), docile (*docilis*), and good-willed (*benevolus*) reader in a traditional vein, but no attention was paid to the individual differences of different recipients. Rather, precepts for writing different kinds of letters were coupled with short examples, and the emphasis was especially on the way in which the salutation and the ending were constructed according to socially accepted rules.[71] Hegendorf's *Methodus* also exemplified a formulaic approach to rhetoric. Unlike Vives's work, its structure was thoroughly pedagogical. Titles on a theme were presented with short pieces of text, tables of things (such as topics to be used), and frequent examples. Its practicality was based on the combination of the visualisation of an extensive set of topics with a number of examples, but it did not discuss *decorum* or issues stemming from the differences between different recipients at all. In participating in the simplification and visualisation of rhetorical theory so elaborately set out by Walter Ong, Hegendorf's treatment was distinctly different from Vives's.[72]

Another work that was sometimes printed with Vives's *De conscribendis epistolis*, and that mentioned him in the dedicatory letter, was *Compendiosae institutiones artis oratoriae* (1537), written by Adriaan van Baarland (1486–1538), who was Vives's friend and an active member of the humanist circles of Louvain. Baarland's short handbook stressed the civic dimension of rhetoric and closely followed classical rhetorical theory in its structure (three genera of rhetoric, five duties of rhetoric, etc.).[73] Here too, the *exordium*, in demonstrative, deliberative, and judicial compositions, was described as a place where the docility, attention, and benevolence of the audience was secured, but no further advice concerning the audience was given.[74] A number of circumstantial (*circumstantiae*) topics such as the cause, time, occasion, education, age, and fortune were discussed, but they were primarily connected with the amplification of a demonstrative speech that praised or blamed things and persons. The treatment of emotions (*affectuus*), although said to be of vital importance for persuasion, was not linked to the differing dispositions of the audience in any way.[75]

This approach can be contrasted to Vives's letter-writing manual, which developed some of the ideas found in Erasmus's *De conscribendis epistolis*. In tune with the standard theory of his time, Erasmus, in his early *Formula*, had still constructed the presentation by and large on traditional building blocks (three genera, five duties of oratory, etc.). Yet he added an introduction in which he questioned a merely rule-based approach. Erasmus posed the question of whether there was an art of letter writing, and claimed that although precepts could be given, one should improvise and turn these precepts to one's advantage by considering things such as 'the case, the times, the occasion' since letters were written to men of 'different origin, rank, and temperament'.[76] This was taken as the starting point of his more exhaustive *De conscribendis epistolis,* where the classical structure was deliberately removed and the exposition was built around the specific requirements of a vast genre of letters. While *decorum* was not a central category as such, the idea that contextual factors, especially the audience, should structure letter writing was very present. As Erasmus put it, when one was writing a letter, one should be 'well acquainted with the nature, character, and moods of the person to whom the letter is being written and their own standing with him in favour, influence, or services rendered'. This was of some help since 'from the accurate examination of all these things they should derive, so to speak, the living model of the letter'.[77] In discussing letters of encouragement, he made the point with some vigour. According to Erasmus, 'the exhortatory letter [...] originates in the emotions', which is why 'we must observe and explore the nature of man's mind, the variety of temperaments, the emotions generated by various circumstances, and the things by which people are attracted or repelled'.[78] If we understood what aroused hope, fear, pity, or other emotions in the recipient, we would know how to address the audience. So, when we knew what triggered hope in the recipient – honours in the ambitious man, for instance – we would concentrate on the honours that resulted from a given action in order to arouse hope.[79] In short, here the audience appeared as a category through which we could think about letter writing in a more flexible manner.

Vives's *De conscribendis epistolis* shared with Erasmus's letter-writing manual an interest in a vast array of letters and meticulous study of the recipient/audience.[80] In the spirit of the exposition of *decorum* in *De ratione dicendi*, it maintained that all persuasion and negotiation of differences should take place under the surface of concord that should only on rare occasions be breached. Many of the themes familiar from *De ratione dicendi* were present. Vives told the reader that all invention, both of letters and of discourse more broadly, was a matter of prudence rather than precepts; that the disposition (*ordo*) of the letter should not follow a fixed order but should be determined by a consideration of the theme (*res*); and that one should regard the subject one was writing about, the person of the writer, and the recipient as decisive factors when setting out to compose a letter.[81] Furthermore, many sections of the work, especially the lengthy part on the *exordium*, abound in advice on the management of the ties between the writer and the recipient.[82] Lastly, fully in accordance with *De ratione dicendi* and *De consultatione*, the focus throughout was on the management of reciprocal relations that conditioned invention, style, and tone rather than on the analysis of questions.

Unlike the more general *De ratione dicendi*, *De conscribendis epistolis* gave very specific advice on preserving concord tailored to different practical problems of letter writing. A good example of this were the recommendations concerning adversarial letters. Naturally, the very definition of letters as a form of conversation (*sermo*) as opposed to rhetoric – a traditional definition underscored by Vives – already softened their adversarial nature. Equally as importantly, his precepts on how to present the *persona* of the orator throughout the treatise stressed the pivotal importance of avoiding any 'semblance of arrogance', which could be achieved if we spoke 'soberly, modestly and with a sense of propriety and restraint' of our own affairs.[83]

Similar ideas were expressed in Vives's depiction of letters of complaint and invectives, in which, he wrote, one should not 'insist too much on the misdeed and [...] pursue the matter in abusive language, but it is a mark of civility and courtesy to give the reason for your complaint'.[84] In such letters, we should be more interested in exploring how to avoid similar confrontations in the future than in venting our disappointment over past actions. Invective was only acceptable if it was 'intended to attack vice and to deter others from that kind of life', in which case the person should still be spared as far as possible. If an invective did not cure vice, this 'dog-like eloquence' (*canina facundia*) should not be allowed.[85] All in all, in letters that concerned matters relating to both the writer and the recipient (such as letters of invective) 'the greatest precaution must be taken not to offend anyone'. This was especially pertinent in letters since they were 'destitute of advocates', which meant that often 'the addressee upon rereading it [the letter] aggravates the injury and as he puts his own construction on it the insult becomes more grievous'.[86] Civility, calmness, and moderation appear as the only way to solve problems involving both parties.

Perhaps the trickiest task for a letter writer was, however, to address issues that pertained to the addressee, especially when the recipient was someone superior to oneself. Here we entered the domain of false praise that had been abundantly discussed within the Erasmian circles at least since Erasmus's own *Panegyricus* (see Chapter 2). Since people did not gladly endure a superior, 'and since all these letters of instruction, admonishment, advice, exhortation, reproof and censure speak from above [...] we must carefully consider who is writing to whom, and on what account'.[87] If the writer was a person of a higher standing, everything was quite straightforward. If, on the other hand, one admonished an equal or someone superior to oneself, a softer tone was needed.[88] The most difficult situation was when we had to reprove a vice. In these cases, both overt and concealed speech had their problems since some 'do not tolerate an open reproof, and do not recognize it if it is disguised'.[89] True to his appreciation of individual differences, Vives argued that 'different medicines must be administered to different temperaments'. He continued by writing that 'if praise for a virtue that one does not possess is beneficial, let praise be given, as some princes, powerful, learned and talented men are praised'.[90] If the recipient did not permit advice even through praise, Vives suggested practical ways of establishing one's authority (e.g. reminding the recipient of friendship) that allowed one to advise through praise. But if correcting someone was your duty, and 'praise goes to his head and he loses control of himself', you should remonstrate with the addressee 'simply and openly' (*simpliciter aperteque*) and justify your decision, so that at least you fulfilled your responsibility.[91] When your advice was destined to fail and to 'prove detrimental to yourself and to others, it will be more prudent not to disturb Camarina'.[92] While the strategy of false praise might be gradually abandoned for more open reproof if the situation so dictated, there were limits to what could be achieved when addressing a superior, which is why certain lines should not be crossed for the sake of your own safety and the common good.

The decorous approach was extended to humour and laughter, which were included in the section on writing about things pertaining to the recipient. Whereas in the 1519 *De initiis, sectis et laudibus philosophiae* Menippus the Phoenician, with his satirical laughter, was praised as an elegant yet relentless foe of vice, in *De conscribendis epistolis* we were told that all offensiveness and vulgarity should be absent and that all jests should be undertaken in the spirit of 'elegance, urbanity, cleverness, and wit'.[93] Ultimately, just as *De ratione dicendi* and *De consultatione*, his precepts on letter writing were highly sensitive to the intellectual and moral qualities of those addressed.

It might not be a coincidence that a close study of the audience was suggested in genres where it was often composed of only one person – such as counsel and letter writing – yet the rhetoric of *decorum* was extended to almost all forms of speaking including preaching. Vives never composed a manual on homiletics, but he clearly thought that *decorum* was an important concept of the rhetoric of the New Testament as well; he incorporated Christ (*Servator*) as an example of the limits of *decorum* and outspokenness in his *De conscribendis epistolis.*[94] The idea of *decorum* in preaching was, however, expanded on in Erasmus's final and most elaborate treatise on rhetoric, *Ecclesiastes* (1535). Naturally, Erasmus had for long explored the principles of *decorum* in his discussions on St Paul's dissimulation and in his rhetorical treatises, such as *De conscribendis epistolis*, that were highly sensitive to contextuality, concord, and the audience. Still, *Ecclesiastes* was the first of his rhetorical works in which *decorum* was treated as a distinct category.[95]

Although the principles of *decorum* could be observed right the way through *Ecclesiastes*, the end of Book Three was specifically dedicated to this subject. Here we are told to take into account the theme, persons, time, and place 'throughout the speech' (*tota oratione*), that *decorum* was a question of 'judgment' (*iudicium*) rather than art, and that the examples of the Apostles showed 'how effective language is when tempered with a prudent civility'.[96] Erasmus gave examples of how the Apostles had to speak in circumstances in which their authority could not be taken for granted since they were addressing an audience of non-Christians, and he connected their success to their mastery of *decorum*, as when Paul spoke about the Christian religion to the Athenians without ever accusing them openly of idolatry.[97] Like Vives, Erasmus regarded cases where one had to admonish those above oneself especially problematic. He offered various ways of softening the reproof, but, just like Vives, warned the preacher not to descend into flattery when addressing the powerful. As Erasmus put it, 'it is seditious to bark openly against princes, but it is foolish and abject to flatter them openly to their face. Some err in the former fault, but many more are guilty of the latter'.[98]

All in all, Vives's attempt to think about rhetoric as a creative practice of *decorum* and not as a formulaic art was a shift in emphasis. While different genres posed specific problems and made different demands on rhetoric, ranging from the transformative potential of preaching to the more instrumental deliberative rhetoric that sought to influence specific decisions, they all partook in this tendency. Across the spectrum of genres, it was suggested that rhetoric was an art of prudence rather than of ready-made precepts and that it had to be tailored to specific situations by taking into account the theme, time, place, speaker, and audience. Within this categorisation, the audience was usually the decisive heading. Moreover, those instances in which one addresses a superior are presented at length, and a recourse to self-hiding, apparent consensus, moderation, politeness, and a subtle use of emotions was recommended.

In condensing interest in the audience and the requirement of politeness and courtesy into the concept of *decorum*, two things were simultaneously achieved. On the one hand, *decorum* provided a means of regulating socially convenient speech by setting the limits within which such speech could appear as acceptable; it upheld concord and society. This can be seen as a major point against the emerging culture of verbal discord (e.g. pamphlets), which frequently violated *decorum* and accepted norms of address. This side had already been evident in Erasmus's criticism of indecorous loquacity in *Lingua* and it was equally denounced in Vives's *De concordia*. On the other hand, it was consistently argued that in all the different rhetorical genres, persuasion only became possible within the parameters of decorous speech. In this sense, the avoidance of an adversarial approach was not just an act of politeness but the only way in which the audience could truly be persuaded through responsible rhetoric. Furthermore, in *De consultatione* and *De conscribendis epistolis,* the civic task of addressing a ruler decorously was perhaps the main issue.

This approach was novel but not without its problems; its stress on particularity and context offered a view of rhetoric that was very difficult to condense into precepts. Its invitation to think about (or rather imagine) the opinions and emotions of the audience as a key to rhetorical invention, disposition, and style did, however, imply that rhetoric could profit more from an analysis of emotions and passions than from a merely linguistic treatment of style and arrangement. Provided one was not satisfied with a typology of typical responses of a limited number of audiences, the audience, or the recipient in the case of letter writing and counselling, could only be understood through a more general enquiry into how judgment and emotional response functioned. This demanded knowledge that was rarely supplied by rhetorical manuals in any detail. The emphasis put on the audience and the unwillingness to provide a typology of common reactions clearly motivated Vives's efforts in *De ratione dicendi* to direct the reader to his treatment of the soul and emotions in *De anima*.

De anima et vita as the Foundation of Moral Philosophy

Vives's *De anima* is in many ways a puzzling work. Despite its adherence to a long tradition that went back to Aristotle's *De anima*, it was the first systematic Northern humanist treatise on the soul and emotions. Although somewhat of an anomaly within the context of Northern humanist educational, rhetorical, and theological literature, its avowed *raison d'être* was to serve precisely as the foundation of ethical, political, educational, and rhetorical concerns of a generation of humanists. Vives himself certainly thought so. In the dedicatory letter, we are told that nothing was 'more excellent' (*praestabilior*) and useful than knowledge of the soul. Since the soul was the 'source and origin' (*fons atque origo*) of good and bad actions, knowing about its operations helped to guide our actions.[99] The knowledge of emotions provided in Book Three of the treatise was said to constitute 'the foundation of all moral philosophy, whether private, or public'; and no other science was 'more suitable' for a prince in particular in 'the due governance of himself, his subjects, and the whole commonwealth'.[100]

This dimension of the treatise has been picked up in the scholarly literature, where its practical, empirical, and ethical approach to the soul has frequently been lauded as original.[101] Despite this recognition, the way in which the link between the understanding of the operations of the soul and moral philosophy was supposed to work is, however, seldom analysed in detail. Lorenzo Casini, the foremost expert on the treatise, acknowledges the ethical dimension of the *De anima*, yet his focus is on placing it in the context of sophisticated internal discussions of the soul rather than on connecting it to mental therapy or rhetorical concerns. In Noreña, the therapy of emotions is a more prominent theme, but while he deals with the social element of therapy (e.g. the role of education in habituation), he does not examine it in the context of rhetoric or the wider Northern humanist understanding of moral philosophy.[102] The omission of the ethical, educational, and political dimensions is quite understandable, considering that Vives was not very explicit about how knowledge of the soul provided the basis for moral philosophy. Yet, if moral philosophy is not emphasised, we risk ignoring the context within which Vives thought that the treatise should be interpreted. In what follows, I suggest that the analysis of the soul reflects, among other things, broader humanist concerns on two levels. First, it can be seen as the foundation of individual ethics and, second, as the culmination of rhetoric, both transformative and non-transformative.

Before these issues can be understood, some preliminary knowledge about the treatise must be established. The basic conceptual framework within which the soul and emotions were discussed had an Aristotelian ring. Vives agreed with Aristotle's view in *De anima* that the soul, in tune with the theory of hylomorphism, was the formal cause that animated a material body. In accordance with this principle, all living beings had a soul: plants had a nutritive soul, animals nutritive and sensitive souls, and human beings possessed these two lower souls as well as an intellective soul.[103] On the basis of Aristotle's *De anima,* medieval treatises had developed a nuanced system of faculty psychology whereby different operations were attributed to separate faculties in an increasingly sophisticated system. Despite the substantial differences between different theories, it was agreed that all propositional reasoning happened in the intellective soul, which processed the representations produced by the internal senses of the sensitive soul (these normally included common sense, imagination, memory, fantasy, estimation); these, for their part, produced representations on the basis of the information received through the external senses. An eclectic exposition of faculty psychology could be found in Vives's *De anima*.[104]

While Vives discussed several technical issues, his account, however, relied heavily on those mental operations that were relevant for moral action; he was concerned about the interplay between the intellective soul (reason, judgment, will), internal senses (especially fantasy), and emotional response. Drawing heavily on a Christian interpretation of an Aristotelian tradition, emotions were primarily described as natural impulses implanted in humans by God for self-preservation and a good life. As he wrote, 'the actions of those faculties that were given to us by nature to follow what is good and to shun away from what is bad are called emotions or affections'.[105] Consequently, the extreme version of Stoic *apatheia* – a complete freedom from emotions – was heavily criticised by Vives, according to whom emotions should be trained and habituated to fulfil their created tasks adequately rather than eradicated.[106] While Vives primarily saw emotions as natural, he also introduced another categorisation that could be found in

Roman rhetorical manuals among other sources. In this theory, mild, ethical emotions were contrasted to strong passions. The categorisation had definite normative connotations since strong passions were perturbations of the soul that threatened the power of reason and rational judgment over human actions.[107] Although much of the treatment in *De anima* was focused on the negative consequences of destructive passions, the Aristotelian framework was, however, largely dominant since most passions, such as pride (*superbia*) or anger (*ira*), were ultimately interpreted as distorted versions of natural emotions that were instituted by God as instruments of self-preservation and perfection.[108] This placed Vives's view on emotions primarily within a Peripatetic framework, albeit with notable differences between Vives and Aristotle in how individual passions were interpreted.[109]

In accordance with a long medieval tradition, emotions, in order to be activated, needed to follow a judgment, some prepared by the rational soul (*iudicium*) and some based on the estimations of the sensitive soul (often *aestimatio*). In the rational soul, reason (*ratio*) – an active discourse – prepared arguments for judgment, the only activity of which consisted in judging what reason had proposed. These judgments were the basis for the activity of the third faculty of the intellective soul, which was responsible for choice: the will (*voluntas*).

The interaction between reason, judgment, and will comprised numerous possibilities for wrong judgment and emotional response. In its practical form (*prudentia*), reason was aided in the assessment of particular objects by the ability of the human mind to grasp the universal truths of natural law, which were employed by practical reason in the assessment of specific issues. This was linked to the medieval theory of *synderesis*, a natural propensity in all humans to recognise truth and goodness.[110] Reason could, however, fail to form a correct conclusion – the goal of practical reason – because of many reasons such as the slowness of the discourse, the complexity of the task at hand, lack of will, darkness of the mind, momentary confusion (*perturbatio*) due to passions, conflicting thoughts, or the activity of fantasy.[111] If the reasoning was correct and assented to by the judgment (which judged both the argumentative discourse and its conclusion), the resolution of the judgment was passed over to the will.

The will could also play a role in erroneous emotional activation. As Casini has suggested, Vives's treatment of the will came close to Jean Buridan's (c.1300–c.1358) mild voluntarist position since they both argued that the will, although free and self-determined, could not will something bad as such or will against something good, that the will could will only something that had been judged good in some way, and that the will could not will a lesser good if a greater good was under consideration.[112] The freedom of the will was, however, quite ambivalent; Vives could draw an analogy with deep medieval roots between the will and the prince (and between the judgment and a counsellor) to portray the will as a capricious, emotional, and disturbing power.[113] Although the will could only assent to what had been judged good, it wielded considerable power over reason and judgment, because some emotions clearly worked within the will itself. It could choose whether to subject a given object to deliberation in the first place, it could divert the attention to something else during the deliberation, and it could decide not to want (*non velle*) something that had been judged good (it could not hate it, but it did not have to act on it). Furthermore, due to the great variety and ambiguity of things, almost everything could be judged good or bad by the reason, which is why the will, just like a prince, would often find a reason to act as it pleases. In these cases, the freedom of the will, which made free humans moral agents for Vives, turned into a tyrannical power that was hard to control.[114]

The problem related to the activation of emotions was not restricted to the intellective soul. As we are told in the part on emotions, all emotions that were not instinctive reactions (such as thirst) 'follow a judgment'.[115] This judgment, however, needed not be produced by the intellective soul. We are informed that a judgment based on 'the representations of the imagination' was sufficient and more frequent.[116] These judgments were the estimations of the sensitive soul, which humans shared with animals, and they were not produced by the propositional argumentation of reason but by the freely associative activity of compositive fantasy.[117] While reliance on an estimation of the internal senses brought humans near to the non-reflective life of animals and was consequently potentially threatening, their power over emotional response was taken as a natural fact throughout Book Three.

De anima, Emotions, and Self-Knowledge

An explanation of the way in which emotional response was actualised through the judgment of reason or the estimation of internal senses, and how emotions posed a threat to the intellective soul, would have been of help to anyone interested in self-understanding and the purification of his/her own actions, both of which were express goals of *De anima*.[118] As is well established, the therapeutic, ethical motivation behind the understanding of emotions had been essential to many classical traditions which strove for the control and direction of emotions (e.g. the Peripatetics) or for their eradication (the Stoics).[119] Socrates, the original spokesperson for self-knowledge, had already linked self-knowledge precisely to the knowledge of the soul in the *First Alcibiades*.[120] In addition to the different schools of Antiquity (Stoics, Peripatetics, Epicureans, Neoplatonists), the ethical interpretation of emotions had been largely adopted by Christian philosophy, in which assenting to erroneous emotional impulses was frequently associated with sin.[121] We are told in the dedicatory letter to *De anima* that the ancient maxim of 'know thyself' (*sese nosse*) – central for Vives throughout his life – should be interpreted as an order to know 'the nature of the soul, qualities, *ingenia*, powers, emotions'.[122] This implied a naturalistic interpretation of self-knowledge. Ideally, this enabled us to inculcate the right emotional dispositions, to evaluate the ways in which judgments were made, to control and direct specific emotions, and to understand what was suitable for us and what was beyond our limits. But this natural understanding was not free of theological, metaphysical, and teleological elements. For to interpret emotions was also to understand the reason they were implanted in us in the first place (this is always stated in the analysis of separate emotions in Book three), which, for its part, presupposed knowledge of our place in the hierarchy of creation and of our nature as an image of God.

All this resonated well in the Erasmian tradition. Within humanist circles, self-knowledge could be interpreted in different ways that gave the emotions varying levels of centrality but that never discarded them completely. On numerous occasions, the control or eradication of passions and emotions was regarded as crucial for ethical self-government, that is, freedom from the slavery of passions. In Erasmus's immensely popular *Enchiridion*, self-knowledge was already of decisive importance. While some readings have found an underlying logic in the *Enchiridion* – most recently, Ross Dealy has read it as a systematic appropriation of Stoicism into Christianity – Erasmus's treatment was quite eclectic, and it was never systematically placed within a clearly defined tradition by the contemporaries.[123] In the *Enchiridion*, self-knowledge was primarily described as a spiritual process. We are told that 'the beginning of this wisdom is to know thyself' and that this wisdom should be asked of God 'with ardent prayer' and from the 'veins of the divine Scripture'.[124] We are reminded that knowledge of our body and state of mind was difficult to attain, and that the war within ourselves, an often employed metaphor in the work, was primarily due to a fight between reason and bodily passions, which could only be remedied through spiritual wisdom.[125]

Despite its spiritual interpretation of self-knowledge, the *Enchiridion* did not, however, rule out knowledge of emotions. Erasmus tells us that self-knowledge included 'knowledge of all the impulses of the soul', and knowledge of how to restrain them and redirect them to virtue.[126] As the idea of redirection implied, the *Enchiridion* did not simply strive for the eradication of emotions. Erasmus knew well the distinction between the Stoic eradication of emotions and the Peripatetic interpretation of affections as potential inducements to wisdom, and, while arguing that there were only superficial differences between these schools, he was clearly against a complete uprooting of the emotions, as his positive attitude to paternal love and other socially constructive affections testified. His account of emotions also paid particular attention to individual propensity to certain emotions because of specific character traits or physical constitution, which implied the importance of their correct interpretation in self-cure.[127] In his rhetorical writings, Erasmus generally took the role of emotions in human motivation for granted but rarely discussed them in any detail. In his *De conscribendis epistolis,* however, he wrote that the emotions, according to many philosophers, had been given to us 'as incentives and guides to perfect virtue', which aligned Erasmus with the Peripatetic tradition.[128] But it should be noted that here, as in many other places, it remained unclear whether the term – *affectus* – comprised all emotions or just socially constructive or moderate ones.

Vives's understanding of moral philosophy also consisted essentially in self-knowledge that could occasion self-cure from vice. This self-cure was systematically described as freedom from harmful passions. In his *Introductio ad Sapientiam,* we are told that wisdom entailed the correct judgment of all things, and that the first step in its attainment was self-knowledge.[129] As in the *Enchiridion,* a normative dichotomy between the mind and passions was established – a dichotomy in which passions were linked to the body and to vice.[130] Vives held that the purification of passions and vice was what transformed us into God-like creatures; and he furthermore stated that 'the greatest thing' (*summum*) in learning and erudition was the philosophy that provided a remedy for the diseases of the soul. The cure, that is, the control of the perturbations of the mind, was not only of great importance for a scholar but it brought him close to the angels and to God. Moreover, the remedies for these diseases were said to be derived not only 'from God and the law and life of the Christ', but also from 'things and from ourselves'.[131] While much of the *Introductio ad Sapientiam* was structured around the dichotomy between wisdom and reason, on the one hand, and passions, on the other, passions referred only to destructive passions (*pathe*), not to all emotional responses, as the stress put on love and other socially constructive emotions made clear.[132]

Vives frequently discussed the purification or control of passions as key to self-government in his other works too such as the Book Four of *De concordia* and in *De pacificatione*.[133] In *De concordia*, these passions were contrasted with socially constructive emotions, which testified to love, benevolence, and concord, and that clearly upheld sociability among humans.[134] As a demonstration of the ambiguity on whether passions should be eradicated or merely controlled, the expressions used by Vives in different texts included the correct ordering of passions (*compositus*), their subjection (*subdere*), putting a bridle on them (*freno*), removing (*abluere*) them, and freeing oneself from them (*liberare*).[135] Yet, while this evasiveness was present in some parts of *De anima,* the treatise, with its Peripatetic interpretation of emotions, aligned itself with the ideals of emotional control, education, and habituation, and never suggested a complete eradication of passions as a viable possibility. In this interpretation, virtue was equivalent to adequate emotional response in specific situations, whereas vice resulted from the activation of wrong passions and emotions in wrong situations.

In this picture, *De anima* was clearly an extension of Vives's life-long struggle with self-cure and an attempt to discuss the dynamics of emotions and passions as the culmination of self-knowledge, which made a virtuous life possible. The treatise most likely presupposed the role of different meditative (one can think of Vives's own *Meditatio de Passione Christi in psalmum XXXVII*), contemplative, and discursive practices (e.g. *De disputatione*, part of *De disciplinis*) in emotional control as a way of reimagining or rethinking oneself and one's emotional response to specific objects or moments. Moreover, regarding the supposed usefulness of the work for ethics and politics, the stress on self-knowledge was also a political argument which wove ethics and politics together in the figure of the prince. As Vives had insisted repeatedly, the ethical self-government of the prince – the control and direction of emotions – was a precondition of virtuous political action (see Chapter 3).

Habituation and Education

Despite the placement of the book in the tradition of therapy and self-knowledge, there are, however, several things that suggest that Vives also, if not primarily, targeted *De anima* at those who could be considered enforcers of self-government in different contexts, such as educators, tutors, or counsellors. What confirmed the suitability of the treatise for such readers was not only Vives's explicit claim in *De disciplinis* and *De ratione dicendi* that the analysis of the soul was the culmination of educational and rhetorical concerns but also the markedly social element of self-government that was built into *De anima*. On the one hand, this referred to the processes of habituation that had partly moulded certain groups of people to judge and react in a certain way, which implied that their self-government was connected to several external factors. On the other hand, this pointed to the ways in which emotions were activated socially and linguistically, which would have been of great use for a rhetorician, counsellor, or a tutor.

Throughout the technical description, there was much to encourage a teacher or a tutor. Both judgments and the estimations of fantasy were deeply embedded in social life and subjected to processes of habituation, which was another major Aristotelian theme of *De anima*. In the *Nicomachean Ethics*, Aristotle had firmly maintained that our moral dispositions are largely the result of processes of habituation and continuous practice, and Vives, in *De anima*, also discussed 'acts' (*actus*) that required 'practice' (*usus*) and maintained that 'of that practice comes into being a habit, which includes readiness and propensity to act'.[136] In a 1538 letter to Simon Grynaeus, Vives wrote that while our talent (*ingenium*) composed the seeds of all good things, they could only be perfected with the help of arts and disciplines. Echoing his *De anima*, he claimed that the operations of our minds and especially our understanding, unlike sense perception, could be habituated to operate better through practice and art.[137] In the part on reason (*ratio*) in *De anima*, Vives told us that the variety of ways in which reason operated in humans was partly due to natural differences in *ingenium*, partly to 'instruction, habits'.[138] He also sharply underlined that to prudence 'science is not enough; it also needs practical experience'.[139]

The processes of habituation were not only restricted to rational procedures but also concerned internal senses and fantasy, the associative patterns of which, though hard to control, possessed some degree of predictability. In a reference to a tradition of artificial memory dating back to *Ad Herennium,* Vives connected the possible use of memory places to the fact that if two things were presented to the fantasy together, the presence of one of them would activate the other one in recollection.[140] He also sustained that the supposedly spontaneous estimations of fantasy were intimately tied to one's convictions and beliefs. As Casini has noted, Vives, in discussing a sudden anger that seemed to anticipate rational judgment, argued that such anger burst out only in relation to 'a firmly rooted conviction' that 'we are good, educated, generous, hardworking, and distinguished, and that we ought to be honoured and revered rather than despised'.[141] This indicated that one's convictions and beliefs played a significant role in the supposedly spontaneous estimations of fantasy and in the ensuing emotional response; when your convictions were altered, emotional response changed. Because of all this, a major implication of *De anima* was that if one taught the mind correct precepts and beliefs and habituated it to activate these precepts at the right moment through experience, one could become a prudent person who was predisposed to the performance of virtue, at least within the limits of one's *ingenium*. This was well in line with the tradition of humanist educational ideals.

The concern with habituation and self-control was also apparent in Vives's discussion of emotions. As Casini has shown, Vives aligned himself with Plutarch against the Stoics on the emergence of strong passions. Whereas the Stoics had claimed that once one had assented to a strong passion, its subsequent development remained largely outside one's control, Plutarch had argued that passions such as anger grow gradually: 'Seneca declares that hatred comes into existence at once. Plutarch rightly denies this for it grows from its own causes'.[142] In associating himself with Plutarch, Vives maintained that once a strong passion was activated, one could still control and direct its later development if one understood its causes and dynamics.

The main implication of *De anima* for emotional control was, however, that the dynamics of individual emotions and judgment were related to a worldview of pride. This connected the naturalness of emotions with more spiritual issues; complete self-control could only be forged through a shift in perspective, through a new understanding of oneself as a humble image of God. Vives's treatment of individual emotions showed how this worked. Regarding anger, one of the most destructive of passions if uncontrolled, he suggested that a powerful remedy to counter it was to hold the opinion that 'almost everyone errs in their judgments of things', which is why they should be pitied rather than despised. It was also important 'not to have an overblown estimation of one's self' and to be aware of all of one's own shortcomings (e.g. vices).[143] What Vives was describing here was a link between pride, judgment, and individual emotional response. His point was that changing one's view of oneself and of others also entailed overcoming pride, which, as we have seen, fed even into the supposedly spontaneous estimations of fantasy and, ultimately, made one prone to strong passions such as anger. He went as far as to suggest that 'peace and concord can coexist with all other vices except for pride'.[144]

Hardly unsurprisingly, within this theory, the powerful, especially the prince, received special attention. In the part of *De anima* on offence (*offensio*), from which all malevolent emotions arose, princes were included in a lengthy list of those especially vulnerable to being offended, since they were 'flattered and praised by everyone, opposed by no one'.[145] This habituated them to wrong judgment and made them incapable of bearing any offences. In the part on pride (*superbia*), we were told that those who were proud wanted praise and no competition. Some princes would like that 'no-one was more powerful than them, not even God'. He can be so proud that he 'considers it right that he is exempted from human law', he even wants to be 'exempted from natural law and, in fact, not to be subject to the mighty and powerful God'.[146] They showed any semblance of friendship only towards those who subjected themselves to them through ascent to their wishes and adulation. When proud people acted humbly, this stemmed from false humility. In the case of princes, false humility was performed only in order to increase their 'power' (*dominatio*), which was the case of classical tyrants such as Marius and Caesar and 'our princes every day'.[147] Effectively, Vives's depiction of the ways in which the powerful were habituated to a frame of mind dominated by pride was in accordance with his claims in *De concordia* and other works that material acquisitiveness, flattery, and wrong education encouraged and sustained erroneous judgments.

De anima as the Culmination of Rhetoric

This information was not only significant for an educator interested in the process of character formation and habituation but also for a rhetorician. As has been indicated, Vives regarded the analysis of emotions as a natural extension of rhetoric, and much of rhetorical theory had taken for granted that there was an intimate link between the emotions and judgments of an audience. But there was only one main reference point in classical rhetoric in which this connection was systematically pursued: Aristotle's *Rhetoric*. Interestingly, whereas the first two books of *De anima* were loosely modelled on Aristotle's *De anima* (and the tradition following it), Book Three on emotions largely followed the second part of Aristotle's *Rhetoric*. Although Vives claimed that he wanted to expose emotions 'more simply and precisely' than what Aristotle had done in the *Rhetoric,* where the focus was on the point of view of a political man, his outline of emotions – with its stress on cognitive criteria and occasions on which emotions were activated – drew on Aristotle's *Rhetoric*.[148]

There were a number of things one could find in Aristotle's *Rhetoric* – which contained Aristotle's most thorough treatment of emotions – on the relationship between emotions, judgments, and persuasion. As Vives knew,

Aristotle's ethical philosophy in the *Nicomachean Ethics* gave a fundamental role to emotions as constituents of virtue and a good life, provided that they, through habituation, had become emotional dispositions to respond adequately at correct moments.[149] In the *Rhetoric*, for its part, the focus was on the rhetorical possibilities of emotions. Aristotle offered his fullest account of different emotions in a part on *pathos* (in Book Two) – one of the three sources of persuasion (the others are *logos* and *ethos*) that concerned the emotional response of the audience.

Aristotle told us that 'the employment of persuasive speech is directed towards a judgment' and that 'emotions are all those affections which cause men to change their opinion in regard to their judgments'.[150] Since emotions served as the primary way to alter the judgments of the audience on the object of a speech, they had to be understood. Consequently, Aristotle offered an analysis of several emotions based on the dispositions of mind, persons, and occasions that usually triggered an emotional response. His point was that if we understood how and in what contexts emotions were activated, we could focus on those aspects of a subject that connected the case/person under discussion to specific emotional dispositions of the audience. As he stated in his lengthy discussion of anger, 'it will be necessary for the speaker, by his eloquence, to put the hearers into the frame of mind of those who are inclined to anger, and to show that his opponents are responsible for things which arouse men to anger and are people of the kind with whom men are angry'.[151] In the end, Aristotle's *Rhetoric* was a cornucopia of information on the dispositions, characters, and instances that produced emotional responses. Furthermore, the *Rhetoric* dealt primarily with practical rhetorical contexts, not with character formation. As Aristotle stated in the *Nicomachean Ethics*, rhetoric taught about public speaking that was directed to a judgment on a specific issue (deliberation about future, judgment about past) or a person (epideictic), but it did not deal with moral education.[152]

Lawrence Green has argued that Renaissance interest in Aristotle's *Rhetoric* was motivated by what it taught about emotions and the emotional reactions of the audience. In addition, Green considered Vives a prominent figure in the reception of the work. Although Green did not focus specifically on Vives, I believe that his overall argument was correct.[153] Aristotle's *Rhetoric* was well known to Vives who appreciated it greatly. Already in *De consultatione* he had constructed his treatment of *ethos* on an appropriation of Aristotle's tripartite division of its sources (prudence, virtue, and goodwill).[154] In his *Censura de Aristotelis operibus*, a brief critical presentation of Aristotle's works printed together with the 1538 Latin edition of Aristotle's *Opera*, he praised the philosopher as the inventor of the art of rhetoric, in whose *Rhetoric* 'nothing seems to be lacking'. Vives also lauded the treatise in *De disciplinis*, not for what Aristotle had to say about the method of invention (that is topics) or moral philosophy, but rather for his views on the 'prudence (*prudentia*) needed in common life'.[155] Although Aristotle's

Rhetoric did not enjoy the same success in the printing world as some of Cicero's works or the *Ad Herennium*, it was available in many Latin editions in the translations of William of Moerbeke or George of Trebizond.[156]

There are reasons to think that Aristotle's *Rhetoric* influenced Vives's view that rhetoric was an art that was essentially based on understanding the emotional dispositions and reactions of the audience. The kind of knowledge Aristotle provides in the *Rhetoric* – and Vives in *De anima* – was essentially a reply to Vives's method of rhetorical invention based on imagining what moved the audience, as outlined in *De ratione dicendi*. But there were also some specific themes that he took from Aristotle. Perhaps the most important of these was the role of the estimation of fantasy in activating emotions, which was grounded in Aristotle's description of emotional response in the *Rhetoric*. In Aristotle's *De anima*, imagination was the central power of the soul that mediated between sense perception and reasoning (all reasoning happened through the mental representations produced by the imagination on the basis of sense perception), but it was denied a role in the activation of emotions.[157] In the *Rhetoric*, on the other hand, Aristotle often emphasised that the mere representations of the imagination could produce emotional response through their own, non-rational evaluation of objects. These representations might work because they spoke to the audience's previously held beliefs or dispositions to evaluate in a certain way, but they did not present rational judgments as such. In Book Two, he defined fear as 'a painful and troubled feeling caused by the impression [*phantasia*] of an imminent evil that causes destruction or pain'.[158] While there is an ongoing philosophical discussion as to what exactly he meant by this, the Latin translation by George of Trebizond fostered the idea that what triggered emotional response was a representation of the imagination, since *imaginatio* was the term that he employed for Aristotle's *phantasia*.[159] One potential implication of this was that the orator who could craft representations of situations/objects/persons so that they spoke to the emotional dispositions or beliefs of the audience would wield considerable power over both the non-rational estimation and the rational judgment of the audience.

This certainly influenced Vives. He knew, of course, the theory of internal sensation, developed by Arab and medieval writers on the basis of Aristotle's *De anima*, which he discussed in his commentaries on Augustine's *De civitate Dei, De disciplinis*, and in *De anima*. The theory (or theories: there were different versions, but they usually involved the *sensus communis, imaginatio, memoria, phantasia*, and *facultas estimativa*) explained how the information received through external senses was turned into a meaningful sensation.[160] It equally explained how internal sensation captured the intentions (*intentiones*) of the perceived object by which it was experienced either as good and beneficial or bad and hostile. Some theories had furthermore discussed how the estimation of the intention of an object perceived or imagined triggered emotional response and initiated animal movement.[161]

But despite the inclusion of the theory in *De anima,* Vives had relatively little to say about it or any of the internal senses other than compositive fantasy, which occasionally stood for the whole of internal sensation in *De anima*.[162] While the treatment of fantasy covered many issues, its relationship to emotional response was driven more by Aristotle's *Rhetoric* than by the theory of internal sensation.[163] Moreover, in some parts, as in the opening sentence in the section on fear, Vives freely paraphrased Aristotle in claiming that 'fear is a *phantasia* of an approaching evil'.[164] In *De anima,* we are told that fantasy could be agitated by words, gestures, and other signs that surpassed the cognition of mere brutes.[165] Vives also gave countless examples of the ways in which a mere representation of fantasy activated emotions in the treatment of particular affections.[166] Quite explicitly, Vives claimed that 'the reign of fantasy is extensively open to all affects'.[167] This almost exclusive focus on fantasy within the theory of internal sensation and the importance given to it in emotional arousal was not that typical of other contemporary treatises. In the works on the soul that were often printed with Vives's *De anima,* such as Philipp Melanchthon's *Commentarius de anima* (1540) – which praised Vives in the introduction – and Vitus Amerbach's (1503–1557) *Quatuor libri de anima* (1542), the discussion on fantasy drew on Galen (Melanchthon) and Aristotle (Amerbach), and neither attributed much centrality to fantasy within the theory of internal sensation or discussed the rhetorical significance of all this.[168]

There were natural differences between Vives's and Aristotle's views of fantasy. More than Aristotle, Vives gave the representations of fantasy a strikingly visual interpretation by linking them to the practice of *enargeia/ evidentia*, that is, vivid visual representations that could move the audience. The idea was that if we could craft a vivid representation of a given object/ person/event, we could direct the emotional response of the audience with regards to the thing in question. The potential of *evidentia* was extensively explored by classical rhetoricians and in Quintilian's *Institutio oratoria,* the crafting of visual representations was essential to the control of the emotional response of the audience.[169] Practices of *evidentia* had been taken up forcefully in Erasmus's *De copia* and *De conscribendis epistolis*, both of which emphasised the role of visuality in various rhetorical tasks ranging from demonstrative rhetoric to letters of advice and encouragement.[170] Similarly, Book Three of Vives's *De ratione dicendi* opened with a treatment of description (*descriptio*) which was about *enargeia*.[171] In this part, we are told that the essence of persons, places, acts, or abstract concepts could not be perceived as such, yet they could be reconstructed through accidental qualities that were perceivable to the senses. These were especially useful when abstract concepts had to be explained 'to the intellectual strength of the people' incapable of propositional understanding.[172] For instance, in talking about philosophy to the people, we should not try to define it but rather to depict it as a beautiful and virtuous lady. While this mirrored Vives's general view that all essences were grasped through their accidents, it had an undeniable rhetorical flavour, as the focus on the *vulgus* implied. Indeed, Vives argued that 'descriptions have great importance for persuasion' because when things, through descriptions, 'were unveiled and disclosed they move us greatly'.[173] He gave an example, drawn from Quintilian, about how to vividly describe the destruction of a city, which illustrated how to depict a concept (sack of a city, war) through its consequences in a way that moved the audience.[174]

Naturally, an Aristotelian interest in emotions could be associated with the purification of the soul through transformative rhetoric in a quite non-Aristotelian vein. As seen, the idea of transforming the ruler had been of decisive importance in the mirror-for-princes genres, and much of religious rhetoric, as epitomised by Erasmus's *Ecclesiastes*, took character formation as its avowed goal.[175] Furthermore, transformative rhetoric had often aspired to contemplation and meditation through visuality and Erasmus's *Institutio principis Christiani* was defined precisely as an attempt to offer 'the picture of a true and upright Christian prince'.[176] Much of Vives's *oeuvre*, ranging from mirror-for-princes and meditative literature to the use of *enargeia* in political treatises such as *De concordia*, had aimed at producing this kind of transformation by crafting an idealised image or, alternatively, a dystopian representation of the disastrous consequences of passional disorders. In this way, visuality and imagination were put into play to portray someone as a humble image of God, as an ideal example of a given *officium*, or to demonstrate the consequences of actions such as the terrors of warfare and the fruits of peace.

It is clear, however, that *De anima* did not just provide information about the possibilities of character transformation. As an extension of rhetorical theory, it could equally help anyone interested in the tradition of classical rhetoric, which was more focused on communicating specific messages persuasively than on the cultivation of *persona*. After all, knowledge of the soul was supposed to be the culmination of *De ratione dicendi*, *De conscribendis epistolis*, and *De consultatione*, all of which were practical appropriations of classical rhetoric. Non-transformative rhetoric could naturally profit from the powers of fantasy by harnessing them to convey a specific message. Vives's own dedicatory letter to Charles V in *De concordia* played with the image of a universal monarch in a highly visual language yet employed this image to argue for dynastic peace and ecclesiastical concord. More generally, his discussion of the significance of material culture and praise for the re-creation of the powerful in *De concordia* implied that visuality both inculcated virtue and played a part in the activation of emotional response in specific instances (Chapter 3).

In addition to visuality and fantasy, a rhetorician reading *De conscribendis epistolis*, *De consultatione*, and *De ratione dicendi* would find other useful information in *De anima*. First, he would encounter an explanation framed in natural philosophy for the pivotal importance of *decorum* in a world in which the audience most likely was controlled by pride. In rhetorical works, the worldview of pride was taken primarily as a natural starting point for persuasion in practical issues, not as an object of reform. Since a human being driven by pride was extremely inclined to feel offended and, consequently, to be overtaken by passion, every effort should be made not to offer him/her any opportunity to take offence. This concerned the way one presented oneself, the subject, and the person of the recipient, and this was especially helpful when one addressed those above oneself. Since destructive passions, when grown to their full power, were hard to control and direct, one should use them carefully even in speaking against a particular issue. We can see that in *De anima*, as in Vives's other writings, he thought of princes as the foremost examples of people dominated by pride.

More concretely, in the analysis of the recipient, his/her emotional and passional dispositions were crucial. In the part of *De ratione dicendi* in which the orator was told to assume the mind of the audience through his/her own imagination, one of the crucial issues was to understand what 'moves them and calms them'.[177] So if an orator had an interpretation about an emotional disposition of the audience towards the object of the discussion or person involved, he/she could open *De anima* to gather more information about the dynamics of a given emotion or passion. Let us think once again of Vives's dedication of *De concordia* to Charles V, which was an attempt to address a ruler whose worldview was assumed to be dominated by a discourse of universal monarchy that likened the powers and qualities of the ruler to those of God. Charles was thus clearly imagined to be under the sway of pride, which goaded him to seek recognition of his supposedly God-like qualities and, if these were not accepted, triggered wrath (*ira*) and envy (*invidia*), as *De concordia* had already implied. In *De anima*, one could learn how pride, as a form of excessive self-love, activated envy towards those who seemed to possess more; wrath, because a proud person 'is never attributed as much as he/she thinks he/she should be'; and a host of other emotions.[178] With the proud, *decorum* was thus required and Vives acknowledged Charles's achievements and their God-like dimension. This admission did not, however, serve to overcome pride and ambition but instead to connect these impulses to goals that Vives presented as solutions to the problems of Europe in his time (the need for a Church council and dynastic peace). In this way, the glory that nurtured pride was linked to a proposed action which resulted in a redirection of harmful passional impulses to something that Vives considered important. Consequently, the deliberator did not transform the audience but rather played with passions in order to enhance a specific action in the context of a particular issue. The dedicatory letter thus exemplified rhetorical *decorum* (not employing *parrhesia* or direct reproof) but, precisely through *decorum*, tied ambition, glory, and pride together with an action which was regarded as good and urgent.

In the end, rhetorical invention did not use commonplaces or pre-existing formulas in composition but relied on a mental reconstruction of the audience that was dependent on the kind of information provided by *De anima*.

If a given audience/recipient could be linked to specific emotional dispositions, an orator would understand how to move it to his/her side by opening Vives's treatise on the soul. This effectively reinstituted the understanding of emotions as the key to persuasion, a view which was to have echoes in the development of early modern rhetorical theory in the sixteenth and seventeenth centuries.[179]

While *De anima et vita* was not Vives's last publication, it certainly was the pinnacle of Vives's moral, political, and rhetorical thought. It fulfilled the quest for a theory of the soul and emotions that could serve as the foundation for ethical and political self-government and as the basis of a renewed rhetoric of *decorum*. In the context of Northern Humanist thought, it was a remarkable work not because it anticipated modern, experimental psychology, but because it was the only Erasmian treatise of the early sixteenth century that built a bridge from humanist concerns with moral philosophy and rhetoric to natural philosophy.

Notes

1. His most ambitious and his most popular works were not necessarily the same. His letter writing manual, *De conscribendis epistolis*, was more successful than any of his larger treatises such as *De disciplinis*, *De ratione dicendi*, or *De anima*; see González González, 2007, 103–11.
2. González González, 2008, 61–4.
3. Vives, 2013, 333, 451; Vives, 1532, 609. The treatises were probably composed more or less simultaneously since *De anima*, although printed in 1538, was already a work in progress by the time *De disciplinis* appeared in print; see Curtis, 2008, 126.
4. The relative originality of the work, which probably made it unsuitable for educational use, is pointed out in most of the scholarly literature on the subject; see Mack, 2005, 66, 91; Mack, 2008, 263, 274–5; Rodríguez Peregrina, 1996, 363–4. For a philosophical reading of the work inspired by Heidegger, see Hidalgo-Serna, 2002. For a philosophical view of style, see Walker, 2017. See also Cooney, 1966.
5. For a similar categorisation of different genres, see George, 1992, 166.
6. Fables, descriptions, and narrations are all part of traditional rhetorical exercises that can be found, for instance, in Aphthonius's widely used *Progymnasmata*.
7. Vives described orations embedded in histories as political; see Vives, 2000, 144: 'Oratio atque orationis sensa erunt plane politica, cuiusmodi esse solent senum in republica prudentum'.
8. For Vives's claim to originality vis-à-vis the classical tradition, see Vives, 2000, 9.
9. Bonilla y San Martín, 1929, 2:147–9. George has also noted this; see George, 1992, 154.
10. Mack does not comment on the reasons in his analysis of *De ratione dicendi*; see Mack, 2005, 84–5; Mack, 2008, 238. George and Rodríguez Peregrina, to whom Vives's mature and reflective attitude to rhetoric in *De ratione dicendi* contrasts with the merely practical interest of his youth, do not comment on the implications of *decorum* either; see George, 1992, 163–5; Rodríguez Peregrina, 2000, LIII. Don Abbott notes the centrality of *decorum* in *De ratione dicendi*, but does not explain the reasons for its centrality, Abbott, 1986, 198–9.

206   *Rhetorical* decorum

A recent interpretation by David Walker has seen the interest in *decorum* as stemming from a new understanding of style as an expression of and exercise in one's character; see Walker, 2017.

11. For more general presentations of the Italian and English background of civil conversation, see Bryson, 1998, 54–6; Peltonen, 2003, 24–6.
12. Vives, 2000, 3: 'Quorum duorum sermo certe fortior est ac validior inter homines [...] mentes ad se allicit et in affectibus dominatur ...'.
13. Vives, 2000, 4: 'Ego vero nihil video conducibilius hominum coetibus quam sit sermo bene instutus atque educatus, nec aliud perinde damnosum, ut importunum, neque locis neque temporibus neque personis accommodatum'.
14. Vives, 2000, 4–5, 100.
15. Vives, 2000, 5–6.
16. Vives, 2000, 8–9; Vives, 2013, 171–5.
17. Vives, 2000, 8: 'nec est aliud perinde societati aptum instrumentum'.
18. Vives, 2000, 9: 'isque plane inter homines regnat, qui maxime est ad dicendum appositus'.
19. Vives, 2000, 9: '... ut non perinde renovemus priscam atque omnino tradamus novam'.
20. For *decorum* and *kairos* in the classical tradition, see Sipiora – Baumlin, 2002. For poetry and *decorum*, see Horace, 1926, 456–9 (1.81–106).
21. Kinneavy, 1986, 82; Baumlin, 2002, 159.
22. Cicero, 1942, 1:100–1, 2:166–9 (1.32.144, 3.60.210–2).
23. Cicero, 1939b, 356–61 (21.69–22.74).
24. Quintilian, 2001, 5:8–59 (11.1).
25. Quintilian, 2001, 5:8–11 (11.1.2–3, 11.1.6).
26. Quintilian, 2001, 5:10–3 (11.1.7): 'Sed totum hoc apte dicere non elocutionis tantum genere constat, sed est cum inventione commune. Nam si tantum habent etiam verba momentum, quanto res ipsae magis!'.
27. Hermogenes, 1987, 101.
28. Trebizond, 1522, 164^r-7^r.
29. Mayans 7:215 (Vives to Hugu); Vives, 2013, 388, 401, 402. The link between Vives and Trebizond on *elocutio* is discussed in Sánchez Manzano, 2014.
30. For poetry, see Vinsauf, 2010, 72. For political speech, see John of Salisbury's *Policraticus*; Salisbury, 1938, 1.5.37.
31. In Erasmus's *De copia*, there is a section on how to talk about appropriateness, but he does not elaborate on *decorum* as a rhetorical principle; see Erasmus, ASD I/6 (*De copia*), 123.
32. Rivius, 1539, [Nn6]^r-[Nn7]^v.
33. Cicero, 1939b, 356–7 (21.70).
34. Cicero, 1913, 94–121 (1.27.93–1.32.117).
35. Erasmus, ASD I/8, 316 (*De civilitate morum puerorum*. CWE 25:273).
36. See, for instance, Vives, 1527a, 22^v (433).
37. Vives, 2000, 110–3.
38. Vives, 2000, 101–4.
39. Mack, 2011, 2; Cicero, 1942, 1:450–5 (2.81.333–83.340). The fact that if the audience is composed of a single person the character should also be considered is briefly mentioned by Cicero.
40. *Ad Herennium*, 16–21 (1.6.9–10); Cicero, 1960a, 40–53 (1.15.20–1.18.26).
41. Quintilian, 2001, 2:204–7 (4.1.52–3).
42. Mack, 2011, 261. Another possibility was to categorise the audience according to the subject matter of rhetoric (judicial, deliberative, and epideictic). This approach did not problematise the audience but rather linked their reactions to the functions of different genres (to judge, deliberate, and laude); see, for instance, Caesarius, 1535, Ciii^r-Ciiii^v.

43. Nebrija, 1529, f[v]ᵛ, f[viii]ᵛ. Vives mentioned Nebrija often in *De disciplinis* but mostly as a specialist in grammar, see Vives, 2013, 94, 364, 370.
44. Vives, 2000, 110–1.
45. See, for instance, Rivius, 1539, [Ff8]ʳ-Gg2ʳ, [Ll8]ʳ-Mm.
46. Vives, 2000, 105–8.
47. Vives, 2000, 104: 'In relatione est comparatio personarum, maior, minor, par in re omni, sanguine, eruditione, virtute, aetate, robore, dignitate, rebus gestis, opibus'; '... videndum quod sit eorum iudicium ad quos dicimus'.
48. Vives, 2000, 104.
49. Vives, 2000, 107: 'Inimicum voco non quem ipse oderis, sed qui te, nam si diligit, etiam si tu odisti, quod tamen est perrarum, pro amico habebitur, nec aliter apud eum dices quam si mutuo cuperitis optime'.
50. Vives, 2000, 115–21.
51. Vives connects the part on goodwill and emotions explicitly to his treatment of the soul, see Vives, 2000, 120.
52. Vives, 2000, 83–4, 125–6: '... ad finem extremum referenda omnia ...'.
53. Vives, 2000, 122: 'Sunt in actione impedimenta [...] ab audientibus in attentione, in ingenio, in affectibus'.
54. Vives, 2000, 126: '... non initio tantum, sed in quacumuque orationis parte ...'.
55. Vives, 2000, 119: '... oblique enim sunt a nobis invadendi, qui vel in dicentem sustulerunt se vel in rem ipsam'.
56. Vives, 2000, 91.
57. Vives, 2000, 91: 'Ante omnia considerandum qui nos simus, qui illi quos agitare volumus aut sedare, quod eorum iudicium de rebus, quibus plurimum tribuunt, quibus parum, in quos affectus sint proclives, a quibus alieni, ex quibus in quos leviter transeant, ex ingenio, persuasionibus, moribus, aetate, sexu, valetudine, habitudine, conditione, loco, tempore, omnibus denique, quae persecuti sumus in *Probabilitate*. Induenda mens illorum et totum ingenium tantisper, dum quae ad rem nostram faciant excogitamus; ponamusque nos illorum loco, id est, contemplamur sedulo, si nos essemus illi, hoc est, si nobis ita esset de rebus persuasum atque illis, quibus tandem in praesenti negotio moveremur aut sedaremur' (Translation from Vives, 2017, 253).
58. Vives, 2000, 95: 'Si in persuadendo dissimulanda est ars, quanto magis in movendo, quod est delicatius'.
59. Vives, 2000, 95–6.
60. Vives, 2000, 83–8.
61. Abbott, 1986, 198–9. Abbott does notice though that *decorum* is not just a virtue of style but 'virtually synonymous with rhetoric'. He does not, however, develop this idea further.
62. Vives, 2000, 10: 'Aptatio tamen tum verborum, tum sensuum, quomodo cuique fini applicabuntur, huius sunt propositi'.
63. Agricola, 1992, 440–1 (3.II).
64. Agricola, 1992, 364–74 (2.XIV).
65. Agricola, 1992, 370–1 (2.XIV), 428–31 (2.XXX); 446–7 (3.III).
66. Erasmus, ASD IV/1, 268 (*Lingua*. CWE 29:294).
67. Erasmus, ASD I/2, 653-5 (*Ciceronianus*. CWE 28:406).
68. Erasmus, ASD I/2, 650 (*Ciceronianus*. CWE 28:400).
69. Vives, 2013, 201: 'aspectu [...] formosam'.
70. Vives, 2013, 180: 'Sed hoc [invenire] certe singularum est artium in sua materia; in uita uero est iudicii, consilii, et quae ex his nascitur, prudentiae, quae nulla comprehendi potest arte'; '... tanquam consultrix et rectrix omnium'. For *decorum* and prudence, see also Vives, 2000, 100–1; Cicero, 1942, 2:168–9 (3.55.212).
71. Celtis, 1537, 105–7.

208 Rhetorical decorum

72. Ong, 2004, see esp. 92–126.
73. It also adds a part on argumentative forms; see Baarland, 1537, 168–71.
74. Baarland, 1537, 156, 161–3, 166.
75. Baarland, 1537, 160–1: 'In ratione affectuum est omnis eloquentiae fructus'.
76. Erasmus, *Formula*, CWE 25:261.
77. Erasmus, ASD I/2, 316 (*De conscribendis epistolis*. CWE 25:74).
78. Erasmus, ASD I/2, 324 (*De conscribendis epistolis*. CWE 25:79).
79. Erasmus, ASD I/2, 325–6 (*De conscribendis epistolis*).
80. For a comparison of Vives and Erasmus on letter writing, see Fantazzi, 2002.
81. Vives, 1989a, 26, 28, 82.
82. Vives, 1989a, 28–34, 46.
83. Vives, 1989a, 38–9. See also 64–6.
84. Vives, 1989a, 60–1: '... imperiosum est nimis malefactum dicere et rem atrocitate verborum insectari'.
85. Vives, 1989a, 62–3: 'Invectivae, si ad insectationem vitii aliosque ab eo genere vitae deterrendos parantur, ferendae sunt'.
86. Vives, 1989a, 64–5: 'Vehementer cavendum est ne quem epistola offendamus'; '... epistola nuda est omnino ac patronis destituta'; 'Ille autem relegendo auget vulnus et maledictum interpretando fit acerbius'.
87. Vives, 1989a, 52–3. Vives follows Quintilian here loosely; see Quintilian, 2001, 5:16–7 (11.1.16).
88. Vives, 1989a, 52–4: '... omnes epistolae – praeceptoria, admonitoria, consultoria, adortatoria, castigatoria, obiurgatoria – tamquam ex alto loquuntur, ideo considerandum accurate qui scribat, cui, qua de re'.
89. Vives, 1989a, 56–7: '... apertam reprehensionem non ferunt, tectam non sentiunt ...'.
90. Vives, 1989a, 56–7: '... variis ingeniis [...] varia est adhibenda medicina ...'; 'Si laus de virtute, quam non habet, prodest, laudetur, quales sunt nonnulli principum et potentum et dcotorum atque ingeniosorum hominum'.
91. Vives, 1989a, 56–7: 'Sin laudibus insolecit ac fit insanior ...'.
92. Vives, 1989a, 58–9: 'Quod si omnino profuturus non es, sed magis irritatione tua et tibi nociturus et aliis, consultius erit Camarinam non movere ...'. Camarina refers to one of Erasmus's adages (*Movere Camarinam*) which warned against inviting trouble. The inhabitants of a town called Camarina dried a fen of the same name against the warning of the oracle. This allowed their enemies to attack them; see Erasmus ASD II/1 (*Adagia*), 174.
93. Vives, 1987, 42–3; Vives, 1989a, 52–3: '... urbanitas, acumen et facetiae ...'.
94. Vives, 1989a, 58–9.
95. For Erasmus and St Paul, see 74–5.
96. Erasmus, ASD V/5, 288, 298 (*Ecclesiastes*. CWE 68:1011).
97. Erasmus, ASD V/5, 292–4. The example is taken from Erasmus's *Paraphrase on Acts* (1524), where St Paul's ability to become all things to all people was already praised; see Erasmus, LB 735E–738C (*Paraphrasis in Acta Apostolorum*, 17:19–34).
98. Erasmus, ASD V/5, 304 (*Ecclesiastes*. CWE 68:1017).
99. Vives, 1959, *Praefatio*, first page.
100. Vives, 1959, *Praefatio*, last page: '... fundamentum uniuersae moralis disciplinae, siue priuatae, siue publicae'. 'nam nec alia ulla est aeque uiro principi conueniens, ad se ac suos, totamque rempublicam rite gubernandam'. See also Vives, 2013, 252, 257.
101. Watson, 1915, 334–5; Casini, 2006a, 16; Noreña, 1989, xv, 71–2, 141; Ebbersmeyer, 2013, 291.
102. Noreña, 1989, 213–8.

103. Vives at times also separates animals into those who had a sensitive soul and those who possessed a cognitive soul capable of higher cognitive processes; Vives, 1959, 1–2; Aristotle, 1957, 67–73, 81–5 (412a–413a, 414a–415a).
104. Vives, 1959, 52–4. For internal sensation, see Casini, 2013. For Arabic and medieval traditions, see Wolfson, 1935, 89–129; Knuuttila – Kärkkäinen, 2013; Park, 1988.
105. Vives, 1959, 146: '... istarmu facultatum, quibus animi nostri praediti a natura sunt ad sequendum bonum, uel uitandum malum, actus dicuntur affectus siue affectiones ...'.
106. Vives, 1959, 147, 191–3. The prevalent view of Stoic *apatheia*, which was criticised by Plutarch, Augustine, and many Renaissance writers such as Melanchthon, did not necessarily do justice to the Stoic view in which a sage was allowed some emotional states, but it had become a commonplace by Vives's time. See Casini, 2006a, 131–8.
107. Vives, 1959, 149.
108. Vives, 1959, 219, 264.
109. The tension between these two discourses is noted in the scholarly literature; see Noreña, 1989, 141–3; Casini, 2006a, 132–3, 137–45.
110. Vives, 1959, 67.
111. Vives, 1959, 66–74. Of these impediments, Vives had frequently emphasised the harmful potential of passions; Mayans 5:347–8 (*De concordia*).
112. Casini, 2006b, 406, 415–6.
113. Saarinen, 2011, 31; Teske, 1994; Teske, 2011; Casini, 2006b, 416.
114. Vives, 1959, 97–104.
115. Vives, 1959, 146: '... iudicii sententiam sequuntur ...'.
116. Vives, 1959, 147: 'sed non semper ad affectum excitandum opus est iudicio illo, quod ex rationum collatione de rebus statuit: illud sufficit, & est frequentius, quod imaginationis moueatur uisis'.
117. There is some confusion in Vives's language. At times he posits a separate estimative act (*facultas aestimativa*) responsible for the judgmental activities of the internal senses. But at times, he discusses the judgments of fantasy without mentioning a separate estimative faculty. This reflects a broader tension in the use of fantasy as one of five internal senses, on the one hand, and as the synonym of all internal sensation, on the other. See Vives, 1959, 31–4, 36, 66.
118. Vives, 1959, *Praefatio*.
119. Sorabji, 2000; Hadot, 2002, 22–74; Nussbaum, 1994.
120. Plato, 1964, 195 (129A).
121. Sorabji, 2000, 8–9; Knuuttila, 2004, 2, 122–5.
122. Vives, 1959, *Praefatio*, second page: 'animi naturam, qualitatem, ingenium, uires, affectiones ...'
123. Dealy, 2017, 4–10, 263–332. For a reading that situates the work in the Neoplatonic framework of Origen, see Tracy, 1996, 32–40; Godin, 1982.
124. LB V:12C (CWE 66:40).
125. LB V:11F–14E (*Enchiridion*).
126. LB V:14F (*Enchiridion*. CWE 66:44).
127. LB V:13F–16D (*Enchiridion*).
128. Erasmus, ASD I/2, 324 (*De conscribendis epistolis*. CWE 25:79).
129. Vives, 1527a, 2r-3v (1–11)
130. Vives, 1527a, 7v-8r (118–9).
131. Vives, 1527a, 11r-12v (206–14): 'Remedia his morbis ex rebus ac nobis ipsis, vel ex deo, vel ex Christi lege ac vita petuntur'.
132. Vives, 1527a, 18r-21r.
133. Mayans 5:331–2 (*De concordia*); Mayans 5:420–1 (*De pacificatione*).

134. Mayans 5:198–9 (*De concordia*).
135. Mayans 5:332, 347 (*De concordia*); Vives, 1527a, 11ʳ-12ʳ.
136. Vives, 1959, 116: 'ex quo usu nascitur assuefactio, in qua insunt & facilitas ad agendum, & pronitas ...'; Aristotle, 1934, 70–5 (1103a–b).
137. Vives, 1978, 605–6 (Ep. 174, Vives to Simon Grynaeus).
138. Vives, 1959, 73: 'Discursuum magna est uarietas, ut sunt diuersissima in hominibus ingenia: partim ex constitutione ipsa naturali, partim ex doctrina, assuefactione ...'. See also Vives, 1527a, 2ʳ (8).
139. Vives, 1959, 66: 'ad prudentiam [...] non sola scientia satis est, experimentis etiam est opus ...'.
140. *Ad Herennium*, 204–25 (3.16.28–3.24.40); Vives, 1959, 54–63 For the tradition of mnemotechnics as an associative practice that connected words and concepts to visual images, see Carruthers, 1990; Yates, 1966.
141. Vives, 1959, 211: 'motus quidam offensionis naturalis [...] non ex iudicio a contemptu orto subito, sed ex illo quod in animo habemus praeceptum, & confirmatum, bonos esse nos, doctos, generosos, industrios, praestantes, oportere nobis honorem exhiberi, & reuerentiam, non oportere nos contemni, ex hoc iudicio informato intus atque infixo subito ira incalescit ...'. See also Casini, 2006a, 155–6.
142. Vives, 1959, 213: 'Seneca totam iram subito dicit existere, cui merito Plutarchus refragatur, crescit enim ex suis causis ...'; Casini, 2006a, 157–9.
143. Vives, 1959, 219: 'Multum ad iram excludendam facit, praecognitum habere & persuasum, homines fere omnes iniquissime de rebus statuere ...'; '... de seipso non magnificam habere existimationem ...'.
144. Vives, 1959, 263: 'Inter omnia uiciorum genera potest constare pax & concordia, superbia excepta ...'.
145. Vives, 1959, 207: '... principes [...] quibus assentantur & abblandiuntur omnes, repugnat nemo'.
146. Vives, 1959, 262: '... ne quis se esset potentior, ac ne Deus quidem ...'; '... exemptum se arbitretur esse oportere humanis legibus ...'; 'exemptos quoque naturae legibus, ne Deo quidem summo & praepotenti subditos ...'.
147. Vives, 1959, 263: '... quottidie nostri principes'.
148. Vives, 1959, 145. 'Aristoteles in Rhetoricis tantum de materia hac exposuit, quantum uiro politico arbitratus est sufficere. Nos pro uirili parte nostra singula argumenti huius subtilius exactiusque persequemur'.
149. Aristotle, 1934, 89–114 (1106–1109b).
150. Aristotle, 1926, 173, 263 (1378a, 1391b).
151. Aristotle, 1926, 185 (1380a).
152. Aristotle, 1934, 629 (1179b).
153. Green, 1994, 3, 5–7.
154. In Vives, these are one's prudence (*prudentia*), honesty (*probitas*), and friendship (*amicitia*); see Vives, 1536, 244, 247; Aristotle, 1926, 17 (1356a), 171 (1378a).
155. Vives, 1538, [a6]ʳ: 'nihil videatur deesse'; Vives, 2013, 402: '... prudentiam uitae communis'.
156. Green – Murphy, 2006, 33; Brandes, 1989, 86–103.
157. Aristotle, 1957, 155–63 (427a–429a).
158. Aristotle, 1926, 201 (1382a). Some have argued that Aristotle's conception of judgment includes both rational beliefs and mere apprehensions; see Sihvola, 1996, 106. For a more thorough discussion on what Aristotle meant, see Knuuttila, 2004, 36–41. See also Dow, 2015, 182–225.
159. The cognitive perspective is defended in Nussbaum; see Nussbaum, 1994, 88–90. For a compositional explanation, see Knuuttila, 2004, 35–8.

160. Thomas Aquinas, 1962, 1:380–1 (i.lxxviii.iiii); Avicenna, 1972, 87–9; Wolfson, 1935; Black, 2000. Sensible objects refer to what can be perceived only by one sense (colour, sound, etc.), while common sensibles are common to all or some senses (movement, number, figure, etc.), and incidental objects are those which do not directly affect the senses (we perceive someone as the son of Diares); see Aristotle, 1957, 101–3 (418a).
161. See Aristotle, 1957, 155–63, 175–9, 181–95 (427a–429a, 431a–431b, 432a–434a); Richardson, 1992, 384–5. For Arabic and medieval traditions, see Wolfson, 1935, 89; Knuuttila – Kärkkäinen, 2013, 132, 142–5; Black, 2000, 59–63, 68–9.
162. Vives distinguishes between passive *imaginatio* and active *phantasia*, which was responsible for the production of mental representations, Vives, 1959, 52–3. While these concepts were semantically close and some used them as synonyms, this categorisation was fairly standard in the theory of internal sensation. Interestingly, Vives employs the term *imaginatio* when he discusses its ability to trigger emotional response. While the correct term in his theory would have been *phantasia*, Latin translations of Aristotle's *Rhetoric* could employ *imaginatio* in this context.
163. Casini has also argued this; see Casini, 2006a, 154–7.
164. Vives, 1959, 242: 'Metus est, inquit Aristoteles, mali appropinquantis phantasia'. In Trebizond's translation: 'Timor, ex imaginatione futuri mali corruptiui [...] dolor'; See Aristotle, 1538, 269.
165. Vives, 1959, 33, 211.
166. Vives, 1959, 172, 194, 249.
167. Vives, 1959, 249: 'Sed hoc phantasiae regnum late per affectiones omnes patet'.
168. Melanchthon, 1550, a5^r, 109^r–13^r; Wolfson, 1935, 71–7. Melanchthon emphasised the importance of heart in the arousal of emotions; see Mack, 2004, 68–9. Amerbach, 1542, 166–72. Much of the discussion draws on Aristotle, 1957, 155–63 (427a–429a).
169. Quintilian, 2001, 3:58–61, 3:374–9 (6.2.26–6.2.32, 8.3.61–8.3.70). See also Aristotle, 1926, 405 (1411b); *Ad Herennium*, 356–9 (4.39.51); Lévy – Pernot, 1997.
170. Erasmus, ASD I/6 (*De copia*), 202–15; Erasmus, ASD I/2 (*De conscribendis epistolis*), 326–7; 513–6.
171. Vives, 2000, 130–7.
172. Vives, 2000, 132: '... ad vulgi [...] intelligentiam ...'.
173. Vives, 2000, 134: 'Multum habent momenti descriptiones ad persuadendum [...] apertae atque evolutae acriter commovent'.
174. Quintilian, 2001, 3:378–9 (8.3.67–9); Vives, 2000, 135. For a description of a thing from its effects, see 132.
175. In *Ecclesiastes*, Erasmus discussed the ability of religious rhetoric to transform secular rulers as well; Erasmus, ASD V/4 (*Ecclesiastes*), 118–20.
176. Erasmus, ASD IV/1 (*Institutio principis Christiani*), 134 (CWE 27:204).
177. Vives, 2000, 91: 'quibus [...] moveremur aut sedaremur'.
178. Vives, 1959, 259–60: '... nunquam sibi tantum tribui existimat, quantum meretur ...'.
179. Green, 1994.

Conclusion

As in many areas of study, scholarship on Vives has found it hard to balance rigorous contextual studies with overall assessments of his place in Renaissance intellectual history. On the one hand, there are a growing number of increasingly specialised studies on different aspects of his life and thought that rarely address broader themes within Renaissance scholarship. On the other hand, there is a long tradition of overemphasising the place of Vives in European philosophical, humanist, and pedagogical traditions that is not attuned to a contextual reading of his work.

The problem has been partly solved by three recent studies on Vives's reception, Enrique González González's and Víctor Gutiérrez Rodríguez's *Los diálogos de Vives y la imprenta. Fortuna de un manual escolar renacentista (1539–1994)*, Valentín Moreno Gallego's *La recepción hispana de Juan Luis Vives* (2006), and Enrique González González's *Una república de lectores* (2007). All have painted a broad fresco of the popularity of Vives's work across the centuries. In tune with modern theoretical developments, all have seen reception as an active engagement with texts that creates meaning relevant to the context of a given historical moment. In focusing on the reception of individual works, they have shown that the intertextuality between Vives's different pieces was largely lost in a reception that was interested in specific treatises and ideas for particular purposes.[1] Unlike Erasmus, who was a controversial figure and linked to a certain approach to theology from early on, the figure of Vives, despite his popularity, was not the subject of public disputes, his work was not associated with a system of thought, and some of his more ambitious treatises, such as *De ratione dicendi*, were not very influential. Consequently, these studies have proved the success of some of Vives's individual works, but because Vives was never attributed a distinct philosophy, they have perhaps done less to show what might have been original in Vives's overall *oeuvre*. In what follows, I will not engage in a detailed analysis of Vives's reception. Instead, I will interpret his work as a reception of several classical and Northern humanist trends and place these in the broader history of rhetoric and political thought. My intention here is not to replace the focus of reception studies on actual practices of reading but to show a side of Vives that was largely forgotten in his

DOI: 10.4324/9781003240457-7

reception and which, I hope, brings out a new dimension of his thought in relation to some of the dominant trends in rhetoric and political thought in the early modern period.

As I have shown in Chapter 1, Vives understood rhetorical theory, education, and practice in close connection with the possibilities of realising an active life at the service of others (a form of *negotium*) ever since his encounter with the art of eloquence in the 1510s. This connection between rhetoric and a life of *negotium* implies, in my view, three things regarding the importance of rhetoric for politics in Vives. First, his political activity and thought were mediated through rhetorical categories. Because of this, his ethical understanding of politics was not merely a plea for a politics of moral reform as a solution to political discord but a critical discourse that was employed to comment on the actions of the powerful and to criticise dynastic warfare. Second, Vives, more than most writers on rhetoric of the time, developed a nuanced understanding of rhetorical *decorum* as an extension of politics since he thought that adversarial rhetoric was not conducive to a successful life of *negotium* or to political concord. Consequently, he reshaped classical rhetorical precepts into new literary and conversational genres that stressed the necessity of disguising aggressive tactics in the spirit of *decorum* as an answer to the religious and civic upheaval and changing political circumstances of the 1520s and 1530s. In this environment, *decorum* regulated speech by promoting erudite Latin and classical beauty against the coarse and uncouth language used in pamphlets. Third, his interest in *decorum* and in the management of the passions and emotions of the audience played a crucial role in extending rhetoric from merely formulaic precepts to the understanding of emotions in the 1530s. Consequently, Vives argued that political concord could best be mediated rhetorically if we understood the dynamics of emotions and passions and adapted our rhetorical activity accordingly.

In this picture, a rhetoric of *decorum* was the key to concord in two ways. First, it suppressed open discord which was an act of concord in itself since it nurtured sociability by establishing constructive emotional ties between the speaker and the audience. In a harmonious discursive atmosphere, the ethical self-government of individuals became possible. Second, under the guise of concord, it enabled effective persuasion since a rhetoric of *decorum*, not adversarial rhetoric, was the only way to convince and move people. *Decorum* thus enabled the performance of a political life of *negotium* by mediating differences of opinion in harmony: it communicated virtue and concord without making discord apparent. This, I believe, demonstrates that the rhetoric of *decorum* was not only developed in the context of politics but that it was thought of as a reply to fundamental questions of politics concerning a life of *negotium* and the functioning of concord in a changed environment.

What then should we make of this conclusion with regards to Vives's place in the broader early modern culture of the time? In order to make sense of this, I believe that the results must be put into the context of several discussions on Renaissance rhetoric, its political implications, and its links to the rise of a new culture of civility.

Some discussions of pivotal importance on Renaissance eloquence are only indirectly connected to politics. On the most general level, there is no agreement on whether Renaissance rhetoric should be seen as a largely immovable discourse or as an active process of reception. While this divide mirrors differences in research projects and the materials analysed, it has led to differing interpretations of the potential originality of individual writers. Wayne A. Rebhorn and Quentin Skinner, in tracing the discourse on rhetoric (Rebhorn) and in building a context for Thomas Hobbes's philosophy (Skinner), have emphasised the largely immutable and classical nature of Renaissance rhetoric. On the other end of the spectrum, Marc Fumaroli, among others, has seen the Renaissance as a period of active reception and appropriation of rhetoric to a myriad of different contexts.[2] This study has argued that the political significance of Vives's rhetoric can only be understood if it is seen as a conscious process of adaptation. He not only saw rhetoric as an art that had to be accommodated again and again for new political, religious, and cultural environments but also acted on this premise in his theoretical writings and in his career as a counsellor.[3]

To understand Vives, or Erasmian rhetoric more broadly, as an active process of reception is not novel *per se*, but this process is rarely analysed as an extension of political considerations. In most scholarship, rhetoric has been seen as a worldview that extends to other disciplines – most notably dialectic, philosophy, and theology – introducing a strong rhetorical element into their very core. Regarding rhetoric and dialectic, it has been well established that interest in rhetorical categories gradually rhetorised dialectic in the writings of Lorenzo Valla, Rudolph Agricola, Juan Luis Vives, and Petrus Ramus among others.[4] In this view, dialectic, the investigation of truth, was turned into an ancillary discipline of rhetoric that provided a basis for the rhetorical practices of writing, arguing, and persuading. In Chapters 1 and 4, I have tried to show that for Vives the debate on dialectic was not merely an abstract issue of semantics but intrinsically linked to an attempt to make arts and knowledge useful for a life of *negotium*. While this is hardly a new argument, with Cesare Vasoli's seminal *La dialettica e la retorica dell'umanesimo* (1968) already connecting Vives's dialectical viewpoints to their utility, much of the discussion on humanist dialectic has taken place on a distinctively philosophical level that, while aware of its social implications, touches upon them only in passing.[5] Even more broadly, the prevalent philosophical interpretation has seen rhetoric as a key to the philosophical and theological worldview of a generation of humanists to which Vives belonged. Whether it is philosophical scepticism that arises from the rhetorical practice of coming up with arguments on both sides of any issue, the rise of the epistemological dialogue, the anti-scholastic and anti-dogmatic theology that relies on the transformative capacities of rhetoric, or literary creativeness, this scholarship has situated rhetoric on a distinctively philosophical, literary, or spiritual level.[6] While these interpretations, many of which were motivated by the post-linguistic-turn interest in rhetoric, have been countered recently by scholars that see rhetoric as antithetical to serious philosophy (e.g. Ross Dealy), they are dominant in our understanding of Erasmian humanism.[7]

This study can be viewed as a comment on these discussions as well as an attempt to shift their emphasis in light of Vives's work. It is, of course, undeniable that Vives's dialectic – which investigates truth – was imbued with rhetorical categories. It is equally true that he gave conversations (*sermo*) between the learned a philosophical role, although this *sermo* was not so much constitutive of truth as a way of clarifying it in the current post-lapsarian epistemological state.[8] But, while these developments were facilitated by the transposition of rhetorical categories to other areas of thought, such as dialectic, philology, theology, or philosophy, rhetoric as a distinctive art was not conceptualised in rhetorical manuals or encyclopaedic treatments (e.g. *De disciplinis*) as a philosophical or spiritual issue but as a practical art that dealt with persuasion. Furthermore, while Vives thought that rhetoric was operative in a range of communicative situations, persuasive possibilities were much more often linked to the civic duties of addressing those above oneself in counsel than to Christian genres such as preaching. His history of rhetoric in *De disciplinis* was civic, he composed rhetorical exercises on political themes, he employed rhetoric in addressing those in power, he wrote a manual on the application of deliberative rhetoric to counsel, and his advice on letter writing elaborated on how to address those superior to oneself. Consequently, his rhetoric of *decorum* can be understood primarily as an attempt to redefine the possibilities of civic rhetoric in a new context.

This is not to say that the stress put on the practicality and civic nature of rhetoric is antithetical to all attempts to place rhetoric within a philosophical framework. Considering political philosophy, some of the views that emphasise rhetoric, given its argumentative flexibility, as contrary to philosophy have effectively shown that rhetorical adaptability was more fundamental than any philosophical commitment for a host of *quattrocento* humanists who were ready to say almost anything their position demanded.[9] This, I would argue, was not the case for Vives nor for some other major humanist of his generation who did possess relatively robust ethical and philosophical commitments. Erasmus was never willing to support the policies of the rulers of his time, and Thomas More and Juan Luis Vives both suffered the wrath of Henry VIII personally for not supporting his projects (the divorce and the Act of Supremacy). As I have argued, the significance of rhetoric was bound together with a broader project to mediate reason in a post-lapsarian reality. But within this broader narrative, rhetoric never lost its practically oriented aspirations to find the best possible means to persuade the audience in a specific deliberation or to transform their views more thoroughly.

Those rare interpretations of Erasmian rhetoric that take into account its civic implications have largely emphasised the ability of epideictic rhetoric to mould the character of those in power.[10] We can definitely discern this element in Vives to whom epideictic rhetoric enabled, among other things, character formation. But as I have argued, the instrumental side of classical rhetoric was also preserved and embedded in much of his advice on rhetorical persuasion and the use of passions. This idea has, I believe, been downplayed in scholarship on Vives and Erasmus, and in some philosophical interpretations of Renaissance rhetoric, it has been explicitly cast aside as uninteresting.[11]

The instrumental idea of rhetoric as an argumentative practice that strove for persuasion has, however, been embraced in civic interpretations of Renaissance rhetoric. In recent scholarship, much of the work on the political dimension of rhetoric has been tied together with a historiography on republicanism in which civic participation was enabled by the argumentative tools offered by the *ars rhetorica*. In this literature, the civic possibility of participating freely in debates is tied to the acceptance of the plurality of opinions and the inevitability of continuous negotiation between citizens who recognise each other as participants in a conversation.[12] While Vives thought that rhetoric enabled a life of *negotium* as did most republican writers, the differences were substantial. Although he shared reference points with the republican tradition (such as Cicero) there is no indication that Vives ever strove for a republican oratorical culture that was regarded as both impossible to achieve and unstable in its outlook. While there were debates (or conversations) between the equal citizens of the Republic of Letters and scholarly circles, in the political realm debates were not conceptualised as between peers who both possessed an equal claim to argue their respective cases. Rather, Vives's understanding of politics underlined it as a place in which an ethically self-governed man of the Republic of Letters engaged with a predominantly corrupt world of capricious rulers and malevolent counsellors, a view flamboyantly evident in Vives's description of the life of an erudite man in *De disciplinis*. This was a world in which the audience was largely understood as a corrupt object of reform or persuasion, which meant that rhetoric was not seen as natural participation in day-to-day politics with actors whose aspirations were recognised, but as engagement with sin and corruption. Thus, while Vives's rhetoric could be flexibly integrated into different theories, some of which had republican undertones, he himself did not envision its use from a republican mindset.[13]

If Vives's idea of rhetoric does not fit easily into republican models, his call for a rhetoric of *decorum* often suited to everyday *sermo* in place of passionate oratory did not, I would argue, deal with the rise of a new code of civility either. Ever since Norbert Elias's ground-breaking *The Civilizing Process*, Erasmian humanism, most notably Erasmus's *De civilitate morum puerilium*, has held a distinct, although much debated, place in the emergence of a culture of civility which, unlike medieval courtly and monastic codes of conduct, was designed for a large aristocratic and urban audience in a broader social setting or civil community. In this literature, the rise of civil conversation has been primarily described as a largely meaningful, polite discourse and it has been interpreted as part of a culture of manners that enhanced adaptation to situations, created ties of reciprocal recognition, and served in the delineation of social boundaries.[14]

While some Erasmian texts became classics in the teaching of manners, Vives's call for *decorum* was predominantly discursive in nature and rarely discussed in the context of a reform of civility and manners. Indeed, his plea for a rhetoric of *decorum* should be seen in the context of humanist understanding of active virtue rather than a move towards a world of politeness devoid of humanist meaning. Although one finds passages on polite manners in Vives's writings, there is no programme of civility, and his focus was much more centred on the interconnections between classical and late medieval models of self-control and piety with civic rhetoric than on manners as such. *Decorum* rather implied that oratorical duties, in historically specific circumstances, were inscribed within a range of practices that often, although not always, drew on *sermo*. While *sermo* created a reciprocal model when employed between a restricted group of humanists, in addressing others outside these circles, such as noblemen or rulers, *sermo* did not imply reciprocity and symmetry in any straightforward way. It was rather a strategic choice that enabled persuasion in an atmosphere of harmony, and highly instrumental language was used to describe those one spoke to. Moreover, Vives's relationship to a life of *negotium* was full of tensions. On the one hand, those places where he operated – such as courts – were systematically seen as corrupt and in need of reform. Because of this, their code of conduct, or that of urban elites, should not be interiorised. On the other hand, this reform was possible only if one adapted one's speech to those circumstances without departing from one's scholarly *gravitas*. Considering all this, Vives's rhetoric of *decorum* appears as a distinctively discursive concept; it deals with the persuasive possibilities of language but cannot be seen as a move to a culture of reciprocal pleasing of an emerging urban and aristocratic elite.

The model outlined here does not necessarily change Vives's place in the internal history of political thought if the concept refers to the traditional field of political theory. In political theory, the sixteenth and seventeenth centuries are described as a time in which new ideas of the reason of state and natural law were formulated. Reason of state, a concept that became popular in the 1580s and was amply discussed in works such as Giovanni Botero's (c.1544–1617) *Ragione di stato* (1589), referred to the obligation of rulers to override law in cases of necessity (what exactly these were was heatedly debated) in view of enhancing the good of the state through political prudence.[15] In the history of natural law, seventeenth-century formulations by Hugo Grotius (1583–1645), Thomas Hobbes (1588–1679), and Samuel Pufendorf (1632–1694) transformed the concept from a teleological ideal of living according to one's true nature to the description of minimal conditions within which different kinds of self-realisations, often based on mere self-preservation, were possible. Both tendencies were often put into the context of major developments in the early modern period: the rise of bureaucratic states and the continuous warfare resulting from religious division.[16] In light of this study, there is no reason to place Vives in the history of these traditions. As I have argued in Chapter 3, he considered the interest of the state or the ruling dynasty a threat to peace and concord and his understanding of natural law fell within thoroughly traditional formulations of Stoic-Christian natural law as life lived according to one's true nature. The critical potential of this discourse was activated in the context of the debates between Dutch towns and the central government on warfare and taxation, but it did not lead to new theoretical formulations on natural law or on the legal boundaries of good rule. Although Vives's emphasis on the contractual nature of power might draw on the conciliarist and constitutionalist tradition, strong at the University of Paris (e.g. John Mair and Jacques Almain), he conceived of politics in decidedly ethical terms and remained suspicious of all attempts to resolve political questions through legal discourse, whether constitutionalist theory or a system of casuistry designed to accommodate ever-more specific situations.

But the transformations of political theory in the late sixteenth and early seventeenth centuries have, in quite another key, also been closely tied together with the claim that in this period, emotions were theorised as the foundation of a political order in remarkably novel ways. Albert Hirschman famously argued that the early modern period signalled a move from the condemnation of several passions as vices to a positive revaluation of their constructive worth. In this way, private vices and destructive passions, rather than being condemned, could be harnessed to the interest of the state as incentives to action, provided that they were managed by playing them against each other in the correct measure.[17] The transformations in natural law, resulting in a more pronounced stress on self-preservation, as opposed to natural Aristotelian sociability, were also analysed as a normative re-evaluation of the emotions on which political life was based. In a similar spirit, much of the ground-breaking work on the relationship between emotions and politics has been centred on this transformative period.[18]

Since Vives relied on traditional discourses of ethical self-government and virtue in his political theory, his relationship to the re-evaluation of passions in politics is complicated. Still, I suggest that we can discern three ways in which he can be placed in a wider narrative in which, as Susan James has claimed, 'the interest in emotions' became part of 'a broader preoccupation in early-modern European culture with the relations between knowledge and control, whether of the self or others'.[19]

First, Vives's *De anima* implied a particularly naturalistic take on the philosophy of ethical self-government which, in comparison with the more spiritual bent of many of Erasmus's writings, claimed that knowledge of emotions was the foundation of moral philosophy. Indeed, it offered one of the most ambitious attempts to extend questions of ethics to detailed analysis of the soul and emotions in Northern humanist thought and, perhaps, in early sixteenth-century thought more generally.

Second, he claimed that rhetoric, rather than a schematic art, was dependent on mastery of emotions, as I have shown in Chapter 5. In doing so, he played a part in a development in which rhetoric was increasingly associated with the understanding of emotions in the later sixteenth and early seventeenth centuries. As Lawrence Green and Peter Mack have shown, the reincorporation of Aristotle's treatment of emotions into rhetorical theory took place in the course of the sixteenth and seventeenth centuries in radically different contexts, ranging from the Jesuits (e.g. Nicolas Caussin, 1583–1651) to Reformed writers (Bartholomäus Keckermann, c.1572–1608, Gerardus Vossius, 1577–1649).[20] One can speculate that in Vives there was an intimate connection between his theory of *decorum* and interest in the audience, on the one hand, and the foundational role of emotions in rhetoric, on the other. For when rhetorical invention was described primarily as a meticulous analysis of the emotional dispositions of the audience, as Vives did, then theory of emotions offered a justification for the necessity of *decorum* and essential knowledge for the invention of persuasive arguments in most rhetorical tasks. Interestingly, Vives did become an authority precisely on *decorum* and could be cited by writers as diverse as John Rainolds (1549–1607) and Nicolas Caussin (1583–1651), the Jesuit author of the gigantic *De eloquentia sacra et humana* (1619).[21]

Third, and most importantly, these developments in rhetoric and ethics can be integrated into a distinctive perspective on political thought when the concept is extended from traditional political theory to cover the cognitive and emotional basis of sociability and politics. As I have tried to show, politics is not just the context in which Vives's views on ethics and rhetorical *decorum* were developed, but these essentially provide an interpretation of the cognitive and emotional foundations of political harmony. The political meaning of what has been stated about rhetoric and emotions can, in my view, be interpreted in two ways.

The first of these two reflects a traditional political model in which successful political life was predicated on the ethical self-government of those in power. In this view, knowledge of emotions enabled their control which, in turn, was a prerequisite for virtuous action in the political realm. As part of rhetoric, emotions facilitated the creation of virtuous dispositions through language (e.g. epideictic rhetoric) and made possible their employment for virtuous action in specific debates through a rhetoric of *decorum*.

The second option poses more of a challenge to ethical politics since, in Vives, there were several elements that point towards developments that were to have echoes in later thought. By the 1530s, Vives, with ample experience of the character and actions of the powerful of the time, had understood that the limits of self-control, at least without divine intervention, were closely linked to natural and cultural factors. Not only were our cognitive and emotional possibilities in the post-lapsarian state stressed as limits of ethical self-government, but we were also continuously told in political, educational, social, and psychological works that the cultural environment in which meaning was constituted contributed decisively to processes of habituation and to our character. Within this system, one could, as Vives did in works such as *De disciplinis*, aspire to transform those cultural patterns within which we were formed since this was the only way in which the ethical self-control of individuals could be forged. His rhetoric of *decorum* could certainly be considered a factor here since it habituated one to a mode of discussion that did not break concord. But within this system, one could, as Vives also often did in his rhetorical works, explore the ways in which politics functioned when people attributed erroneous meanings to things and were motivated by wrong kind of judgments and passions. Here the ethical ideal was embodied in a humanist counsellor, tutor, teacher, or a member of the Republic of Letters who had to understand the less-than-perfect realities of politics in order to deal with them. Political concord, at least in the short term, was no longer thought of as the result of the ethical self-governance of those in power but as the result of the rhetorical activity of their counsellors who, through crafty handling of emotions, directed political actions. This system did not deal with long-term reform but was more interested in the immediate possibilities of rhetoric in particular situations.

This perspective was largely a built-in element of rhetorical works and as such divulged to further generations through works such as *De conscribendis epistolis*. Yet it is fair to say that it was not fully theorised; it remained full of ambiguities concerning the corrupting tendencies of *negotium*, and its exact relationship to the reform project is underdeveloped. Yet it is here that we find ideas about using bad passional dispositions, such as ambition, to good ends or playing certain emotions against each other, a view that was to become increasingly central for later political and rhetorical thought. This model pointed to the limits of ethical politics and to much more complicated ways of conceptualising it as a cognitive and emotional practice.

Notes

1. Moreno Gallego, 2006, 21–2, 783–95; González González, 2007, 10–3, 395–402.
2. Rebhorn stresses the internal coherence of Renaissance rhetoric but is aware of the differences between classical and Renaissance interpretations of rhetoric. See Rebhorn, 1995 8–14; Skinner, 1996, 40; Fumaroli, 1980; Fumaroli, 1999.
3. This point has been made by George and Rodríguez Peregrina; see George, 1992, 114; Rodríguez Peregrina, 2000, LIII, CVII.
4. Ashworth, 1974, 8–18; Jardine, 1988; Vasoli, 1968.
5. Mack, 1993; Nauta, 2009; Waswo, 1987; Spranzi, 2011
6. Kahn, 1985; Chomarat, 1981; Margolin, 1999.
7. Dealy, 2017, 3–4.

8. Needless to say, philosophical *sermo* is reserved to an exclusive group of scholars.
9. Seigel, 1966; Hankins, 1995, 325–30; Hankins, 2003–2004, 121–2.
10. Stacey, 2007, 196–204; Vickers, 1988, 54, 289–91.
11. For a strong formulation of this idea, see Grassi, 1980, 18.
12. Pocock, 1975, 59–63; Skinner, 1996, 9–10, 15–6.
13. See note 36, 42.
14. Elias, 1994, 43–5; Bryson, 1998, 276–83; Peltonen, 2003, 5, 18–9, 24–6; Thomas, 2018, 18–21. For an interpretation that stresses the political dimension of civic conversation in the courtly context, see Fumaroli, 1983, 258–9. For an interpretation that connects the disappearance of humanist virtue with the rise of commerce, see Pocock, 1983, 240–1; Peltonen, 2003, 305.
15. Burke, 1991, 479–81.
16. Tuck, 1979, 67–8, 76, 126–7, 157–9; Haakonssen, 1999, xiv–xvi; Hochstrasser, 2000, 2–4; Saastamoinen, 2004.
17. Hirschman, 1977, 9–31.
18. James, 1997; Kahn – Saccamano, 2006.
19. James, 1997, 2.
20. Green, 1994; Mack, 2011, 187–92, 195; 203–4.
21. Caussin, 1657, 145–6; Rainolds, 1986, 98.

Bibliography

Printed Primary Source

Ad Herennium, trans. H. Caplan (Cambridge, MA: Harvard University Press, 1954).
Agricola, Rudolph. *De formando studio* (Antwerpen: Merten de Keyser, 1532).
Agricola, Rudolph. *De inventione dialectica libri tres* (Tübingen: Niemeyer, 1992).
Agricola, Rudolph. *Letters*, eds. and trans. A. Van der Laan – F. Akkerman (Tempe: Arizona Center for Medieval and Renaissance Studies, 2002).
Agrippa, Cornelius. *De incertitudine et vanitate scientiarum et artium* (Paris: Pierre, 1531).
Amerbach, Vitus. *Quatuor libri de anima* (Strasbourg: Kraft Müller, 1542).
Aristotle. *The "Art" of Rhetoric*, trans. J. H. Freese (Cambridge, MA.: Harvard University Press, 1926).
Aristotle. *Ethica, cum commentariis* (Paris: Petit, 1530).
Aristotle. *Metaphysics, Books I–IX*, trans. H. Tredennick (Cambridge, MA.: Harvard University Press, 1933).
Aristotle. *Nicomachean Ethics*, trans. H. Rackham (Cambridge, MA: Harvard University Press, 1934).
Aristotle. *Rhetorica*, in Aristotle. *Opera quae quidem extant omnia*, 2 vols. (Basel: Oporinus, 1538), 241–303.
Aristotle. *On Interpretation*, in Aristotle. *On Categories: On Interpretation; Prior Analytics*, trans. H. P. Cooke – H. Tredennick (Cambridge, MA: Harvard University Press, 1938).
Aristotle. *On the Soul*, in Aristotle. *On the Soul: Parva naturalia; On Breath*, trans. W. S. Hett (Cambridge, MA: Harvard University Press, 1957), 2–203.
Aristotle. *Posterior Analytics*, in Aristotle. *Posterior Analytics: Topica*, trans. H. Treddenick (Cambridge, MA: Harvard University Press, 1960a), 2–261.
Aristotle. *Topica*, in Aristotle. *Posterior Analytics: Topica*, trans. H. Treddenick (Cambridge, MA: Harvard University Press, 1960b), 272–739.
Augustine. *De civitate Dei* (Basel: Johann Froben, 1522).
Augustine. Contra Faustum Manichaeum, in Augustine. *Opera omnia*, 8 vols. (Paris: Garnier, 1886).
Augustine. *De doctrina Christiana* (Turnhout: Brepols, 1962).
Avicenna. *Liber de anima seu sextus de naturalibus* (Louvain: Peeters, 1972).
Baarland, Adrian. *Compendiosae institutiones artis oratoriae*, in Vives. *De conscribendis epistolis* (Köln: Gymnich, 1537), 155–71.

Bade, Josse. 'Iodocus Badius Ascensius domino Adae Kempensi', introductory letter to Balbi, Johannes. *Catholicon seu universale vocabularium ac summa grammatices* (Paris: Josse Bade/Jean Petit, 1506).
Bade, Josse. 'Disquisitio Ascensiana', in Cicero. *Rhetoricorum ad Caium Herennium libri quattuor cum eruditissimis elucidationibus* (Paris: Bade & Petit, 1508a).
Bade, Josse. 'Iodocus Badius Ascensius Wolfardo Largouirgio', in Cicero. *Rhetoricorum ad Caium Herennium libri quattuor cum eruditissimis elucidationibus* (Paris: Bade & Petit, 1508b).
Bade, Josse. 'Epistola nuncupatoria', in Valla, Lorenzo. *Dialectice* (Paris: Bade, 1509).
Bade, Josse. *Introductio in Grammaticen* (Paris: Bade & Petit, 1510a).
Bade, Josse. 'Iodoci Badii Ascensii in oratoriam institutionem Isagogica collectanea', in Cicero. *Ad Caium Herennium Rhetorici seu de institutione oratoria libri IIII* (Paris: Bade, 1510b).
Bakker, Paul J. J. M. 'The Statutes of the Collège de Montaigu: Prelude to a Future Edition', *History of Universities* XXII:2 (2007), 76–111.
Basil. 'Address to Young Men on the Right Use of Greek Literature', in Padelford, F. M. (ed.). *Essays on the Study and Use of Poetry by Plutarch and Basil the Great* (New York: H. Holt and Company, 1902), 99–120.
Bérauld, Nicolas. *Praelectio et commentaire à la Silve Rusticus d'Ange Politien (1518)*, eds. G. A. Bergère – A. Bouscharain – P. Galand-Hallyn – O. Pedeflous (Genève: Droz, 2015).
Beroaldo, Filippo. *Opusculum eruditum quo continetur Declamatio philosophi medici et oratoris de excellentia disceptantium* (Paris: Jean Barbier/Denis Roce, 1514).
Bonilla y San Martín, Adolfo. *Clarorum Hispanensium epistolae ineditae*, in *Revue hispanique* (1901), 181–308.
Budé, Guillaume. *Annotationes in quatuor et viginti pandectarum libros* (Paris: Bade, 1508).
Budé, Guillaume. *De transitu Hellenismi ad christianismum, libri tres* (Paris: Estienne, 1535).
Budé, Guillaume. *Le livre de l'institution du prince* (Paris: Foucher, 1547).
Caesarius, Johannes. *Rhetorica in septem libros sive tractatus digesta* (Köln: Johann von Aich, 1535).
Cantiuncula, Claudius. *Topica* (Basel: Andreas Cratander, 1520).
Castiglione, Baldassare. *Il libro del cortegiano, nuovamente con diligenza revisto per Lodovico Dolce* (Venezia: Girolamo Scoto, 1556).
Caussin, Nicolas. *De eloquentia sacra et humana* (Lyon: Candy, 1657).
Celtis, Konrad. *Epitome in rhetoricam Ciceronis, & non inutile scribendarum epistolarum compendium* (Ingolstad: Apian, 1532).
Celtis, Konrad. *Methodus* in Vives. *De conscribendis epistolis* (Köln: Gymnich, 1537), 104–18.
Cicero. *Opera rhetorica, oratoria et forensia, premisso indice et Ad Caium Herennium rhetoricorum libri IIII. De inventione que et vetus rhetorica libri II. Topicorum ad Brutum* (Paris: Bade, 1511).
Cicero. *De officiis*, trans. W. Miller (Cambridge, MA: Harvard University Press, 1913).
Cicero. *Academica*, trans. H. Rackham, in Cicero. *De natura deorum – Academica* (Cambridge, MA: Harvard University Press, 1933), 406–659.

224 Bibliography

Cicero. *Brutus*, trans. H. M. Hubbell, in Cicero. *Brutus – Orator* (Cambridge, MA: Harvard University Press, 1939a), 1–296.
Cicero. *Orator*, trans. H. M. Hubbell, in Cicero. *Brutus – Orator* (Cambridge, MA: Harvard University Press, 1939b), 306–509.
Cicero. *De oratore I–III*, 2 vols., trans. E. W. Sutton – H. Rackham (Cambridge, MA: Harvard University Press, 1942).
Cicero. *De inventione*, trans. H. M. Hubbell, in Cicero. *De inventione, De optimo genere oratorum, Topica* (Cambridge, MA: Harvard University Press, 1960a), 1–346.
Cicero. *De topica*, trans. H. M. Hubbell, in Cicero. *De inventione, De optimo genere oratorum, Topica* (Cambridge, MA: Harvard University Press, 1960b), 382–459.
Cicero. *Tusculanae disputationes, trans.* J. E. King (Cambridge, MA: Harvard University Press, 1960c).
Cicero. *De amicitia*, trans. W. A. Falconer, in Cicero. *De senectute, De amicitia, De divinatione* (Cambridge, MA: Harvard University Press, 1971), 108–211.
Cicero. *Philippics: 1–6*, trans. and ed. S. Bailey (Cambridge, MA: Harvard University Press, 2009).
Clichtove, Josse. 'Judocus Clichtoueus Aeportuensis Theobaldo parvo insigni doctori Theologo salute', in Badius et al. *In epistolarum compositionem compendium isagogicum brevitate et facilitate praeditum* (Paris: 1501).
Clichtove, Josse. *De laude monasticae religionis opusculum* (Paris: Estienne, 1513).
De Vocht, Henry (ed.). *Literae virorum eruditorum ad Franciscum Craneveldium, 1522–1528* (Louvain: Louvain Librairie Universitaire, 1928).
Elyot, Thomas. *The Boke Named the Governor* (London: Thomas Berthelet, 1531).
Erasmus, Desiderius. *Epistolae aliquot illustrium virorum ad Erasmum Roterodamum et huius ad illos* (Louvain: Thierry Martens, 1516).
Erasmus, Desiderius. *Farrago nova epistolarum Des. Erasmi Roterodami ad alios, & aliorum ad hunc* (Basel: Froben, 1519).
Erasmus, Desiderius. *Ciceronianus*, in Erasmus. *Familiarium colloquiorum opus, multis nominibus utilissimum, nuper ab autore correctum, cum accessione colloquiorum aliquot, quae nunc primum nova prodeunt. Item Ciceronianus eiusdem, per eundem emendatus & auctus, cum nonnullis aliis* (Basel: Froben, 1529).
Erasmus, Desiderius. *Apologia. Ad Jacobum Latomum de linguis*, in Erasmus, Desiderius. *Opera omnia*, 10 vols., ed. Jean Leclerc (Leiden: Vander, 1703–1706, hereafter LB), IX:79–106.
Erasmus, Desiderius. *Enchiridion*, in LB V:2–66.
Erasmus, Desiderius. *De libero arbitrio*, in LB IX:1215–1248.
Erasmus, Desiderius. *Paraclesis*. in LB V:137–44.
Erasmus, Desiderius. *Paraphrasis in Acta Apostolorum*, in LB VII:659–770.
Erasmus, Desiderius. *Opus epistolarum Des. Erasmi Roterodami: denuo recognitum et auctum*, 12 vols., eds. Percy Stafford Allen – Helen Mary Allen – Heathcote William Garrod (Oxford: Clarendon, 1906–1958).
Erasmus, Desiderius. *Adagia*, in Erasmus. *Opera omnia Desiderii Erasmi Roterodami* (Amsterdam: Elsevier, 1969– hereafter ASD), II/1-9.
Erasmus, Desiderius. *Ciceronianus*, in ASD, I/2:599–710.
Erasmus, Desiderius. *Colloquia, in ASD I/3*.
Erasmus, Desiderius. *De bello Turcico*, in ASD V/3:31–82.
Erasmus, Desiderius. *De civilitate morum puerorum*, in ASD I/8:315–41.
Erasmus, Desiderius, *De conscribendis epistolis*, in ASD I/2:205–579.

Erasmus, Desiderius. *De copia*, in ASD I/6.
Erasmus, Desiderius. *De pueris statim ac liberaliter instituendis*, in ASD I/2:21–78.
Erasmus, Desiderius. *De ratione studii*, in ASD I/2:111–51.
Erasmus, Desiderius. *Ecclesiastes*, in *ASD V/4*.
Erasmus, Desiderius. *Institutio principis Christiani*, in ASD, IV/1:133–219.
Erasmus, Desiderius. *Lingua*, in ASD IV/1:233–370.
Erasmus, Desiderius. *Moriae encomium*, in ASD IV/3:67–195.
Erasmus, Desiderius. *Querela pacis*, in ASD IV/2:61–100.
Erasmus, Desiderius. *Sileni Alcibiadis*, in ASD II/5:159–90.
Erasmus, Desiderius. *Formula conficiendarum epistolarum*, in *Collected Works of Erasmus*, 72 vols. (Toronto: University of Toronto Press, 1974–. Hereafter CWE), 25:258–67.
Gattinara, Mercurino di. *Autobiografia* (Rome: Bulzoni, 1991).
Gellius, Aulus. *Attic Nights*, 3 vols., trans. J. C. Rolfe (Cambridge, MA: Harvard University Press, 1927).
Gerson, Jean. *Oeuvres complètes*, ed. P. Glorieux (Paris: Desclee, 1960–1973).
Guarino, Battista. *De modo et ordine docendi ac discendi* (Strasbourg: Mathias Schürer, 1514).
Guarino, Battista. 'A Program of Teaching and Learning', in Kallendorf, Craig (ed.). *Humanist Educational Treatises* (Cambridge, MA: Harvard University Press, 2002), 261–309.
Hegendorf, Christoph. *De instituenda vita, et moribus corrigendis juventutis, paraeneses* (Haguenau: Setzer, 1529).
Hermogenes. *On Types of Style*, trans. C. W. Wooten (Chapel Hill: University of North Carolina Press, 1987).
Homer. Odyssey, vol. 1, trans. A. T. Murray (Cambridge, MA: Harvard University Press, 1919).
Horace. *Ars poetica*, in Horace. *Satires. Epistles. The Art of Poetry*, trans. H. R. Fairclough (Cambridge, MA: Harvard University Press, 1926), 442–90.
Hutten, Ulrich von. *Cum Erasmo Roterodamo, presbytero, theologo, expostulatio* (Strasbourg: Schott, 1523).
IJsewijn, Jozef et al. (eds.). Litterae ad Craneveldium Balduinianae, *Humanistica Lovaniensia* 4 vols (1992–1995), XLI–XLIV.
Isocrates. *Epistola ad Demonicum*, in Isocrates. *Praecepta Isocratis per eruditissimum virum Rudolphum Agricolam Graeco sermone in Latinum traducta* (Wittenberg: Johann Rhau-Grunenberg, 1508).
Latomus, Jacobus. *De trium linguarum et studii theologici ratione dialogus* (Antwerpen: Michael Hillen, 1519.
Lefèvre d'Étaples, Jacques, 'Jacbous Stapulensis reverendo patri Johanni Rellico', introductory letter to Aristotle. *Liber ethicorum Aristotelis*, ed. Jacques Lefèvre (Paris: Jean Granjon, 1504), Aii.
Lefèvre d'Étaples, Jacques, 'Iacbous Faber, Fortunato suo', in Trapezuntius (ed.). *Dialectica* (Strasbourg, Schürer, 1509), Aiir–Aiiiv.
Luther, Martin. *De servo arbitrio*, in *Luthers Werke*, vol. 18 (Weimar: Hermann Böhlaus Nachfolger, 1908), 600–787.
Luther, Martin. *Temporal Authority: To What Extent Is Should Be Obeyed*, in *Luther's Works*, vol. 45, ed. W. I. Brandt (Philadelphia: Fortress Press, 1966).
Luther, Martin. *To the Christian Nobility of the German Nation Concerning the Reform of the Christian Estate*, in *Luther's Works*, vol. 44, ed. J. Atkinson (Philadelphia: Fortress Press, 1980).

Macrobius, *Opera*, vol. 2, *Commentarii in Somnium Scipionis*, ed. J. Willis (Stuttgart/ Leibniz: Teubner, 1994).
Macrobius, *Saturnalia*, vol. 1, trans. Robert A. Kaster (Cambridge, MA: Harvard University Press, 2011).
Mair, John. Johannes Maior Alexandro Stevvard, dedicatory letter to Mair, John. *Quartus Sententiarum* (Paris: Poncet Le Preux, 1509), ii[r].
Mair, John. *In quartum Sententiarum questiones utilissimae suprema ipsius lucubratione enucleatae cum duplici tabella videlicet alphabetica materiarum decisarum in fronte et quaestionum in calce* (Paris: Josse Bade, 1516).
Melanchthon, Philipp. *Necessarias esse ad omne studiorum genus artes dicendi, declamatio* (Köln: Cervicornus, 1523).
Melanchthon, Philipp. *Commentarius de anima* (Wittenberg: Seitz, 1550).
Melanchthon, Philipp. *Elementorum Rhetorices libri duo*, in Melanchthon. *Opera omnia: Opera philosophica. Part 2, Principal Writings on Rhetoric*, eds. W. P. Weaver – S. Strohm – W Volkhardt (Berlin: De Gruyter, 2017a), 269–408.
Melanchthon, Philipp. *De rhetorica libri tres*, in Melanchthon. *Opera omnia: Opera philosophica. Part 2, Principal Writings on Rhetoric*, eds. W. P. Weaver – S. Strohm – W Volkhardt (Berlin: De Gruyter, 2017b), 33–176.
More, Thomas. *Utopia*, eds. E. Surtz – J. H. Hexter (New Haven: Yale University Press, 1965).
More, Thomas. *Thomas Morus Martino Dorpio*, in More. *Complete Works of St Thomas More*, vol. 15, ed. D. Kinney (New Haven: Yale University Press, 1986).
More, Thomas. *Utopia*, eds. G. M. Logan – R. M. Adams (Cambridge: Cambridge University Press, 2002).
Mosellanus, Petrus. *Oratio de variarum linguarum cognitione paranda* (Basel: Johann Froben, 1519).
Murmellius, Johannes. *Libri duo, literarum studiosis utilissimi; alter de artibus tum liberalibus tum mechanicis, alter continet Paraenesin ad ingenuarum artium studia* (Deventer: De Borne, 1515).
Nani Mirabelli, Domenico. '*Epistola Nuncupatoria*', in Nani Mirabelli. *Polyanthea* (Paris: Josse Bade - Petit, 1512).
Nebrija, Antonio de. *Artis rhetoricae compendiosa coaptatio, ex Aristotele, Cicerone et Quintiliano* (Alcalá de Henares: Eguía, 1529).
Pace, Richard. *De fructu qui ex doctrina percipitur* (Basel: Johann Froben, 1517).
Pico della Mirandola, Giovanni. '*Ioannes Picus Baptistae Mantuano*', in Spagnuoli, Battista (Mantuanus). *Prima pars operum: in qua sunt Alphonsus. Triumphus. Panegyris Roberti Sanseverinatis et sylvae* (Paris: Bade, 1507).
Pico della Mirandola, Giovanni. '*Iohannes Picus Mirandulanus Hermolao Barbaro suo*', in Della Mirandola, Pico. *Auree epistole* (Antwerpen: Thierry Martens, 1509), B[i][r]-Cii[r].
Plato. *Alcibiades I*, in Plato. *Charmides – Alcibiades I and II – Hipparchus – The Lovers – Theages – Minos – Epinomis*, ed. and trans. W. R. M. Lamb (Cambridge, MA: Harvard University Press, 1964), 93–224.
Plato. *The Republic*, 2 vols., ed. and trans. C. Emlyn-Jones – W. Preddy (Cambridge, MA: Harvard University Press, 2013).
Plutarch. *Quo pacto dignosci possit advlator ab amico*, in Erasmus. *Institutio principis Christiani* (Basel: Froben, 1516), fols. P[3]–Y[r].
Plutarch (Pseudo-Plutarch). '*De liberis educandis*', in Plutarch. *Moralia*, vol. 1, ed. and trans. F. C. Babbitt (Cambridge, MA: Harvard University Press, 1966), 2–71.

Bibliography 227

Quintilian. *Institutio oratoria*, 5 vols., trans. D. A. Russell (Cambridge, MA: Harvard University Press, 2001).

Rainolds, John. *John Rainolds's Oxford Lectures on Aristotle's Rhetoric*, ed. and trans. Lawrence Green (Newark: University of Delaware Press, 1986).

Regius, Raphael. '*Annotationes*', in Quintilian. *Oratoriarum institutionum libri XII* (Paris: Bade & Petit, 1515).

Reisch, Gregor. *Margarita philosophica* (Freiburg im Breisgau: Johann Schott, 1503).

Rhenanus, Beatus. '*Beatus Rhenanus Ioanni Kierhero*', in Trapezuntius. *Dialectica* (Strasbourg, Schürer, 1509), Aii^v.

Rhenanus, Beatus. '*Beatus Rhenanus Lucae Paliuro tubeaquensi*', in Guarini, Battista, *De modo et ordine docendi ac discendi* (Strasbourg: Mathias Schürer, 1514).

Ringelberg, Joachim Sterck van. *Lucubrationes, vel potius absolutissima kyklopaideia: nempe liber de ratione studii, utriusque linguae grammatice, dialectice, rhetorice mathematice, & sublimioris philosophiae multa* (Basel: Westheimer, 1538).

Rivius, Johannes. *De dialectica libri VI. De rhetorica libri II. De periodis, libellus I* (Leipzig: Nicolaus Wolrab, 1539).

Salisbury, John of. *Policraticus. Frivolities of Courtiers and Footprints of Philosophers*, ed. and trans. J. B. Pike (Minneapolis: University of Minnesota, 1938).

Seneca. *Epistles*, vol. 2, trans. Richard M. Gummere (Cambridge, MA: Harvard University Press, 1920).

Seneca. De otio, trans. J. W. Basore, in Seneca. *Moral Essays*, vol. 2 (Cambridge, MA: Harvard University Press, 1965), 180–201.

Sturm, Johannes. *De amissa dicendi ratione, ad Franciscum Frossium jurisconsultum libri duo* (Strasbourg: Wendelin Rihel, 1538a).

Sturm, Johannes. *De literarum ludis recte aperiendis liber* (Strasbourg: Wendelin Rihel, 1538b).

Sturm, Johannes. 'The Advice of Johann Sturm on What Organization to Give to the Gymnasium of Strasbourg', in Spitz, L. – B. Tinsley (eds.). *Johannes Sturm on Education* (St Louis: Concordia Pub House, 1995a), 61–7.

Sturm, Johannes. 'On the lost art of speaking', in Spitz, L. – B. Tinsley (eds.). *Johannes Sturm on Education* (St Louis: Concordia Pub House, 1995b), 121–32.

Sturm, Johannes, 'The Correct Opening of Elementary Schools of Letters', in Spitz, L. – B. Tinsley (eds.). *Johannes Sturm on Education* (St Louis: Concordia Pub House, 1995c), 71–118.

Sulpitius Victor. *Institutiones oratoriae in Veterum aliquot de arte rhetorica* (Basel: Froben, 1521), 83–154.

Tacitus. *Dialogus de oratoribus*, in Tacitus. *Agricola, Germania, Dialogue on Oratory* (Cambridge, MA: Harvard University Press, 1913), 229–347.

Thomas Aquinas. *Summa theologiae*, 3 vols., ed. P. Caramello (Torino: Marietti, 1962).

Tournoy, Gilbert – Monique Mund-Dopchie (eds.). *La correspondence de Guillaume Budé et Juan Luis Vives* (Leuven: Leuven University Press, 2015).

Trebizond, George of. *Dialectica* (Strasbourg: Matthias Schürer, 1509).

Trebizond, George of. *Rhetoricorum libri, in quibus quid recens praestitum, proxima facie indicabit liminaris epistola* (Basel: Valentin Curio, 1522).

Trithemius, Johann. *De scriptoribus ecclesiasticis* (Paris: Berthold Rembolt, 1512).

Tunstall, Cuthbert. *Cutheberti tonstalli, in laudem matrimonii oratio, habita in sponsalibus Mariae potentissimi regis Angliae Henrici octavi filiae, et Francisci Christianissimi Francorum regis primogeniti* (Basel: Froben, 1519).

228 *Bibliography*

Valdés, Alfonso de. *Diálogo de las cosas ocurridas en Roma* (Madrid: Espasa-Calpe, 1956).
Valla, Giorgio. *De expedita argumentandi ratione libellus* (Basel: Froben, 1519).
Valla, Lorenzo. *Laurentii Valle repastinatio dialectice et philosophie*, ed. Gianni Zippel (Padua: Antenore, 1982).
Vergerio, Pier Paolo. 'De ingenuis moribus et liberalibus adulescentiae studiis liber', in Kallendorf, Craig (ed.). *Humanist Educational Treatises* (Cambridge, MA: Harvard University Press, 2002), 3–91.
Verulanus, Sulpitius. *De epistolarum compositione opusculum* in Bade, Josse. *In epistolarum compositionem compendium isagogicum brevitate et facilitate praeditum* (Paris: Bade, 1501), Avii^v-Bvii^v.
Vinsauf, Geoffrey of. *Poetria nova*, trans. M. F. Nims (Toronto: Pontifical Institute of Mediaeval Studies, 2010).
Virgil. *Aeneid*, 2 vols., ed. and trans. F. H. Rushton (Cambridge, MA: Harvard University Press, 1999–2000).
Vitruvius, *De architectura*, 2 vols., trans. F. Granger (Cambridge, MA: Harvard University Press, 1931–1934).
Vives, Juan Luis. *Obras completas*, ed. L. Riber, 2 vols. (Madrid: Aguilar, 1947–1948).
Vives, Juan Luis. *Somnium. Est praefatio ad Somnium Scipionis Ciceronis Eiusdem Vigilia. Quae est enarratio Somnii Scipionis Ciceronis* (Basel: Froben, 1521).
Vives, Juan Luis. *Commentarii ad divi Aurelii Augustini De civitate Dei*, in Augustine. *De civitate Dei* (Basel: Johann Froben, 1522).
Vives, Juan Luis. *Ad Adrianum De tumultibus Europae*, in Vives, Juan Luis. *De Europae dissidiis, & Republica* (Brügge: Hubertus de Croock, 1526a), IIv–Xr.
Vives, Juan Luis. *Ad Henricum Angliae Regem De Rege Galliae capto*, in Vives, Juan Luis. *De Europae dissidiis, & Republica* (Brügge: Hubertus de Croock, 1526b), XIv–XIIIv.
Vives, Juan Luis. *Ad Henricum De regni administratione, bello, & pace*, in Vives, Juan Luis. *De Europae dissidiis, & Republica* (Brügge: Hubertus de Croock, 1526c), XIIIr–XXIIIv.
Vives, Juan Luis. *De Europae dissidiis et bello Turcico*, in Vives, Juan Luis. *De Europae dissidiis, & Republica* (Brügge: Hubertus de Croock, 1526d), XXIIIr–XLIIIIr.
Vives, Juan Luis. *Vives Thomae Cardinali*, in Vives, Juan Luis. *De Europae dissidiis, & Republica* (Brügge: Hubertus de Croock, 1526e), XLVv–XLVIIr.
Vives, Juan Luis. *Vives Ioanni Episcopo Lincolniensi*, in Vives, Juan Luis. *De Europae dissidiis, & Republica* (Brügge: Hubertus de Croock, 1526f), LXXr–LXXIIIv.
Vives, Juan Luis. *Introductio ad Sapientiam*, in Vives, Juan Luis. *Introductio ad Sapientiam satellitium sive symbola, epistolae duae de ratione studii puerilis* (Paris: Simon de Colines, 1527a), 2–31.
Vives, Juan Luis. *Satellitium sive Symbola*, in Vives, Juan Luis. *Introductio ad Sapientiam satellitium sive symbola, epistolae duae de ratione studii puerilis* (Paris: Simon de Colines, 1527b), 32–48.
Vives, Juan Luis. *De ratione studii puerilis* in Vives, Juan Luis. *Introductio ad Sapientiam satellitium sive symbola, epistolae duae de ratione studii puerilis* (Paris: Simon de Colines, 1527c), 49–64.
Vives, Juan Luis. *De disciplinis libri XX* (Köln: Gymnich, 1532).
Vives, Juan Luis. *De consultatione liber I*, in Vives, Juan Luis. *Rhetoricae, sive de recte dicendi ratione libri tres, Eiusdem de consultatione liber I* (Basel: Thomas I Platter & Balthasar Lasius, 1536), 233–72.

Vives, Juan Luis. *De Aristotelis operibus censura*, in Aristotle. *Aristotelis Stragiritae, philosophorum omnium facile principis opera* (Basel: Oporinus, 1538), [a3]r–[a7]v.

Vives, Juan Luis. *Familiarium colloquiorum formulae, sive linguae Latinae exercitatio* (Antwerpen: Guilielmus Montanus, 1539).

Vives, Juan Luis. *Sapiens*, in Vives, Juan Luis. *Opera omnia*, vol. 1 (Basel: Episcopus, 1555), 296–300.

Vives, Juan Luis. *De anima et vita*, ed. M. Sancipriano (Torino: Bottega d'Erasmo, 1959).

Vives, Juan Luis. *Epistolario*, ed. and trans. J. J. Delgado (Madrid: Editora nacional, 1978).

Vives, Juan Luis. *In pseudodialecticos*, ed. C. Fantazzi (Leiden: Brill, 1979).

Vives, Juan Luis. *Praefatio in Leges Ciceronis*, in Vives. *Ioannis Lodovici Vivis Valentini praefatio in leges Ciceronis et aedes legum*, ed. C. Matheeussen (Leipzig: Teubner, 1984a), 2–15.

Vives, Juan Luis. *Aedes legum*, in Vives. *Ioannis Lodovici Vivis Valentini praefatio in leges Ciceronis et aedes legum*, ed. C. Matheeussen (Leipzig: Teubner, 1984b), 16–30.

Vives Juan Luis. *De initiis, sectis et laudibus philosophiae*, in Vives. *Early Writings*, eds. C. Matheeussen – C. Fantazzi – E. George (Leiden: Brill, 1987), 1–57.

Vives, Juan Luis. *De conscribendis epistolis*, ed. C. Fantazzi (Leiden: Brill, 1989a).

Vives, Juan Luis. *Declamationes Sullanae, Part One*, ed. E. George (Leiden/Boston: Boston, 1989b).

Vives, Juan Luis. *De communione rerum*, in Vives, Juan Luis. *Opera omnia*, 8 vols., ed. Gregorio Mayans y Siscar (Valencia: Monfort, 1782–1790, hereafter Mayans), 5:464–82.

Vives, Juan Luis. *De concordia et discordia in humano genere*, in Mayans 5:187–403.

Vives, Juan Luis. *De conditione vitae sub Turca*, in Mayans 5:447–60.

Vives, Juan Luis. *De pacificatione*, in Mayans 5:404–46.

Vives, Juan Luis. *De subventione pauperum*, in Mayans 4:420–94.

Vives, Juan Luis. *Veritas fucata sive de licentia poetica, quantum poëtis liceat a veritate abscedere*, in Mayans 2:517–31.

Vives, Juan Luis. *Praelectio in Convivia Francisci Philelphi*, in Vives, Juan Luis. *Early Writings*, vol. 2, eds. J. IJsewijn – A. Fritsen – C. Fantazzi (Leiden: Brill, 1991a), 144–51.

Vives, Juan Luis. *Praelectio in quartum Rhetoricorum ad Herennium*, in Vives, Juan Luis. *Early Writings*, vol. 2, eds. J. IJsewijn – A. Fritsen – C. Fantazzi (Leiden: Brill, 1991b), 126–37.

Vives, Juan Luis. 'Vita Ioannis Dullardi per Ioannem Lodovicum Vivem Valentinum', in Vives, Juan Luis. *Early Writings*, vol. 2, eds. J. IJsewijn – A. Fritsen – C. Fantazzi (Leiden: Brill, 1991c), 14–5.

Vives, Juan Luis. *Clipei Christi descriptio*, in Vives, Juan Luis. IJsewijn, J. – A. Fritsen – C. Fantazzi (eds.). *Early Writings*, vol. 2 (Leiden: Brill, 1991d), 109–25.

Vives, Juan Luis. *Del arte de hablar*, ed. J. M. Rodríguez Peregrina (Granada: Universidad de Granada, 2000).

Vives, Juan Luis. *De disciplinis: Savoir et enseigner*, trans. and ed. T. Vigliano (Paris: Les belles lettres, 2013).

Vives, Juan Luis. *De ratione dicendi*, trans. and ed. David J. Walker (Leiden: Brill, 2017).

Secondary Literature

Abbott, Don. 'La retórica y el Renacimiento: an overview of Spanish Theory', in Murphy J. J. (ed.). *Renaissance Eloquence Studies in the Theory and Practice of Renaissance Rhetoric* (Berkeley: California University Press, 1983), 95–104.

Abbott, Don. 'Juan Luis Vives. Tradition and Innovation in Renaissance Rhetoric', *Central States Speech Journal* 37: 4 (1986), 193–203.

Abellán, José Luis. *Historia crítica del pensamiento español. Vol. II. La edad de oro* (Madrid: Espasa-Calpe, 1986).

Abellán, José Luis. *Erasmismo español* (Madrid: Espasa-Calpe, 2005).

Adams, Robert P. *The Better Part of Valor. More, Erasmus, Colet, and Vives on Humanism, War and Peace, 1496–1535* (Seattle: University of Washington Press, 1962).

Ashworth E. J. *Language and Logic in the Post-Medieval Period* (Dordrecht: Reidel, 1974).

Ashworth E. J. 'Changes in Logic Textbooks from 1500 to 1650: The New Aristotelianism', in Kessler, E – C. H. Lohr – W. Sparn (eds.). *Aristotelismus und Renaissance: in memoriam Charles B. Schmitt* (Wiesbaden: Harrassowitz, 1988), 75–87.

Baker, Patrick. *Italian Renaissance Humanism in the Mirror* (Cambridge: Cambridge University Press, 2015).

Baker-Smith, Dominic. 'Civitas Philosophica: Ideas and Community in Thomas More', in Cousins, A. D. – D. Grace (eds.). *A Companion to Thomas More* (Madison: Fairleigh Dickinson University Press, 2009), 165–77.

Baron, Hans. *The Crisis of the Early Italian Renaissance: Civic Humanism and Republican Liberty in an Age of Classicism and Tyranny* (Princeton: Princeton University Press, 1955).

Bataillon, Marcel. *Érasme et l'Espagne*, vol. 1 (Genève: Droz, 1991a).

Bataillon, Marcel. '*Humanisme chrétien et littérature, Vivès moqué pare Resende*', in Bataillon. *Érasme et l'Espagne*, vol. 3 (Genève: Droz, 1991b).

Baumann, Uwe. 'The Humanistic and Religious Controversies and Rivalries of Thomas More (1477/8-1535: A Typology of Literary Forms and Genres?', in Lines, D. A. – M. Laureys – J. Kraye (eds.). *Forms of Conflict and Rivalries in Renaissance Europe* (Göttingen: V & R unipress, 2015).

Baumlin, James. 'Ciceronian Decorum and the Temporalities of Renaissance Rhetoric', in Sipiora, P – J. S. Baumlin (eds.). *Rhetoric and Kairos: Essays in History, Theory, and Praxis* (Albany: State University of New York Press, 2002), 138–64.

Baylor, Michael. 'Political Thought in the Age of the Reformation', in Klosko, George (ed.). *The Oxford Handbook of the History of Political Philosophy* (Oxford: Oxford University Press, 2011), 227–45.

Bedouelle, Guy. *Lefèvre d'Étaples et l'intelligence des Ecritures* (Genève: Droz, 1976).

Bejczy, István. 'Historia prestat omnibus disciplinis. Juan Luis Vives on History and Historical Study', *Renaissance Studies* 17 (2003), 69–83.

Berger, Harry, Jr. *The Absence of Grace* (Stanford: Stanford University Press, 2000).

Bevir, Mark. *The Logic of the History of Ideas* (Cambridge: Cambridge University Press, 1999).

Bianchi, Luc. 'Renaissance Readings of the Nicomachean Ethics', in Lines, D. A – S. Ebbersmeyer (eds.). *Rethinking Virtue, Reforming Society, New Directions in Renaissance Ethics, c. 1350–c.1650* (Turnhout: Brepols, 2013), 131–67.

Bietenholz, Peter G. 'Ethics and Early Printing: Erasmus' Rule for the Proper Conduct of Authors', *Humanities Association Review* 26 (1975), 180–95.

Bietenholz, Peter G. (ed.). *Contemporaries of Erasmus, a Biographical Register of the Renaissance and Reformation*, vols. 1–3 (Toronto: University of Toronto Press, 1985–1987).

Bietenholz, Peter G. *Encounters with Radical Erasmus: Erasmus' Work as a Source of Radical Thought in Early Modern Europe* (Toronto: University of Toronto Press, 2009).

Black, Deborah. 'Imagination and Estimation: Arabic Paradigms and Western Transformations', *Topoi* 19 (2000), 59–75.

Black, Robert. *Humanism and Education in Medieval and Renaissance Italy: Tradition and Innovation in Latin Schools from the Twelfth to the Fifteenth Century* (Cambridge: Cambridge University Press, 2001).

Blair, Ann. *Too Much to Know: Managing Scholarly Information before the Modern Age* (New Haven/London: Yale University Press, 2010).

Blockmans, Wim. 'Charles's Ideals, Pragmatism and Strategy: An Impossible Mission', in Martínez Millán, J. – I. J. Ezquerra Revilla (eds.). *Carlos V y la quiebra del humanismo politico en Europa (1530-1558)*, vol. 1 (Madrid: Sociedad Estatal para la Conmemoración de los Centenarios de Felipe II y Carlos V, 2001), 179–90.

Blockmans, Wim. *Emperor Charles V* (Oxford: Oxford University Press, 2002).

Bonilla y San Martín, Adolfo. *Luis Vives y la filosofía del Renacimiento*, 3 vols. (Madrid: Rubio, 1929).

Bradshaw, Brendan. 'More on Utopia', *Historical Journal* 24:1 (1981), 1–27.

Bradshaw, Brendan. 'Transalpine Humanism', in Burns, J. H. – M. Goldie (eds.). *The Cambridge History of Political Thought 1450–1700* (Cambridge: Cambridge University Press, 1991), 95–131.

Brandes, Paul Dickerson. *A History of Aristotle's Rhetoric, with a Bibliography of Early Printings* (Metuchen: Scarecrow Press, 1989).

Brandi, Karl: *Kaiser Karl V* (München: Verlag F. Bruckmann, 1959).

Bryson, Anna. *From Courtesy to Civility: Changing Codes of Conduct in Early Modern England* (Oxford: Clarendon, 1998).

Burke, Peter. 'Tacitism, Scepticism, and Reason of State', in Burns, J. H. – M. Goldie (eds.). *The Cambridge History of Political Thought 1450–1700* (Cambridge: Cambridge University Press, 1991), 477–98.

Butler, Leslie. 'From the History of Ideas to Ideas in History', *Modern Intellectual History*, 9:1 (2012), 157–69.

Calero, Francisco. 'Estudio Introductorio', in Vives, Juan Luis. *Obras políticas y pacifistas* (Madrid: Ediciones Atlas, Madrid 1999), 11–59.

Cappelli, Guido. 'Machiavelli e l'umanesimo politico del Quattrocento', *Res Publica*, 20:1 (2017), 81–92.

Carlsmith, Christopher. *A Renaissance Education: Schooling in Bergamo and the Venetian Republic, 1500–1650* (Toronto: University of Toronto Press, 2010).

Carruthers, Mary. *The Book of Memory: A Study of Memory in Medieval Culture* (Cambridge: Cambridge University Press, 1990).

Casini, Lorenzo. *Cognitive and Moral Psychology in Renaissance Philosophy: A Study of Juan Luis Vives' De anima et vita* (Uppsala: Universitetstryckeriet, 2006a).
Casini, Lorenzo. 'Juan Luis Vives' Conception of Freedom of the Will and Its Scholastic Background', *Vivarium* 44 (2006b), 396–417.
Casini, Lorenzo. 'Self-Knowledge, Scepticism and the Quest for a New Method: Juan Luis Vives on Cognition and the Impossibility of Perfect Knowledge', in Maia Nieto, J. R. – G. Paganini (eds.). *Renaissance Scepticisms* (Dordrecht: Springer, 2009), 33–60.
Casini, Lorenzo, 'Renaissance Theories of Internal Senses', in Knuuttila, S. – J. Sihvola (eds.). *Sourcebook for the History of the Philosophy of Mind, Philosophical Psychology from Plato to Kant* (Dordrecht: Springer, 2013), 147–56.
Castro, Américo. *España en su Historia. Cristianos, Moros y Judíos* (Buenos Aires: Editorial Losada, 1984).
Cave, Terence. *The Cornucopian Text: Problems of Writing in the French Renaissance* (Oxford: Clarendon, 1979).
Charlier, Yvonne. *Érasme et l'amitié: d'après sa correspondence* (Paris: Les Belles lettres, 1977).
Chomarat, Jacques. *Grammaire et rhétorique chez Érasme* 2 vols. (Paris: Les Belles Lettres, 1981).
Coleman, Janet. *A History of Political Thought. From the Middle Ages to the Renaissance* (Oxford: Blackwell, 2000).
Coleman, Janet. 'Are There Any Individual Rights or Only Duties?', in Korkman, P. – V. Mäkinen (eds.). *Transformations in Medieval and Early-Modern Rights Discourse* (Dordrecht: Springer, 2006), 3–36.
Coleman, Janet. 'Medieval Political Theory, c.1000–1500', in Klosko, George (ed.). *The Oxford Handbook of the History of Political Philosophy* (Oxford: Oxford University Press, 2011), 180–205.
Cools, Hans. 'The Impact of Charles V's Wars on Society in the Low Countries. A Brief Exploration of the Theme', in Martínez Millán, J. – I. J. Ezquerra Revilla (eds.). *Carlos V y la quiebra del humanismo politico en Europa (1530–1558)*, vol. 1 (Madrid: Sociedad Estatal para la Conmemoración de los Centenarios de Felipe II y Carlos V, 2001), 315–20.
Cooney, James Francis. *De ratione dicendi: a Treatise on rhetoric by Juan Luis Vives* (a Thesis defended at the Ohio State University, 1966).
Copeland, Rita – Ineke Sluiter. *Medieval Grammar and Rhetoric: Language Arts and Literary Theory, AD 300–1475* (Oxford: Oxford University Press, 2009).
Copenhaver, Brian P. 'Translation, Terminology, and Style in Philosophical Discourse', in Schmitt, C. – Q. Skinner – E. Kessler – J. Kraye (eds.). *The Cambridge History of Renaissance Philosophy* (Cambridge: Cambridge University Press, 1990), 75–110.
Coseriu, Eugenio. 'Zur Sprachtheorie von Juan Luis Vives', in Mönch, W. – W. Dierlamm (eds.). *Aus der Französischen Kultur- und Geistesgeschichte. Festschrift Walter Mönch* (Heidelberg: Kerle 1971), 234–55.
Cox, Virginia – John O. Ward. 'Preface', in Cox – Ward (eds.). *The Rhetoric of Cicero in Its Medieval and Early Renaissance Commentary Tradition* (Leiden/ Boston: Brill, 2006), xv–xvii.
Crousaz, K. *Érasme et le pouvoir de l'imprimerie* (Lausanne: Éditions Antipodes, 2005).

Cummings, Brian. *The Literary Culture of the Reformation: Grammar and Grace* (Oxford: Oxford University Press, 2007).
Cummings, Brian. 'Erasmus and the Invention of Literature', *Erasmus Yearbook* 33 (2013), 22–54.
Curtis, Cathy. 'The Best State of Commonwealth: Thomas More and Quentin Skinner', in Tully, J. – A. Brett (eds.). *Rethinking the Foundations of Modern Political Thought* (Cambridge: Cambridge University Press, 2006), 93–112.
Curtis, Cathy. 'The Social and Political Thought of Vives', in Fantazzi, Charles (ed.). *A Companion to Juan Luis Vives* (Leiden: Brill, 2008), 113–76.
Curtis, Cathy. 'Advising Monarchs and Their Counsellors: Juan Luis Vives on the Emotions, Civil Life and International Relations', *Parergon* 28:2 (2011), 29–53.
Damen, Mario. 'Education or Connections? Learned Officials in the Council of Holland and Zeeland in the Fifteenth Century', in Goudriaan, K. – J. van Moolenbroek – A. Tervoort (eds.). *Education and Learning in the Netherlands, 1400–1600* (Leiden: Brill, 2003), 51–67.
D'Amico, John. *Theory and Practice in Renaissance Textual Criticism: Beatus Rhenanus between Conjecture and History* (Berkeley: University of California Press, 1988).
D'Amico, Juan Carlos. 'Mercurino Arborio de Gattinara et le mythe d'un empire universel au service de Charles Quint', in Crémoux, F. – J-L. Fournel (eds.). *Idées d'empire en Italie et en Espagne (XIVe–XVIIe siècle)* (Mont-Saint-Aignan: Publications des universités de Rouen et du Havre, 2010).
Dealy, Ross. *The Stoic Origins of Erasmus' Philosophy of Christ* (Toronto: University of Toronto Press, 2017).
De Bom, Erik. 'Realism vs Utopianism. The Problem of the Prince in the Early-Modern Netherlands', in Van Ruler, H. – G. Sissa (eds.), *Utopia, 1516–2016, More's Eccentric Essay and Its Activist Aftermath* (Amsterdam: Amsterdam University Press, 2016), 109–42.
De Gandillac, Maurice. 'Lefèvre d'Étaples et Charles de Bouvelles', in *L'humanisme français au début de la Renaissance* (Paris: Vrin, 1973), 155–71.
De la Garanderie, Marie. *Christianisme et lettres profanes* (Paris: Honoré Champion, 1995).
De la Pinta y Llorente, Miguel – José María de Palacio y de Palacio. *Procesos Inquisitoriales contra la familia judía de Luis Vives* (Madrid: Instituto Arias Montano, 1964).
De Schepper, Marcus, 'April in Paris (1514): J. L. Editing B. Guarinus', in Sacré, D. – G. Tournoy (eds.). *Myricae. Essays of Neo-Latin Literature in Memory of Jozef IJsewijn* (Leuven: Leuven University Press, 2000), 195–206.
De Vocht, Henry. *Monumenta humanistica lovaniensia. Texts and Studies about Louvain Humanists in the First Half of the XVIth Century: Erasmus, Vives, Dorpius, Clenardus, Goes, Moringus* (Louvain: Librairie Universitaire, 1934).
De Vocht, Henry. *History of the Foundation and the Rise of the Collegium Trilingue Lovaniense, 1517–1550* (Bruxelles: Bibliothèque de l'Université, 1951).
Del Nero, Valerio. *Linguaggio e filosofia in Vives. L'organizzazione del sapere nel 'De disciplinis' (1531)* (CLUEB, Bologna 1991).
Del Nero, Valerio. 'The *De disciplinis* as a Model of a Humanistic Text', in Fantazzi, Charles (ed.). *A Companion to Juan Luis Vives* (Leiden/Boston: Brill, 2008a), 177–226.

Del Nero, Valerio. 'A Philosophical Treatise on the Soul: *De anima et vita* in the Context of Vives's Opus', in Fantazzi, Charles (ed.). *A Companion to Juan Luis Vives* (Leiden/Boston: Brill, 2008b), 277–314.
Dixhoorn, Arjan van. 'Chambers of Rhetoric: Performative Culture and Literary Sociability in the Early Modern Northern Netherlands', in Dixhoorn, A. – S. Speakman Sutch (eds.). *The Reach of the Republic of Letters*, vol. 1 (Leiden/Boston: Brill, 2008), 119–58.
Dow, Jamie. *Passions and Persuasion in Aristotle's Rhetoric* (Oxford: Oxford University Press, 2015).
Dumolyn, Jan. 'Justice, Equity and the Common Good: The State Ideology of the Councillors of the Burgundian Dukes', in Boulton, J. – J. Veenstra (eds.). *The Ideology of Burgundy, the Promotion of National Consciousness 1364–1565* (Leiden: Brill 2006), 1–20.
Duke, Alastair. *Reformation and Revolt in the Low Countries* (London: Hambledon Press, 1990).
Dust, Philip. *Three Renaissance Pacifists. Essays in the Theories of Erasmus, More, and Vives* (New York: Peter Lang, 1987).
Ebbersmeyer, Sabrina. 'Passions for this Life', in Lines, D. A. – S. Ebbersmeyer (eds.). *Rethinking Virtue, Reforming Society* (Turnhout: Brepols, 2013), 277–304.
Eden, Kathy. *Hermeneutics and the Rhetorical Tradition* (New Haven: Yale University Press, 1997).
Eisenstein, Elizabeth L. *The Printing Revolution in Early Modern Europe* (Cambridge: Cambridge University Press, 1983).
Elias, Norbert. *The Civilizing Process* (Oxford: Blackwell, 1994).
Fantazzi, Charles. 'Vives versus Erasmus on the Art of Letter Writing', in Van Houdt, T. – J. Papy – G. Tournoy – C. Matheeussen (eds.). *Self-Presentation and Social Identification. The Rhetoric and Pragmatics of Letter Writing in Early Modern Times* (Leuven: Leuven University Press, 2002), 39–56.
Fantazzi, Charles. 'Vives's Parisian Years', in Celenza, C. S. – K. Gouwens (eds.). *Humanism and Creativity in the Renaissance* (Leiden/Boston: Brill, 2006).
Fantazzi, Charles. 'Vives and the *emarginati*', in Fantazzi, Charles (ed.). *A Companion to Juan Luis Vives* (Leiden: Brill, 2008), 65–112.
Fantazzi, Charles. 'The Erasmus-Vives Correspondence', in Ryle, Stephen (ed.). *Erasmus and the Renaissance Republic of Letters* (Turnhout: Brepols, 2014), 145–57.
Farge, James K. *Orthodoxy and Reform in Early Reformation France* (Leiden: Brill, 1985).
Farge, James K. *Le Parti conservateur au XVIe siècle: Université et Parlement de Paris à l'époque de la Renaissance et de la Réforme* (Paris: Les belles lettres, 1992).
Fenlon, Dermot. 'England and Europe: Utopia and its Aftermath', *Transactions of the Royal Historical Society* XXV (1975), 115–35.
Ferguson, Wallace K. 'Introduction', in CWE 1, ix–xxiii.
Fernández-Santamaría, J. A. *The State, War and Peace, Spanish Political Thought in the Renaissance 1516–1559* (Cambridge: Cambridge University Press, 1977).
Fernández-Santamaría, J. A. *The Theater of Man: J.L. Vives on Society* (Philadelphia: American Philosophical Society, 1998).
Fubini, Riccardo. *Politica e pensiero politico nell'Italia del Rinascimento. Dallo stato territoriale al Machiavelli* (Firenze: EDIFIR, 2009).
Fumaroli, Marc. *L'âge de l'éloquence* (Genève/Paris: Librairie Droz, 1980).

Fumaroli, Marc. 'Rhetoric, Politics, and Society: From Italian Ciceronianism to French Classicism', in Murphy, James J. (ed.). *Renaissance Eloquence* (Berkeley: University of California Press, 1983), 253–73.

Fumaroli, Marc. 'Préface', in Fumaroli, Marc (ed.). *Histoire de la rhétorique dans l'Europe moderne (1450–1950)* (Paris: PUF, 1999), 1–16.

Furey, Constance M. *Erasmus, Contarini, and the Religious Republic of Letters* (New York: Cambridge University Press, 2006).

Gadoffre, Gilbert. *La révolution culturelle dans la France des humanistes* (Genève: Librairie Droz, 1997).

Galand, Perrine. 2015. 'Introduction', in Bérauld, Nicolas (ed.). *Praelectio et commentaire à la Silve Rusticus d'Ange Politien (1518)* (Genève: Droz, 2015), xv–xl.

Galasso, Giuseppe. 'Lettura Dantesca e lettura umanistica nell'idea di imperio del Gattinara', in Martínez Millán, J. – I. J. Ezquerra Revilla (eds.). *Carlos V y la quiebra del humanismo político en Europa (1530–1558)*, vol. 1 (Madrid: Sociedad Estatal para la Conmemoración de los Centenarios de Felipe II y Carlos V, 2001), 93–114.

Garanderie, Marie-Madeleine de La. 'Introduction', in La Garanderie (ed.). *La correspondance d'Érasme et de Guillaume Budé* (Paris: J. Vrin, 1967), 9–47.

García Cárcel, Ricardo. 'El perfil del rey' in García Cárcel, Ricardo (ed.). *Historia de España, Siglos XVI y XVII* (Madrid: Cátedra, 2003), 29–40.

Garin, Eugenio. *Scienza e vita civile nel Rinascimento italiano* (Laterza: Bari 1965).

Garin, Eugenio. *L'Education de l'homme moderne. La pédagogie de la Renaissance (1400–1600)* (Paris: Fayard, 1968).

George, Edward. 'Introduction', in Vives. George (ed.). *Declamationes Sullanae, Part one* (Leiden/Boston: Brill, 1989a), 1–11.

George, Edward. 'The Declamationes Syllanae of Juan Luis Vives: sources and departures', *Humanistica Lovaniensia, Journal of Neo-Latin studies* XXXVIII (1989b), 124–51.

George, Edward. 'Rhetoric in Vives', in Mestre, Antonio (ed.). *Opera omnia Ioannis Lodovici Vivis Valentini, I: Volumen introductorio* (Valencia: Generàlitat Valenciana, 1992), 113–77.

George, Edward. 'Rhetorical Strategies in Vives' Peace Writings: The Letter to Charles V and *De concordia*', in Tournoy, G. – D. Sacré (eds.). *Ut granum sinapis. Essays on Neo-Latin Literature in Honour of Jozef IJsewijn* (Leuven: Leuven University Press, 1997), 249–63.

George, Edward. 'Review of The Theater of Man: J. L. Vives on Society by José A. Fernández Santamaría', *Renaissance Quarterly* 52:4 (1999), 1156–8.

George, Edward. 'Suadendo, admonendo, hortando, precando. Rhetoric and peacemaking in Juan Luis Vives' *De pacificatione*', in Schur, R – R. Green (eds.). *Acta Conventus Neo-Latini Abulensis* (Tempe: Arizona Center for Medieval and Renaissance Studies, 2000), 253–64.

George, Edward. 'Author, Adversary, and Reader: A View of the *de Veritate Fidei Christianae*', in Fantazzi, Charles (ed.). *A Companion to Juan Luis Vives* (Leiden: Brill, 2008), 65–112.

George, Edward. 'Captive Greeks and Deluded Europeans: Notes on Juan Luis Vives's De conditione vitae Christianorum sub Turca (1529)', *eHumanista* 26 (2014), 508–29.

Geri, L. *A colloquio con Luciano di Samosata: Leon Battista Alberti, Giovanni Pontano ed Erasmo da Rotterdam* (Roma: Bulzoni, 2011).

Gilly, Carlos. 'Erasmo, la reforma radical y los heterodoxos radicales españoles', in Martínez Romero, Tomás (ed.). *Les lettres hispàniques als segles XVI, XVII i XVIII* (Castelló de la Plana: Publicacions de la Universitat Jaume I, 2005), 225–376.

Godin, André. 'The *Enchiridion militis Christiani*: The modes of an Origenian appropriation', *Erasmus of Rotterdam Society Yearbook* 2 (1982), 47–71.

Gómez-Hortigüela, Ángel. *El Pensamiento filosófico de Juan Luis Vives* (Valencia: Institució Alfons Magnanim, 1998).

González González, Enrique. *Joan Lluís Vives. De la Escolástica al Humanismo* (Valencia: Generalitat Valenciana, 1987).

González González, Enrique. 'Vives: un humanista judeoconverso en el exilio de Flandes', in Dequeker, L. – W. Verbeke (eds.). *The Expulsion of the Jews and Their Emigration to the Southern Low Countries (15th–16th C.)* (Leuven: Leuven University Press, 1998), 35–82.

González González, Enrique – Víctor Gutiérrez Rodríguez. *Los diálogos de Vives y la imprenta. Fortuna de un manual escolar renacentista (1539–1994)* (Valencia: Alfonso el Magnànim, 1999).

González González, Enrique. 'The Encounter of Luis Vives and Hadrianus Barlandus in Louvain 1514? – 1515', *Lias* 30:2 (2003), 177–212.

González González, Enrique. *Una república de lectores. Difusión y recepción de la obra de Juan Luis Vives* (México: Plaza y Valdés, 2007).

González González, Enrique. 'Juan Luis Vives, Works and Days', in Fantazzi, Charles (ed.). *A Companion to Juan Luis Vives* (Leiden/Boston: Brill, 2008), 15–64.

González González, Enrique. 'Juan Luis Vives sur les presses parisiennes et le dialogue *Sapiens* (1514)', *Réforme, humanisme, Renaissance* 80:1 (2015), 39–67.

Goudriaan, Koen. 'The Gouda Circle of Humanists', in Goudriaan, K. – J. van Moolenbroek – A. Tervoort (eds.). *Education and Learning in the Netherlands, 1400–1600* (Leiden: Brill, 2003), 155–77.

Goudriaan, Koen – Jaap van Moolenbroek – Ad Tervoort. 'Introduction', in Goudriaan – van Moolenbroek – Tervoort (eds.). *Education and Learning in the Netherlands, 1400–1600* (Leiden: Brill, 2003), 1–11.

Grafton, Anthony – Lisa Jardine. *From Humanism to the Humanities: Education and the Liberal Arts in Fifteenth- and Sixteenth-Century Europe* (London: Duckworth, 1986).

Grant, John N. 'Erasmus' Adages', in CWE 30, 1–83.

Grassi, Ernesto. *Rhetoric as Philosophy* (Carbondale: Southern Illinois University Press, 1980).

Green, Lawrence D. 'Aristotle's Rhetoric and Renaissance Views on the Emotions', in Mack, Peter (ed.). *Renaissance Rhetoric* (London: Palgrave McMillan, 1994), 1–26.

Green, Lawrence D. – Murphy, James Jerome. *Renaissance Rhetoric, Short Title Catalogue 1460–1700* (Aldershot: Ashgate, 2006).

Greenblatt, Stephen. *Renaissance Self-Fashioning from More to Shakespeare* (Chicago: The University of Chicago Press, 1980).

Grendler, Paul F. *Schooling in Renaissance Italy: Literacy and Learning, 1300–1600* (Baltimore: John Hopkins University, 1991).

Grendler, Paul F. *Renaissance Education between Religion and Politics* (Aldershot: Ashgate, 2006).

Guy, Alain. *Vivès ou l'humanisme engagé* (Paris: Seghers, 1972).

Guy, John. *Thomas More* (London: Arnold, 2000).
Gwyn, Peter. *The King's Cardinal, the Rise and Fall of Thomas Wolsey* (London: Barrie & Jenkins, 1990).
Haakonssen, Knud. 'Introduction', in Haakonssen (ed.). *Grotius, Pufendorf and Modern Natural Law* (Dartmouth: Ashgate, 1999).
Haas, Guenther. *Concept of Equity in Calvin's Ethics* (Waterloo, Ontario: Wilfrid Laurier University Press, 1997).
Haddock, Bruce. *A History of Political Thought: from Antiquity to the Present* (Oxford: Polity Press, 2008).
Hadot, Pierre. *Exercises spirituels et philosophie antique* (Paris: Albin Michel, 2002).
Hale, John. *The Civilization of Europe in the Renaissance* (New York, Touchstone, 1995).
Halkin, Léon E. *Érasme parmi nous* (Paris: Fayard, 1987).
Hankins, James. 'The Baron thesis after forty years: Some recent studies on Leonardo Bruni', *Journal of the History of Ideas* 56:2 (1995), 309–38.
Hankins, James. 'Humanism and the Origins of Modern Political Thought', in Kraye, Jill (ed.). *The Cambridge Companion to Renaissance Humanism* (Cambridge: Cambridge University Press, 1996), 118–41.
Hankins, James. *Humanism and Platonism in the Italian Renaissance*, 2 vols. (Roma: Edizioni di Storia e Letteratura, 2003–2004).
Hankins, James. *Virtue Politics: Soulcraft and Statecraft in Renaissance Italy* (Cambridge, MA: Belknap Press, 2019).
Havu, Kaarlo. 'Ethos, authority and worldly reputation in the Erasmian Republic of Letters', *Renaissance Studies* 33:5 (2019), 789–807.
Headley, John M. *The Emperor and His Chancellor: A Study of the Imperial Chancellery under Gattinara* (Cambridge: Cambridge University Press, 1983).
Headley, John M. 'The Emperor and His Chancellor: Disputes over Empire, Administration and Pope (1519–1529)', in Martínez Millán, J. – I. J. Ezquerra Revilla (eds.). *Carlos V y la quiebra del humanismo politico en Europa (1530–1558)*, vol. 1 (Madrid: Sociedad Estatal para la Conmemoración de los Centenarios de Felipe II y Carlos V, 2001), 21–36.
Hexter, J. H. *More's Utopia. The Biography of an Idea* (New York: Princeton University Press, 1952).
Hidalgo-Serna. 'Introduzione, La retorica filosofica di Juan Luis Vives', in Vives, Juan Luis. *De ratione dicendi* (Napoli: La città del sole, 2002), vii–liv.
Hillerbrand, Hans J. *The Division of Christendom* (Louisville: Westminster John Knox Press, 2007).
Hirschman, Albert O. *The Passions and the Interests* (Princeton: Princeton University Press, 1977).
Hochstrasser, Tim. *Natural Law Theories in the Early Enlightenment* (Cambridge: Cambridge University Press, 2000).
Hoffmann, Manfred, 'Erasmus on Free Will: An Issue Revisited', *Erasmus of Rotterdam Society Yearbook* 10 (1990), 101–21.
Hoffmann, Manfred. *Rhetoric and Theology: The Hermeneutic of Erasmus* (Toronto: University of Toronto Press, 1994).
Huppert, George. *Les bourgeois gentilshommes* (Chicago: University of Chicago Press, 1977).
Huppert, George. *Public Schools in Renaissance France* (Urbana, IL: University of Illinois Press, 1984).

238 Bibliography

Hyrkkänen, Markku. 'All History Is, More or Less, Intellectual History: R. G. Collingwood's Contribution to the Theory and Methodology of Intellectual History', *Intellectual History Review* 19:2 (2009), 251–63.

IJsewijn, Jozef. 'The Coming of Humanism in the Low Countries', in Oberman, H. – T. Brady (eds.). *Itinerarium Italicum; the Profile of the Italian Renaissance in the Mirror of Its European Transformations* (Leiden: Brill, 1975), 193–301.

IJsewijn, Jozef. 'J.L. Vives in 1512–1517: A Reconsideration of Evidence', *Humanistica Lovaniensia* 26 (1977), 82–100.

IJsewijn, Jozef. 'Humanism in the Low Countries', in Rabil Jr, A. Jr (ed.). *Renaissance Humanism; Foundations, Forms, and Legacy*, vol. 2 (Philadelphia: University of Pennsylvania Press, 1988), 156–215.

James, Susan. *Passion and Action: The Emotions in Seventeenth-Century Philosophy* (Oxford: Oxford University Press, 1997).

Jardine, Lisa. 'The Place of Dialectic in Sixteenth Century Cambridge', *Studies in the Renaissance* 21 (1974), 31–62.

Jardine, Lisa. 'Humanistic Logic', in Schmitt, Charles (ed.). *Cambridge History of Renaissance Philosophy* (Cambridge: Cambridge University Press, 1988), 173–98.

Jardine, Lisa. *Erasmus, Man of Letters: the Construction of Charisma in Print* (Princeton: Princeton University Press, 1993).

Jonsen, Albert – Stephen Toulmin. *The Abuse of Casuistry. A History of Moral Reasoning* (Berkeley: University of California Press, 1988).

Kahn, Victoria. *Rhetoric, Prudence and Skepticism in the Renaissance* (Ithaca: Cornell University Press, 1985).

Kahn, Victoria – N. Saccamano. 'Introduction', in Kahn, V. – N. Saccamano – D. Coli (eds.). *Politics and Passions, 1500–1850* (Princeton: Princeton University Press, 2006), 6–10.

Kahn, Victoria – N. Saccamano – D. Coli (eds.). *Politics and Passions, 1500–1850* (Princeton: Princeton University Press, 2006).

Karant-Nunn, Susan, 'Alas, a Lack, Trends in the Historiography of Pre-University Education in Early Modern Germany', *Renaissance Quarterly* 43:4 (1990), 788–98.

Karlin, Louis – Jordan Teti. 'A Trace of Equity in Utopia? On Raphael's Reformulation of Classical Equity', *Moreana* 54:1 (2017), 19–35.

Kaukua, Jari – Thomas Ekenberg (eds.), *Subjectivity and Selfhood in Medieval and Early Modern Philosophy* (Switzerland: Springer, 2016).

Kelley, Donald. 'Law', in Burns, J. H. – M. Goldie (eds.). *The Cambridge History of Political Thought 1450–1700* (Cambridge: Cambridge University Press, 1991), 66–94.

Kempshall, Matthew. *Rhetoric and the Writing of History, 400–1500* (Manchester: Manchester University Press), 2011.

Kennedy, Teresa. *Elyot, Castiglione, and the Problem of Style* (New York: Peter Lang, 1996).

Kinney, Arthur. 'Inhabiting Time: Sir Thomas More's *Historia Richardi Tertii*', in Cousins, A. D. – D. Grace (eds.). *A Companion to Thomas More* (Madison: Fairleigh Dickinson University Press, 2009), 114–26.

Kinneavy, James. 'Kairos: A Neglected Concept in Classical Rhetoric', in Moss, Dietz (ed.). *Rhetoric and Praxis: The Contribution of Classical Rhetoric to Practical Reasoning* (Washington, DC: The Catholic University of America Press, 1986), 79–105.

Kisch, Guido. *Erasmus und die Jurisprudenz seiner Zeit* (Basel: Helbing & Lichtenhahn, 1960).
Knecht, R. J. *The Rise and Fall of Renaissance France 1483–1610* (Malden: Blackwell, 2001).
Knott, Betty I. 'Introductory Note', in CWE 28, 324–36.
Knuuttila, Simo. *Emotions in Ancient and Medieval Philosophy* (Oxford: Clarendon Press, 2004).
Knuuttila, Simo – Pekka Kärkkäinen, 'Medieval Theories', in Knuuttila, S. – J. Sihvola (eds.). *Sourcebook for the History of the Philosophy of Mind: Philosophical Psychology from Plato to Kant* (Dordrecht: Springer, 2013), 61–79.
Knuuttila, S. – J. Sihvola (eds.). *Sourcebook for the History of the Philosophy of Mind: Philosophical Psychology from Plato to Kant* (Dordrecht: Springer, 2013).
Koenigsberger, H. G. *Monarchies, States Generals and Parliaments: The Netherlands in the Fifteenth and Sixteenth Centuries* (Cambridge: Cambridge University Press, 2001).
Kohut, Karl. 'Vives, la Guerra y la paz', *eHumanista* 26 (2014), 539–68.
Kolsky, Stephen. *Courts and Courtiers in Renaissance Northern Italy* (Aldershot: Ashgate, 2003).
Koryl, Jakub, 'Erasmianism, Mediterranean Humanism and Reception History: The Case of Jerzy Liban of Legnica at the University of Cracow', *Studi Slavistici* X (2013), 43–68.
Kraye, Jill – M.W.F. Stone (eds.). *The Cambridge Companion to Renaissance Humanism* (Cambridge: Cambridge University Press, 1996).
Kraye, Jill. *Humanism and Early Modern Philosophy* (London: Routledge, 1999).
Kraye, Jill. 'Pico on the Relationship of Rhetoric and Philosophy', in Dougherty, M. V. (ed.). *Pico della Mirandola: New Essays* (Cambridge: Cambridge University Press, 2008), 13–36.
Kristeller, Paul Oskar. *Renaissance Thought and Its Sources* (New York: Columbia University Press, 1979).
Kristeller, Paul Oskar. 'Humanism and Moral Philosophy', in Rabil Jr, A. (ed.). *Renaissance Humanism: Foundations, Forms, and Legacy*, vol. 3 (Philadelphia: University of Pennsylvania Press, 1988), 271–309.
Kristeller, Paul Oskar. 'Humanism', in Schmitt, C. – Q. Skinner – E. Kessler – J. Kraye (eds.). *The Cambridge History of Renaissance Philosophy* (Cambridge: Cambridge University Press, 1990), 111–38.
Lange, F. A. 'Vives', in Schmid, K. A. – W. Schrader (eds.). *Encyklopädie des gesammten Erziehungs- und Unterrichtswesens*, vol. 9 (Leipzig: Fues's Verlag, 1887).
Laureys, Marc – Roswitha Simons – Arnold Becker. 'Towards a Theory of the Humanistic Art of Arguing', in Laureys – Simons (eds.). *The Art of Arguing in the World of Renaissance Humanism* (Leuven: Leuven University Press, 2013).
Leites, Edmund. 'Casuistry and Character', in Leites (ed.). *Conscience and Casuistry Early Modern Europe* (Cambridge: Cambridge University Press, 1988), 119–33.
Levi. A. H. T. 'Introduction', in CWE 27, ix–xxx.
Lévy, Carlos – Laurent Pernot (eds.). *Dire l'évidence* (Paris: L'Harmattan, 1997).
Loades, David. 'Charles V and the English', in Martínez Millán, J. – I. J. Ezquerra Revilla (eds.). *Carlos V y la quiebra del humanismo politico en Europa (1530–1558)*, vol. 1 (Madrid: Sociedad Estatal para la Conmemoración de los Centenarios de Felipe II y Carlos V, 2001), 247–58.

Lochman, Daniel – Maritere López. 'Introduction: The Emergence of Discourses', in Lochman, D. – M. López – L. Hudson (eds.). *Discourses and Representations of Friendship in Early Modern Europe, 1500–1700* (Burlington, VT: Ashgate, 2011), 1–28.
Logan, George. 'Utopia and Deliberative Rhetoric', *Moreana* 31 (1994), 103–20.
Maas, Coen. 'Batavia and the Historiographical Canon in Holland', in Van Miert, Dirk (ed.). *The Kaleidoscopic Scholarship of Hadrianus Junius (1511–1575). Northern Humanism at the Dawn of the Dutch Golden Age* (Leiden: Brill, 2011), 38–68.
Mack Peter. *Renaissance Argument: Valla and Agricola in the Tradition of Rhetoric and Dialectic* (Leiden/New York: Brill, 1993).
Mack, Peter. *Elizabethan Rhetoric: Theory and Practice* (Cambridge: Cambridge University Press, 2002).
Mack, Peter. 'Early Modern Ideas of Imagination: The Rhetorical Tradition', in Nauta, L. – D. Pätzold (eds.). *Imagination in the Later Middle Ages and Early Modern Times* (Leuven: Peeters, 2004), 59–76.
Mack, Peter. 'Vives's *De ratione dicendi*: Structures, Innovations, Problems', *Rhetorica: A Journal of the History of Rhetoric* 23:1 (2005), 65–92.
Mack, Peter. 'Vives's Contributions to Rhetoric and Dialectic', in Fantazzi, Charles (ed.). *A Companion to Juan Luis Vives* (Leiden/Boston: Brill, 2008), 227–76.
Mack, Peter. *A History of Renaissance Rhetoric 1380–1620* (Oxford: Oxford University Press, 2011).
Mahlmann-Bauer, Barbara. 'Catholic and Protestant Textbooks in Elementary Latin Conversation. Manuals of Religious Combat or Guide to Avoiding Conflict', in Campi, E. et al. (eds.). *Scholarly Knowledge. Textbooks in Early Modern Europe* (Genève: Droz, 2008), 341–90.
Majeske, Andrew J. *Equity in English Renaissance Literature: Thomas More and Edmund Spenser* (New York: Routledge, 2006).
Mallet, Michael – Christine Shaw. *The Italian Wars 1494–1559* (Harlow/New York: Pearson, 2012).
Mann Phillips, Margaret. *The 'Adages' of Erasmus* (Cambridge: Cambridge University Press, 1964).
Mansfield, Bruce. *Erasmus in the Twentieth Century: Interpretations c. 1920–2000* (Toronto: University of Toronto Press, 2003).
Margolin, Jean-Claude. 'Conscience européenne et réaction à la menace turque d'après le *De dissidiis Europae et bello Turcico*', in Buck, August (ed.). *Juan Luis Vives* (Hamburg: Hauswedell, 1982), 107–40.
Margolin, Jean-Claude. 'L'apogée de la rhétorique humaniste (1500–1536)', in Fumaroli, Marc (ed.). *Histoire de la rhétorique dans l'Europe moderne (1450–1950)* (Paris: PUF, 1999), 191–258.
Marlow A. N. – B. Drewery. 'Introduction', in Rupp, G. – P. Watson (eds.). *Luther and Erasmus. Free Will and Salvation* (London: John Knox Press, 1969), 1–32.
Martínez Millán, José (ed.). *Instituciones y elites de poder en monarquia hispana durante el siglo XVI* (Madrid: Ediciones de la Universidad Autónoma de Madrid, 1992).
Martínez Millán, José. 'Conseillers et factions curiales durant le règne de l'empereur Charles Quint (1500–1558)', in Michon, Cédric. *Conseils et conseillers dans l'Europe de la Renaissance* (Tours: Presses universitaires François-Rabelais, 2012), 109–45.

Martínez Millàn, José – Manuel Rivero Rodríguez. 'La coronación imperial de Bolonia y el final de la "Vía flamenca', in Martínez Millán, J. – J. I. Ezquerra Revilla (eds.). *Carlos V y la quiebra del humanismo politico en Europa (1530–1558)*, vol. 1 (Madrid: Sociedad Estatal para la Conmemoración de los Centenarios de Felipe II y Carlos V, 2001), 131–50.

Martinich, A. P. 'A Moderate Logic of the History of Ideas', *Journal of the History of Ideas* 73:4 (2012), 609–25.

Matheeussen, Constant. 'Das rechtsphilosophische Frühwerk des Vives', Buck, August (ed.). *Juan Luis Vives* (Hamburg: Hauswedell, 1982), 93–106.

Matheeussen, Constant. 'Quelques remarques sur le *De subventione pauperum*', in IJsewijn, J. – Á. Losada (eds.). *Erasmus in Hispania et Vives in Belgio* (Louvain: Peeters, 1986), 87–97.

Matheeussen, Constant. 'El humanismo de los Países Bajos y Juan Luis Vives', in Puig de la Bellasca, Ramón. *La discapacidad y la rehabilitación en Juan Luis Vives* (Madrid: Real Patronato de Prevención y de Atención a Personas con Minusvalía, 1993), 28–45.

Matheeussen, Constant. 'Vives et la problématique sociale de son temps, son attitude envers la mendicité et le vagabondage', in Fernández Nieto, F. J. – A. Melero Bellido – A. Mestre (eds.). *Luis Vives y el humanismo Europeo* (Valencia: Universitat de València, 1998).

Mayans y Siscar, Gregorio. *Vita Vivis*, in Mayans 1:2–219.

Mazzocco, Angelo. *Interpretations of Renaissance Humanism* (Leiden: Brill, 2006).

McConica, James. *English Humanists and Reformation Politics under Henry VIII and Edward VI* (Oxford: Clarendon Press, 1965).

McCutcheon, Elizabeth. 'More's Rhetoric', in Logan, George (ed.). *The Cambridge Companion to Thomas More* (Cambridge: Cambridge University Press, 2011), 46–68.

Ménager, Daniel. 'Erasmus, the Intellectuals and the Reuchlin Affair', in Rummel, Erika. *Biblical Humanism and Scholasticism in the Age of Erasmus* (Leiden/Boston: Brill, 2008), 39–54.

Menéndez Pelayo, Marcelino. 'Historia de los heterodoxos españoles. Erasmistas y protestantes', in Sánchez Reyes, Enrique (ed.). *Edición nacional de las obras completas de Menéndez Pelayo*. vol. 37 (Madrid, Consejo Superior de Investigaciones Científicas, 1948).

Menéndez Pelayo, Marcelino. '*Ciencia española*, tomo 3', in Sánchez Reyes, Enrique (ed.). *Edición nacional de las obras completas de Menéndez Pelayo*, vol. 58 (Santander: Consejo Superior de Investigaciones Científicas, 1953–1954).

Menéndez Pidal, Ramón. *Idea imperial de Carlos V* (Buenos Aires/México: Espasa-Calpe, 1946).

Mesnard, Pierre. *L'essor de la philosophie politique* (Paris: Boivin, 1936).

Michon, Cédric. *Les conseillers de François Ier* (Rennes: Presses universitaires de Rennes, 2011).

Michon, Cédric. 'Introduction. Conseils et conseillers en Europe (v. 1450–v. 1550)', in Michon, Cédric (ed.). *Conseils et conseillers dans l'Europe de la Renaissance* (Tours: Presses universitaires François-Rabelais, 2012), 9–20.

Miglietti, Sara. 'Meaning in a Changing Context: Towards an Interdisciplinary Approach to Authorial Revision', *History of European Ideas* 40:4 (2014), 474–94.

Monfasani, John. *George of Trebizond: A Biography and a Study of His Rhetoric and Logic* (Leiden: Brill, 1976).

Monfasani, John. 'Toward the Genesis of the Kristeller Thesis of Renaissance Humanism: Four Bibliographical Notes', *Renaissance Quarterly* 53:4 (2000), 1156–73.
Monzón i Arazo, August. 'Humanismo y derecho en Joan Lluís Vives', in Mestre, Antonio (ed.). *Opera omnia Ioannis Lodovici Vivis Valentini, I: Volumen introductorio* (Valencia: Generàlitat Valenciana, 1992), 263–316.
Moreno Gallego, Valentín. *La recepción hispana de Juan Luis Vives* (Valencia: Generalitat Valenciana, 2006).
Moss, Ann. *Printed Commonplace Books and the Structuring of Renaissance Thought* (Oxford: Oxford University Press, 1996).
Moss, Ann. *Renaissance Truth and Latin Language Turn* (Oxford: Oxford University Press, 2003).
Mout, M. E. H. N. 'Introduction', in Mout, M. E. H. N. – H. Smolinsky – J. Trapman (eds.). *Erasmianism: Idea and Reality* (Amsterdam: North-Holland, 1997).
Murphy, James Jerome. *Rhetoric in the Middle Ages: A History of Rhetorical Theory from Saint Augustine to the Renaissance* (Berkeley: University of California Press, 1974).
Murphy, James Jerome. *Latin Rhetoric and Education in the Middle Ages and the Renaissance* (Aldershot: Ashgate, 2005).
Nauert, Charles. 'Humanist Infiltration into the Academic World: Some Studies of Northern Universities', *Renaissance Quarterly* 43: 4. (1990), 799–812.
Nauert, Charles. 'Humanism as Method, Roots of Conflict with the Scholastics', *Sixteenth Century Journal* XXIX:2 (1998), 427–38.
Nauert, Charles. *Humanism and the Culture of Renaissance Europe* (Cambridge: Cambridge University Press, 2006).
Nauta, Lodi. *In Defense of Common Sense: Lorenzo Valla's Humanist Critique of Scholastic Philosophy* (Cambridge, MA: Harvard University Press, 2009).
Nauta, Lodi. 'The Order of Knowing. Juan Luis Vives on Language, Thought and the Topics', *Journal of the History of Ideas* 76:3 (2015), 325–45.
Noreña, Carlos. *Juan Luis Vives* (The Hague: Martinus Nijhoff, 1970).
Noreña, Carlos. *Juan Luis Vives and the Emotions* (Carbondale: Southern Illinois University Press, 1989).
Nussbaum, Martha. *The Therapy of Desire: Theory and Practice in Hellenistic Ethics* (Princeton: Princeton University Press, 1994).
O'Malley, John. *The First Jesuits* (Cambridge, MA: Harvard University Press, 1993).
O'Neill, Daniel. 'Revisiting the Middle Way: The Logic of the History of Ideas after More Than a Decade', *Journal of the History of Ideas* 73:4 (2012), 583–92.
Ong, Walter. *Ramus: Method and the Decay of Dialogue* (Chicago: The University of Chicago Press, 2004).
O'Rourke Boyle, Marjorie. *Rhetoric and Reform: Erasmus' Civil Dispute with Luther* (Cambridge, MA: Harvard University Press, 1983).
Ortega y Gasset, José. *Vives-Goethe* (Madrid: Revista de occidente, 1961).
Ossa-Richardson, Anthony. *A History of Ambiguity* (Princeton: Princeton University Press, 2019).
Overfield, James. *Humanism and Scholasticism in Late Medieval Germany* (Princeton: Princeton University Press, 1984).
Pabel, Hilmar. 'Review of The Theater of Man: J. L. Vives on Society by José A. Fernández Santamaría', *The Sixteenth Century Journal* 30:2 (1999), 487–9.
Padley, G. A. *Grammatical Theory in Western Europe 1500–1700* (Cambridge: Cambridge University Press, 1976).

Papy, J. 'The Reception of Agricola's *De inventione dialectica* in the Teaching of Logic at the Faculty of Arts in the Early Sixteenth Century', in Akkerman, F. – A. J. Vanderjagt – A. H. Van der Laan (eds.). *Northern Humanism in European Context, 1469–1625* (Leiden: Brill, 1999), 167–85.

Papy, J. (ed.). *The Leuven Collegium Trilingue 1517–1797: Erasmus, Humanist Educational Practice and the New Language Institute: Latin, Greek, Hebrew* (Leuven: Peeters, 2018).

Park. K. 'The Organic Soul', in Schmitt et al. (eds.). *The Cambridge History of Renaissance Philosophy* (Cambridge: Cambridge University Press, 1988), 464–84.

Pascoe, Louis. *Jean Gerson: Principles of Church Reform* (Leiden: Brill, 1973).

Peltonen, Markku. *The Duel in Early Modern England: Civility, Politeness, and Honour* (Cambridge: Cambridge University Press, 2003).

Peltonen, Markku. *Rhetoric, Politics, and Popularity in Pre-Revolutionary England* (Cambridge: Cambridge University Press, 2012).

Périgot, Béatrice. *Dialectique et littérature: Les avatars de la dispute entre Moyen Âge et Renaissance* (Paris: Honoré Champion Éditeur, 2005).

Perreiah, Alan. 'Humanist Critiques of Scholastic Dialectic', *Sixteenth Century Journal* XIII:3 (1982), 3–33.

Pettegree, Andrew. *The Book in the Renaissance* (New Haven: Yale University Press, 2010).

Pippidi, Andrei. *Visions of the Ottoman World in Renaissance Europe* (Oxford: Oxford University Press, 2013).

Pocock, John. *The Machiavellian Moment* (Princeton: Princeton University Press, 1975).

Pocock, John. 'Cambridge Paradigms and Scotch Philosophers: A Study of the Relationship between the Civic Humanist and the Civil Jurisprudential Interpretation of Eighteenth-Century Social Thought', in Hont, I. – M. Ignatieff (eds.). *Wealth and Virtue: The Shaping of Political Economy in the Scottish Enlightenment* (Cambridge: Cambridge University Press, 1983), 232–52.

Pollnitz, Aysha. *Princely Education in Sixteenth-Century Britain* (Cambridge: Cambridge University Press, 2015).

Post, R. R. *The Modern Devotion. Confrontation with Reformation and Humanism* (Leiden: Brill, 1968).

Rabil Jr, A. 'Desiderius Erasmus', in Rabil Jr, A. (ed.). *Renaissance Humanism: Foundations, Forms, and Legacy*, vol. 2 (Philadelphia: University of Pennsylvania Press, 1988a), 216–64.

Rabil Jr, A. (ed.). *Renaissance Humanism: Foundations, Forms, and Legacy*, 3 vols. (Philadelphia: University of Pennsylvania Press, 1988b).

Radice, Betty. 'Introductory Note', in CWE 27, 290–1.

Rebhorn, Wayne A. 'Baldesar Castiglione, Thomas Wilson, and the Courtly Body of Renaissance Rhetoric', *Rhetorica* (1993), 241–73.

Rebhorn, Wayne A. *The Emperor of Men's Mind, Literature and the Renaissance Discourse of Rhetoric* (Ithaca: Cornell University Press, 1995).

Rebhorn, Wayne A. *Renaissance Debates on Rhetoric* (Ithaca: Cornell University Press, 2000).

Remer, Gary. *Humanism and the Rhetoric of Toleration* (University Park: Pennsylvania State University Press, 1996).

Renaudet, A. *Préréforme et humanisme à Paris pendant les premières guerres d'Italie (1494–1517)* (Paris: Champion, 1916).

Rice, Eugene F., Jr. 'Introduction', in Lefèvre, Jacques. Rice, Jr. (ed.). *Prefatory Epistles of Jacques Lefèvre d'Etaples*, (New York: Columbia University Press, 1972).
Rice Henderson, Judith. 'Must a Good Orator Be a Good Man? Ramus in the Ciceronian Controversy', in Oesterreich, P. L. – T. O. Sloane (eds.). *Rhetorica movet* (Brill: Leiden, 1999), 43–56.
Richardson, Glenn. *Renaissance Monarchy: The Reigns of Henry VIII, Francis I and Charles V* (London/New York: Arnold, 2002).
Richardson, H. 'Desire and the Good in *De anima*', in Nussbaum, M. – R. Rorty (eds.). *Essays on Aristotle's De anima* (Oxford: Clarendon, 1992), 381–99.
Ridder-Symoens, Hilde. 'Milieu social, études universitaires et carrière des conseillers au Conseil de Brabant', in Asaert, G. et al. (eds.). *Recht en Instellingen in de oude Nederlanden tijdens de Middeleeuwen en de Nieuwe tijd* (Leuven: Universitaire Pers, 1981), 257–301.
Ridder-Symoens, Hilde. 'Training and Professionalization', in Reinhard, Wolfgang (ed.). *Power Elites and State Building* (Oxford: Oxford University Press, 1996), 149–72.
Rodríguez Peregrina, José Manuel. 'La retórica clásica en el *De disciplinis* de Luis Vives', *Florentia Iliberritana* 6 (1995), 417–31.
Rodríguez Peregrina, José Manuel. 'Algunas consideraciones en torno al *De Ratione Dicendi* de Luis Vives', *Humanistica Lovaniensia: Journal of Neo-Latin Studies* 45 (1996), 348–71.
Rodríguez Peregrina, 'Introducción', in Vives, *Del arte de hablar* (Granada: Universidad de Granada, 2000), XIII–CXLVI.
Roest, Bert. 'Rhetoric of Innovation and Recourse to Tradition in Humanist Pedagogical Discourse', in Gersh, S. – B. Roest (eds.). *Medieval and Renaissance Humanism: Rhetoric, Representation, and Reform* (Leiden/Boston: Brill, 2003), 115–48.
Rosa di Simone, Maria. 'Admission', in Ridder-Symoens, Hilde (ed.). *A History of the University in Europe*, vol. 2 (Cambridge: Cambridge University Press, 1996).
Rummel, Erika. *Erasmus and his Catholic Critics*. 2 vols. (Nieuwkoop: De Graaf, 1989).
Rummel, Erika. *The Humanist-Scholastic Debate in the Renaissance & Reformation* (Cambridge, MA: Harvard University Press, 1995).
Rummel, Erika. 'Political and Religious Propaganda at the Court of Charles V: A Newly Identified Tract by Alfonso de Valdés', *Historical Research* 70:171 (1997), 23–33.
Rummel, Erika. 'Erasmian Humanism in the Twentieth Century', in Shaffer, Elinor (ed.). *Comparative Criticism: Humanist Traditions in the Twentieth Century* (Cambridge: Cambridge University Press, 2001), 57–67.
Rummel, Erika. *The Case against Johann Reuchlin: Social and Religious Controversy in Sixteenth-Century Germany* (Toronto: University of Toronto Press, 2002).
Rummel, Erika. 'Introduction', in Rummel (ed.). *Biblical Humanism and Scholasticism in the Age of Erasmus* (Leiden: Brill, 2008), 1–14.
Rummel, Erika. 'Secular Advice in Erasmus's Sacred Writings', *The European legacy: Toward New Paradigms* 19:1 (2014), 16–26.
Saastamoinen, Kari. 'Pufendorf and the Stoic Model of Natural Law', in Blom, H. – L. C. Winkel (eds.). *Grotius and the Stoa* (Assen: Royal van Gorcum, 2004).
Saarinen, Risto. *Weakness of Will in Renaissance and Reformation Thought* (Oxford: Oxford University Press, 2011).

Sánchez Manzano, María Asunción. 'Juan Luis Vives sobre la elocución retórica: conceptos y composición del parrafo', *eHumanista* 26 (2014), 468–85.
Sancipriano, Mario. *Il pensiero psicologico e morale di G. L. Vives* (Florence: Sansoni, 1958).
Sancipriano, Mario. 'Introduzione', in Vives. Sancipriano, M. (ed.), *De anima et vita* (Torino: Bottega d'Erasmo, 1959), iii–vii.
Scott, Alison. 'More's Letters and "the Comfort of the Truth"', in Cousins, A. D. – D. Grace (eds.). *A Companion to Thomas More* (Madison: Fairleigh Dickinson University Press, 2009), 53–76.
Sebastiani, Valentina. *Il privilegio di pubblicare Erasmo. Johannes Froben (1460 c.–1527), Stampatore di Basilea* (Florence: EUI thesis, 2010).
Seidel Menchi, Silvana. *Erasmo in Italia 1520–1580* (Torino: Bollati Boringhieri, 1987).
Seigel, Jerrold. '"Civic Humanism" or Ciceronian Rhetoric', *Past and Present* 34 (1966), 3–48.
Severi A. 'Introduzione', in Spagnoli, Battista. Severi, A. (ed.), *Adolescentia* (Bologna: Bup, 2010).
Sharpe, Kevin. 'Virtues, Passions, and Politics in Early Modern England', *History of Political Thought* 32:5 (2011), 773–98.
Sihvola, Juha. 'Emotional Animals: Do Aristotelian Emotions Require Beliefs?', *Apeiron* 29:2 (1996), 105–44.
Sinz, William. 'Vives's Treatises on the Arts', *Studies in the Renaissance* 10 (1963), 68–90.
Sipiora, P. – J. S. Baumlin, (eds.). *Rhetoric and Kairos: Essays in History, Theory, and Praxis* (Albany: SUNY Press, 2002).
Skinner, Quentin. *The Foundations of Modern Political Thought*, 2 vols. (Cambridge: Cambridge University Press, 1978).
Skinner, Quentin. 'Sir Thomas More's *Utopia* and the Language of Renaissance Humanism', in Pagden, Anthony (ed.). *The Languages of Political Theory in Early-Modern Europe* (Cambridge: Cambridge University Press, 1987), 123–57.
Skinner, Quentin. 'Political Philosophy', in Schmitt, C. – Q. Skinner – E. Kessler – J. Kraye (eds.). *The Cambridge History of Renaissance Philosophy* (Cambridge: Cambridge University Press, 1990), 387–452.
Skinner, Quentin. *Reason and Rhetoric in the Philosophy of Hobbes* (Cambridge: Cambridge University Press, 1996).
Skinner, Quentin. *Visions on Politics*, vols. 1–3 (Cambridge: Cambridge University Press, 2002).
Skinner, Quentin. 'Paradiastolae', in Adamson – Alexander – Ettenhuber (eds.). *Renaissance Figures of Speech* (Cambridge: Cambridge University Press, 2007), 149–64.
Skinner – Van Gelderen, (eds.). *Freedom and the Construction of Europe* (Cambridge: Cambridge University Press, 2013).
Snyder, Jon R. *Dissimulation and the Culture of Secrecy in Early Modern Europe* (Berkeley, CA/London: University of California Press, 2009).
Sorabji, Richard. *Emotion and Peace of Mind: From Stoic Agitation to Christian Temptation* (Oxford: Oxford University Press, 2000).
Sowards, J. K. 'Introduction', in CWE 71, ix–li.
Spies, Marijke. *Rhetoric, Rhetoricians and Poets* (Amsterdam: Amsterdam University Press, 1999).

Spranzi, Marta. *The Art of Dialectic between Dialogue and Rhetoric: The Aristotelian Tradition* (Amsterdam: John Benjamins Pub. CO, 2011).

Stacey, Peter. *Roman Monarchy and the Renaissance Prince* (Cambridge: Cambridge University Press, 2007).

Stahl, William H. 'Introduction', in Macrobius (ed.). *Commentary on the Dream of Scipio* (New York: Columbia University Press, 1990), 1–66.

Stayer, James M. *The German Peasant's War and Anabaptist Community of Goods* (Montreal: McGill-Queen's University Press, 1991).

Stone, M. W. 'Scrupulosity and Conscience: Probabilism in Early Modern Scholastic Ethics', in Braun, H. – E. Vallance (eds.) *Contexts of Conscience in Early Modern Europe* (Basingstoke: Palgrave MacMillan, 2004), 1–16.

Strosezki, Christoph. 'From the Microcosm to the Macrocosm: Ethos and Policy in Vives', *eHumanista* 26 (2014), 530–8.

Struever, Nancy. 'Political Rhetoric and Rhetorical Politics in Juan Luis Vives (1492–1540)', in Struever, Nancy (ed.). *The History of Rhetoric and the Rhetoric of History* (Aldershot: Ashgate Variorum, 2009), 243–58.

Surtz, Edward – J. H Hexter. 'Introduction', in *The Complete Works of Thomas More*, 4 vols. (New Haven: Yale University Press, 1965), xv–cxciv.

Tervoort, Ad. *The Iter Italicum and the Northern Netherlands: Dutch Students at Italian Universities and their role in the Netherlands' Society (1426 – 1575)* (Leiden: Brill, 2005).

Teske, Roland. 'The Will as King over the Powers of the Soul: Uses and Sources of an Image in the Thirteenth Century', *Vivarium* 32:1 (1994), 62–71.

Teske, Roland. 'Henry of Ghent on Freedom of the Human Will', in Wilson, Gordon A. (ed.). *A Companion to Henry of Ghent* (Leiden-Boston: Brill, 2011), 315–35.

Thomas, Keith. *In Pursuit of Civility: Manners and Civilization in Early Modern England* (London: Yale University Press, 2018).

Tilmans, Karin. *Historiography and Humanism in Holland in the Age of Erasmus: Aurelius and the Divisiekroniek of 1517* (Nieuwkoop: De Graaf, 1992).

Tilmans, Karin. 'The Burgundian-Habsburg Netherlands (1477–1566)', in Van Gelderen, M. – Q. Skinner (eds.). *Republicanism, a Shared European Heritage*, vol. 1 (Cambridge: Cambridge University Press, 2002), 107–45.

Todd, Margo. *Christian Humanism and the Puritan Social Order* (Cambridge: Cambridge University Press, 1987).

Tournoy, Gilbert. 'Juan Luis Vives and the World of Printing', *Gutenberg-Jahrbuch* 69 (1994), 128–48.

Tracy, James D. *The Politics of Erasmus: A Pacifist Intellectual and his Political Milieu* (Toronto: University of Toronto Press, 1978).

Tracy, James D. *Holland under Habsburg Rule, 1506–1566: The Formation of a Body Politic* (Berkeley: University of California Press, 1990).

Tracy, James D. 'Erasmus among the Postmodernists', in Pabel, Hilmar (ed.). *Erasmus' Vision of the Church* (Kirksville, MO: Sixteenth Century Journal Publishers, 1995), 1–40.

Tracy, James D. *Erasmus of the Low Countries* (Berkeley: University of California Press, 1996).

Tracy, James D. 'Erasmus, Coornhert and the Acceptance of Religious Disunity in the Body Politic: A Low Countries Tradition?', in Berkvens-Stevelinck – Israel – Posthumus Meyjes (eds.). *The Emergence of Tolerance in the Dutch Republic* (Leiden: Brill, 1997), 49–62.

Tracy, James D. *Emperor Charles V, Impresario of War* (Cambridge: Cambridge University Press, 2002).
Tuck, Richard. *Natural Rights Theories* (Cambridge: Cambridge University Press, 1979).
Tuck, Richard. 'Humanism and Political Thought', in Goodman, A. – A. MacKay (eds.). *The Impact of Humanism on Western Europe* (New York: Longman, 1990), 43–65.
Universal Short Title Catalogue (USTC, https://www.ustc.ac.uk/).
Vanautgaerden, Alexandre. *Érasme typographe: humanisme et imprimerie au début du XVIe siècle* (Genève: Droz, 2008).
Vanautgaerden, Alexandre. 'Les lettres de Dirck Martens, imprimeur d'Érasme', in Ryle, Stephen (ed.). *Erasmus and the Renaissance Republic of Letters* (Turnhout: Brepols, 2014), 105–44.
Vanderjagt, Arjo. *Qui sa vertu anoblist. The Concepts of noblesse and chose publicque in Burgundian Political Thought* (Groningen: J. Miélot, 1981).
Van der Poel, Marc. 'Observations on J. L Vives's Theory of Deliberative Oratory in *De consultatione*', in Dalzell, A. – C. Fantazzi – R. J. Schoeck (eds.). *Acta Conventus Neo-Latini Torontonensis* (Binghamton, NY: Medieval & Renaissance Texts & Studies, 1991).
Van Gelderen, Martin. *The Political Thought of the Dutch Revolt 1555–1590* (Cambridge: Cambridge University Press, 1992).
Van Gelderen, Martin – Quentin Skinner (eds.). *Republicanism, a Shared European Heritage*, vols. 12 (Cambridge: Cambridge University Press, 2002).
Vasoli, Cesare. *La dialettica e la retorica dell'Umanesimo* (Milano: Feltrinelli, 1968).
Vermeir, René. 'Je t'aime, moi non plus. La nobleza flamenca y España en los siglos XVI–XVII', in Yun Casalilla, Bartolomé (ed.). *Las redes del imperio: élites sociales en la articulación de la Monarquía Hispánica, 1492–1714* (Madrid: Marcial Pons, 2009), 313–37.
Vermeir, Maarten. 'Erasmus and the Joyous Entry', *Erasmus Studies* 34:2 (2014), 144–53.
Vickers, Brian. *In Defence of Rhetoric* (Oxford: Oxford University Press, 1988).
Vigliano, Tristan. 'Introduction', in Vives, Juan Luis. *De disciplinis* (Paris: Les belles lettres, 2013), XI–CXLV.
Waith, Eugene. *Patterns and Perspectives in English Renaissance Drama* (Newark: University of Delaware Press, 1988).
Walker, David. 'Introduction' in Vives, Juan Luis. Walker, D. (ed.). *De ratione dicendi* (Leiden: Brill, 2017).
Waquet, Françoise. 'Qu'est-ce que la République des lettres? Essai de sémantique historique', *Bibliothèque de l'école des chartes* 147 (1989), 473–502.
Waquet, Françoise. *Le latin ou l'empire d'un signe: XVIe-XXe siècle* (Paris: Albin Michel, 1998).
Ward, John O. 'Renaissance Commentators on Ciceronian Rhetoric', in Murphy, James, J (ed.). *Renaissance Eloquence Studies in the Theory and Practice of Renaissance Rhetoric* (Berkeley: University of California Press, 1983), 126–73.
Waswo, Richard. *Language and Meaning in the Renaissance* (Princeton: Princeton University Press, 1987).
Watson, Foster. 'Introduction', in Vives, Juan Luis. *Vives, on Education: A Translation of the De tradendis disciplinis of Juan Luis Vives* (Cambridge: Cambridge University Press, 1913), xvii–clvii.

Watson, Foster. 'The Father of Modern Psychology', *Psychological Review* 22:5 (1915), 333–53.
Watson, Alan. *Law Making in the Later Roman Republic* (Oxford: Clarendon Press, 1974).
Weaver, William. 'Volume Introduction', in Melanchthon. *Opera omnia: Opera philosophica. Part 2, Principal Writings on Rhetoric* (Berlin: De Gruyter, 2017), xxxiii–liv.
Weijers, Olga. *La disputatio à la Faculté des Arts de Paris (1200–1350 environ): esquisse d'une typologie* (Turnhout: Brepols, 1995).
Weijers, Olga. *In Search of the Truth. A History of Disputation Technique from Antiquity to Early Modern Times* (Turnhout: Brepols, 2013).
Weithman, Paul. 'Augustine's Political Philosophy', in Kretzmann, N. – E. Stump (eds.). *The Cambridge Companion to Augustine* (Cambridge: Cambridge University Press, 2001), 234–52.
White, Paul. *Jodocus Badius Ascensius: Commentary, Commerce and Print in the Renaissance* (Oxford: Oxford University Press, 2013).
Wolfson, Harry Austrin. 'The Internal Senses in Latin, Arabic, and Hebrew Philosophic Texts', *Harvard Theological Review* XXVIII:2 (1935), 69–133.
Yates, Frances A. *The Art of Memory* (London: Routledge and Keegan Paul, 1966).
Yoran, Hanan. *Between Utopia and Dystopia: Erasmus, Thomas More, and the Humanist Republic of Letters* (Lanham: Lexington Books, 2010).
Zagorin, Perez. *Ways of Lying: Dissimulation, Persecution, and Conformity in Early Modern Europe* (Cambridge, MA: Harvard University Press, 1990).
Zappala, Michael. 'Vives's *De Europae Dissidiis et Bello Turcico*, the Quattrocento Dialogue and "Open" Discourse', in Dalzell, A. – C. Fantazzi – R. J. Schoeck (eds.). *Acta Conventus Neo-Latini Torontonensis* (Binghamton, NY: Medieval & Renaissance Texts & Studies, 1991).
Zijlstra, Samme. 'Studying Abroad. The Student Years of Two Frisian Brothers at Cologne and Douai', in Goudriaan, K. – J. van Moolenbroek – A. Tervoort (eds.). *Education and Learning in the Netherlands, 1400–1600* (Leiden: Brill, 2003), 297–313.

Index

academic milieus of Paris 20
Accursius 102
active life 9, 42–44, 162–166, 213, 216
Ad Adrianum VI Pontificem de tumultibus Europae 110, 111–112
Ad Herennium 27, 28–30, 32, 42, 80, 198
Adrian of Utrecht, Pope 110
Africanus, Scipio 75, 87, 114–116
Agricola, Rudolph: credibility of argumentation 41; *De inventione dialectica* 39–42, 153, 155, 184; system for analysing terms 41
Alexander of Aphrodisias 123
Alexander the Great 127
Amerbach, Vitus 202; *Quatuor libri de anima* 202
Amstelredamus, Alardus 39–40
Anabaptist sect 128
ancient theology *(prisca theologia)* 25
Andrelini, Fausto 25
Anglo-Habsburg relations 110
Aquinas, Thomas 101, 120
Aristotle 25, 32, 39, 154; *The Art of Rhetoric* 29; *Censura de Aristotelis operibus* 200; concept of *epikeia* 99, 100–101; *De anima* 192, 199, 201; ethical philosophy 200; *ethos* and *pathos* 85, 200; on humanist dialectic 36–37; *Nicomachean Ethics* 31, 63, 197, 200; *Organon* 153; *phantasia* 201; *Posterior Analytics* 155; *Rhetoric* 29, 82, 143, 155, 199–201
Artaxerxes, King 100
auctores 23–24, 28
Augustine 67, 71; on concord 121; *De civitate Dei* 65–66, 97, 100, 104, 120–121, 201; *De doctrina Christiana* 82; idea of political authority 121; understanding of secular power and peace 122

Baarland, Adriaan van 186
Bade, Josse 22, 26, 31–32, 40; *Epistolarum compositionem compendium isagogicum* 30; *Inquiry (Disquisito Ascensiana)* 27; *Introductio in Grammaticen* 26; *Introductio in grammaticen* 23; *Praenotamenta* 27
Balbi, Girolamo 25
Balbi, Iohannes 22; *Catholicon* 22
Barbaro, Ermolao 22, 35
Bataillon, Marcel 6; *Érasme et l'Espagne* 6
Battle of Pavia 110
Bérault, Nicolas 19–21, 26, 66
Bietenholz, Peter 70
Boethius's *Topics* 154–155
Bois, François du 22; *Progymnasmatum* 22
Bonilla y San Martín, Adolfo 3, 7, 15n11
Botero, Giovanni 217
Budé, Guillaume 3, 60, 63–67, 84, 106; *Annotationes* 40; *Annotationes in Pandectarum libros* 25, 98–99; *De asse* 65; *L'institution du Prince* 100
Burgundian Netherlands 105–106, 158

Calero, Francisco 7
Campeggi, Lorenzo 71
Cantiuncula, Claudius 39
Casini 191, 193, 198
Castiglione, Baldassare 107, 166, 177

Celtis, Konrad 145, 186; *Methodus conficiendarum epistolarum* 186
Charles of Burgundy 127
Charles V 9, 64, 75, 104, 106–108, 113–114, 117–119, 137, 203–204; actions 117; demonstrations of power, military success, and virtue 118; imperial plans 117; politics 118; rise to imperial throne 118
Chièvres family 66, 107–108
Chomarat, Jacques 6, 11, 70; *Grammaire et rhétorique chez Érasme* 6
Christian ethical philosophy, 8–9
Christian humanism 5
Christians, discord and warfare between 114
Christian truth 27
Chrysostom 123
Cicero 28, 31, 37–38, 46, 121, 185; *Ad Herennium* 201; on *aequitas* 99; *Brutus* 40; *De amicitia* 63; on *decorum* 177–180; *De inventione* 28, 30–31, 80, 154; *De officiis* 30; *De oratore* 29; *De re publica* 74, 97; description of rhetoric as a power or force 144; as a model of a citizen 43–44; orations 46; on oratorical ability 30; *Partitiones Oratoriae* 28; rhetorical philosophy of 77; *Somnium Scipionis* 74–75, 87; *Topica* 28, 154; treatment of disposition 80
Ciceronianism 150–152, 185
Cimmerian darkness of scholasticism 61
Cimmerians 88n13
City of God 121
classical rhetorical theory 27–32, 142–144
Clement VII, Pope 117
Clichtove, Josse 21, 23
Colet, John 159
Collège de Montaigu 20, 22, 158–159
Collegium Trilingue 35
Concordia ordinum 121
contemporary rhetorical theory 144–147
conversation *(sermo)* 62–63, 69, 84, 165, 177, 181, 183, 188, 215, 217
counselling 76–78, 83–84
Cranevelt, Franciscus 65–66
Croy, Guillaume de 66, 107–109
Curtis, Cathy 108

Dante's *Monarchy* 117
Dati, Agostino 22
declamations 45–49, 164
decorum 2, 8, 10, 15n6, 47, 70–71, 73–74, 151, 156, 185–187, 203–205, 213, 217, 219; rhetoric of 176–184, 189–190, 213, 216–217
De disciplinis 3–4, 10, 14n2, 44, 63, 76, 103, 127, 177; background of 137–139; dialectical topics 153–156; elementary education and rhetorical confrontation 160–162; history of rhetoric 139–142; ideal of extensive education 158; life of an erudite man 44, 63, 68–69, 166, 216; life of *negotium* 162–166; practical exercises 163–164; practical suggestions for education 156–160
De Europae dissidiis et bello turcico 110–111, 113–116
De Rege Galliae capto 110, 112, 114
De regni administratione, bello, & pace 110, 112–113
Despauterius, Johannes: *Ars versificatoria* 26
d'Étaples, Jacques Lefèvre 21, 25, 31, 35, 37, 40
dialectic 33, 214–215; criticisms on 37–39; distinction of humanist and scholastic 35–36; humanist 39–42; teaching of 155
dialectical invention 152–156, 163
dialectical judgment 163
dialectical reasoning 22–23
Donatus: *Ars Grammatica* 22; *Ars minor* and *Ars maior* 22
Dorp, Martinus 34–36, 38–40; on Erasmus's *Novum Instrumentum* 35
Dust, Philip 7

eclecticism 24
education: elementary education and rhetorical confrontation 160–162; ideal of extensive 158; practical suggestions for 156–160; *see also De disciplinis*
Elyot, Thomas 166; *The Boke named the Governour* 166
emotional control 196–198
emotional dispositions 2, 11–13, 182–184, 200–201, 204–205, 219
emotions 1, 194–197
emotions and passions 84–87
enargeia 112, 118, 125, 202–203

enarratio 23–24, *25*
Enchiridion 34, 195
Erasmian educational reformers 158
Erasmian humanism 5, 10, 13, 33, 60, 79, 107, 215
Erasmian Republic of Letters 59–78; contributions from humanist circles 62; as form of self-interpretation 62; friendship and conversation *(sermo)* 62–63, 69–70; social and cultural link 60; tension between truth and ethics 71–72
Erasmian rhetoric 11, 214, 216
Erasmian worldview 34
Erasmus, Desiderius 3–6, 26, 49; *Adagia* 7, 30, 44; *Ciceronianus* 67, 151–152; *Colloquia* 30, 44; conception of friendship 62–63, 88n20; contextual aspect of speech 70; criticism of scholastic theology 102; *De conscribendis epistolis* 30, 70, 76, 80, 162, 179, 187, 195, 202, 220; *De copia* 29, 45, 70; on decorum 71, 189–190; *De libero aribtrio* 122; denunciation of tyranny 45; *De pueriis instituendis* 146, 158–159; *De ratione studii* 34, 39, 146, 159; *Dulce bellum inexpertis* 44–45, 116; *Ecclesiastes* 148, 189–190, 203; *Enchiridion militis Christiani* 34, 195; *Encomium Moriae* 34, 60, 71; *Epistolae ad diversos*, 64; *Epistolae aliquot selectae ex Erasmicis*, 64; ethical theology 101; *Farrago* 88n18; *Formula conficiendarum epistolarum* 186; *Hyperaspistes* 122; ideal ruler 75; idea of ethical dissimulation 70–71; idea of power 104, 119; *Institutio principis Christiani* 7, 46, 75, 83, 100–101, 104–105, 107, 109, 126, 164, 203; introductory letter to *Declamationes* 64; *Opus epistolarum* 64; *Panegyricus* 75; *Paraclesis* 34, 70; philosophy of Christ *(philosophia Christi)* 4, 33–34, 44, 74, 76–77; popularity 62; preface to *Tusculanae Quaestiones* 74; printed disputes 68; *Querela pacis* 76, 107, 119–120; relationship between humanists and scholastics 34–35; on rhetorical interventions 7; self-presentation 16n22; *Sileni Alcibiadis* 71; transformative *sermo* 11, 75, 82; treatment of political themes 45; use of proverbs 44–45; *Utilissima consultatio de bello Turcis inferendo* 116; Vives's relationship with 67
Erasmus, Man of Letters: The Construction of Charisma in Print (Jardine) 62
ethical dissimulation 70–71
ethical self-control and virtue 2, 4, 7, 9, 13, 98, 100–101, 110, 194–197
ethics (private moral philosophy) 1, 197
ethos 60–61, 66, 81–85, 127, 200
evidentia see enargeia
exemplary dialogues 44
exordium 180, 182, 184, 186, 188

Faculty of Arts 21–22, 35, 163
fantasy 125, 194, 197–198, 201–203
Fantazzi, Cahrles 14; *In pseudodialecticos* 14
Ferdinand, Prince 46, 64, 66
Fernández-Santamaría, José A. 7, 123–124, 138
Fichet, Guillaume: *Rhetorica* 28
Filelfo, Francesco 24; *Convivia Mediolaniensia* 24–25, 32
Fisher, Bishop 106
flatterer, recognising a 83–84
Fonseca, Archbishop Alonso de 107
Fonteius, Marcus 47, 86
friendship 62–63, 83–84, 88n20; general obligations of 63; spiritual 63
Fumaroli, Marc 6, 214
Fundanus, Quintus 47–48

Gaguin, Robert 25; *Ars versificatoria* 26
Gattinara, Mercurino di 107, 117–118
Gellius, Aulus 24; *Attic Nights (Noctes Atticae)* 25
George, Edward 10, 46, 118
George of Trebizond 29; *Dialectica* 39–40, 153, 155; *Rhetoric* 31; *Rhetoricorum libri V* 29, 178–179
Gerson, Jean 31
Giles of Rome 31
Gillis, Pieter 77
González González, Enrique 20, 212
grammar teaching: implications 22; influence of humanist handbooks 22–27; prescriptive rules for 24; semantics and dialectical reasoning 22–23; tools of *quaestio* (question) and *disputatio* (disputation) 23
grammatical commentaries 23
Green, Lawrence 200, 219
Grotius, Hugo 217

Guarino, Battista 23–24; *De ordine docendi ac studendi* 23–24, 145
Gutiérrez Rodríguez, Víctor 212

habituation process 197–199
Hankins, James 1, 13
Hegendorf, Christoph 145–146; *Methodus scribendi epistolas* 186
Henry VIII 4, 9, 106, 110–112
historiography 3, 5
Hobbes, Thomas 214, 217
Hoffmann, Manfred 6
humanism 20–21, 50n11; public support of 66–69
humanism-scholasticism debate 61, 88n10
humanist commonplaces and wisdom 44
humanist dialectic 39–42, 152–156
Hutten, Ulrich von 68

Jewish diet 71
Joâo III, King 165
Jonas, Justus 71
Jouenneaux, Guy de 22
justice *(aequitas)* and honour 99–101

knowledge (circle of arts) 24–25
know thyself 124, 194–195
Kristeller, Paul Oskar 5, 16n16, 50n11

language teaching 23
Latin schools 157, 160–161
Latomus, Bartolomeus 153; *Epitome* 153
Latomus, Jacobus 48, 60–61
Lax, Gaspar 19, 21
learned piety *(docta pietas)* 34
Lee, Edward 60, 63
Lepidus, Aemilius 47–48
letter writing 30
Louis of Flanders, Lord of Praet 78, 108
love 82–83
Luther, Martin 66, 68, 71, 121; debate between Erasmus and 122; *On Temporal Authority and the Limitations in Obeying It* 122

Mack, Peter 10, 176, 219
Macrobius 24; commentaries on *Somnium Scipionis* 75; *Saturnalia* 25
Madrid, Treaty of 1526 113, 117–118
Magnus, Albertus 101

Mair, John 21–23, 31
Manrique, Alonso 107
Marck, Érard de la 75
Margarita philosophica 81, 144
Martens, Thierry 33, 39, 42
Mary of Burgundy 105
Matheeussen, Constant 102
Maximilian of Austria, Archduke 105
Mayans y Siscar, Gregorio 14, 176; *Opera omnia* 14
Melanchthon, Philipp 146–150; *Commentarius de anima* 202
Mirabelli's *Polyanthea* 32
Mirandola, Giovanni Pico della 22, 26, 35
moral philosophy 30, 191–194
moral poetry 26
More, Thomas 3–4, 6, 35–36, 38, 63–66, 106, 109, 176, 215; on counsel and counselling 76; life of *otium* and *negotium* 76; *Utopia* 7, 74, 76–78, 100, 126, 164
Mosaic dietary laws 70–71
Mosellanus's *Oratio de variarum linguarum cognitione* 36
Müntzer, Thomas 128
mystical wisdom *(sapientia)* 25

Nebrija, Antonio de 66, 181
Neo-Platonism 25
Noreña, Carlos 3, 7–8, 117, 123, 137, 192; *Juan Luis Vives* 3
Northern humanism 2–7, 9–10, 65, 79, 137–139, 191–192, 219

Overfield, James 88n10

Pace, Richard 106
Parisian experience of Vives 20–27; deficiencies of Parisian academic life 21
Parra, Juan de la 64
Peasant Revolt 128
Pelayo, Marcelino Menéndez 3
peroration 182, 184
Perotti, Niccolò 22; *Cornucopiae* 23
Philip, Archduke 75
Plato 32, 73–74, 147; *Republic* 103
Plutarch 198; *De discrimine adulatoris & amici* 83–84
Pocock, John 5
poetry 25–26
political concord and discord, causes and consequences of 119–128, 213

political life 44
political theory 7, 12, 217–219
politics 5–8, 12, 218–220; connection between ethical self-government and 13
politics (public moral philosophy) 1
Poliziano, Angelo 151; *Sylva* 26
Polypragmon 113–114
primus theologus 25
Pro divo Carolo 117
project of peace 105–110
proverbs 24, 30, 44
Pufendorf, Samuel 217

Quintilian 28, 31, 37–38, 48, 84–85, 142–147; definition of orator 70, 82, 142; ideal orator 165; *Institutio oratoria* 28–29, 45, 48, 81, 154, 178, 180, 202

Rebhorn, Wayne A. 6, 214
religious rhetoric 71, 203
Renaissance humanism 3
Renaissance rhetoric 5–7, 214, 216
Republic of Letters 59, 62–64, 67, 106–107, 137, 166
rhetoric 3, 5–14, 214; ambivalence of 147–150; *ars rhetorica* 28; Christian understanding of 27–32; civic dimension of 9–10; classical 6; as cognitive power 31; connection between politics and 6–14; in context of God's providential plan 11; of criticism 110–116; in *De causis* 139–144, 156; of decorum 178–184; discrepancies between classical rhetoric and Christian eloquence 31–32; genres of 29; importance in forensic and civic matters 31; nature of 27–28; Plato's attack on 32; political counsel and 76–78; of praise and blame 29; religious 71; Renaissance treatises on 29–31; of Roman and Greek orators 28–29, 32; speech and 11; transformative capacities of 28, 74–76
rhetorical handbooks 42
rhetorical invention 153–154, 185, 191, 201, 204
Rodríguez Peregrina, José Manuel 14
Roman Law 99, 102–103
Roman models of concord 121
Roman orators 28

sacred theology 19, 26
salvation 122
Sancipriano, Mario 14
satire 19, 27, 34, 68
Saxoferrato, Bartolus de 102
scholasticism 20–21, 61
self-cultivation, self-government, self-transformation 124–125
self-knowledge, self-cure 194–197
self-reflection 124
semantics 22–23, 36
Seneca the Elder: *Controversies* 164; *Declamations* 45
Skinner, Quentin 5, 13, 214
Socrates 43, 71, 194
Spagnoli, Battista 26
speaker's authority 80–84
speculative grammar 22
spiritual friendship 63
spiritual or ethical self-transformation 7, 75
spiritual poetry 26
St. Paul 70–71, 82, 190
Stoic ethics 8, 87, 165, 192, 195
Stoic philosophy 123
Struever, Nancy 11
Sturm, Johannes 140, 157; curriculum for Latin schools 160; *De literarum ludis recte aperiendis* 157, 162
Sulla 47–48, 86; tyrannical dictatorship 47
Sulpicius, Servius 40

Tacitus's *Dialogus de oratoribus (Dialogue on the Orators)* 29, 141
Thrasymachus 103
Tiresias 113–115
Todd, Margo 2
Tracy, James 76, 104
transformative rhetoric and speech 11, 27, 28, 31, 70, 74–76, 82, 112, 190, 203
Treaty of Cambrai 118, 137
Treaty of London, 1518 106
trivium 9, 20–21
trivium, teaching of: dialectic 32–39; grammar 21–27; rhetoric 27–32
truth 69–74, 164
Tunstall, Cuthbert 106, 125
Turks, crusade against 116

universal monarchy 104, 117–119
Universal Short Title Catalogue (USTC) 14

Valdés, Alfonso de 107; *Diálogo de las cosas acaecidas en Roma* 117–118
Valencian *Studium generale* 63
Valla, Giorgio 154
Valla, Lorenzo 22, 35, 37; *Dialectice (Repastinatio dialecticae et philosophiae)* 39, 145; *Elegantiae linguae latinae* 22
Vasoli, Cesare 214
Vergara, Juan de 72, 107
Vergerio, Pier Paolo 159
Vergil, Christian 26
Verulanus, Sulpitius 30; *De epistolarum compositione opusculum* 30
Villedieu, Alexandre de 22; *Doctrinale* 22
Virués, Alonso de 107
Vives, Juan Luis 1–2; academic texts 97; adoption of *sine querela* 68; *Aedes legum* 97–102; *Argumentum Somnium Scipionis Ciceroniani* 97; attitude towards ethics, politics, and rhetoric 3, 5–14; causes and consequences of concord and discord 119–128; on Cicero's eloquence 43, 152; on civic life 44; *Clipei Christi descriptio* 72; commentaries on Augustine's *De civitate Dei* 39, 65, 67, 78, 100, 103, 120, 123; constructive idea of disputations 160; criticisms 9; critique of contemporary rhetorical education 150; *De anima et vita* 1–4, 8, 12, 175, 191–194, 196–205; *De causis* 139, 142, 156; *Declamationes Syllanae* 9, 20, 43, 45–49, 60, 64, 86, 97, 164; *De communione rerum* 128; *De concordia & discordia in humano genere* 4, 14, 68–69, 98, 101, 116–128, 150, 196, 203–204; *De conscribendis epistolis* 4, 11, 30, 70, 76, 80, 138, 162, 174–175, 179, 186–189, 191, 195, 202–203, 220; *De consultatione* 10–11, 78–87, 115, 118, 188–189, 203; decorous adjustment of truth 74; *De disciplinis* 3–4, 10, 14, 44, 68, 76, 100, 103, 127, 128, 137–166, 177, 185, 197, 200, 215; *De Europae dissidiis et bello Turcico* 110, 113; *De Europae dissidiis & Republica* 97, 109–116; defence of free will 123; definition of orator 82; definition of rhetoric 144; *De pacificatione* 84, 104, 196; depiction of the prudent, educated man 165–166; *De ratione dicendi* 10, 14, 79, 174–188, 202–204; *De subventione pauperum* 98, 108, 126; *De tradendis disciplinis* 138, 157, 163, 165; discourse on virtues and duties 111; discussion of emotions and passions 84–87; distrust of strong passions 85; in divorce negotiations 4, 109; dynamics of debate 68–69; emotional interpretations of individual events 126–127; *epikeia/aequitas* 98–101; ethical politics 105; eulogy of Adrian's papacy 111–112; family background 4; final years 174–175; God's grace and assistance 123–124; grammar teaching and poetry 20–27; habituation process 197–199; handling of his own image 67–68; ideals of justice *(aequitas)* and honour 100–101; ideas on jurisprudence 102–105; importance of *decorum* 177, 185–186, 190–191; on institutions 8; internalisation of natural law 101; interpretation of *decorum* 2, 8, 10, 12, 14, 216–220; interpretation of *epikeia* 98–100; *Introductio ad Sapientiam* 124, 125, 196; *In Leges Ciceronis praefatio* 40, 44, 97, 101–102; letters to Cranevelt 66, 104, 174; *Meditationes in septem Psalmos penitentiae* 72; method of rhetorical invention 201; moral code 76; Northern humanism 2–7; notions of peace and concord 116; *Opera* 19–20; *Opuscula* 33, 35, 60, 97, 98; on the *Organon* 37; political interventions 12, 105, 213; political texts 97–98; political views 7–9; *Pompeius fugiens* 97; pre-political scheme of vices and passions 120; on princes and princely rhetoric 78–80; *In pseudodialecticos* 21, 33, 35–39, 60, 61, 64, 68–69, 150; as public arbitrator between Erasmus and Budé 64–65; publishing of private letters 110–114, 119; purification of passions and vice 196; on Radical reformers 127–128; relationship between law and politics 98–105; relationship between rhetoric and political thought 8–14; relationship

of rhetoric to philosophy 143–144; relationship with Erasmus 66–67; relationship with princes 78; rules of *sermo* 62–63, 69; *Sapiens* 19, 21, 25–26, *27*, 32; *Satellitium animi* 125; *Somnium et Vigilia* 74–75, 97; against Stoics 192, 198; theory of monarchy 8–9, 104–105, 117–118; theory of soul and emotions 1, 8, 13, 192–197; understanding of moral philosophy 196; use of *ethos* 66; *Veritas fucata* 72–73; views on dialectic 36–39, 152–156; *Vigilia* 75–76, 87

Vocht, Henry De 3

wisdom 20, 24–26, 146–147
Wolsey, Cardinal 66, 106–107

Printed in the United States
by Baker & Taylor Publisher Services